GOVERNING ACCESS TO
ESSENTIAL RESOURCES

———

GOVERNING ACCESS TO ESSENTIAL RESOURCES

EDITED BY

Katharina Pistor
and Olivier De Schutter

COLUMBIA UNIVERSITY PRESS

NEW YORK

Columbia University Press
Publishers Since 1893
New York   Chichester, West Sussex
Copyright © 2016 Columbia University Press
All rights reserved

Library of Congress Cataloging-in-Publication Data
Governing access to essential resources / edited by Katharina
Pistor and Olivier De Schutter
pages cm
Includes bibliographical references and index.
ISBN 978-0-231-17278-3 (cloth : alk. paper)
ISBN 978-0-231-54076-6 (e-book)
1. Environmental policy—Cross-cultural studies. 2. Environmental management. 3. Environmental law. 4. Natural resources—Management. 5. Water resources
development. 6. Water resources—Management. 7. Conservation of natural
resources. I. Pistor, Katharina, editor. II. Schutter, Olivier de, editor.

GE170.G675 2015
363.7—dc23

2015005508

Columbia University Press books are printed on permanent and
durable acid-free paper.

This book is printed on paper with recycled content.

Printed in the United States of America
c 10 9 8 7 6 5 4 3 2 1

Cover design: Noah Arlow

References to Internet Web sites (URLs) were accurate at the time of writing.
Neither the author nor Columbia University Press is responsible for URLs
that may have expired or changed since the manuscript was prepared.

CONTENTS

GOVERNING ACCESS TO
ESSENTIAL RESOURCES

PART I

Analytical Framework

CHAPTER 1

Introduction

TOWARD VOICE AND REFLEXIVITY

Olivier De Schutter and Katharina Pistor

The allocation of scarce resources defines the field of economics. This book is also concerned with the allocation of scarce resources, but its emphasis is on essential resources: resources that are either absolutely necessary for the survival of every human being, which include drinking water, basic food, clothing and shelter, or indispensable for minimum existence in a given society, which may include land, electricity, or other resources.[1] The shift of focus from goods in general to essential resources brings to the fore normative aspects of resource maintenance and allocation and calls for a critical reassessment of existing governance regimes and their distributional effects—or a shift form the tragedy of the commons to the tragedy of exclusion.

We observe three trends in the allocation of scarce, essential resources worldwide today. First, essential resources, in particular drinking water and arable land, are becoming ever more scarce. The dire predictions made most famously by the Club of Rome forty years ago (Meadows et al. 1972)—that economic growth would surpass the carrying capacity of the planet without changes in the management of scarce resources—may well be materializing in our century (Millennium Ecosystem Assessment 2005). In other words, humankind may face *absolute* scarcity of essential resources in the foreseeable future if levels of consumption continue to increase in proportion to rising incomes. Second, human-made constraints, including legal institutions and social practices, create (quite purposefully) scarcity for some even as others continue to enjoy in abundance. Property rights are the most obvious example of an institution that creates *relative* scarcity. Nation-states and other jurisdictional boundaries have the same effect, with the implication that some resources are inaccessible in some regions. Paradoxically, opposite arrangements—the removal of barriers to the free flow of goods, services, and capital—may also result in scarcity. This is the case when the superior purchasing power of some actors excludes others from access. Third and related, the market mechanism has become the preferred mechanism for allocating scarce, including essential, resources, not least for its seemingly neutral operation. The smooth functioning of the market in turn depends on legal arrangements that facilitate exclusion, thereby setting the stage (without further interventions) for pricing out those without sufficient purchasing power. Denying people access to essential resources they cannot afford is not a market failure: it is the logical outcome of market forces.

We posit that jointly these trends already exclude the most vulnerable members of humankind from access to essential resources and threaten to leave more behind as scarcity increases. This is intolerable on normative grounds. A just society and a just world require that all humans have the capability to live the lives they have reason to value (Sen 1999; Nussbaum 2011). This calls for more than meeting peoples' basic needs but certainly includes it. Approximating justice, we contend, is possible. But it requires forms of governance that embrace normative principles, such as Voice and Reflexivity, which are distinct from the sole pursuit of efficiency. *Voice* is defined here as the ability to collectively choose the rules by which social groups wish to be governed; *Reflexivity* as the ability to question one's preferences in the light of competing claims and to accommodate such claims in a collective-learning process.

This introductory chapter develops the conceptual framework for the contributions that follow, which critique the framework; they offer insights from other disciplines and literatures or apply them to, among others, the operations of common law, the struggle over property rights in contemporary China, and access to water in the slums of Mumbai or the arid West of the United States. These studies demonstrate that context matters both for determining what resources shall be deemed "essential" and what governance devices might be available (or not) to ensure universal access to them. The specific institutional arrangements for realizing Voice and Reflexivity will therefore vary considerably, but this is true more generally for institutions that affect individual and social behavior.

Most of the contributions in the book focus on specific countries or regions within countries. This, however, should not distract from the fact that in our globalized world scarce resources are increasingly allocated across the borders of national or subnational polities. This implies that local or national institutional arrangements are rarely sufficient to ensure Voice and that additional efforts must be made to ensure Reflexivity to achieve justice on a global scale. This is a major challenge for future global governance, one that is only too often sidestepped by leaving resource allocation primarily to the market mechanism.

The remainder of this chapter is organized as follows. We first introduce the basic building blocks for our framework: essential resources, the determinants of scarcity, Voice, and Reflexivity. Second, we situate our framework within the dominant literature on resource allocation in law and economics and the literature on common-pool resources. Third, we introduce the other contributions to this volume and explain how they relate to the framework developed in this chapter.

ESSENTIAL RESOURCES

For the purpose of the current book project, we label resources essential if they are indispensable for survival; at a minimum this includes drinking water, adequate food, and shelter. Water is the most obvious case of an essential resource, as deprivation will lead to death within days. Still, drinking water can be more or less clean, a source of health or harbinger of disease. It would be absurd to call for pristine springwater for all as much as this might be normatively desirable; a more moderate claim, but one that would improve the current state of the world in relative terms (Sen 2009), is that all should have access to water that is safe for immediate consumption. The right to clean water has meanwhile been recognized by a UN resolution,[2] but without stipulating a minimum threshold for cleanliness—indicating the politically divisive nature of this seemingly straightforward issue.

Other resources pose additional challenges; take the example of land. For rural households in the developing world, where many still reside in extreme poverty, access to food and water is inextricably linked to land; in such conditions, land itself becomes an essential resource. In contrast, most city dwellers can live comfortable lives without controlling the land their apartment buildings occupy—though their tenure security ultimately depends on the security of a right to land, if only indirectly. The qualification of any particular resource as "essential" beyond the needs for bare survival is thus context specific. In more affluent societies, education, health care, or electricity (consider the effects Hurricane Sandy had on New York when it shut down electricity for part of the city) may be considered essential resources as well. Their classification is determined by shared norms about what resources a just society should make available to all irrespective of purchasing power (Walzer 1983; Elster 1993).

In short, essentiality is a normative concept and, as such, malleable and context specific. For some this may seem to weaken its explanatory power. We take a different position and emphasize that resources have not only an "objective" market value that can be determined by the pricing mechanisms but also a normative value that rests on principles of justice. There is an old, lively, and ultimately unresolvable debate as to whether justice shall be measured in absolute or relative terms, which we will not recapitulate here. Suffice to say that even proponents of absolute justice would agree that societies vary in how they prioritize claims to resources and that this influences social behavior. Economic and normative value may but need not be correlated. For some resources and "under certain very special assumptions" (Arrow 1974, 20) it may be perfectly justifiable and indeed preferable to rely exclusively on the pricing mechanism. For others, this would by morally repugnant; other considerations, including "distributive justice" (Arrow 1974), are therefore called for to modify or even replace the pricing mechanism. We propose that essential resources fall into the latter category. In what follows we mostly ignore resources other than those required to cover basic needs, in particular water and land; not because we do not believe that the concept of essential resources cannot be extended to them (we do), but for the purpose of analytical clarity.

The concept of essential resources thus overlaps but is not identical with the notion of basic needs developed by the International Labor Organization (ILO) in the 1980s.[3] Our approach is distinct in three ways. First, we suggest there is not a single, objective standard for categorizing certain resources as "essential"; instead what is essential is highly context specific. Second, we seek to shift emphasis from the goods or resources in question to the ability of individuals and groups to partake in deliberation and the design of governance mechanisms. Satisfying the need to access essential resources cannot simply be a technocratic, top-down process but requires involvement of the people concerned precisely because appropriate governance tools are resource and context specific. Indeed, unless greater attention is paid to the question of governance—to inputs in decision making rather than simply to the outputs understood as the satisfaction of basic needs—the default solution will be to promote economic growth in the hope that all boats will be lifted. Yet we have learned from the past thirty years that the "trickle-down" effect hoped for is less effective than is frequently asserted; even more troubling, the means by which economic growth is promoted, that is, the creation of private property rights, the removal of obstacles to free trade, and so on, can in fact create obstacles for ensuring access to essential resources.

THE DETERMINANTS OF SCARCITY

Scarcity is ubiquitous and the very essence of a competitive market economy. Scarcity of essential resources, however, can be deadly—for those denied access or engulfed in riots and warfare over access. Governing access to essential resources in a peaceful and equitable manner is of utmost importance, but to develop workable solutions we need to understand the determinants of scarcity. It is useful to distinguish between absolute and relative scarcity and between natural and human-made scarcity. We note that most scarcity is relative rather than absolute and that by implication scarcity is almost always the product of human action or inaction. Nonetheless, there is strong evidence that per capita availability of water and arable land is in decline globally (Lambin and Meyfroidt 2011). This is not to say that other sources for food might not be found or that it may not become feasible in the near future to turn saltwater into drinking water at reasonable costs. It does mean, however, that the most obvious and historically most widely used solution to meet demand for essential resources, namely migration to or the conquest of as yet undiscovered or unused resources is diminishing. Estimates suggest that fewer than 450 million hectares of arable land remain (one-third in surface of the land that is already cultivated) and that this resource is likely to be exhausted within the next several decades (Lambin and Meyfroidt 2011). Indeed, taking into account the ecological and social costs of converting yet unused land into cultivated land, this figure should be drastically lowered: there simply is not much land left to satisfy the increase in demand for agricultural commodities (Lambin et al. 2013).

Beyond instances of absolute scarcity, essential resources are scarce only in relative terms, that is, they are human-made and result mostly from politics and institutional choice (Allouche 2011). Even if flooding destroys crops or droughts deplete drinking water in some parts of the world, these resources are typically still available elsewhere. Supplying them to people in distressed regions of the world is a matter of logistics, costs, and political will, not scarcity. The most effective response to acute scarcity, namely self-help in the form of migration to parts of the world where essential resources are still abundant, is severely restricted by political institutions. Where essential resources can be found, other peoples reside and protect their rights and interests by legal and physical boundaries. Virtually all territory and most shorelines on this planet have been enclosed by nation-states that guard entry to their territories, increasingly with physical fences and walls.

Pointing out that scarcity of essential resources is mostly human-made is not new, but this apparently simple assertion has a number of ramifications. First, it highlights the importance of institutions that ensure accountability. Amartya Sen famously asserted that famines are the result not necessarily of food scarcity but of a lack of entitlements for people to demand food (Sen 1999). He concluded that the ability of the people to hold governments accountable is a key safeguard against extreme deprivation: famines, he noted, are rare in democracies. Yet in many countries those most vulnerable to conditions of scarce essential resources lack effective Voice because the political regime suppresses public opinion. The countries that house most of the world's poor today tend to be controlled by autocratic regimes (Collier 2007). Transitions to democracy are fragile, especially at the lower end of the income scale (Przeworski and Limongi 1993). Less well understood is why some countries make it against these odds and others revert to autocratic regimes or collapse into "failed" states. The latter is often attributed to bad domestic institutions, but there is growing evidence that resource scarcity itself may be an aggravating factor for political instability. Indeed, food insecurity contributes to weakening political regimes (Maystadt, Trinh Tan, and Breisinger 2014): There is some evidence that the forced migration of two million people from drought-affected regions played a role in the civil conflict in Syria (Gleick 2014). Thus, lack of access to essential resources is both a consequence and potentially a cause for authoritarian solutions to prevent societies from falling apart.

Even what may seem to be technical problems can be redefined as failure of accountability. Consider, for instance, waste as another human-made contributor to scarcity. Leaking water pipes, unnavigable rural roads to transport food from villages into cities, or the lack of cooling facilities to preserve harvested food on its way to consumers are its most obvious manifestations. These are symptoms of bad policy choice and governance failure in the form of misallocating resources that would otherwise be available to maintain infrastructure; being unable to collect tax or other revenue to fund infrastructure and its maintenance; or choosing institutions that undermine rather than strengthen normative principles of sharing and Voice.

Second, human-made scarcity can have its source in both formal and informal, or customary, arrangements. Even in a country such as India, where democracy has long been established and famines have indeed been rare, Sen's own research has pointed to the "missing 100 million women" (Sen 1990)—that is, the highly unequal treatment of females, evidenced by sex-related abortions, stunted growth, and premature death. A long list of statutory interventions in India since independence has brought about some change but has not fundamentally altered the social norms that condone sex-based discrimination (Pistor, Haldar, and Amirapu 2009). Comparative research on property in land in different parts of the world similarly shows that women often have inferior rights that are derived from and subordinated to those of their husbands, fathers, brothers, even sons, as illustrated by the fact that women lose access to land altogether when one of their male relatives dies (Deininger 2003). As a result, some multinational organizations are now advocating woman empowerment as a means for alleviating hunger (Asian Development Bank 2013).

Third, scarcity can be the result of expanding markets and removing boundaries between jurisdictions. As a result of economic globalization, competition for resources has become global, pitting populations with widely divergent purchasing power against one another. Indeed, whereas the causes of food insecurity are manifold (they include changes in the rate of urbanization, soil degradation, droughts or other changes in climate patterns as well as resource constraints), one increasing concern is the propensity of net-food-importing countries over the past decade to acquire land in foreign countries on a large scale rather than relying on the global trade system (De Schutter 2011). Since the 1980s, many countries with highly volatile agricultural production cycles have abandoned storage facilities in the expectation—and with the policy backing of multilateral institutions, such as the World Bank—that global commodities markets would always grant them access to food. They are now realizing that the unfettered operation of the market mechanism exposes those most desperate for food to the volatility of global market prices, as evidenced by the global food crisis of 2008. This realization explains at least in part the recent shift from relying on trade to acquiring arable land or land with substantial natural resources, including water in recent years (Allouche 2011).

This illustrates a more general point: Excessive reliance on the market mechanism can result in relative scarcity. In principle, the pricing mechanism is a useful indicator of scarcity and forces people to adjust their behavior, cut back on waste, and manage a resource more effectively. Yet prices are an indicator of demand, as expressed by those with purchasing power, rather than of needs: The richer you are, the more votes you have in influencing the allocation of resources. As noted by Scitovsky, this means that the marketplace is analogous to a plutocracy: It is "the rule of the rich," he wrote, "where each consumer's influence on what gets produced depends on how much he spends" (Scitovsky 1992, 8). Thus, the pricing mechanism can price out people who lack sufficient bargaining power. While this may be acceptable for many goods, it is not acceptable when it comes to essential resources. Many countries allocate water through public utilities and frequently offer water for free (at least to cover basic needs). Where the market mechanism has been employed in the provisioning of water, it is typically attenuated by regulations and governance mechanisms that set priorities for water consumption and curb speculation and monopolization. Examples include water banks in California during periods of drought and water markets in European countries (see Casado-Pérez in this volume). Effectively restricting market mechanisms requires well-functioning political and legal institutions. Where these are lacking, the combination of demographic shifts, urbanization, and the commodification of land through titling programs can result in the widespread reallocation of access to essential resources from the destitute to the well-off and well connected (Durand-Lasserve in this volume).

Markets are backed by legal rules, which contribute to scarcity—and not by accident but by design: The delineation of property rights over resources is meant to exclude others from access so as to enable the legal owner to put the asset to the most highly valued use. Any property regime, including communal property, excludes some to the benefit of others. Exclusion is thus at the very core of property regimes, whether individual or collective, public or private (Hall, Hirsch, and Murray Li 2011). Yet, exclusion does not have to be absolute. Indeed, most developed legal systems attenuate the right to exclude by taking account of competing claims and normative concerns. Hanoch Dagan has shown in his work on common-law property (Dagan 2012, and this volume) that courts and legislatures developed property law that has proved to be quite responsive to competing claims; they have endorsed access and sharing constraints in areas as varied as intellectual property rights (mandatory licensing rules), marriage (sharing obligations in marriage and upon divorce), and land (the right to passage). This is not a unique feature of the common law but can also be found in civil law jurisdictions (Mattei 2000).

The development of a contestable property regime that is responsive to competing claims is, however, far from universal. It presupposes that power relations are not too unequal and that the norm-setting processes—that is, the political system—allow ample space for contestation of norms and for changing priorities in response to changing circumstances rather than limiting themselves to defending once-established rights (see also Cox in this volume). The latter, however, has become the rallying cry for property rights and their spread to other parts of the world by zoning and titling programs (World Bank 2010). This ideological shift was precipitated by the collapse of the former socialist world and the promotion of markets based on individualized property rights with the absolute right to exclude as the governance solution for all social ills. The "Washington Consensus" (Williamson 1990) formulated in the early 1990s is the most powerful manifestation of this shift at the global level. And yet, the World Bank, one of the key proponents of the Washington Consensus, had to concede less than two decades later that the recipes of the Washington Consensus did not produce the envisioned growth and prosperity (World Bank 2005). Indeed, we suggest that the measures endorsed by these policies, including widespread privatization and titling and zoning of land without built-in institutional mechanisms that ensure responsiveness to competing claims and changing circumstances, has contributed to the increasing scarcity of essential resources for the world's poor.

The institutionalization of private property in countries around the globe raises important questions as to if and how past institutional choices can be modified to take account of the normative principles embodied in Voice and Reflexivity. Institutions are path dependent (North 1990). For the most part, they change only incrementally; it often takes dramatic events, such as wars or revolutions, to profoundly change historical paths (Olson 1982). Lack of responsiveness, however, can prove fatal for a regime and destabilize entire societies. Karl Polanyi famously linked the rise of totalitarian regimes in the first half of the twentieth century to displacement of the rural poor in preindustrial England and their plight in the process of industrialization. According to him, it is the gradual erosion of all protective features of societies by the "satanic mill" of commodification that leads societies to seek to restore protection, even if only at the price of authoritarianism (Polanyi 1944). Terra Lawson-Remer makes a similar point by showing strong property rights for elites are positively correlated with economic growth and development, but those of marginalized groups are negatively correlated (Lawson-Remer 2011). She also contends that the reallocation of property rights in favor of elites has resulted not infrequently in civil unrest or war, which have at times undone the advances made with the help of a private property regime.

Several contributions to the volume highlight the difficulty of altering established regimes. Michael Cox shows that regimes that have stabilized around a first-come-first-serve rule for making use of riparian water have exacerbated the degradation of underground water resources in times of prolonged drought: Those excluded from access to riparian water have drilled their own wells and drained underground resources. Recent research suggests that tapping into underground water accounts for 75 percent of the documented loss of the Colorado River basin.[4] Nikhil Anand discusses how the physical infrastructure of Mumbai's municipal water system built during colonial rule has deprived the majority of the city's contemporary dwellers of access to the system. They navigate survival by buying water from private sellers, by pressuring city councilmen in return for electoral support, or at times by resorting to violence. But they have, as of now, not been able to change the infrastructure or the rules and practices that deny them full access rights. Further, Vamsi Vaku-labharanam shows that even where weaker constituencies are granted legal rights under the Indian constitution, these rights are often flagrantly violated by a coalition of public and private interests against which they are largely powerless. These examples show that a legal rule or regime on its own is unable to prevent the deplorable outcome of denying the most vulnerable access to essential resources and thereby contributing to their destitution or even death. The absence of open contestation over access rights, the political will and institutional capacity to mitigate economic and social power relations both domestically and globally, undermines the efficacy of isolated legal rules.

SCARCITY IN A GLOBALIZED WORLD

There is perhaps no better illustration of human-made scarcity of essential resources than the imbalances we find in the current wave of globalization. In sharp contrast to the globalization of the pre–World War I period, the current process of globalization has prioritized the movement of goods and capital over that of individuals. As states have imposed ever more severe restrictions on population flows, they have taken away one of the most powerful devices for humans to deal with scarcity: migration to places where relevant resources are abundant or more accessible. International agreements have protected the free flow of goods services and capital through multilateral agreements such as those placed under the umbrella of the World Trade Organization (WTO) or through a growing web of bilateral investment treaties (BITs); in contrast, the free movement of persons has been largely left out.[5] Restricting the movement of persons thus remains the one undisputed power (and, arguably, liability) of sovereigns in a globalized world. Capital can freely chase higher yields by moving in and out of commodity and other markets, but humans are not free to search for more hospitable places to feed their families when they lose access or can no longer afford the prices for resources essential for their survival. The task of addressing their needs is left to the nation-states where they reside—whether or not those nation-states have the political will or retain the economic or institutional capacity to do so.

In fact, international law has increasingly been designed to restrict the capacity of sovereign states to accommodate domestic constituencies and denies them the possibility to contest rights granted to outsiders even if they are directly affected by them. An example is the transnational property regime for protecting foreign investors. It was meant to protect foreign investors against expropriation, but as it has evolved, the regime has overshot its original target by giving foreign investors the power to block domestic legal change that could affect their rights, including change aimed at furthering distributive justice, including a more equitable allocation of essential resources. Under the thousands of BITs that comprise this regime, foreign investors can sue host countries in arbitration tribunals outside their countries for damages if their investments have been infringed (Suda 2006; Roberts 2013). Cases have been brought not only for outright expropriation (which has become a rarity these days) but for legislative or regulatory change to protect the environment or to create more equitable conditions for marginalized groups in society. The hearings are not public and are presided over by arbiters with little knowledge of the host countries' duties (Roberts 2013) toward their own populations even in cases where such duties are imposed by human rights treaties.

There are good reasons for protecting investors against arbitrary state action by host country governments. Yet the prioritization of the rights of foreign investors over those of domestic constituencies becomes problematic when this leads to denying the latter access to essential resources on which their livelihoods depend, as in the famous case of the *Sawhoyamaxa Indigenous Community v. Paraguay*, in which Paraguay alleged before the Inter-American Court of Human Rights that it could not give effect to the indigenous community's property rights over their ancestral lands because, among other reasons, these lands now belonged to a German investor who was protected by a BIT.[6] There is a growing recognition for the need of grounding these treaties in broader social objectives, but these goals are yet to be transposed into actual treaty language. In the meantime, states are often reluctant to infringe investor rights, as they fear expensive arbitral disputes and potentially huge liabilities.

Thomas Pogge has taken this argument a step further and posited that our international legal order violates the very same human rights it endorses as universal (Pogge 2005). His critique targets the rules governing the recognition of states and their governments, which are oblivious to the often violent means those entities used to acquire power; the agreements establishing the World Trade Organization, which commit members to free trade and sustain unfair rules for poor countries; and other aspects of the rules that sustain our international economic order. We agree with Pogge that some international legal instruments entrench existing power relations to the detriment of the world's poor—such as the Agreement on Trade-Related Intellectual Property Rights (TRIPs) with regards to intellectual property rights or BITs that can be used by foreign investors to threaten states with liabilities for general welfare-enhancing policies that seem to infringe their rights. In effect, they can hold states hostage. The effects of many other international rules or instruments, however, are arguably more ambivalent. Pogge is correct that the rules on state recognition frequently end up endorsing a group of robber barons who were successful in their power grab. The claim is reminiscent of Charles Tilly's comparison of war making and state making as organized crime (Tilly 1985)—legitimated ex post by whoever comes out victorious. And yet international law is no longer oblivious to the internal conduct of states to the extent it once was. Humanitarian interventions have been legitimated (if not legalized), and international criminal justice has been institutionalized, albeit imperfectly. Finally, and most relevant to the concerns raised in this volume, governments are not expected to remain passive in the face of extreme deprivation faced by their populations: As stipulated by the Committee on Economic, Social and Cultural Rights, it is now accepted that even the poorest states should discharge "a minimum core obligation to ensure the satisfaction of, at the very least, minimum essential levels of each of the rights" listed in the International Covenant on Economic, Social and Cultural Rights, including the right to food, housing, water, and essential medicines (CESCR 1990, para. 10). This requirement under international human rights law can be traced to the impact of the then rapporteur of the committee, Philip Alston, who urged the committee to "find a way of conveying to states the fact that priority must be accorded to the satisfaction of minimum subsistence levels of enjoyment of the relevant rights by *all* individuals" (Alston 1987, 359–360). As a matter of international law, ensuring access to essential resources is thus no longer left to the discretion of sovereign nation-states: It has become part and parcel of international human rights law.

We do recognize, however, that these principles are rarely enforced. We are also in agreement about the importance of identifying arrangements that pose the greatest impediments to a more just order. A major source of concern is the demise of multilateralism: the shift away from seeking multilateral solutions that would address human rights concerns in the context of free trade and investment protection toward the negotiation of bilateral agreements (see also De Schutter et al. 2012). Imbalances in the parties' respective bargaining powers (as larger economies by definition have more to bring to the table than smaller economies) tend to produce outcomes that are severely skewed toward the interests of the most powerful players. Consider the likely effects of BITs on the allocation of essential resources. Investors who bought land in foreign countries to export food or water will be able to invoke these treaties to protect their investments even if their actions contribute to scarcity of essential resources in the country where they are harvesting them. Where their rights conflict with those of domestic constituencies (such as indigenous people who live on the land that has been sold or for which mining concessions have been granted, as in the case of *Sawhoyamaxa Indigenous Community* cited earlier), any attempts by host countries to protect the latter create the risk of liability to foreign investors affected by this change. From our vantage point, any regime that creates vested rights for some without leaving room for Voice to those affected by it or that fails to incorporate mechanisms for enhancing Reflexivity is a governance failure.

VOICE

We argue that Voice and Reflexivity should be relied on as normative principles to guide the governance of essential resources. Voice captures the ability of *all* members of a group, community, or society to claim their share in resources essential to their survival. Reflexivity is the correlate of Voice; it stands for the capacity to question one's preferences in the context of changing circumstances. Reflexivity requires that collective-action mechanisms be established to redefine interests and rights in a process of institutional reform that acknowledges competing claims and accommodates them to the fullest extent possible.

The concept of Voice is borrowed from Hirschman (1970), who famously identified "exit, voice and loyalty" as the possible range of options for members in organizations, both public (including states) and private. Voice is not identical with voting; the case of water management in Mumbai's slums (Anand in this volume) suggests that the right to vote does not guarantee access to drinking water, even though it can help exert pressure on officials who have to stand for election. More generally, Voice stands for the normative proposition that people should have a say in the rules by which they are governed—especially when it comes to governing access to resources critical for their survival. Cafaggi and Pistor use the term "regulatory capabilities" to capture the notion of regulatory self-determination (Cafaggi and Pistor 2014). Regulatory capabilities are an extension of individual capabilities, the claim to live the life one has reason to value, as defined by Sen (1999) and Nussbaum (2011). Individual capabilities can be effectively realized only if institutions are put in place that empower individuals to develop their innate abilities. Leading a healthy life requires access to clean water, basic food, shelter, and health; education is a prerequisite for knowledge, reasoning, and participation in public life, including but not limited to elections. Providing these goods and setting up the institutions that govern them is a collective not an individual undertaking; this is what makes institutions that enhance individual capabilities "public goods" in the true sense of the phrase. And yet, only too often is the public excluded from framing governance domains and creating governance regimes that determine access rights and the scope of participation or Voice.

This exclusion is obvious when international treaties are signed following secret negotiations and without any involvement of branches of government other than the executive. The mere fact that in most countries legislatures have to ratify an international treaty for it to become formally binding does not ensure actual deliberation or influence by democratically elected lawmakers. They are effectively left with a take it or leave it option. Exclusion also occurs when governing elites establish institutions at the domestic level without any attempt to encourage participation or to subject them to standard mechanisms of accountability or, indeed, when regulatory powers are delegated to private actors. This practice is problematic, because it undermines basic forms of self-governance; when applied to essential resources it is arguably abusive. Historically, legal rules that ensure a modicum of inclusiveness of property rights have evolved in "open-access orders," that is, under conditions of fairly pluralistic political regimes with room for deliberation (North, Wallis, and Weingast 2009). This has helped mitigate conflicts between holders of potentially exclusive control rights and competing claimants (see Dagan in this volume). In contrast, closed- or limited-access orders have reserved framing and enforcement powers for the political elites, which only too often exercise it in an arbitrary fashion (see Pils in this volume).

Insisting on Voice challenges both the unfettered operation of markets and authoritarian or paternalistic regimes. A particularly difficult case is the transnational context, in which institutional structures for organizing and expressing Voice are largely absent. Indeed, current trends emphasize the importance of depoliticizing international law and institutions in the name of efficiency; they do so at the expense of contestability and publicness, ingredients we deem critical for self-governance. Further, in today's world states are no longer the primary agents of governance. There is a burgeoning literature on the rise of the "new global rules" (Büthe and Mattli 2011) and on transnational private regulation (Cafaggi 2011). It documents the rise of private and nongovernmental actors in defining regulatory standards that are often vindicated by states or domestic regulators. The right to regulatory self-determination is therefore a claim directed at any actor—private, public, or hybrid—with the power and influence to frame regulatory domains. Applying this principle in practice will require new approaches to governance that take into account the specifics of the regulatory domain (i.e., a water reserve, a lake, or forest that offers economic opportunities to some and is the basis of subsistence for others) and the stakes involved.

The concept of essential resources requires every governance regime to include those dependent on the resource to partake in the design of the governance regime that establishes their access rights. Depending on circumstances, these rights may be temporal or limited in geographical or quantitative terms. The choice of the exclusion benchmark will affect the relative inclusiveness of the governance regimes. Every property regime is necessarily based on exclusion (Hall, Hirsch, and Murray Li 2011); the critical question is not only *where* to draw the line but *how*—in particular, how porous or amenable is such a line to future change? As Edda Schlager points out in her contribution to this volume, some regimes use quantitative benchmarks ("How much can be harvested?"), while others apply pluralist approaches ("How many different uses can be sustained?"). The latter has greater potential than the former to evolve into an "architecture of inclusion" (Sturm 2006) that is commensurate with the normative claim of Voice to ensure access, because it invites different forms of usages and their contestation.

Voice does not necessarily call for direct participation—just as democratic governance is not equivalent with direct democracy. Instead it calls for deliberative governance (Sen, 1999), and no preestablished right can be absolutely immune against such deliberation. If the use of underground water resources depletes water reserves on which entire cities, states, or countries depend, then actual use must be moderated and property rights, insofar as they legitimate unrestricted use, must be curtailed. Otherwise, the exercise of these rights will give rise to a new form of the tragedy of the commons (Hardin 1968)—one in which private property rights result in the unsustainable exploitation of essential resources. Similarly, if land is expropriated for infrastructure projects, then the dispossessed who lived off the land should be afforded Voice in determining how they should be compensated: by current market value, a stake in the project, or compensation in kind, such as reallocation. This would allow them to choose the option most suited to their circumstances, including access to alternative sources to meet their demands for essential resources or to employment or migration options that would offer alternative avenues for meeting their needs (Lehavi and Licht 2007). Most legal systems offer "adequate compensation" for expropriation based on the market value of the claimed property. Employing alternative forms of compensation presupposes that those to be dispossessed are sufficiently organized to express their preferences—a difficult task, especially when they have heterogeneous interests and face collective-action problems (Olson 1971). To effectuate Voice in these cases, special arrangements are required. An interesting example comes from India: In the aftermath of violent uprisings against large-scale expropriation for the benefit of infrastructure development, rural land departments encouraged landowners to join cooperatives as a means of self-organization and increasing their bargaining power (Balakrishnan 2013).

REFLEXIVITY

Reflexivity complements and expands on the notion of Voice: As we use it, the concept refers to the capacity of actors to actively participate in governance processes that allow them to *reshape their preferences* in the light of a broadened range of alternatives. Reflexivity thus stands for the capability to reimagine solutions and update interests in light of competing claims, changing circumstances, and mutual learning processes (De Schutter and Lenoble 2010). The concept takes as a point of departure the relative weakness of Voice of the most vulnerable constituencies in most societies. Simply registering what the poor and marginalized say about their condition or changes they most desire ignores the fact that their evaluation may be shaped by existing social norms (da Cunha and Junho Pena 1997). Extensive research suggests a psychological tendency to adapt one's preferences to one's situation (Elster 1982, 1983). Furthermore, the poor may have only limited imagination for altering their current predicament. Clearly, adaptive preferences are a useful survival strategy for those who have little choice (Kahneman, Diener, and Schwarz 1999) and allows them to "make the best" of the set of circumstances with which they are confronted (Teschl and Comim 2005). There is, however, no reason that these beneficial effects should be limited only to social groups that lack Voice or resources to change their circumstances on their own. The notion of Reflexivity acknowledges a dialectic relationship between individual preferences that reflect existing institutional arrangements and processes of institutional change that offer alternatives.

The inclusion of Reflexivity in the governance of essential resources distinguishes ours from the "basic needs" approach that has influenced discussions concerning poverty reduction since the 1970s (Stewart 1985, 1995). At least in part in response to this approach, Sen emphasized the imperative of individuals having an adequate set of capabilities and suggested that development could be measured as the expansion of capabilities.[7] Capabilities are distinct from the actual *achievements* or *functionings* of the individual, that is, a person's "doings" or "beings."

They refer instead to the *possibilities* an individual has to lead a life which he or she values:

> A functioning is an achievement, whereas a capability is the ability to achieve. Functionings are, in a sense, more directly related to living conditions, since they are different aspects of living conditions. Capabilities, in contrast, are notions of freedom, in the positive sense: what real opportunities you have regarding the life you may lead. (Sen 1987, 36)

The capabilities approach respects the plurality of conceptions of a good life more than approaches that focus exclusively on individuals' income or actual achievements, their material condition. It emphasizes the need to provide individuals with the means to make significant choices and refrains from imposing goals or values as if they were desirable in themselves. Instead, it places the value of freedom (or individual choice) among the values that make a life valuable: If one individual has a choice between different styles of life and chooses one of those styles, his or her situation is more desirable than that of another individual who has attained precisely the same style of life and corresponding standard of living but without the freedom to choose.

And yet, the capabilities approach leaves open the determinants of individual choice, in particular the ability of individuals to make choices that are informed not simply by existing institutional arrangements but by an awareness of the possibilities of alternative arrangements that could result from collective-learning processes. Institutions or processes that allow for collective learning and the search for novel means for governing the allocation of resources are critical for Reflexivity. Such institutions could help mediate between conflicting interests. Indeed, one of the key advantages of reflexive governance is that it moves beyond mutual learning (Sabel and Zeitlin 2008) to focus on the process for discovering solutions and addressing conflicts between competing claims.

The concept is applicable well beyond essential resources but is particularly pertinent in this context. Access to essential resources is a moral imperative that imposes obligations on those with control rights over these resources or those whose actions might affect supply and access. Their rights, we suggest, are morally bounded by the legitimate needs of others to receive access to these resources. To effectuate these rights, legal and institutional arrangements must be put in place that encourage a permanent redefinition of access rights in the light of the need to accommodate conflicting claims on resources. This presupposes that social actors are capable of imagining solutions that can strike an appropriate balance between conflicting interests and in this process redefine their own preferences.

Reflexive governance may sound utopian, yet there is ample evidence that social groups are quite capable of governing resources in ways that are both inclusive (ensuring limited access for all) and sustainable (avoiding depletion of the resource in question). Dealing with competing claims that do not stand in a clear hierarchical fashion to one another is nothing new to social practice or law. Common-pool resource management (Ostrom 1990) offers many examples. Moreover, courts in several jurisdictions have recognized the need to reconcile competing claims and have developed appropriate doctrinal vehicles. A prominent example is the doctrine of *practical concordance* that Germany's Constitutional Court has developed (Brugger 1994; Hesse 1995, 172). It holds that in cases where competing claims are protected by different constitutional norms with neither given explicit priority, a compromise must be found that curtails each right but only to the extent necessary for the other right to receive recognition as well. Practical concordance is not a silver bullet but a way of reconciling inevitable conflicts between rights and values that cannot be resolved by imposing hierarchies or priorities. It is also distinct from balancing, because it takes into account what may be called the declining marginal utility of recognizing rights: Once a right has been recognized to a certain degree, any greater amount of recognition would only marginally benefit the right holder while potentially negatively affecting conflicting claims. The idea of *practical concordance* tends to prioritize equal distribution in resolving conflicting claims. It calls for institutional imagination to maximize the possibility of upholding both claims simultaneously rather than sacrificing one for the other, which may require both rights to be compromised.

This approach contrasts with approaches that seek to sidestep the challenges of complexity by narrowing the scope of each policy intervention to a one-dimensional problem. If it were indeed always possible to unbundle competing normative goals and subject them to different policy strategies (Tinbergen 1956), there would be no need for practical concordance. Unbundling, however, is infeasible where conflicts among competing claims are "inherently unresolvable" (Arrow 1958, 91) from a welfare-optimization perspective. Such problems require normatively grounded rather than efficiency-grounded reconciliation and recognition that no claim is absolute.

Such normatively grounded solutions presuppose shared values and an authority to enunciate them. As Hadfield and Weingast have suggested, law or a legal authority does not necessarily require a full-blown state; sufficient is some agent deemed legitimate by the community to announce binding rules that can be enforced by members of the community (Hadfield and Weingast 2012). The critical element here is community, because any claim for equitable access presupposes at least a modicum of community (Dubet 2014). Communities, however, are not given but are socially constructed. Benedict Anderson has labeled the nation-state an "imagined community" (Anderson 1991). For people living in villages and small townships in early modern times with little information about villagers and townspeople further away than the nearest marketplace, the notion that they were part of a single "nation" must have indeed appeared far-fetched, perhaps even more so than claims about the emergence of a global cosmopolitan community (Appiah 2007) in today's world with its advanced information technology. The important insight of Anderson's analysis is that the rise of the nation-state required not only new modes of governance and organization but (also) a shared identity and destiny both within and beyond nation-states. These are long-term processes of social constructions and reconstruction. Indeed, to this day we witness nation-building efforts, for example, in fragmented India (Guha 2007) or in Europe, where attempts to create a "demos" made of citizens that could shift loyalties from the nation-state to the European Union are still under way (van Middelaar 2013). It is, however, not inconceivable to create a sense of community *beyond* nation-states. Take, for example, the Committee on World Food Security (CFS) that was formed in 2009 in Rome (De Schutter 2012). It started as an intergovernmental body but following the global food crisis in 2007–2008 was transformed into a multistakeholder forum that now includes states, international organizations such as the WTO or the World Bank, and private-sector participants and philanthropic agencies. The CFS plays a critical role in monitoring food security and investigating the causes of food insecurity.[8]

Institutional arrangements or legal rules alone may not be sufficient for achieving the normative ends of universal access to essential resources. Reflexivity is doomed, however, without institutions that reward and foster notions of other-regarding preferences (Blair and Stout 2001). Institutional arrangements that emphasize rights and call for their uncompromising enforcement in the name of efficiency and legal certainty not only fail to do so, they undermine the normative fabric required for

Reflexivity. We do not go as far as arguing that property rights or the pricing mechanism are incompatible with Reflexivity, but they need to be tamed. The enforcement of rights could be made contingent on their compatibility with other norms; alternatively, ex post intervention may help complete contracts or governance regimes that are left incomplete for failure to address such contingencies. Consider the case of agricultural markets: Natural disasters can make it impossible for many to perform in accordance with contracts committed to ex ante. An externally imposed debt moratorium can bring relief in such circumstances by completing contracts that failed to provide for relief in times of natural disasters or other exogenous shocks (Bolton and Rosenthal 2002). A common objection to such interventions is moral hazard. Nonintervention, however, can force those struck by natural or human-made disaster into destitution or worse. In short, justice may demand intervention from time to time, even if this comes at the expense of efficiency.

DEPARTURES FROM EXISTING DISCOURSES

As mentioned above, the allocation of scarce resources is associated primarily with the field of economics. Indeed, the economic analysis of property rights has dominated policy circles and much of academia for the last few decades. In this section we seek to differentiate our approach from this dominant paradigm. We recognize that other literatures in sociology, anthropology, and environmental studies have also contributed to these debates, and we believe that many of the insights they have produced are highly relevant to addressing our questions. A full review of all relevant literatures would, however, go beyond the scope of this introductory chapter. We hope that the interdisciplinary background of the other contributors to this volume and the diversity of analytical frameworks they bring to bear will fill this gap.

The notion of essential resources contrasts with the dominant approach to property, which links principles of allocation to physical characteristics of the goods in question, not to normative principles.[9] Subtractability and excludability are the criteria used for determining the nature of goods (Ostrom 2003). A good is subtractive if consumption by one person subtracts from the consumption of others (Samuelson 1954; Musgrave 1959). It is excludable if, because of its nature, institutions, or technology, it is feasible to exclude others from access to and use of the good. Collective-action problems arise, according to the classic account,

Table 1.1 Typology of Goods

	Consumption is Subtractive	Consumption is *not* Subtractive
Exclusion is feasible.	Private goods	
Exclusion is not feasible.	Common-pool resource	Public goods
Exclusion is economically inefficient.	Anticommons	
Exclusion threatens survival.	Essential resources	

Source: Authors' compilation following fig. 1 in Ostrom (2003, 241).

when goods are subtractive but not excludable, resulting in the "tragedy of the commons" (Hardin 1968), wherein resources that all can freely access will be overexploited and eventually depleted to the detriment of all. The common answer to this problem is to privatize the commons and vest the owner of the asset with the right to exclude.

Table 1.1 builds on Ostrom (2003, 241) in classifying goods, but differentiates between excludability that is economically inefficient—what Michael Heller has termed the "tragedy of the anticommons" (Heller 1998)—and excludability that is not desirable because it deprives fellow human beings of resources that satisfy basic needs, that is, essential resources.

The governance of essential resources raises issues that extend further than the need to ensure increased productivity in the exploitation of the said resource. It calls attention to distributional equity as well as to sustainability—that is, the compatibility of current uses with the satisfaction of the basic needs of future generations, in accordance with the famous definition of the 1987 Brundtland report (United Nations 1987). In other words, though efficiency matters in the governance of resources, we argue that it should be promoted with the proviso that nobody should be excluded from resources that are essential for satisfying basic needs; further, the exploitation of the resource today should not jeopardize the ability of future generations to satisfy their needs. Governing access to essential resources therefore requires different approaches than those economists tend to associate with conventional classifications of public, private, or common goods. In fact, the standard governance regimes applied to private or public goods tend to fall short when applied to *essential*, scarce resources.

To illustrate this, we present a taxonomy of different governance regimes generally associated with different types of goods (see table 1.2).

Table 1.2   Typology of Property Rights Regimes

	Individual Property	Centralized Property	Communal Property
Private goods	X	X	X
Public goods	o	X	X
Common-pool resources	o	o	X
Anticommons	o	X	X
Essential resources	o	o	o

Note: "X" is used to indicate the compatibility between a good and a governance regime, and "o" is used to indicate incompatibility.

Private goods are typically slated for individual property rights to ensure their efficient use; public goods for centralized (state) property regimes; and common-pool resources for centralized or communal property regimes. Finally, the problem of the anticommons (when exclusion is technically feasible but creates inefficient delays) is addressed by central intervention with private property rights, that is, by the state exercising the power of eminent domain (Heller 2008). However, communal forms of property could feasibly address this problem. These governance regimes constitute the repertoire of regimes under which all resources are most commonly managed. It is important to understand the limitations that this classical approach faces and why the dominant regimes leave a number of questions unanswered.

The juxtaposition of goods and governance regimes in table 1.2 shows that some goods are compatible with more than one governance regime. Specifically, private goods can be governed in the alternative by individual, centralized, or communal property rights. This is particularly true for land. Though it was treated for much of human history as a common and unlimited resource, land has also been governed as centralized state, communal, and individual property. The versatility of private goods in relation to governance regimes contrasts with the incompatibility of essential, scarce resources with *any* governance regime (see table 1.2). Individual property rights over such resources are problematic, because their dominant mechanism, that is, the ability to exclude others (Coase 1960; Demsetz 1966), is morally repugnant when exclusion violates basic needs. Centralized property rights pose their own problems, because the power of central control does not guarantee universal access or effective use (Umbeck 1981; Campbell and Lindberg 1990; Firmin-Sellers 1995). Finally, communal property rights presuppose communities with the capacity of collective governance (Ostrom 1990; Ellickson 1991; Schlager and Blomquist 1998)[10]—conditions that may not be present where constituencies with heterogeneous interests and varying power seek access to the same resource, whether locally or globally.

Over the past thirty years, individual property rights have been favored as the optimal governance solution for most resources, including essential resources such as land (Deininger 2003). Titling programs promoted by multilateral and bilateral development agencies have extended the geographical remit of individual property rights by penetrating a larger number of countries in the developing world (World Bank 2010). Control rights over land are increasingly allocated to the highest bidder across national boundaries in a market-driven process, ostensibly in the name of promoting the most efficient use of resources (Coase 1960). Under private property rights regimes, individual control rights over land will determine who has access to these essential and increasingly scarce resources and whether they are harvested in a sustainable fashion.

Experience with land privatization suggests that this can take a substantial toll on millions of peasant smallholders and forest dwellers who are being deprived of the basis of their sustenance (Cotula et al. 2009; Zoomers 2010; De Schutter 2011). Moreover, while private property regimes have been traditionally justified by their contribution to increases in productivity, they provide no assurance of sustainability, that is, the preservation of essential resources in the interest of future generations (Beddoe et al. 2009). Finally, whereas private ownership and the allocation of land through market mechanisms were intended to translate into higher productivity, this hope did not always materialize. Those who place the highest bid on the land, it was reasoned, surely were best equipped to maximize production resulting from the use of land. In reality, some owners are tempted to hoard land without using it to increase total output but instead to speculate on further price increases (De Schutter 2011). To the extent that economic efficiency is associated only with effects on price (Demsetz 1966), this outcome is, of course, efficient, but it violates the normative principles put forward in this paper.

The alternatives to individual property regimes in the classic repertoire do not fare much better when applied to essential resources. Centralized control is the ultima ratio for dealing with the problem of scarcity, as demonstrated time and again in times of war or emergencies, when governments requisition critical assets and resort to rationing. These cases also exemplify the problems associated with centralized control: abuse of power and mismanagement of resources. Any government that has the power to decide on the allocation of resources also has the power to determine who may benefit from them and to exclude others at its whim (Binswanger, Deininger, and Feder 1995). Moreover, government control often suffers from mismanagement, as bureaucratic management and accountability structures frequently fall short of the governance tasks at hand.

Communal property regimes also face limitations when applied to essential resource management. Governance mechanisms that ensure the survival of the community do not always ensure that its weakest members have equal access to essential resources. Discrimination against girls and women, minorities, or others deemed "outcasts" remains only too common. Communal property regimes face another problem in today's world. The scarcity of essential resources now plays out at the global level: With the emergence of a transnational market for land (World Bank 2010; De Schutter 2011), water, and carbon, the competition for control of these resources pits actors located in different jurisdictions against one another; similarly, with climate change and increasing pressure on natural resources, the management of essential resources must take into account not only the interests of local users but also of constituencies far afield whose basic needs would otherwise be difficult to meet. Furthermore, externalities may result from how one community chooses to manage the resources over which it exercises control. The unsustainable use of a resource may affect the ability of other communities to satisfy their basic needs (i.e., where shifts in land use increase greenhouse gas emissions or agricultural production pollutes shared groundwater reserves). To be effective in the global context, communal governance regimes would need to expand their remits to the global community. In other words, even when localized communal regimes ensure effective governance of essential resources, they do not address the problem that these resources are distributed unevenly around the globe, where such communal regimes are not operable.

In addition, each of the property regimes associated with the classic approach assumes institutional arrangements for its operation that may or may not be present (see table 1.3). The efficacy of individual property regimes depends on their delineation and legal validation (Benda-Beckman 1995; Hodgson 2003) and on markets and the operation of the price mechanism. Yet transactions in real property are conducted typically not in transparent, liquid markets but in private deals characterized

Table 1.3   Conditions for Effective Property Regimes

Individual Property	Centralized Property	Communal Property
Clear delineation of rights	Effective management	Shared norms of reciprocity and community
Market	Information	Information
Enforceability	Authority	Long time horizon
		Low monitoring and compliance costs

by asymmetries in information and power: The value that is attached to the resources exchanged is typically determined not by some objective standard related to the relative use to the transacting parties but by the bargaining power the parties to the transaction can exert on each other.

Effective public asset management and accountability systems must be in place to avoid the typical pitfalls of centralized regimes, that is, arbitrariness and waste. Resources should instead be managed in the public interest, and opposing interests of different communities or geographically dispersed groups should be reconciled (De Schutter 2012). This requires information about how resources are managed, knowledge about how to improve their management, and mechanisms for implementing reforms. Moreover, the central manager must have both the authority and legitimacy to manage these resources, lest shirking, corruption, and theft will erode them. At the global level, no such regime exists.

Finally, decentralized communal property regimes may not be transposable to governing essential resources at the global level. This would require the development of shared, general norms of reciprocity and community. Experience with divided jurisdiction over the same watershed or lake system suggests that common management of such a resource is difficult although not entirely infeasible (Ostrom 2010). While powerful arguments have been made that cosmopolitanism is feasible (Appiah 2007)—as announced by the growth of global social movements (Miller 2006)—the challenges facing multilateralism today suggest that its full realization will remain aspirational for some time to come. The efficacy of communal property regimes depends on a fairly long-term horizon as well as sufficiently powerful incentives for a community to invest in collective governance—a substantial challenge in a world characterized by high levels of heterogeneity, mobility, and the absence of institutional arrangements that would give Voice to the diverse interest groups.

In summary, the classical approach focuses on efficient use of a resource and neglects considerations of distributive justice. It also makes heroic assumptions about the rationality of individuals and about the predominance, in choosing their course of conduct, of utilitarian considerations based on fixed self-interest.[11] We argue that for essential resources, a normative approach is required that embraces Voice and Reflexivity as the guiding principles for designing and adapting governance over time.

We now turn to the other contributions in this volume. They can be divided into three groups: those that wrestle with the concept of essential resources and seek to understand how it can be operationalized for different assets or in different contexts; others that tackle questions of Voice and Reflexivity; and finally, case studies that explore actual governance of essential resources in various regional contexts or that suggest alternative approaches.

ESSENTIAL RESOURCES: CHALLENGES AHEAD

Derek Hall in his contribution "Land's Essentiality and Land Governance" problematizes the concept of essentiality by applying it to the case of land. He argues that land is not only a critical resource for the survival of each human being; rather, land also needs to be understood in its spatial and territorial dimensions. As such, land is a source not only of individual but of collective survival. Further, the claim that all should have access to essential resources does not resolve the legal question of whether access requires ownership or other forms of property rights or whether a specific plot of land might be substituted for another. This implies that context matters not only for defining what resources shall be deemed essential but also for determining the rights or causes of actions that follow. Further, for some groups land is essential for their social identity. Depriving them of a specific piece of land challenges their survival as a group and often fuels conflict. By the same token, identity-based claims often stake out exclusion claims that deprive others of access to the land. Last but not least, the normative claim of essentiality is in tension with processes of economic and social differentiation embedded in the operation of global capitalism. In short, Hall argues that while land is often deemed essential for those directly dependent on it, it differs from other resources associated with guaranteeing basic needs such as water, food, and shelter because of the complex nature of this asset and its varying roles in the lives of individuals and collectives. Drawing attention to essentiality is thus not a panacea for solutions; it is only the beginning of an inquiry into a set of complex issues that require context-specific analysis.

In "Governing Boundaries: Exclusion, Essential Resources, and Sustainability" Edella Schlager urges a broader conceptualization of essential resources that focuses not only on demand—access to and the allocation of scarce essential resources—but also on supply. Potable water depends on lakes and watersheds, that is, on environmental infrastructures rather than human-made institutions. Ensuring the maintenance of this infrastructure is critical for the sustainability of essential resources. On the demand side the more familiar problem of how to govern access to common-pool resources arises; this is typically managed by quantitative restrictions and the like. Failure to manage demand can exhaust the resource, resulting in the well-known tragedy of the commons, but so can failure to ensure supply. Thus, Schlager argues that at a deeper level, the tragedy of exclusion we postulate is actually a twin crisis of the failure to prevent overusage of a common-pool resource *and* to protect the supply of environmental services. Quantitative restrictions on resource extraction alone are insufficient for avoiding this twin crisis. Instead, a shift toward considering how many different usages and/or users shall be recognized and protected is required.

While Schlager emphasizes the importance of the physical infrastructure, Hanoch Dagan's chapter focuses on the law, or the social infrastructure, for governing essential resources. In "Property Theory, Essential Resources, and the Global Land Rush," he claims that property rights and market competition can be reconciled with the notion of essential resources. In his view the classification of resources as essential does not raise questions and concerns that are fundamentally different from a properly understood and normatively guided property discourse. Dagan asserts that the dominant theoretical view of property rights—as depicted in our literature review—is mostly prescriptive rather than descriptive: The emphasis on exclusion and individual autonomy does not reflect the state of the common law or other legal systems for that matter. The legal systems in developed market economies tend to be much more accommodating to competing normative and social claims, and the actual operation of property law is more inclusive than is often assumed. More generally, property can be reimagined to incorporate values such as Voice and Reflexivity, and the market could and should be enlisted to pursue these goals. To this end, auctions could be designed to ensure there is sufficient buyer competition, or antitrust law could be brought to bear to counter monopolies. Dagan concedes that not all of these mechanisms are available in all legal systems, much less in the transnational realm. Yet he insists that, in principle, they could be put in place and that existing legal institutions offer important models as guidance.

Nikhil Anand's contribution, "MultipliCity: Water, Rules, and the Making of Connections in Mumbai," suggests that the supply of essential resources can be curtailed not only by the physical nature of the environmental infrastructure but equally by human-made physical and social infrastructures. Indeed, the human-made infrastructure is often just as unbending as nature in compelling those seeking access to devise costly circumvention strategies. He analyzes the municipal water system of Mumbai, originally built during English colonial rule and at the time supplying water exclusively to English settlers. While the physical scope was expanded over time, this system still serves only parts of the city. Millions of slum dwellers living in Mumbai today are excluded from access, as the plumbing does not reach their settlements and legal rules deny access to those unable to document settlement prior to 1995. To get around the constraints of plumbing and law, settlers bargain with councilmen in return for their vote in municipal elections, negotiate with engineers, pool households able to pay for the supply of water, or turn to violence. Full privatization of water is vehemently resisted irrespective of possible gains in terms of reliability, mostly because it would undermine this complex set of relations on which settlers have come to rely. Anand thus extends Hall's insight that classifying resources as essential may help clarify the normative stake but does not lead directly to institutionally operative solutions. As it turns out, even drinking water, the least disputed of essential resources, raises a host of complex issues that require a deep understanding of context-specific social structures and power relations. An important insight of this work is that Voice and Reflexivity is only loosely related to whether essential resources are governed by public or private regimes (markets or bureaucrats). While the vote in (public) municipal elections enhances the bargaining power of settlers, personal relations and bargaining, including the pricing mechanism, play an equally important role.

BEYOND VOICE AND REFLEXIVITY

Eva Pils in "Voice, Reflexivity, and Say: Governing Access to and Control of Land in China" uses land use and reallocation practices in China to shed new light on the notion of essentiality and the claim that

Voice and Reflexivity offer guidance for addressing questions of fundamental injustice. She places our framework into a broader philosophical discourse and associates it with Peter Singer and others who developed a global theory of responsibility. This leads her to warn against the consequentialism and utilitarianism associated with that body of work. Most importantly, she warns against focusing too much on the distributional consequences of property rights that honor the right to exclude while overlooking injustice in the process of redistribution. China serves as an interesting example, because it features state actors who, in the name of development (but not infrequently for personal gain), use state power to expropriate individuals. These practices are deeply unjust. They deprive the affected individuals of access to essential resources, and as illustrated by the fact that many owners have committed suicide in response to such injustice, they rob people of their human dignity. Voice and Reflexivity, according to Pils, fall short of guarding against injustice in general. Rather, people must be given much greater "say" in their lives—including the right to exclude the state from interference with their rights save for exceptional circumstances.

Alain Durand-Lasserve offers an interesting comparison with Pils's analysis of land rights in China. He studies peri-urban areas and hinterlands of West African cities and argues that any formalization of rights to land needs to take account of social practices and highly uneven bargaining power of different actors. Zoning and titling programs introduced by the World Bank and other developing agencies that ignore these practices are bound to fail, or worse, they tend to accelerate the concentration of land in favor of the elites. Durand-Lasserve presents an analytical framework for diagnosing land use and allocation practices that takes account of tenure security and property rights but also of the channels through which land is reallocated, given these initial conditions. Moreover, he highlights the importance of a well-run land administration for limiting graft and capture. Only too often bureaucrats collude with well-heeled agents wishing to obtain formal title for land acquired in informal markets, or from parties with weaker rights. Put differently, Voice, Reflexivity and Pils's "Say" can be undermined not only by a powerful state but also by rampant corruption, with the legal title to land itself becoming an item for purchase by the better off. Aid organizations only too often play into the hands of this system, as they make assumptions about market efficiency and the operation of law that are at odds with practices on the ground.

Michael Dwyer's analysis of land-titling efforts in Cambodia points in a similar direction. In "Redirecting Regulation? Land Titling and Cambodia's Post-neoliberal Conjuncture," he documents the failure of ambitious land-titling schemes in the aftermath of Cambodia's civil war. The World Bank's land-titling operation closed down in 2009, after it fell seriously behind target numbers. The civil war had disrupted informal land tenure and formal property rights alike. After the war the government allowed farmers to apply for recognition of title, which quickly evolved into a system of quasi titles. At the same time, the government sought to spur economic development by granting concessions to timber-extraction companies. As Dwyer shows, newly emergent smallholdings on one hand and large-scale land control via concession agreements on the other set the stage for a sharply bifurcated property regime that not infrequently gave rise to conflicts. Alternative programs aimed at granting land rights to collectives (villages) were marginalized as bureaucrats dragged their feet or preempted the programs by claiming land as state owned for the purpose of reallocating it to more lucrative uses. More successful were programs whereby state land was redistributed to the poor. In short, Dwyer argues that governing essential resources requires more than minimum regulation in the form of zoning or titling programs, which are oblivious to domestic and global power relations. A superior approach would be to emphasize the multiplicity of normative goals—equity and sustainability in addition to economic productivity—and to empower local actors to effectively voice these concerns.

Like Dwyer, Vamsi Vakulabharanam emphasizes the dynamics of economic processes unleashed by neoliberal policies that spur cycles of primitive capital accumulation—in this case natural resource mining in rural India. In "Erosion of Essential Resources in India: A Bottom-Up View," he compares the fate of different legal protections for landholders when confronted with powerful interests of private investors who are often in collusion with state officials. India has a complex legal regime for property rights, with different rights for different constituencies. People who have been recognized as "scheduled tribes" under the Indian constitution have important procedural rights meant to protect their social identity—rights that go well beyond the procedural hearings granted to village governments in which only ordinary peasants are concerned. Tribal veto powers are anything but cosmetic: They have in fact been frequently and successfully litigated at the federal level. However, mining concessions and other privileges are granted at the state level, and it is the state government that benefits from investments by way of fees, taxation, and economic spillovers (i.e., employment) that may result (if indeed they are forthcoming). The comparative analysis of how peasants and tribal people fared in Andhra Pradesh when their land was found to be of interest to large mining companies reveals that differences in legal protection make little difference in outcome. Law is not simply set aside, but loopholes are exploited in ways that render largely toothless the Voice they were meant to protect. Further, the economic value at stake and the lack of any mechanism to force the internalization of social costs such as environmental degradation and health hazards creates few incentives for investors or state officials to incorporate the interests of tribes or peasants into their strategies. Vakulabharanam concludes from this analysis that institutional design is futile when confronted with the logic of global capitalism.

In contrast, Michael Cox's work on two communities in the arid West of the United States shows that ex ante institutional design can generate divergent outcomes. One community—the San Luis Valley in Colorado—adheres to the principle of "first come, first served" for allocating riparian water rights, a principle that was widely adopted for westbound migration in the eighteenth century and has subsequently been incorporated into the law of many states. The other community, acequias in Taos, New Mexico, uses collectively monitored temporal sharing arrangements. In times of water abundance both systems work reasonably well. In times of water scarcity the first produces substantial negative externalities. While those who come first can ensure their economic survival, those further down the line are left with the choice of abandoning agriculture or resorting to self-help. To avoid economic disaster many have drilled their own water wells, relying on the legal principle that property owners can indiscriminately exploit subsoil resources irrespective of the effect on a common-pool resource, such as a shared river basin. In contrast, temporal sharing arrangements have been more adaptive to changes in environmental circumstances as communities rely on existing practices to adapt their water needs. Based on this analysis, Cox urges consideration of the long-term effects of institutional choices and their adaptability to changing circumstances. This analysis calls attention to the fact that while conventional property rights theories assume that most social problems can be resolved through bargaining, once rights have been clearly allocated (as implied by the Coase theorem derived from the work of Ronald H. Coase [1960]), under conditions of absolute scarcity individual property rights may exacerbate problems rather than offer solutions.

GOVERNING ESSENTIAL RESOURCES IN ACTION

The remaining contributions present accounts of how essential resources are governed in different parts of the world. Some are empirical, while others sketch out normative solutions based on evidence, historical precedents, or theoretical insights gained from field research.

Vanessa Cassado-Pérez, in "Go with the Flow: Lessons from Water Management and Water Markets for Essential Resources," investigates water markets. In line with Dagan's arguments, she suggests that the market mechanism can be put to use for allocating scarce water resources as long as it is properly governed. Her empirical evidence is drawn primarily from developed market economies—California and western Europe. There, priorities for water usage are determined ex ante and incorporated in legislation that governs both primary water allocations and secondary markets where water rights can be traded. Further, these jurisdictions benefit from a legacy of reasonably well-functioning legal institutions that can be employed for determining specific rights to water and ensuring their enforcement.

Scott McKenzie complements Cassado-Pérez by focusing on the ecology of water. In "Ecology: Water Governance's Missing Link," he shows that governance regimes that emphasize human rights, water basin management, or the ecology of water not only lead to different governance solutions but affect the sustainability of this essential resource. He thus confirms Schlager's insight that failure to account for environmental constraint contributes to the tragedy of exclusion associated with human-made governance regimes. Importantly, McKenzie identifies possible solutions for avoiding or prolonging the effects of absolute scarcity, most important among them are strategies for reusing water and politics that make these strategies palatable.

John Hursh's "Water Scarcity in Morocco: Voice, Narrative, and Essential Resource Governance" takes the analysis of water management to Morocco. This country has a tradition of water scarcity, but climate change, intensive agriculture, and an expanding tourism industry have put additional pressure on this essential resource. Government policies tend to favor irrigated agriculture and tourism, which help fuel economic growth and development, over other usages. Recent years, however, have seen greater emphasis on social programs that broaden water access, including to women. Water use associations have played a critical role in this regard. Hursh emphasizes that this shift is largely a result of a change in the narrative on water and water management. He suggests that this is an important additional mechanism beyond Voice and Reflexivity.

Nilhari Neupane takes the problem of governing access to essential resources to the international stage in "Solving Transborder Water Issues in Changing Climate Scenarios of South Asia." Many countries share a common river or water basin. Their location determines ease of access and use potentially at the disadvantage of neighboring countries and their people. Power relations, however, can reverse the effects of physical geography. In his account, India, which is situated downstream on the Ganges basin, has used its regional power to gain greater access to water for irrigation and electricity at the expense of Nepal, its upstream neighbor, and Bangladesh, its downstream neighbor. He employs a principal-agent model to show that cooperation can produce superior outcomes for all concerned as compared with the single-minded exploitation of hegemony. In the model, principal and agent share a common resource but trade access for services. A contractual solution providing for sharing is the optimal outcome. Even as reality deviates from this outcome, the model offers some hope that contracting mechanisms can be employed to advance the normative goals associated with Voice and Reflexivity.

Laila Macharia shows how the process of negotiation of a new social contract and a constitution can be used to broaden the Voice of communities over land rights. In "Voice and Reflexivity in Essential Resources: Reforming the Community Land Regime in Kenya," she attributes conflicts of land access and use rights to the history of colonialism and the tension between community land rights and property regimes imposed during colonial rule. Following independence, community rights were converted into private rights without resolving conflicts over competing claims. Following the breakout of violence after the contested 2007 elections, a new constitution was drafted, and land reform became one of its central features. Community-based organizations participated in the drafting process and were thus able to voice their grievances and aspirations. Moreover, institutions were created to monitor the process of land reform—creating the possibility for continuing dialogue and thus Reflexivity. Much will depend on how these organizations are run. However, this case offers some perspective on how processes of institutionalization can further inclusion and contribute to social peace.

Moving from the positive to the normative accounts, Manase Kudzai Chiweshe's "Do Traditional Institutions Matter in Participatory Essential Resource Governance Systems in Zimbabwe?" seeks to broaden our search for alternatives to individualized property rights for governing essential resources by harnessing social knowledge and practices from traditional societies. He argues that in Zimbabwe local chieftains hold the authority needed for effective governance, indeed that this authority could be used to raise awareness for Voice and Reflexivity. While he concedes that in the past chieftains have often discriminated against women and other minorities, this does not mean that these institutions could not be updated to an evolving normative framework. Most importantly, as community-based institutions they could assert the needs of the community and play a critical role in the internal allocation of scarce resources.

Finally, James Krueger, in "Local Corporations: An Organizational Form to Reduce Information Costs and Maintain Supportive Resources," asserts that absolute scarcity poses a fundamental challenge to humankind. He agrees with our argument that Voice and Reflexivity depend on communities and develops a framework for creating communities with the capacity to govern in accordance with these normative principles. Specifically, he advocates a system of layered governance, with local corporations that control essential resources occupying a role as intermediaries. These local corporations should retain some control over entry and exit; include multiple stakeholders who share collective responsibility for the entity; and employ governance regimes that promote good governance.

CONCLUSION

How we frame problems sets the stage for finding solutions. The challenge of allocating scarce resources can be framed as a question related exclusively to the economic value of the resource as expressed by the pricing mechanism. Alternatively, it can be framed as a question of equity in accessing essential resources. Moving from asset to users (current and future ones) and shifting the focus from efficiency to essentiality is, in effect, an exercise in reframing: It restates the problem as a potential tragedy of exclusion (deprivation from essential resources) rather than a tragedy of the commons (unsustainable depletion of shared resources) or the anticommons (inefficient hoarding).

This shift does not come without costs. Most importantly, the classification of a resource or asset as essential does not map directly onto any specific governance solution. Rather, it calls for further inquiry into the political, economic, and social contexts to find solutions that will achieve the normative outcome. For some this complication will appear too costly. Defining property rights and using pricing mechanisms for allocative purposes in line with the Coase theorem offers a much simpler and, therefore, a perhaps more appealing solution. Yet rarely do property rights operate in the real world as depicted in these simple models. As Coase himself insisted, social costs are part and parcel of human existence, which is why the initial allocation of rights and the institutions that govern their reallocation are both critical (Coase 1960). Property rights are part of a complex social fabric and stem from power relations that affect the allocation of assets and control over access. Where formal legal regimes effectively mitigate power and ensure a modicum of inclusion, they tend to be the product of political and social contestation within complex institutional arrangements that foster contestation.

Complexity in governance, we suggest, should not be avoided but embraced. Governing access to resources that are both scarce and essential is complicated normatively, politically, and institutionally. No governance regime is likely to provide a simple solution or to last forever. We therefore do not advocate a specific institutional fix or a search for an optimum; what is optimal in one context may be inoperable elsewhere due to different social or environmental conditions. Instead, we emphasize the normative principles that should govern the access to essential resources: Voice and Reflexivity. These are open-ended concepts that can and should be institutionalized in different ways. They are critical ingredients for deliberative democracy but are meant to offer normative guidance beyond domestic polities—the only domain where democracies have been successful as of today. And they point toward a "thick" property regime, where rights can be contested, competing claims made, and institutional arrangements reconfigured over time to take account of changing circumstances and the reflexive adaptation of self-interests. We contrast this with the "thin" concept of well-defined property rights allocated by the pricing mechanism to produce efficient outcomes. By focusing on a single dimension of assets and resources, that is, their price, the task of thin property rights seems much easier. Yet they fail to address critical social problems, namely how to ensure that all whose survival depends on a resource will have adequate access. If water, food, or shelter is allocated exclusively by the pricing mechanism, some other mechanism has to kick in to avoid the logical outcome of freewheeling markets—pricing out those who lack sufficient purchasing power. Such mechanisms—whether tax policies, subsidies, or public provisioning of essential resources to the most needy—are not available everywhere, and even where they are, they offer only a partial solution. Paying heed to the principles of Voice and Reflexivity ensures that normative concerns are addressed not only as an afterthought—that is, once negative externalities (market failures) have become apparent—but at the framing stage of governance regimes. Given path dependency (Cox in this volume), it is difficult to dislodge regimes once they have been entrenched and fortified by legal protections.

The leading property rights theories in economics have been motivated by a search for internalizing the costs of externalities. For Demsetz (1966) and many others, private property rights were the answer to this problem. Demsetz saw very clearly that private owners would seek to externalize the effects of their actions. However, he suggested that this secondary effect could be managed through owners—who would be less numerous and therefore face fewer collective-transaction costs—bargaining with one another. The problem he did not address is what would happen to those excluded from resources now controlled by the new owners should their survival depend upon it. This is the problem we have posed for the present volume.

We did not expect to find a silver bullet solution, and we clearly did not. However, we hope that by reframing the issue and offering evidence from around the world on the operation of different property regimes and arrangements developed to cope with increasing scarcity of water and arable land, we set the stage for new kind of debate: one that takes seriously the externalities created by any governance regime and seeks to find solutions that internalize them based on widely shared normative principles.

NOTES

1. Thus, in societies where subsistence farmers have no alternative but agricultural production to make a living, land can be considered an essential resource. This would not be the case in societies where people can readily earn their living as wage labor.

2. See UN Resolution 64/292 on "The Human Right to Water and Sanitation," 28 July 2010.

3. The ILO proposed the following definition of basic needs in 1982: "First, certain minimum requirements of a family for private consumption: adequate food, shelter and clothing, as well as certain household equipment and furniture. Second, they include essential services provided by and for the community at large, such as safe drinking water, sanitation, public transport and health, educational and cultural facilities" (ILO 1982, 1). These "basic needs" in turn have influenced the definition of the "essential content" of the social rights recognized in the International Covenant on Economic, Social and Cultural Rights, including housing, food, and essential medicines (De Schutter 2013).

4. See American Geophysical Union (2014).

5. The European Union with its guarantee of free movement of persons is a rare exception; but even there the principle is coming under increasing political pressure.

6. See Inter-American Court of Human Rights, case of the Sawhoyamaxa Indigenous Community v. Paraguay (judgment of 29 March 2006, Series C, No. 146).

7. Sen himself was initially reluctant to identify such "basic capabilities," in particular because different societies might value capabilities differently and because the "basic needs" of one society may not correspond to the "basic needs" of another (see Alkire 2002).

8. This was recently acknowledged by the outcome document of the Rio+20 UN Conference on Sustainable Development, where the world leaders noted "the important work and inclusive nature of the Committee on World Food Security" (United Nations 2012, para. 115).

9. Note that this approach is in tension with classical philosophers who are often referred to to justify this position. For a critique of the association of John Locke with neoclassical approaches to property, see Waldron (2012); for a restatement of Adam Smith's conception of individuals and markets in light of his broader conception of justice and metaphysics, see Herzog (2013).

10. Note that according to Schlager and Blomquist, heterogeneous groups can engage in collective governance if there is substantial jointness in the production of governance outcomes and capturability is minimized. See Schlager and Blomquist (1998).

11. In her work on common-pool resources, Elinor Ostrom questioned the rationality assumption, but she did remain wedded to a certain extent to the idea that the physical nature of the good (including a common-pool resource such as a fishery) should be the departure point to determine how the good should be governed: Instead, we are concerned with the alignment between the nature of the needs the good should serve to meet and the norms governing how the good is managed and allocated.

REFERENCES

Alkire, Sabina. 2002. *Valuing freedoms: Sen's capability approach and poverty reduction*. New York: Oxford University Press.

Allouche, Jeremy. 2011. "The Sustainability and Resilience of Global Water and Food Systems: Political Analysis of the Interplay Between Security, Resource Scarcity, Political System, and Global Trade." *Food Policy* 36: S3–S8.

Alston, Philip. 1987. "Out of the Abyss: The Challenges Confronting the New U.N. Committee on Economic, Social and Cultural Rights." *Human Rights Quarterly* 9: 332–381.

American Geophysical Union. 2014. "Satellite Study Reveals American West Using Up Underground Resources." News release 24 July. http://news.agu.org/press-release/satellite-study-reveals-parched-u-s-west-using-up-underground-water.

Anderson, Benedict. 1991. *Imagined Communities: Reflections on the Origin and Spread of Nationalism*. London: Verso.

Appiah, Kwame Anthony. 2007. *Cosmopolitanism: Ethics in a World of Strangers.* New York: Norton.

Arrow, Kenneth. 1958. "Tinbergen on Economic Policy." *American Statistical Association Journal* March: 89–97.

———. 1974. *The Limits of Organization.* New York: Norton.

Asian Development Bank. 2013. *Gender Equality and Food Security: Women's Empowerment as a Tool Against Hunger.* Manila.

Bankrolling, Sai. 2013. "Highway Urbanization and Land Conflicts: The Challenges of Decentralization in India." *Pacific Affairs Journal* 86(4): 785–811.

Benda-Beckman, Franz. 1995. "Anthropological Approaches to Property Law and Economics." *European Journal of Law and Economics* 2 (3): 309–336.

Binswanger, Hans B., Klaus Deininger, and Gershon Feder. 1995. "Power, Distortions, Revolt, and Reforming Agricultural Land Relations." In *Handbook of Development Economics*, ed. Jere Behrman and T. N. Srinivason. Amsterdam: Elsevier: 2659–2772.

Blair, Margaret M., and Lynn A. Stout. 2001. "Trust, Trustworthiness, and the Behavioral Foundations of Corporate Law." *University of Pennsylvania Law Review* 149 (6):1735–1810.

Bolton, Patrick, and Howard Rosenthal. 2002. "Political Intervention in Debt Contracts." *Journal of Political Economy* 110 (5): 1103–1134.

Brugger, Winfried. 1994. "Legal Interpretation, Schools of Jurisprudence, and Anthropology: Some Remarks from a German Point of View." *American Journal of Comparative Law* 42 (2): 395–421.

Büthe, Tim, and Walter Mattli. 2011. *The New Global Rulers: The Privatization of Regulation in the World Economy.* Princeton, N.J.: Princeton University Press.

Cafaggi, Fabrizio. 2011. "New Foundations of Transnational Private Regulation." *Journal of Law and Society* 38 (1): 20–49.

Cafaggi, Fabrizio, and Katharina Pistor. 2015. "Regulatory Capabilities: A Normative Framework for Assessing the Distributional Effects of Regulation." *Regulation & Governance* (forthcoming) (online version published September 2014).

Campbell, John R., and Leon N. Lindberg. 1990. "Property Rights and the Organization of Economic Activity by the State." *American Sociological Review* 55 (5): 634–647.

Coase, Ronald H. 1960. "The Problem of Social Cost." *Journal of Law and Economics* 3: 1–44.

Collier, Paul. 2007. *The Bottom Billion: Why the Poorest Countries Are Failing and What Can Be Done About It.* Oxford: Oxford University Press.

Committee on Economic, Social and Cultural Rights. 1990. General Comment No. 3, "The Nature of States Parties' Obligations." Article 2(1). E/1991/23, annex 3, UN ESCOR supp. (no. 3), p. 83. 1991.

Cotula, Lorenzo, Sonja Vermeulen, Rebeca Leonard, and James Keeley. 2009. *Land Grab or Development Opportunity? Agricultural Investment and International Land Deals in Africa.* Rome: IIED/FAO/IFAD.

da Cunha, P. V., and Junho Pena, M.V. 1997. *The Limits and Merits of Participation.* Washington, D.C.: World Bank.

Dagan, Hanoch. 2012. "Pluralism and Perfectionism in Private Law." *Columbia Law Review* 112: 1409.

Deininger, Klaus. 2003. *Land Policies for Growth and Poverty Reduction, World Bank Policy Research Reports*. Washington, D.C.: World Bank.

Demsetz, Harold. 1966. "Toward a Theory of Property Rights." *American Economic Review* 57 (May): 347–359.

De Schutter, Olivier. 2011. "The Green Rush: The Global Race for Farmland and the Rights of Land Users." *Harvard International Law Journal* 52 (2): 504–559.

——. 2012. "Reshaping Global Governance: The Case of the Right to Food." *Global Policy* 3 (4): 480–484.

——. 2013. "Economic, Social and Cultural Rights as Human Rights: An Introduction." In *Economic, Social and Cultural Rights as Human Rights*, ed. O. De Schutter, xiii–lxi. Cheltenham, U.K.: Elgar.

De Schutter, Olivier, and Jacques Lenoble. 2010. *Reflexive Governance: Redefining the Public Interest in a Pluralistic World*. Oxford: Hart.

De Schutter, Olivier, Jo Swinnen, and Jan Wouters. 2012. *Foreign Direct Investment and Human Development. The Law and Economics of International Investment Agreements*. London: Routledge.

Dubet, François. 2014. *La préférence pour l'inégalité. Comprendre la crise des solidarités*. Paris: Seuil.

Ellickson, Robert C. 1991. *Order Without Law—How Neighbors Settle Disputes*. Cambridge, Mass.: Harvard University Press.

Elster, Jon. 1982. "Sour Grapes—Utilitarianism and the Genesis of Wants." In *Utilitarianism and Beyond*, ed. A. K. Sen and B. Williams. Cambridge: Cambridge University Press, 219–238.

——. 1983. *Sour Grapes: Studies in the Subversion of Rationality*. Cambridge: Cambridge University Press.

——. 1993. *Local Justice: How Institutions Allocate Scarce Goods and Necessary Burdens*. New York: Russell Sage Foundation.

Firmin-Sellers, Kathryn. 1995. "The Politics of Property Rights." *American Political Science Review* 89 (4): 867–882.

Gleick, P. H. 2014. "Water, Drought, Climate Change, and Conflict in Syria." *Weather, Climate and Society* 6: 331–340.

Guha, Ramachandra. 2007. *India After Gandhi. The History of the World's Largest Democracy*. New York: HarperCollins.

Hadfield, Gillian, and Barry R. Weingast. 2012. "What Is Law? A Coordination Model of the Characteristics of Legal Order." *Journal of Legal Analysis* 4 (2): 471–515.

Hall, Derek, Philip Hirsch, and Tania Murray Li. 2011. *Powers of Exclusion: Land Dilemmas in Southeast Asia*. Honolulu: National University of Singapore Press/ University of Hawaii Press.

Hardin, Garrett. 1968. "The Tragedy of the Commons." *Science* 162: 1243–1248.

Heller, Michael. 1998. "The Tragedy of the Anti-Commons." *Harvard Law Review* 111: 621–688.

——. 2008. *Gridlock Economics: How Too Much Ownership Wrecks Markets, Stops Innovation, and Costs Lives*. New York: Basic.

Herzog, Lisa. 2013. *Inventing the Market: Smith, Hegel, and Political Thought.* Oxford: Oxford University Press.

Hesse, Konrad. 1995. *Grundzüge des Verfassungsrechts der Bundesrepublik Deutschland.* 20th ed. Heidelberg: Müller.

Hirschman, Albert O. 1970. *Exit, Voice, and Loyalty: Responses to Decline in Firms, Organizations, and States.* Cambridge, Mass.: Harvard University Press.

Hodgson, Geoffrey M. 2003. "The Enforcement of Contracts and Property Rights: Constitutive Versus Epiphenomenal Conceptions of Law." *Revue Internationale de Sociologie* 13 (2): 375–391.

International Labor Organization. 1982. *Target Setting for Basic Needs.* Geneva.

Kahneman, Daniel, E. Diener, and N. Schwarz. 1999. *Well-Being: The Foundations of Hedonic Psychology,* New York: Russell Sage Foundation.

Lambin, Eric F., and Patrick Meyfroidt. 2011. "Global Land Use Change, Economic Globalization, and the Looming Land Scarcity." *Proceedings of the National Academy of Sciences USA* 108 (9): 3465–3472.

Lambin, Eric F. et al. 2013. "Estimating the World's Potentially Available Cropland Using a Bottom-Up Approach." *Global Environmental Change* 23(5):892–901.

Lawson-Remer, Terra. 2011. "Property Insecurity, Conflict, and Long-Run Growth." Unpublished manuscript on file with the author.

Lehavi, Amnon, and Amir Licht. 2007. "Eminent Domain, Inc." *Columbia Law Review* 107: 1704.

Mattei, Ugo. 2000. *Comparative Law and Economics.* Ann Arbor: University of Michigan Press.

Maystadt, Jean Francois, Jean-Francois Trinh Tan, and Clemens Breisinger. 2014. "Does Food Security Matter for Transition in Arab countries?" *Food Policy* 46: 106–115.

Meadows, Donella H., Dennis L. Meadows, Joergen Randers, and William W. Behrens III. 1972. *The Limits to Growth: A Report for the Club of Rome's Project on the Predicament of Mankind.* New York: Universe.

Millennium Ecosystem Assessment (2005). *Ecosystems and Human Well-Being: Synthesis.* Washington, D.C.: Island Press.

Miller, Richard. 2006. "Global Institutional Reform and Global Social Movements: From False Promise to Realistic Hope." *Cornell International Law Journal* 39: 501–514.

Musgrave. 1959. *The Theory of Public Finance.* New York: McGraw-Hill.

North, Douglass C., John Joseph Wallis, and Barry R. Weingast. 2009. "Violence and the Rise of Open-Access Orders." *Journal of Democracy* 20 (1): 55–68.

North, Douglass Cecil. 1990. *Institutions, Institutional Change, and Economic Performance.* Cambridge: Cambridge University Press.

Nussbaum, Martha. 2011. *Creating Capabilities: The Human Development Approach.* Cambridge, Mass.: Belknap.

Olson, Mancur. 1971. *The Logic of Collective Action: Public Goods and the Theory of Groups.* Rev. ed. Cambridge, Mass.: Harvard University Press.

——. 1982. *The Rise and Decline of Nations: Economic Growth, Stagflation, and Social Rigidities.* New Haven, Conn.: Yale University Press.

Ostrom, Elinor. 1990. *Governing the Commons—The Evolution of Institutions for Collective Action*. Cambridge: Cambridge University Press.

———. 2003. "How Types of Goods and Property Rights Jointly Affect Collective Action." *Journal of Theoretical Politics* 15 (3): 239–270.

———. 2010. "Beyond Market and States: Polycentric Governance of Complex Economic Systems." *American Economic Review* 100 (June): 641–672.

Peterson, Luke Eric. 2005. *The Global Governance of Foreign Direct Investors: Madly Off in All Directions. Friedrich Ebert Stiftung Occasional Paper Series* 19 (2005).

Pistor, Katharina, Antara Haldar, and Amrit Amirapu. 2009. "Social Norms, Rule of Law, and Gender Reality: An Essay on the Limits of the Dominant Rule of Law Paradigm." In *Global Perspectives on the Rule of Law*, ed. James Heckmann, Robert L. Nelson, and Lee Cabatingan. New York and London Routledge, 241–278.

Pogge, Thomas. 2005. "Recognized and Violated: The Human Rights of the Global Poor." *Leiden Journal of International Law* 18 (4): 717–745.

Polanyi, Karl. 1944. *The Great Transformation: The Political and Economic Origins of Our Time*. Boston: Beacon.

Przeworski, Adam, and Fernando Limongi. 1993. "Political Regimes and Economic Growth." *Journal of Economic Perspectives* 7 (3): 51–69.

Roberts, Anthea. 2013. "Clash of Paradigms: Actors and Analogies Shaping the Investment Treaty System." *American Journal of International Law* 107: 45–94.

Sabel, Charles, and Jonathan Zeitlin. 2008. "Learning from Difference: The New Architecture of Experimentalist Governance in the European Union." *European Law Journal* 14 (3): 271–327.

Samuelson, Paul A. 1954. "The Pure Theory of Public Expenditure." *Review of Economics and Statistics* 36 (November): 387–389.

Schlager, Edella, and William Blomquist. 1998. "Heterogeneity and Common Pool Resource Management." In *Designing Institutions for Environmental Resource Management*, ed. Edna Tusak Lohman and D. Marc Kilgour. Elgar. pp. 101-113. Cheltenham, UK

Scitovsky, Tibor. 1992. *The Joyless Economy. The Psychology of Human Satisfaction*. New York: Oxford University Press.

Sen, A. K. 1987. *The Standard of Living*, ed. G. Hawthorn, Cambridge: Cambridge University Press.

Sen, Amartya. 1990. "100 Million Women Are Missing." *New York Review of Books*, 20 December.

———. 2009. *The Idea of Justice*. Cambridge, Mass.: Harvard University Press.

Sen, Amartya K. 1999. *Development as Freedom*. New York: Random House.

Stewart, Frances. 1985. *Planning to Meet Basic Needs*. London: Macmillan.

———. 1995. "Basic Needs, Capabilities and Human Development." *Greek Economic Review* 17: 83–96.

Sturm, Susan P. 2006. "The Architecture of Inclusion: Advancing Workplace Equity in Higher Education." *Harvard Journal of Law & Gender* 29 (2) (June).

Suda, Ryan. 2006. "The Effect of Bilateral Investment Treaties on Human Rights Enforcement and Realization." In *Transnational Corporations and Human Rights*, ed. Olivier De Schutter, 73–160. Oxford: Hart.

Teschl, Miriam, and Comim, Flavio. 2005. "Adaptive Preferences and Capabilities: Some Preliminary Conceptual Explorations." *Review of Social Economy*. 63 (2): 229–247.

Tilly, Charles. 1985. "War Making and State Making as Organized Crime." In *Bringing the State Back In*, ed. Peter Evans, Dieter Rueschemeyer, and Theda Skocpol, 169–191. Cambridge: Cambridge University Press.

Tinbergen. 1956. *Economic Policy: Principles and Design*. Amsterdam: North-Holland.

Umbeck, John. 1981. "Might Makes Rights: A Theory of the Formation and Initial Distribution of Property Rights." *Economic Journal* 29 (January): 38–59.

United Nations. 1987. "Report of the World Commission on Environment and Development: Our Common Future." A/42/427. 4 August.

——. 2012. "The Future We Want." Outcome document of the United Nations Conference on Sustainable Development, held in Rio de Janeiro, 20–22 June 2012. Annex to UN General Assembly Resolution 66/288. 27 July. http://daccess-dds-ny.un.org/doc/UNDOC/GEN/N11/476/10/PDF/N1147610.pdf?OpenElement.

van Middelaar, Luuk. 2013. *The Passage to Europe. How a Continent Became a Union*. New Haven, Conn.: Yale University Press.

Waldron, Jeremy. 2012. *The Rule of Law and the Measure of Property* Cambridge: Cambridge University Press.

Walzer, Michael. 1983. *Spheres of Justice*. New York: Basic.

Williamson, John. 1990. "What Washington Means by Policy Reform." In *Latin American Adjustment: How Much Has Happened?*, ed. John Williamson. Washington, D.C.: Institute for International Economics, 7–40.

World Bank. 2005. *Economic Growth in the 1990s: Learning from a Decade of Reform*. Washington, D.C.

——. 2010. *Rising Global Interest in Farmland*. Washington D.C.

Zoomers, Annelies. 2010. "Globalisation and the Foreignisation of Space: Seven Processes Driving the Present Global Land Grab." *Journal of Peasant Studies* 37 (2): 429–447.

PART II

Essential Resources: Challenges Ahead

CHAPTER 2

Land's Essentiality and Land Governance

Derek Hall

In the introduction to this volume, Olivier De Schutter and Katharina Pistor make a strong case that resources that are essential to human beings need to be governed in different ways than other kinds of goods. "Essential resources," they write, include those (like food and water) that are undeniably necessary for human survival and those that, within a given society, are either "indispensable for minimum existence" or recognized by "shared normative values and intuitions of justice" as ones that "a just society should make available to all irrespective of purchasing power." The essentiality of a resource in their framework can be context dependent: It can be a consequence of the conditions people find themselves facing or the nature of the society in which they live. De Schutter and Pistor argue further that because of the fundamental role that essential resources play in human life, denial of access to them is morally unacceptable, and governance regimes need to ensure that everyone who is dependent on these resources can access them.

In this chapter I seek to contribute to the development of the "essential resources" framework by focusing on one resource in particular: land. De Schutter and Pistor state that land (more specifically, arable land) is an essential resource not for everyone but for rural households in developing countries who depend on it for their ability to collect water and to grow or harvest food. While I agree with this formulation, I also argue that land differs from other resources in ways that complicate applying the "essential resources" concept to it and that contribute to the tensions and dilemmas often accompanying efforts to ensure that everyone dependent upon land has access to it. In the first section of the chapter, I argue that a full understanding of land's essentiality in human life requires acknowledging its roles not just as a productive resource but as space and as territory. Such an analysis suggests, among other things, that the concept of essentiality may need to be expanded to incorporate the survival of human groups in addition to that of individuals. In the second section, I consider the application of De Schutter and Pistor's moral and governance arguments about access to essential resources and highlight some of the implications of the context-specific nature of land's essentiality. I argue that governing access to land as an essential productive resource is complicated by the extent to which rural households can have property rights to land without access and access without property rights, and by the fact that even people for whom access to specific land is essential can reasonably choose to give up that access. I also find that land's characteristics (including its threefold role in human life) raise unusually difficult questions regarding where the land that could fulfill the moral imperative of granting access would come from and what people might have to do to claim that access.

My analysis of the relationship between land's status as an essential resource and the moral claims people can make for access to land overlaps with broader debates over rights to land and land reform (Borras 2007, chap. 1; De Schutter 2010, 21; UN Human Rights Council 2012, paras. 68, 74; Suárez 2013, 241–243). I would like to emphasize at the outset that this chapter should not be construed as a general discussion of those themes, as it deals primarily with moral claims to accessibility in land's essential (though context-dependent) role as a resource. It does not take up other arguments for land rights and land reform that are based on, for instance, the righting of historical injustices, the maintenance of peasant communities and cultures, or the relative efficiency of smallholder production.

I would like here to provide quick definitions of some of the key terms used in the paper. My definitions of property and access follow those used by Jesse Ribot and Nancy Peluso. They cite C. B. Macpherson as defining *property* as "a right in the sense of an enforceable claim to some use or benefit of something," and themselves define an *enforceable claim* as "one that is acknowledged and supported by society through law, custom, or convention." Property for them is one element of the broader concept of access, which entails "the ability to benefit from things —including material objects, persons, institutions, and symbols" (Ribot and Peluso 2003, 155, 154). I define *exclusion*, finally, in the way Philip Hirsch, Tania Murray Li, and I defined it in our book *Powers of Exclusion* (2011, 7): "the ways in which people are *prevented* from benefiting from things." Exclusion is thus the opposite of access.

LAND'S THREE ROLES: PRODUCTIVE RESOURCE, SPACE, AND TERRITORY

Land's multifaceted place in human life has been commented upon widely (Borras 2007, 4, 24). I organize my own analysis around land's roles as productive resource, as space, and as territory. I take up the productive resource role first, because it is the focus of the analysis of land in De Schutter and Pistor's introductory chapter and, more broadly, because it is the main approach taken in studies of the relationship between land and livelihood. *Productive resource* here denotes those land uses that are highly dependent on land's material qualities, especially its soil and water resources (which can be transformed and augmented by human activity) in addition to mineral deposits. Key land uses that depend on land's material characteristics include agriculture, some forms of aquaculture, pastoralism, (agro)forestry, and the collection of nontimber forest products.[1] Analyses of land's use as a productive resource are usually organized around the property rights that people hold in it, and especially ownership, rental, and commons rights. These rights (including rights of access, of use and management, of extraction of goods, and of alienation) are diverse, can be distributed among different people and groups, and are recognized to different extents by governments and communal tenure systems (Schlager and Ostrom 1992; Hall 2013, 16–18). Even individual or household rights are thus not restricted to rights of full private property recognized by governments.

As De Schutter and Pistor argue, arable land can be seen to be essential for many rural households in the global South who rely on access to it to grow or harvest food and to collect water. Exclusion from land (as productive resource) in such conditions can thus be fatal. However, in this context, two points of ambiguity attend use of the term "exclusion." The first is ambiguity over whether such exclusion means not having property rights to land or not being able to access (benefit from) it. The second is whether exclusion refers to people being excluded from some specific piece of land or from any land at all. Discussions of exclusion from land as a resource often implicitly focus on the condition of not having property rights to any land, or what is usually called *landlessness*. The definitions introduced above, however, suggest that exclusion should be taken to mean being prevented from productively accessing either any specific piece of land or any land at all. While exclusion understood in these ways often has troubling or terrible consequences, exclusion in the specific-piece-of-land sense is also essential to almost any productive use of land by anyone (Hall et al. 2011, 4). Even poor rural households need some way to exclude most forms of access by most other people if they are to grow crops on or otherwise productively use land. This need to exclude does not imply the need for absolute property rights in the land; rights of way and rights to glean, for instance, need not interfere much with agricultural land uses or water collection. The key point, however, is that the normative desirability or otherwise of different forms of exclusion needs to be analyzed in the context of concrete situations and with respect to what Hirsch, Li, and I call exclusion's "double edge."

While land's role as a productive resource—allowing access to growing or gathering food and to water—makes it essential to some people in some contexts, land's role as space makes it essential to everyone in some very direct ways. The simplest is that few human activities can be carried out without some kind of access to land. Someone completely deprived of access to land must be floating on the water, and there cannot be many people who have lived their whole lives that way. Li (2014, 591) writes that "land supports every aspect of human and non-human life, so complete exclusion from its affordances is not possible." While there can be extreme cases of this kind of complete exclusion—for instance, refugees who, having put to sea, are prevented from disembarking anywhere—virtually everyone has some kind of access to land. In addition to this most fundamental issue of having a place to stand, land qua space is also indispensable for a variety of other activities essential to the survival of most (in some cases all) people. First, people need access to land to get from one place to another. Property claims over land used for movement and transportation vary, but in contemporary societies much of it is owned (and transportation infrastructure is provided) by the state, and people have what is essentially a property right (in the sense of a recognized and enforceable claim) to pass over it. Second, people whose livelihood depends on the purchase of consumption goods need access to the land where shops and markets are located, land that will often be someone else's private property. Third, access to shelter requires access to land, which may be achieved through ownership, rental, or common rights in the land itself, but may also be limited to the right of spatial access (as when people stay in a hotel). Fourth, people who make their living from waged work need to be able to enter the land where their place of employment is located.

Under what conditions might access to land for movement, shopping, and work be denied? (I do not discuss the more common denial of access to land for shelter here.) Many people in most societies are deprived of such access by virtue of being in prison or enslaved, and the movements of women are often severely restricted by patriarchal norms. Outside of those circumstances, what would prevent people from using space in these ways? During processes of land conversion, people who do not want to give up their land can find themselves surrounded by land belonging to, say, a plantation or a new urban development. Under such conditions, people cannot leave home without trespassing. A study from Indonesia describes developers building walls around the houses of people unwilling to sell their land (Ferguson and Hoffman 1993, 63; for a similar example in the context of plantation development, see Barney 2004, 329). More commonly, people may not be completely deprived of access to land for movement but may not be able to access specific trails and roads that are critical to their livelihoods. This can happen, for instance, to pastoralists who depend on long-distance seasonal migration. Infrastructure that is not accessible to people with restricted mobility can make it difficult or impossible for those people to access land for movement even when they have the right to use it. Fear of physical attack (including gendered and racialized violence and warfare) can also put land to which people might have a right of access out of their effective reach. Finally, as De Schutter and Pistor emphasize in the introduction, international borders constitute obstacles to access to land for movement. The risks people take to evade these obstacles speak to the potentially essential role of cross-border movement in human lives.

While roads and paths are usually on land held by the state or in common, markets, shops, and places of employment are often on private property. Self-interest suggests that shopkeepers will want to let shoppers into their stores and that employers will make the place of employment available to their employees, so access in these cases is not usually a problem. But there are exceptions. Shops may carry signs proclaiming that the owner reserves the right to refuse service to anyone, and some high-end shopping areas are effectively off limits to the poor. Meanwhile, employers may lock their employees out during labor disputes as a means of putting pressure on them (just as striking employees will seek to deny access to the workplace to replacement workers). Racial, ethnic, and gender discrimination, too, can make shops and employment inaccessible.

In addition to its roles as productive resource and space, land can be seen to be essential to human life (though in a way different from that highlighted in the introduction) through its role as territory. Most political and ethnic identities involve a strong territorial component—a deep connection to some particular area of land—and people will often feel that some form of authority over this land is essential to their minimal existence, and even survival, as a group. One implication of this is that people may see land to be "essential" to them even if it is far from where they live and they expect never to access, use, or even see it. This may be because the land is seen as particularly important for the group's identity—the (imagined) site of its origins, for instance, or the home of conationals—but it may also simply be because they see the land as theirs (Hall 2013, 11–14, 34). The dominant contemporary way in which this relationship between land and group identity is expressed is through the sovereign territorial form of (nation-) state. However, other forms of territorial identity, including nonmajority nationalisms and ethnic identifications, are also enormously important in this respect. Indigenous rights to authority and control over territory, too, are increasingly being recognized in domestic and international law (Hall 2013, 147–150).

These different forms of territorial association can lead to various conflicts over and exclusions from land between groups, many of which pose existential challenges to the groups involved. One type is conflict (including war) between states (Hall 2013, chap. 2). A second is conflicts involving ethnic groups and indigenous peoples within and across the borders of states, including those between majority populations and states (especially in settler states) and indigenous peoples. In some of these conflicts, the idea that territory is essential to a group's identity has included the drive to subjugate, expel, or even eliminate other groups. That is, the essentiality of the territory for one group is understood to require its denial to others. While some states are coming to see the relationship between national and indigenous/ethnic minority rights and territory in less zero-sum terms than they have in the past, historical conflicts over this relationship have of course been extensive and brutal. These conflicts, too, are not just between indigenous peoples and "the state." Individual households from majority populations in settler states will very often hold state-recognized property rights to land on territory claimed by indigenous peoples. While some of these rights have been held for many generations, many such claims are ultimately based on land grabs. When the claims of these households are challenged by indigenous people, the response will usually be not just in terms of property rights but of nationality and identity—of the state and nation's territorial claim to the land.

What conclusions about land's essential qualities can be drawn from this analysis of land as resource, space, and territory? While thinking of land as in some respects essential is certainly correct, a comparison with other key essential resources highlighted in the introduction suggests some of the complexities and ambiguities of this judgment. Someone deprived of water will die within a very few days; someone deprived of food, within weeks. People can live without shelter in some climates, but going without it raises the possibility of death by exposure and of suffering physical violence, theft, and arrest. While the case of shelter is not as categorical as those of food and water, being deprived of any of these things is straightforwardly and catastrophically negative. Land's essential qualities, on the other hand, depend more heavily on one's definition of "essential." The most straightforward way in which access to land is essential is when its lack leads to death by drowning; being prevented from moving from place to place can also have fatal consequences. People may feel their identity as a group is threatened by lack of access to and authority over the land they see as their territory. As De Schutter and Pistor point out, finally, many rural households in the South are dependent for their livelihoods on access to land as a productive resource, and members of those households may face death (especially through starvation or exposure) if deprived of it—though this is not necessarily the case, as discussed below. It should be noted here, too, that loss of access even in this productive resource context can be accompanied by the loss of important aspects of one's identity—one's status as a member of a community, for instance, or as a peasant or farmer.

COMPLEXITIES, TENSIONS, AND DILEMMAS OF GOVERNING ACCESS TO LAND AS AN ESSENTIAL RESOURCE

De Schutter and Pistor develop a powerful moral claim for access to essential resources, writing, for instance, that "nobody should be excluded from resources to satisfy basic needs" and that "denying humans access to essential resources is morally repugnant." With respect to land specifically, their argument implies not a positive right of access to land for everyone (since land's essentiality is context dependent) but rather for people who depend upon land as a resource for survival because, again, they rely on it for growing or gathering food and/or for collecting water. Their argument, further, is not that people have a moral claim to full or absolute property rights in some land but rather that people have a right to access the land for essential purposes. De Schutter and Pistor are particularly interested in the ways in which multiple users can access the same resources and in responses to resource scarcity that involve access that is limited temporally, geographically, or quantitatively. They also argue that voice and reflexivity are critical elements of frameworks for the governance of essential resources.

In this section, I develop the points made above about land's essential qualities to analyze some of the complexities, tensions, and dilemmas potentially attendant upon a positive right to land access for rural people who are dependent on land for their survival. I develop these arguments in part by means of a comparison with the other essential resources—food, water, and shelter. First, I suggest that land is unusual as an "essential" resource in the extent to which people can have property rights to it that they cannot benefit from, can benefit from it without having property rights to it, and can benefit from giving up access to it. Second, I argue that land's unusual characteristics as a resource raise difficult questions regarding where the land that could fulfill a positive right to land would come from, and what people might have to do to claim that right.

A key aspect of land considered as an essential resource is the extent to which people can have quite "full" property rights (especially ownership and commons claims) to it without being able to benefit much from those claims. Other resources, of course, are not necessarily usable "on their own." Many foods can be eaten "as is," but many (including key staples) need to be cooked, and thus require cooking utensils and fuel. Shelter on its own should keep the weather at bay, but it may need to be heated, other utilities may need to be paid for, and continued possession often requires making mortgage, rent, and tax payments. Water is even more complex on this score. Having (potable) water will usually mean being able to drink it (and thus to benefit from its most essential function), but even drinking may depend on access to containers and infrastructure. This is even more the case with respect to uses like irrigation and energy generation, which require access to a wide range of other assets. In general, however, while having an enforceable claim to food, shelter, and water may not be enough to benefit fully from them, it will generally go some distance toward fulfilling their essential roles of preventing death by thirst, starvation, or exposure.

Land's use for agriculture in particular, but for other purposes as well, is similar to water's nondrinking uses in this respect.[2] As Ribot and Peluso point out, people may have rights to benefit from land without being able to derive benefits from it; they can have property without access. Actually benefiting from land depends on being able to mobilize "structural and relational mechanisms of access," including technology, capital, markets, labor, knowledge, authority, social identity, and the negotiation of other social relations (Ribot and Peluso 2003, 160). Without access to these, a rural household dependent on land may not have seeds to plant, the labor and knowledge required to farm, tools to work with, storage for produce, connections through which crops can be sold, or the money to solve any of these problems. Further, under modern conditions in which rural households need to sell at least some of their crop to earn money to pay for essential goods and to pay taxes, it will often not be sufficient to have enough access to these mechanisms to produce food for survival; households, rather, may need to be able to produce at least somewhat competitively.

The relationship between access to "structural and relational mechanisms" and the ability actually to benefit from land is particularly important because of its implications not just for the use of land by households that receive it but also for the reasons that rural households lose their land in the first place. Concerns about the global "land grab" over the last five years have appropriately focused much policy attention on the ways in which rural people in the South are deprived of their access to land through political and forceful means. Rural households also, however, lose their land through less high-profile but no less powerful processes of agrarian differentiation that derive from debt, illness, bad luck, and the inability to produce competitively for the market (Akram-Lodhi 2012). These latter processes have two implications regarding a positive right to land access for rural households that are dependent on it. The first is the question of whether households that are no longer dependent on arable land (because they have recently lost their access to it) but would like to return to farming should have the right to receive land in order to do so. If so, one must ask how far back in time that process of "restitution" should extend. In other words, the definition of rural household will need to have a temporal component.

The second implication is that the project of allocating access to land to people for whom it is essential needs to be clearly understood as being opposed not just to forceful dispossession but to tendencies toward agrarian differentiation that are deeply embedded in capitalist social relations. That is, it needs to engage with the question of how people who have once lost their land will not have this happen again if they gain access to new land. The potential consequences of making land available to people who do not have the wherewithal to work it have long been argued. In an English Parliamentary debate in 1657 over the possibility of allocating land to soldiers, one Colonel Sydenham expressed his opposition by saying, "They are poor, and if you assign lands to them they must sell again" (quoted in Hill 1961, 151). This is one of the reasons that many land reforms prohibit the sale of land by beneficiaries, but such regulations are difficult to enforce (Borras 2007, 38). None of this is an argument against the need for land access, but it does suggest that in order to be meaningful, such access will need to be accompanied by the right to various forms of support. Rights along these lines are included in, for instance, (especially) articles 5, 6, and 7 of the draft Declaration on the Rights of Peasants and Other People Working in Rural Areas under discussion at the UN's Human Rights Council (2012, 22–27).[3]

Just as people can have property in land without being able to access (benefit from) it, so they can have access to land without what are usually considered to be the necessary property rights (ownership, rental, commons) to it. This is true in the spatial sense described earlier—people can benefit by moving across land and accessing shops and places of employment and recreation on it without having any more claim to it than the right of spatial access. More crucially in this context, it is also true with respect to land's role as a productive resource. Large numbers of landless rural households in the South access land through agricultural labor markets. While they do not themselves own, rent, or hold in common the land they work, they do access it in Ribot and Peluso's terms—that is, they are able to benefit from it by receiving a wage:

> Even though someone may have no access to a resource through property rights and may not have the capital to buy technology or to engage in commercial transactions giving her or him rights to a resource, she or he may gain resource access by entering into a working relationship with the resource access controller, the holder of a permit, or other market-based access mechanism (2003, 167).

Waged agricultural labor often involves exploitative relations of debt and patron-clientelism, and the wages it pays are often insufficient to support a household (Li 2011; UN Human Rights Council 2012, paras. 15–17, 38–40). From the point of view of a conceptual analysis of the ways in which land is essential to livelihoods, however, the central issue here is that many rural households in the South have livelihoods that are based on access to rural land as a productive resource, but gain that access through labor rather than through property claims. Such access, indeed, seems to fit with the interest in multiple and overlapping ways of allocating and benefiting from scarce essential resources stressed in the introduction to this volume. The question is thus whether and under what conditions, given typical problems like poor remuneration and lack of voice and reflexivity, land-dependent households' access to arable land through labor relations can satisfy the right to access to land in its essential capacity.

Land is unusual as an essential resource, third, because even people from rural households dependent for their survival on access to it can reasonably decide to give that access up. Membership in a rural household dependent on arable land is not necessarily something that one carries throughout one's life. People may shift from livelihoods that depend on working rural land to ones that do not, most notably by moving (temporarily or permanently) to cities, but also through entering the service or manufacturing sectors closer to home or in other rural areas (see Rigg 2006). For many people, such moves will involve little choice and may be a consequence of having been forcibly dispossessed of their land. Loss of access to land, however, differs from loss of access to other essential resources, because people can decide that leaving agriculture (including by more or less voluntarily selling their land) is on balance a positive option for them (or their children). It can thus make sense for people who are dependent for their livelihoods on access to productive rural land to give up that access in a way that it could never make sense for them to give up access to food, water, or shelter.

Another way to make this point is by thinking about a pair of quotations in a World Bank–published book by Martin Ravallion and Dominique van de Walle titled *Land in Transition: Reform and Poverty in Rural Vietnam*. The authors make the striking arguments that since the decollectivization and creation of a market in rights to land in Vietnam in the late 1980s and early 1990s, "rising landlessness has been a positive factor in poverty reduction in Vietnam as a whole" and that "slightly more than half of the increase in landlessness is directly associated with falling poverty, as rural households that moved out of poverty also moved out of farming" (2008, 148, 139; see also Akram-Lodhi 2010). These statements may or may not be correct, but they are not straightforwardly absurd; it is possible to imagine livelihood trajectories that see people increasing their life chances by exiting farming. If one were to replace the word "landlessness" in these quotations with "food-lessness," "waterlessness," or "homelessness," they would be nonsensical.

These points have at least two implications for thinking about the governance of land as an essential resource. First, while everyone requires food, water, and shelter to survive, land qua productive resource is, as De Schutter and Pistor argue, essential mainly to rural people who depend on access to it for their livelihoods. Allocating land access to these households thus implies some way of determining who they are. While De Schutter and Pistor also suggest that land is an essential resource "in societies that rely on subsistence farming without alternatives for displaced farmers to make a living" but not in those "where people can readily earn their living [from] wage labor," such distinctions are not easy to make. Rural households commonly pursue diverse and spatially complex livelihood strategies that incorporate not only subsistence-oriented agricultural activities but waged labor and remittances. In such cases, decisions would need to be made about, for instance, whether children of a farming household who have spent ten years working in the city (or in another country) and now wish to return to their villages would have a right to access some arable land. Figuring out the membership of the groups, communities, and societies referred to in De Schutter and Pistor's definition of voice—deciding who is inside and who is outside—will thus be of enormous importance. Similar issues arise with respect to the draft Declaration on the Rights of Peasants and Other People Working in Rural Areas mentioned earlier: If people are to have certain rights by virtue of being peasants or other rural workers, then it becomes necessary to determine who they are (and are not). Civil society organizations participating in discussions of the draft Declaration at the UN Human Rights Council, for instance, have emphasized the need to consider peasants now residing in towns, cities, and slums (UN Human Rights Council 2014, para. 34; see also Edelman 2013).

Second, there are also potential dilemmas involved in efforts to protect rural people from the negative impacts of land markets, efforts that often involve restrictions on rights of alienation. De Schutter and Pistor write that "zoning and titling programs promoted by multilateral and bilateral development agencies have extended the geographical remit of individual property rights by penetrating a larger number of countries in the developing world," and such moves have very often helped to expand the scope of land markets and commodification. Land sales and markets arise, however, not only from the imposition of private property categories "from above" but from decisions made (though certainly not in conditions of their own choosing) by landholders "from below." The literature on rural land relations in Southeast Asia (the region with which I am most familiar) shows no shortage of cases of landholders selling land in clear opposition to the wishes of state actors, particularly in situations in which the land is not zoned for sale (perhaps because it is classified as agricultural and subject to rules regarding conversion) and/or the state does not recognize the land-holder's rights (Hall et al. 2011). Trying to limit the spread of land markets can thus involve opposing not just the penetration of capitalist forms but the priorities of rural households. Restrictions on private property rights in land could, for instance, prevent people who have been counting on selling their land (perhaps because they are growing too old to work it and their children are not going to be farmers) from doing so. Frameworks for governing the allocation of access to land to rural households may also need to determine whether it would extend to people who have more or less voluntarily decided to sell their land. It seems difficult, on the one hand, to argue that people who have chosen to sell a valuable asset, and perhaps benefited substantially from that sale, should then be able to claim a right to receive new land. On the other hand, the distinction between basically voluntary sales and ones driven by distress (along the lines of those discussed earlier) will often be extremely difficult to make.

Finally, I turn to the challenges involved in finding land to allocate to land-dependent rural households that lack access to it. I approach this issue from the perspective of two important arguments made in De Schutter and Pistor's chapter: first, that most resource scarcity "is local and relative rather than absolute," and second, that the governance of essential resources needs to incorporate the access rights of multiple users. The second point is critical with respect to land. Different essential uses can be accommodated on the same piece of land. The farming rights of one group can coexist with the gleaning rights of another, the water access rights of a third, and the right of way of a fourth. Such multiple land uses are already widespread. At the same time, there are limits to overlapping use. Only so many people, for instance, can intensively cultivate the same piece of land at once.

I begin my discussion of where land for essential purposes might be found by comparing land, again, with other essential resources. A first distinction can be made between food and shelter as what might be called "producible" resources—ones people can make more of—and land and water as "nonproducible" resources.[4] As demand for food and shelter increases, more crops can be raised and more buildings built. Increased supply may not keep up with demand, and distribution may be highly unequal, but expanding production is at least possible. The amount of food produced globally every year and the total number of dwellings in the world are both much higher now than they were a century ago. Water and land, on the other hand, cannot (usually) be produced, and the amount of both in the world is basically constant.[5] One consequence is that while expanded demand for access to food and shelter can be met through expanded supply, the provision of access to land and water will more often involve redistributing those resources from preexisting users. The argument for doing this will often be compelling and simple, as in cases in which large amounts of land are being unproductively hoarded by large landholders. In other situations, however, more painful dilemmas will be associated with such redistributions.

These issues are made more intense with respect to land by a further distinction within the "nonproducible" resources: water can be moved, while land (usually) cannot. It is often possible to make up for insufficient water supply in one area by bringing water in from somewhere else. These movements can take place over long distances but are perhaps even more important locally (through, for instance, irrigation projects and the provision of potable water infrastructure). Land, however, cannot be moved around in this way. This raises the question of whether a guarantee of access to productive land for rural households includes a guarantee that that land will be made available locally—close enough to home, that is, that the household will not have to relocate. If so, then the question of where the land is to come from may be acute. All reasonably productive local land may already be held by groups with strong claims to it, including other households (who may have come into possession of their land in part through outcompeting the households now deprived of access), broader village groups (in the case of common land), other villages, or ethnic or indigenous peoples. In areas where most arable land is devoted to relatively small-scale farming, the question of agrarian differentiation returns to the fore: Should claims to land for land-dependent households be seen as strong enough that they should overturn the dynamics of differentiation through redistributions away from relatively more successful households? If, on the other hand, rural households may have to relocate in order to gain access to land, then both the dislocations this will cause for those households and the ways in which this will happen will be of the first order of importance. State programs of making land available on what are often called "frontiers" have a painful history and very often involve the prioritization of nationally framed claims to land over the territorial and property claims of ethnic groups and indigenous peoples who have historically lived in the areas in question.

A final issue in relation to the provision of land as an essential resource is the extent to which land should be seen to be "substitutable." A comparison with other essential resources will help to highlight this issue. As long as water is of reasonable quality and purity, one liter of it will be more or less as good as another, at least for the purposes of drinking, washing, and irrigation. Food is also fairly substitutable, but less so than water—people prefer some kinds of food over others, may not know how to prepare unfamiliar foods, and refuse to eat some foods entirely. Shelter is extremely heterogeneous in terms of quality, amenities, and location, and people also obviously have attachments to their own homes. Land is perhaps even less substitutable than shelter. Land varies enormously in its usability for different purposes and in its location. A hectare of fertile, irrigated rice paddy near a major road is not the same as a hectare of desert miles from the closest settlement. The relationship between land and identity is also unusually intense, and this connection exists at various levels, including the household, the community, the ethnic group or indigenous people, the nation, and the state. All of these problems of substitutability have long bedeviled efforts to compensate people displaced by development projects (roads, dams, harbors and airports, power plants, etc.) for the loss of their land. Finding land that is both unused and more or less "equivalent," in both the productive and the identity senses, is usually impossible, and people far too often find themselves dumped onto land that is poor in quality, that they do not know how to farm, and that is far from their old homes.

CONCLUSIONS

This paper has taken up two questions: In what ways is land essential to human life? And what are the implications of land's status in that respect for its governance, especially with respect to arguments for the allocation of land access to land-dependent rural households in the South? I have suggested that land's "essentiality" needs to be understood in terms of its roles as space, productive resource, and territory. I have also made the case that while land is certainly essential to the livelihoods of rural households dependent on it (in the sense that being deprived of it may threaten their survival), it remains different from food, water, and shelter in this respect. Land's role as an essential productive resource for rural households involves complexities, tensions, and dilemmas because (1) property rights in land are neither necessary nor (2) sufficient for productive access to land; (3) people can reasonably decide that dispossessing themselves of their land will be beneficial to them (and trying to guarantee land to rural households may thus be inextricably tied to preventing those households from doing things that they would otherwise like to do); (4) determining who is dependent on land is difficult and administratively complicated; (5) land is neither producible nor movable, and providing access to it thus raises tough questions of redistribution; and (6) because land's "substitutability" is unusually low, and specific pieces of land are important to people.

Rural farming households' access to land is jeopardized by a wide range of dynamics—from land-grabbing to transformations in global commodity markets to environmental change to intravillage competition—at work across much of the global South. Land's essential role in reproducing farming households as farming households and in keeping their members alive is under threat. Policies and governance approaches that seek to respond to these threats should operate under a presumption in favor of maintaining and expanding the land access of rural households and of providing the other kinds of resources that those households need to benefit from that land, and these approaches should be supported against the political resistance they always encounter. Nothing in this paper is meant to question the enormous importance of agrarian reform and the expansion of access to land for rural households in situations in which, for instance, land distribution is highly unequal and poverty is severe (De Schutter 2010, 20–21). Finally, to say that efforts to rearrange the governance of land access in terms of moral arguments deriving from land's context-dependent status as an essential resource will involve multiple challenges is not to argue against the project or the motivations behind it. Tensions, complexities, and dilemmas are common to most governance projects, and the key role of context in land relations means that in many cases positive measures will be relatively straightforward. The critical thing, I would suggest, is to be aware of the challenges.

NOTES

I am grateful to the participants in the "Governing Access to Essential Resources" workshop (Columbia Law School, 20–21 June 2013), and especially to Olivier De Schutter, Katharina Pistor, and Edella Schlager, for their very helpful comments. All errors are my own.

1. Mining, in addition to oil and gas extraction, also falls under this heading, but I do not discuss them in this paper.

2. I am grateful to participants at the Columbia workshop for their insights on the land-water comparison here.

3. This document is based very closely on the Declaration of the Rights of Peasants—Women and Men published by La Vía Campesina in 2009 and available at http://viacampesina.net/downloads/PDF/EN-3.pdf. See also Edelman and James 2011.

4. This distinction is similar to that drawn by Karl Polanyi (1957) between real and fictitious commodities. Real commodities, for Polanyi, are things that are not just for sale on the market but that were produced in order to be so sold. Fictitious commodities are things for sale on the market that were not originally created for sale. Polanyi's three key fictitious commodities are land, labor, and money. My analysis here does not depend on the commodity status of resources—it is possible to build dwellings and grow food in noncommodified ways—but the distinction is a related one.

5. This statement is, no doubt, too blunt. New land is constantly being created through silt deposits and the human labor of land reclamation, though the total amount of this new land relative to the world's total land area is small. Large-scale Chinese government projects referred to as "land creation" in a recent paper involve the leveling of hills and mountains and the filling in of valleys (Li, Qian, and Wu 2014). Creating "new" water may be effectively impossible, but saltwater can be converted into freshwater, which for most human purposes means that "new" water has come onstream. More generally, investments in land clearance, irrigation, transportation, and water distribution and storage infrastructure mean that the amount of effectively available/usable land and water in the world is much higher now than it was one hundred years ago. The basic point, however, still stands.

REFERENCES

Akram-Lodhi, A. Haroon. 2010. "Review Essay: Land, Labour and Agrarian Transition in Vietnam." *Journal of Agrarian Change* 10 (4): 564–580.

——. 2012. "Contextualising Land Grabbing: Contemporary Land Deals, the Global Subsistence Crisis and the World Food System." *Canadian Journal of Development Studies* 33 (2): 119–142.

Barney, Keith. 2004. "Re-encountering Resistance: Plantation Activism and Smallholder Production in Thailand and Sarawak, Malaysia." *Asia Pacific Viewpoint* 45 (3): 325–339.

Borras, Saturnino M., Jr. 2007. *Pro-Poor Land Reform: A Critique*. Ottawa: University of Ottawa Press.

De Schutter, Olivier. 2010. "The Right to Food." Report presented to the 65th General Assembly of the United Nations, A/65/281. 11 August.

Edelman, Marc. 2013. "What Is a Peasant? What Are Peasantries? A Briefing Paper on Issues of Definition." Briefing paper prepared for the first session of the Intergovernmental Working Group on a United Nations Declaration on the Rights of Peasants and Other People Working in Rural Areas, Geneva. 15–19 July.

Edelman, Marc, and Carwil James. 2011. "Peasants' Rights and the UN System: Quixotic Struggle? Or Emancipatory Idea Whose Time Has Come?" *Journal of Peasant Studies* 38 (1): 81–108.

Ferguson, Bruce W., and Michael L. Hoffman. 1993. "Land Markets and Effect of Regulation on Formal-Sector Development in Urban Indonesia." *Review of Urban and Regional Development Studies* 5 (1): 51–73.

Hall, Derek. 2013. *Land*. Cambridge: Polity.

Hall, Derek, Philip Hirsch, and Tania Murray Li. 2011. *Powers of Exclusion: Land Dilemmas in Southeast Asia*. Singapore/Honolulu: National University of Singapore Press/University of Hawaii Press.

Hill, Christopher. 1961. *The Century of Revolution, 1603–1714*. Edinburgh: Nelson.

Li, Tania Murray. 2011. "Centering Labor in the Land Grab Debate." *Journal of Peasant Studies* 38 (2): 281–298.

——. 2014. "What Is Land? Assembling a Resource for Global Investment." *Transactions of the Institute of British Geographers* 39 (4): 589–602.

Li, Peiyue, Hui Qian, and Jianhua Wu. 2014. "Accelerate Research on Land Creation." *Nature* 510 (5 June): 29–31.

Polanyi, Karl. 1957. *The Great Transformation: The Political and Economic Origins of Our Time*. Boston: Beacon.

Ravallion, Martin, and Dominique van de Walle. 2008. *Land in Transition: Reform and Poverty in Rural Vietnam*. Washington, DC: World Bank.

Ribot, Jesse C., and Nancy Lee Peluso. 2003. "A Theory of Access." *Rural Sociology* 68 (2): 153–181.

Rigg, Jonathan. 2006. "Land, Farming, Livelihoods and Poverty: Rethinking the Links in the Rural South." *World Development* 34 (1): 180–202.

Schlager, Edella, and Elinor Ostrom. 1992. "Property-Rights Regimes and Natural Resources: A Conceptual Analysis." *Land Economics* 68 (3): 249–262.

Suárez, Sofia Monsalve. 2013. "Editor's Introduction: The Human Rights Framework in Contemporary Agrarian Struggles." *Journal of Peasant Studies* 40 (1): 239–253.

United Nations Human Rights Council. 2012. "Final Study of the Human Rights Council Advisory Committee on the Advancement of the Rights of Peasants and Other People Working in Rural Areas." A/HRC/19/75. 24 February.

——. 2014. "Report of the Open-ended Intergovernmental Working Group on a Draft United Nations Declaration on the Rights of Peasants and Other People Working in Rural Areas." Twenty-Sixth Session, A/HRC/26/48. 11 March.

CHAPTER 3

Governing Boundaries

EXCLUSION, ESSENTIAL RESOURCES, AND SUSTAINABILITY

Edella Schlager

The only thing worse than being exploited by capitalism is not being exploited by capitalism.
— Joan Violet Robinson

I begin with this epigraph by Joan Violet Robinson, a mid-twentieth-century Cambridge University economics professor, because it succinctly and elegantly captures the notion that two seemingly contradictory ideas can hold true at once. Revising Robinson's saying allows me to capture the basic theme of this paper: The only thing worse than being excluded from an essential resource is not being excluded from an essential resource. While not as attention grabbing as Robinson's phrasing, it does capture two key concepts around which I build this paper. First, I consider essential resources. De Schutter and Pistor (2014:1) provide a working definition: "We label resources essential if they are indispensable for survival; at a minimum, this includes drinking water, adequate food, and shelter." Resources that people directly consume to meet their basic needs are indeed essential. However, just as indispensable for survival are environmental services, such as water cleansing and soil regeneration that make potable water and wholesome food possible. The two types of resources, environmental services and common-pool resources, are tightly linked. For many people, including New York City's residents and visitors, potable water, a common-pool resource, depends on the continued functioning of water-cleansing capabilities, an environmental service of the Catskill watershed. Likewise, the means to produce food depends on nutrient recycling and soil formation (Millennium Ecosystem Assessment 2005).

Environmental services may be thought of as public goods. If they are available, people may not be readily, if at all, excluded from their use and enjoyment. Indeed, the values of environmental services are realized when many people enjoy them. In contrast, food and potable water may be thought of as flows of units from a common-pool resource, which when captured are private goods (Ostrom, Gardner, and Walker 1995). In order to sustain flows of units from common-pool resources, exclusion must be carefully governed (Ostrom 1990; Schlager and Ostrom 1992). The value of common-pool resources are realized when exclusion (and use) is carefully limited so as to sustain the resources.

These inextricably linked essential resources raise distinct and seemingly contradictory exclusion challenges, the second concept on which I build my argument. On the one hand, the value of environmental services is realized through open access. On the other hand, the productivity and value of common-pool resources require limited access. Exclusion is often thought of in terms of boundaries: who may enter and enjoy a resource and who may not (Smith 2002). De Schutter and Pistor (2014) emphasize the latter in focusing on deprivation and denial of essential resources, or what they term the "tragedy of exclusion." However, who may enter and enjoy a resource is bound up with the denial of essential resources. Pushing a fisher out of a fishery for want of a license compels him or her to search for another fishery to access. Shutting down a farmer's water diversion for lack of a water right impels him or her to search for an alternative water source. Denying access does not eliminate the demand; rather, demand may be redirected to related resources with lower entry barriers. Thus, entry and exit among linked essential resources, such as different sources of water or different species of fish, allows a more complete analysis of the role of exclusion and supports the reframing of policies in ways that may better realize productivity and sustainability of essential resources.

In the next section, I apply Frischmann's (2012) concept of infrastructure to expand the notion of essential resources to encompass environmental services. Applying the concept of infrastructure to essential resources clarifies the interactions between environmental services and common-pool resources and how entry and exit play out differently across the two essential resource types. The third section is devoted to the policy implications of expanding the notion of essential resources to encompass both environmental services and common-pool resources. The section begins with a brief review of conventional natural resources policy before contrasting it with the policies suggested by an infrastructure lens. Policies devoted to protecting the supply of environmental services are distinct from policies that address the demand for common-pool resource flows. An environmental infrastructure lens, however, highlights how less exclusion from environmental services and more exclusion among linked common-pool resources are complements that act to dampen the tragedy of exclusion.

ENVIRONMENTAL INFRASTRUCTURE AND ESSENTIAL RESOURCES

Frischmann (2012) provides a definition of infrastructure that distinguishes it from the types of goods that infrastructure makes possible. Infrastructure is characterized by three conditions: It may be "accessed and used concurrently by multiple users for multiple uses"; it is not used up or incorporated into final outputs; and it is used to produce all types of goods, including social, public, and private (Frischmann 2012, 61–63). Distinguishing between infrastructure and the different types of uses and users of infrastructure that create a multitude of types of goods highlights the distinction between infrastructure supply of, as well as the demand for, the many types of goods infrastructure makes possible. Emphasizing the demand for many different types of goods made possible by infrastructure supports infrastructure supply, because its full value is accounted for and the public goods and common-pool resources it provides are recognized and protected.

Essential resources are made possible by environmental infrastructures such as lakes, watersheds, ocean fisheries, and deserts. Environmental infrastructures or ecosystems, not humans, produce public goods and common-pool resources. Public goods produced by environmental infrastructures, such as water quality or soil formation, may be referred to as environmental services (Millennium Ecosystem Assessment 2005).[1] Common-pool resources are stocks and flows of units, such as fish or trees (Ostrom et al. 1995), and when appropriated by humans are what Frischmann (2012) calls private goods.[2] Individuals capture the value of such goods, either through direct consumption or as inputs into the production of other private goods. For instance, a water company may divert water from a river and deliver the water to homes, where people directly consume it for bathing and cooking, and to farmers who use it for irrigating vegetable crops, which the farmers then sell in markets.

The goods and resources produced by an environmental infrastructure are intertwined and interacting, and people enjoy the benefits of both environmental services and common-pool resources simultaneously. For instance, fishers benefit from ocean water whose quality is adequate to support aquatic life, such as shellfish, which fishers harvest but which are also key in filtering water and maintaining its quality. The dynamic interactions between common-pool resources (e.g., shellfish) and environmental services (e.g., water quality) mean that both are necessary for meeting basic needs and human well-being. Growing crops, harvesting wildlife, and drawing upon potable water supplies depend on a host of environmental services such as soil formation, water filtering, and aquatic and riparian habitat.[3] Thus, essential resources include private goods that people directly consume as well as public and common-pool resources that make private goods possible.

Using the concepts of public goods and common-pool resources helps to clarify the different exclusion implications of these intertwined goods produced by environmental infrastructure. When supplied, environmental services, as public and social goods, are difficult to exclude users from and are enjoyed without being consumed. People who withdraw drinking water from a river or stream share in the quality of the water in the stream. People living in and around the wetlands and floodplains of a river share in the flood control benefits provided. Access to these essential resources depends on their continued supply. Their continued supply depends on the protection of the productivity of the environmental infrastructures that produce them—specifically, the various components of the infrastructure in addition to their interactions and linkages that create environmental services. Avoiding the tragedy of exclusion requires supporting the supply of environmental services.

In contrast, the tragedy of exclusion regarding the appropriable flows from common-pool resources centers on demand, not supply. Negative externalities generated by multiple uses and users diminish the value of the flows of goods, perhaps to the point of exhaustion. Conflicts over access to the value of the flows of common-pool resources constitute the tragedy of exclusion. Failure to supply *environmental services* and failure to appropriately regulate the negative externalities created by the demand for *common-pool resources* are the twin tragedies of exclusion for essential resources. Policies that address supply *and* demand are required to ensure access and enjoyment of essential resources.

"HOW MUCH?" POLICIES AND ESSENTIAL RESOURCES

In the United States, natural resources policies have largely focused on increasing the supply of or regulating the demand for common-pool resources at the expense of supplying the public goods of environmental services. The manner in which demand for common-pool resources is defined is narrow, with an emphasis on "how much?" How much is available? How much can be taken? How much must remain? These questions are typically asked on a single species and stock basis and typically only when evidence suggests that demand may exceed supply. In addition, demand regulations are often matched with efforts to increase supplies, such as regulating salmon harvesting while also investing heavily in fish hatcheries. If increasing supply is not feasible, then regulating demand often results in a "race to capture," as resource users exploit unregulated dimensions of harvesting effort. In the end, negative externalities predominate for users racing to harvest as well as for users and uses whose demands are either not recognized or who make use of closely related common-pool resources that are affected. The consequences are well known and destructive. Intense conflict over defining how much may be harvested, which is often framed as a zero-sum game, pits different uses or users against one another.

The destructive "how much can be harvested?" dynamic is well documented in commercial ocean fisheries, forests, and grazing lands (Grafton 2010; Glazier 2011; Grossman and Bryner 2012). Even international efforts to cap and reduce greenhouse gas emissions have tended toward the calculation of how much can be deposited into the atmosphere before critical thresholds are exceeded (Prins et al. 2010). A similar dynamic unfolded around water, a scarce resource in the arid western United States. As is typical of such an approach, a particular type of use is privileged over others, such as off-stream diversions to support agriculture and cities or in-stream uses of hydropower and flood control. These restrictions with respect to use almost always come at the expense of environmental services and common-pool resources dependent on in-stream flows. Valuable uses and users, such as riparian and aquatic habitat, have historically been precluded, as have the species dependent on such habitats. In western watersheds the "how much?" question has had the effect of preventing specific types of uses of watersheds, of encouraging negative externalities, and of interrupting and degrading the supply of environmental services.

FROM "HOW MUCH?" TO "HOW MANY?"

Tear et al. (2005), in a paper titled "How Much Is Enough? The Recurrent Problem of Setting Measurable Objectives in Conservation," lucidly capture "how much?" thinking. Clearly concerned that science and scientists do not play a more central role in meeting ecological conservation objectives, the authors propose a process that would place scientists front and center in answering the "how much is enough?" question. Society, through an unspecified collective choice process, would establish general conservation goals. Scientists would lead the effort to realize those goals first by translating them into measurable, empirical objectives, grounded in science and not political or economic feasibility. The objectives would be treated as hypotheses, with implementation supported by intensive monitoring that would allow scientists to evaluate the hypotheses and revise the objectives in light of results.

Tear and his colleagues appear to make a hard-nosed argument for how to engage in "how much?" policies more effectively. However, the case studies these scholars approvingly point to as successful examples of the "how much?" approach suggest something different: an approach that supports many different uses and users of environmental infrastructure. The three case studies involve salmon recovery in the Pacific Northwest, Florida's wildlife habitat conservation system, and the Nature Conservancy's Southern Rocky Mountain Ecoregion conservation program. The first case more comfortably fits within a conventional "how much?" approach—how many salmon to return to streams—but the other two cases do not. Rather, the goal in each case is to protect and recover many different uses and users of environmental infrastructure. The seemingly hard-nosed scientific management approach is not used to define specific quantities of flows but to determine whether adequate levels of protection have been realized. Furthermore, a "how much?" approach does not entirely disappear; rather, it is reoriented and placed in the service of protecting environmental infrastructure. In particular, it becomes part of a monitoring process to determine how many uses and users are part of a particular environmental infrastructure.

"HOW MANY?" POLICIES

PART I. EXCLUSION AND GOVERNANCE

As addressed in the first section, environmental infrastructure produces a host of different environmental services that benefit many users and uses. However, because "nature" is the provider of environmental services and the ways in which nature produces those services are not well understood, easily measured, or valued, emphasis has been placed on the demand for and use of specific dimensions of the environmental services. The uses that can be privatized, such as timber or fish, are given much attention, but almost no regard is given to the negative externalities that are generated and how those externalities undermine the provision of environmental services. To correct that imbalance and to protect the production of environmental services requires a reframing of policies and policy approaches. The goal of environmental infrastructure policies should be to allow many different uses.[4] By allowing for a diverse range of uses the protection of environmental services will be heightened.

"How many?" policies can be divided into three broad categories; the first two are the focus of this section and the third will be taken up in the next section. First, careful scrutiny must be given to any use or user that would preclude or severely undermine environmental services. Policy tools should be available that facilitate the resolution of conflicts over uses, and some particularly destructive uses should be banned. For instance, Arizona water law does not recognize the hydrologic connection between rivers, streams, and groundwater basins, allowing groundwater pumping to dry up streams and impair river flows (Glennon 2002). The San Pedro watershed, located in the southeastern corner of the state, is slowly losing its surface flows, with dire consequences for aquatic and riparian species and habitat. One of the few undammed rivers in the Southwest, the San Pedro is home to hundreds of species and is a major migratory bird flyway. Local watershed groups have formed and actively sought to develop policy tools that would allow regulation of groundwater pumping near sensitive riparian areas, but their efforts have not produced policy reform. In March 2013, an administrative law judge affirmed the Arizona Department of Water Resources decision to issue a groundwater permit to the water company that will serve a proposed 7,000-home development to be built near the river. If the development is fully built, the pumping of approximately 3,000 acre-feet of water annually will further imperil stream flows (Davis 2013; Karp 2013). Prioritizing specific uses of environmental infrastructure, even to the point of allowing those uses to undermine the productivity of environmental infrastructure, is an unacceptable practice under a "how many?" policy approach.

Second, policy tools that protect environmental services are key to a "how many?" approach. Spatial planning, zoning, and regulation recognize and coordinate many uses and users of environmental infrastructure. For instance, large-scale habitat conservation plans, whether they are land based or marine based, address a variety of uses by granting different levels of protection for distinct ecoscapes. The Sonoran Desert Conservation Plan covering much of Pima County, Arizona, is the master plan guiding development. The plan is also currently under review for a section 10 permit under the federal Endangered Species Act of 1973. If granted, the permit will allow public and private organizations to disturb habitat for road building or home building and still be in compliance with the Endangered Species Act. The plan consists of a combination of open-space requirements, a land conservation system, and high levels of protection for particularly sensitive areas, such as riparian areas ("Pima County's Multi-species Conservation Plan" 2012). Marine protected areas play a similar role to that of large-scale habitat conservation plans.

A "how many?" approach reorients policies from a focus on how much can be taken to how many uses and users of environmental infrastructure can be recognized and protected. Recognizing and protecting the environmental services provided by infrastructure resolves one of the tragedies of exclusion related to essential resources. The value of environmental services as social and public goods can be enjoyed by many, but for that to occur, environmental services must be supplied. Ensuring continued access to and enjoyment of environmental services requires the protection of the productivity of environmental infrastructures that supply essential resources.

PART II. ENTRY, EXIT, AND GOVERNANCE

This section returns to the demand for common-pool resources and private goods with an emphasis on managing spillovers across common-pool resources rather than on how much can be harvested. Spillover effects, or negative externalities, occur when the actions of users of a common-pool resource impose costs on users of adjacent or linked common-pool resources. For instance, harvesting timber may lead to siltation of streams, negatively affecting aquatic habitat and the species such habitat supports. Paying attention to spillover effects and adequately governing them is crucial for a workable "how many?" policy approach. A "how many?" policy approach encourages many uses and users of environmental infrastructure, setting the stage for increasing numbers of conflicts and spillover effects that must be addressed. Managing spillovers will also have the effect of limiting or dampening "how much?" issues. Reducing spillovers almost invariably places limits on how much can be harvested, encouraging the sustainability of common-pool resource flows.

It may be tempting to think of managing spillovers as a governance issue. However, a number of legal scholars have pointed to the interaction between exclusion, more specifically entry and exit, and how entry and exit rules interact with managing uses and spillovers (Dagan and Heller 2001; Smith 2002, 2008). The right of exclusion is a rich and multifaceted concept covering boundaries and governance. A right of exclusion provides resource users with the security to invest in governing arrangements that both limit and coordinate users of a shared resource. Exclusion also allows resource users to enjoy the benefits their governing arrangements make possible.[5]

Dagan and Heller (2001) explicitly link entry, exit, and governance in their search for a liberal commons. A liberal commons allows individuals to reap the economic and social benefits of cooperation while protecting their autonomy and liberty through relatively easy exit. Exit, as Dagan and Heller (2001) note, has a powerful effect on individual behavior. It protects the liberty of the individual while disciplining the actions of the collective. The burdens imposed by the collective will be limited so as not to drive away members. While autonomy and liberty are protected, easy exit is likely to undermine cooperation. Individuals may act opportunistically, enjoying the benefits of cooperation generated by the collective without contributing to the creation of those benefits. In turn, individuals may become less trusting and trustworthy, fearing the effects of easy exit. While Dagan and Heller (2001) are optimistic about a properly designed legal context limiting opportunistic behavior, their point is well taken. Entry, exit, and governance are closely intertwined.

Spillover effects undermine access to and use of essential resources. Drying up a neighbor's well by lowering the water table through one's own pumping or polluting a stream by not keeping one's cattle from causing bank erosion are examples. Addressing and limiting spillovers protects access to essential resources; however, managing spillovers requires attention to entry, exit, and governance. Entry and exit requirements provide the context for governance—from shaping levels of cooperation among users to influencing the types of use rules adopted to constrain spillovers.

For instance, western states have used compacts, or "treaties," to govern the use of shared river basins, particularly to divide up the water in rivers among states. While physical entry is a combination of geography and state boundaries, entry into a compact is voluntary. States negotiate water allocation agreements grounded in the compact clause of the U.S. Constitution. Once a compact is adopted, which requires the consent of member states' legislatures and governors and the U.S. Congress and president, the compact becomes the law of the member states as well as U.S. law.

The barriers for states to exit a compact are quite high.[6] Termination of the compact requires unanimous consent of its members. If the compact is terminated, the water baseline is the infrastructure and water allocations put in place by the compact, not the water baseline that existed prior to the compact. The reasons for high exit barriers are likely several, such as protecting infrastructure investments that were made based on the presence of the compact and limiting opportunistic behavior on the part of upstream states. Droughts are common in the West, and at some point water officials in upstream states will be called upon to do something that they would not otherwise choose to do. During times of high water scarcity, when their citizens are clamoring for water, they must shut down water diversions so that citizens of another state may access and use that water.[7]

Entry, exit, and governance are tightly intertwined in interstate river compacts, which coordinate states' uses of shared rivers. Recent developments highlight how entry and exit affect governance. Many interstate river compacts were adopted prior to widespread pumping and use of groundwater. By the 1970s, groundwater pumping was having measurable effects on river and stream flows. Upstream states' water officials were reluctant to shut down wells. Downstream states' water officials forced action by enforcing interstate river compacts before the U.S. Supreme Court. In these cases the court recognized the hydrologic connection between ground and surface water, requiring upstream states to regulate pumping, that is, to address spillover effects, so that downstream states received their required surface water allotments. Thus, one way to read the history of western interstate river compacts is that they are a means of governing demand for water by addressing spillovers across state borders and between different but connected sources of water.

Recognizing and requiring that spillover effects between two connected sources of water be addressed has prompted a revolution in groundwater governance within upstream states. Historically, states did not regulate wells in any meaningful way. Would-be well owners needed only to obtain a permit. Since the adverse court rulings on groundwater, entry, exit, and use rules have been devised and revised for ground and surface water (Schlager and Heikkila 2011).

Entry and exit, two of the dimensions of exclusion, are interdependent with governance. Entry and exit set the stage for governance, and governance in turn affects how entry and exit play out. Entry and exit are central in addressing spillover effects created by users and uses of related common-pool resources. Addressing spillover effects protects those whose use of a common-pool resource is impaired by spillovers. In addition, limiting or reducing negative externalities typically has the effect of limiting demand. Whether the demand is for irrigation water or for disposing of waste in a stream, the reduction of the negative externalities created by those activities typically also involves the reduction of those activities themselves. This relationship, in turn, serves to protect a variety of uses and users of common-pool resources. Regulating entry and exit among common-pool resources may also have positive consequences for environmental services and the environmental infrastructure that produces those services. Managing spillover effects limits destructive uses that harm users of linked common-pool resources, and in so doing provides some protection for social and public goods and those dependent on such goods for their livelihoods.[8]

CONCLUSION

Returning to the epigraph but modifying it slightly, "the only thing worse than being excluded from environmental services is not to be excluded from common-pool resources" captures two related exclusion tragedies that exhibit different dynamics. The two are related because environmental services and common-pool resources are provided by the same environmental infrastructure. They exhibit different dynamics because they entail different types of "goods." Environmental services such as water purification, flood control, and soil regeneration are public goods. As public goods, if they are available, many people may partake of their value. Thus, the tragedy of exclusion in relation to environmental services is a tragedy of supply. Degrading or extinguishing environmental services deprives people of their value. Common-pool resources such as rivers, groundwater basins, fish stocks, and forests—unlike public goods—are rivalrous or subject to crowding. This typically occurs when people convert the flows of common-pool resources into private goods, such as harvesting fish or diverting water from a stream. The tragedy of exclusion in relation to common-pool resources is a tragedy of demand. Unchecked crowding or unregulated use leads to the dissipation of the value of resource flows. In both instances, people are deprived of essential resources.

To address the two related exclusion tragedies requires attention to *supply* of environmental services produced by environmental infrastructure and *demand* for private goods provided by common-pool resources (which are also produced by environmental infrastructure).[9] Conventional natural resource policies primarily attend to demand for the products of common-pool resources, historically stimulating demand and more recently regulating demand. Also, until recently, natural resource policies did not address the supply of environmental services. Policies addressing demand have been relatively narrow, focusing on regulating a single stock or species with little regard for the effects on related common-pool resources or environmental services. Characterized as "how much?" policies because of the emphasis on defining how much of a stock or species may be harvested without depleting it, such policies have privileged specific uses and users to the neglect of many other uses and users (Benson and Craig 2014).

Following Frischmann's (2012) infrastructure policy logic, I reframe natural resources policy approaches from "how much?" to "how many?" to emphasize and highlight the supply of environmental services. A "how many?" approach would forbid uses that are destructive of environmental services and, consequently, uses that would eliminate many other types of users and uses. In addition, a "how many?" approach would also recognize and protect as many uses and users of environmental infrastructure as is feasible. This would often mean the use of different forms of land use or ecosystem planning and zoning that would coordinate uses and limit their impact on one another. The goal is to protect the supply of environmental services and, by doing so, allow many users to enjoy the value of these public goods.

A "how many?" policy approach has implications for the demand for flows of common-pool resources. Allowing many users and uses of environmental infrastructure places a premium on addressing spillover effects. Reducing spillover effects among users of common-pool resources requires attention to the interactions between entry, exit, and use of such resources rather than the current emphasis on how much can be appropriated. Reducing spillover effects protects many users and uses of common-pool resource flows. Thus, protecting the supply of environmental services and carefully regulating entry, exit, and use of common-pool resources addresses both exclusion tragedies.

NOTES

1. The Millennium Ecosystem Assessment's definition of ecosystem is similar to Frischmann's definition of infrastructure. According to the report: "An ecosystem is a

dynamic complex of plant, animal, and microorganism communities and the nonliving environment interacting as a functional unit" (Millennium Ecosystem Assessment 2005: v). The report identifies four categories of ecosystem, or environmental, services: provisioning, regulating, cultural, and supporting. For the purposes of my argument, I treat provisioning services as common-pool resources and the remaining categories as public goods.

2. Frischmann (2012) does not include common-pool resources in the typology of goods provided by infrastructure.

3. While environmental services are critical for human well-being in general, some forms of them are crucial for economically poorer people, who do not possess the resources to replace environmental public goods with human-constructed public goods, such as dams for flood control or water treatment plants for potable water.

4. This goal mirrors Frischmann's (2012) infrastructure policy goal of encouraging many users and uses.

5. Fennell (2009) defines the benefits from exclusion as "use value" or "consumption value."

6. Many western interstate river compacts contains some version of the following clause: "This compact shall remain in effect until modified or terminated by unanimous action of the states and in the event of modification or termination all rights then established or recognized by this compact shall continue unimpaired." Arkansas River Compact of 1949 (C.R.S. §§ 37-69-101 to 37-69-106 [1949]).

7. In *Hinderlider* v. *La Plata River and Cherry Creek Ditch Co.* (304 U.S. 92 [101Colo73; 70 P.2d849]), the U.S. Supreme Court held that compact law supersedes state law. State officials are bound by compacts and are not allowed to avoid their compact obligations when those obligations become inconvenient.

8. For a thoughtful and thought-provoking analysis of efficiency and fairness issues surrounding the regulation of negative externalities, see Rose (2000).

9. Frischmann (2012) builds his theory on human-constructed infrastructures. He makes a detailed sand compelling case that conventional economic theory has emphasized supply to the neglect of demand. In relation to environmental infrastructure the opposite holds. Demand for flows from common-pool resources has been emphasized to the neglect of supply. Thus, in the environmental infrastructure setting, policies need to be revised to better reflect supply-and-demand needs and reframed in terms of reducing negative spillover effects.

REFERENCES

Benson, Melinda Harm, and Robin Kundis Craig. 2014. "The End of Sustainability." *Society and Natural Resources: An International Journal.* Published online May 7, 2014. http://dx.doi.org/10.1080/08941920.2014.901467.

Dagan, Hanoch, and Michael Heller. 2001. "The Liberal Commons." *Yale Law Review* 110:551–623.

Davis, Tony. 2013. "Quirk in Water Law Allows SV Project to Move Ahead." *Arizona Daily Star*, March 15.

De Schutter, Olivier, and Katharina Pistor. 2014. "Governing Access to Essential Resources." Scoping Paper, Columbia Global Centers, Mumbai, India.

Fennell, Lee Anne. 2009. "Adjusting Alienability." *Harvard Law Review* 122:1402–1465.

Frischmann, Brett. 2012. *Infrastructure: The Social Value of Shared Resources*. Oxford: Oxford University Press.

Glazier, Edward, ed. 2011. *Ecosystems-based Management of Fisheries in the Western Pacific*. Chichester, UK: Wiley-Blackwell.

Glennon, Robert. 2002. *Water Follies: Groundwater Pumping and the Fate of America's Fresh Water*. Washington, D.C.: Island Press.

Grafton, R. Quentin, ed. 2010. *Handbook of Marine Fisheries Conservation and Management*. Oxford: Oxford University Press.

Grossman, Mark, and Gary Bryner. 2012. U.S. Land and Natural Resources Policy. 2d ed. Amenia, N.Y.: Greyhouse.

Karp, Hannah. 2013. "A Water Dispute Nears a Boil in Arizona." *Wall Street Journal*, February 16, A3.

Millennium Ecosystem Assessment. 2005. Ecosystems and Human Well-Being: Synthesis. Washington, D.C.: Island Press.

Ostrom, Elinor. 1990. *Governing the Commons*. Cambridge: Cambridge University Press.

——. 2000. "The Danger of Self-Evident Truths." *Political Science and Politics* 33 (1): 33–44.

——. 2005. *Understanding Institutional Diversity*. Princeton, N.J.: Princeton University Press.

Ostrom, Elinor, Roy Gardner, and James Walker. 1995. *Rules, Games, and Common Pool Resources*. Ann Arbor: University of Michigan Press.

"Pima County's Multispecies Conservation Plan." November 2012. Pima County, Arizona.

Prins, Gywn, et al. 2010. "The Hartwell Paper: A New Direction for Climate Policy After the Crash of 2009." University of Oxford and London School of Economics, U.K. http://eprints.lse.ac.uk/27939/

Schlager, Edella, and Elinor Ostrom. 1992. "Common Property and Natural Resources: A Conceptual Analysis." *Land Economics* 68 (3): 249–252.

Schlager, Edella and Tanya Heikkila. 2011. "Left High and Dry? Climate Change, Common Pool Resource Theory, and the Adaptability of Western Water Compacts" *Public Administration Review*. 71(3): 461–470.

Smith, Henry E. 2002. "Exclusion Versus Governance: Two Strategies for Delineating Property Rights." *Journal of Legal Studies* 31 (S2): 453–487.

——. 2008. "Governing Water: The Semicommons of Fluid Property Rights." *Arizona Law Review* 50:445–450.

Tear, Timothy, Peter Kareiva, Paul L. Angermeier, Patrick Comer, Brian Czech, Randy Kautz, Laura Landon, David Mehlman, Karen Murphy, Mary Ruckelshaus, et al. 2005. "How Much Is Enough? The Recurrent Problem of Setting Measurable Objectives in Conservation." *BioScience* 55 (10): 835–849.

CHAPTER 4

Property Theory, Essential Resources, and the Global Land Rush

Hanoch Dagan

Securing access to essential resources is a major human rights concern. It should also be a major concern of property law and theory. As Olivier De Schutter and Katharina Pistor insist, "drinking water, adequate food, and shelter" as well as land (insofar as access to it is necessary for growing food or drawing water, as is the case for many rural households in the developing world) are all "indispensable for survival." Depriving people from access to such resources violates their basic needs and is thus "morally repugnant."

De Schutter and Pistor pose challenges on three fronts: the conceptual, the normative, and the programmatic. They argue that we need "to rethink the *concept* of property in relation to [essential] resources." They urge us to move beyond the concern of ensuring the increased productivity of such resources, taking seriously both the goal of fair access and that of sustainability and further considering the addition of a fourth goal: ensuring "the collective right of communities to self-determine their way of life." Finally, they acknowledge the programmatic challenge of translating these prescriptions into concrete policy measures, laying stress on two main problems. One touches on the potential conflicts between these normative goals, which requires devising strategies able to ensure their proper accommodation. The other derives from competition, which they perceive as a lingering impediment to success. De Schutter and Pistor therefore invite us "to rethink the scope of market mechanisms and the use of defensive mechanisms against the potentially erosive effects of market forces on access to essential resources."

My approach in addressing these challenges is interpretive. I agree that the conventional conceptual map of property is inadequate, that welfare maximization should not be our sole guide, and that the current structure of developing transnational markets is troublesome. But I claim we can face all three challenges—conceptual, normative, and programmatic—by reclaiming the (Western) conception of property and enlisting the market. Rather than rejecting property or shunning competition, I suggest adopting a charitable reinterpretation of them. In what follows, I hope to demonstrate the promising yield of this exercise for members of rural communities whose reliance on access to land is threatened by large-scale transfers of land to which they do not hold formal title.

I claim that, properly interpreted, our conception of property is a loose framework for an array of institutions governing a diverse set of interpersonal relationships regarding different types of resources. Thus, property itself invites a dynamic reimagination of these institutions' contours. I also argue that, notwithstanding the prevailing tendency to discuss property through the prism of only one particular value, notably aggregate welfare and independence, property can, should, and in fact does serve a pluralistic set of liberal values that also includes labor, personhood, community, and distributive justice. I further contend that all these property values weigh heavily in favor of recognizing the rights of those whose (individual and collective) identity, and even survival, depend on access to essential resources. Finally, I maintain that subscribing to the values and structural pluralism of property may be crucial in addressing both these programmatic difficulties. Deciphering the possible underpinnings of property's pluralism can point to proper strategies for addressing conflicts of values, and recognizing this multiplicity may point out how market alienability can be recruited for enhancing rather than hindering the proper governance of access to essential resources.

My approach is not risk free, so I begin by acknowledging its possible drawbacks. The history of property is complicated. Against the optimistic examples of synthesis and accommodation that I will highlight, property also obstructed the realization of the liberal values just mentioned, notably by neglecting the interests of the have-nots and by its tendency to put everything up for sale. Embracing property—or, more specifically, our Western way of thinking about property on which I rely—may therefore be perceived as too conservative. More specifically (and critically), taking cues from the internal structure of property institutions may entrench established social practices and unduly marginalize radical innovations. It may end up as an apologetic exercise, co-opting the hegemonic way of thinking about collective-action problems as if they inevitably need to be addressed with "modest pessimism about human motivation," thus possibly exacerbating our blindness to more utopian alternatives (Purdy 2013).

I do not deny these possible risks, but the alternative of discarding our accepted ideals of property and markets is onerous as well. By neglecting the possibility of mining these ideals for happier practices, champions of the access to essential resources cause may allow the practitioners and beneficiaries of "land-grabbing" to capture the powerful brand names of property and markets, thus undermining their own goals.[1] In other words, given the cultural power of property and markets, losing the battle over their proper interpretation would by default needlessly exacerbate our predicament. The alternative I offer is very different from accepting the (largely corrupt) manifestations of property and markets ideals in contemporary transnational markets. Quite the contrary, unpacking the ideals underlying these contingent social practices is potentially challenging, because it requires at the very least a respectable universalistic facade. This idealized picture can be and often is a fruitful source of social criticism, setting standards our current practices do not necessarily live up to. The idealism of our social world, even if hypocritical, is a significant source in any critical engagement (Dagan 2011, chap. 4; see also Walzer 1987).

STRUCTURES

The standard conceptual apparatus of property offers a well-worn trilogy of ownership forms. Private property is defined "around the idea that contested resources are to be regarded as separate objects each assigned to the decisional authority of some particular individual (or family or firm)" (Waldron 1996, 6). Common property designates resources that are owned or controlled by a finite number of people who manage the resource together and exclude outsiders (Ostrom 1990, 222n23). Finally, state (or collective) property stands for a regime in which "in principle, material resources are answerable to the needs and purposes of society as a whole" (Waldron 1996, 40). Property theorists acknowledge that none of these ideal types is present in pure form and use them only as placeholders for their justificatory and normative debates. But this trilogy has become so entrenched as to seem almost natural, beyond serious contestation or elaboration (Dagan and Heller 2001, 555).

Property law, however, never complied with this architecture. To be sure, many property theorists try to explain (or explain away) the numerous hybrid forms as variations on a common theme or peripheral exceptions to a robust core (e.g., Penner 1997; Merrill and Smith 2007). But the multiplicity of property can be suppressed or marginalized along these lines only if, somewhat arbitrarily, we set aside large parts of what constitutes property law, at least as evident in the conventional understandings of the case law, the Restatements, and the academic discourse. Rather than complying with this canonical tripartite straitjacket, property exemplifies the structural pluralism of private law through a large number of distinct institutions, each governing a specific social context or resource and typified by a particular configuration of owners' entitlement, with a particular property value or a balance of values serving as its regulative principle (Dagan 2012).

Thus, some property institutions, such as the fee simple absolute, are structured along the lines of the Blackstonian view of property as "sole and despotic dominion." These institutions are atomistic and vindicate people's negative liberty. Liberal societies justifiably facilitate such property institutions, which serve both as a source of personal well-being and as a domain of individual freedom and independence. In other property institutions, such as marital property, a more communitarian view of property may dominate, with property as a locus of sharing. There are many others along the strangers-spouses spectrum, and shades and hues of these property institutions will thus be found. In these various categories of cooperative property institutions, both liberty and community are of the essence, and the applicable property configuration includes rights as well as responsibilities. This variety is rich both between and within contexts: It provides more than one option for people who want, for example, to become homeowners, engage in business, or enter into intimate relationships (Dagan 2011, chaps. 1, 3–4, 8–10; 2012).

Indeed, property law supports a wide range of institutions that facilitate the economic and social gains made possible by cooperation. Some of these institutions, such as a close corporation, are mostly about economic gains, including securing efficiencies of economies of scale and risk spreading, with social benefits merely a pleasant side effect. Others are more (or at least equally) about interpersonal relations, with the attendant economic benefits perceived as helpful by-products rather than as the primary good of cooperation. Either way, the whole point of the elaborate governance structures these doctrines prescribe is to facilitate cooperative rather than competitive relationships. Not surprisingly, then, the exclusion conception of property is particularly inapt for understanding these important property institutions.

Property institutions vary not only according to the social context but also according to the nature of the resource at stake. The resource is significant, because its physical characteristics crucially affect its productive use. Thus, for example, the fact that information consumption is generally nonrivalrous implies that when the resource at hand is information, use may not always necessitate exclusion. The nature of the resource is also significant in that society approaches different resources as variously constitutive of their possessors' identities. Accordingly, resources are subject to different property configurations: While owners' control is vigilantly preserved in cases of constitutive holdings such as homeownership, utilitarian considerations (which at times override owners' dominion) take precedence when more fungible resources, such as patents or shares traded on national securities exchanges are concerned.

The pluralist understanding of property law is, at least in its common-law rendition, inherently dynamic (Dagan 2011, chap. 1). While existing property institutions are often the starting point of analysis, they are never frozen. Rather, as institutions structuring and channeling people's relationships, they are subject to ongoing, albeit properly cautious, normative and contextual reevaluation and to possible reconfiguration. The conservative baseline of this approach derives both from the pragmatic reality that existing rules cannot be abandoned completely and from the recognition that existing law represents a cumulative judicial and legislative experience that deserves respect. In turn, the forward-looking perspective of this endeavor is premised on an understanding of law as a dynamic enterprise. Its content unfolds through challenges to the desirability of the normative underpinnings of our private law institutions; their responsiveness to their social context; their effectiveness in promoting their contextually examined, normative goals; and the sufficiency of the repertoire that property law offers for any given type of human pursuit.

At times this process helped to fill gaps in the law by prescribing new rules that further bolstered and vindicated these goals. At other times it pointed out "blemishes" in the existing doctrine, rules that undermine the most defensible account of such a property institution, which should be reformed so that it lives up to its own ideals. This reformist potential has yielded different types of legal reforms throughout the history of property. In some cases the reform was relatively radical—the abolition of a property form (as was the case, for all practical purposes, with the fee tail form[2]) or an overall reconstruction of its content (as with leaseholds or marital property). More moderate options are sometimes in order, such as restating the doctrine pertaining to a property form in a way that brings its rules closer to its underlying commitments and, in the process, removes indefensible rules (the best example here probably comes from the gradual transformation of servitudes).

Property's pluralism and the dynamic adjustment of the repertoire of property institutions to the pertinent social context and the relevant resource reveal an ambiguity in our conceptual task. In one sense, we surely need to rethink property in order to face the enormous (and vastly important) challenge of governing access to essential resources. And yet, we do *not* need to rethink the *concept* of property. Properly interpreted, property as we know it already implies that once we identify essential resources as a distinct category and further appreciate the distinctiveness of social context for the development of the transnational markets in which this category is situated, we should indeed develop a new property institution properly tailored for the tasks at hand. At its best property calls for, or at least responds to rather than rejecting or resisting, such institutional innovation.[3]

It may be instructive to compare our challenge with the most important development in American land law in the last century: the emergence of common-interest communities, a property institution that is by now a major form of land ownership. After some resistance in the courts and some adjustment of people's expectations, common-interest communities "have grown greatly in number and spread to all corners of the United States" (Dukeminier et al. 2014, 937). This property institution has already dramatically changed the reality of property for millions, since it typically entails features alien to the traditional fee simple absolute, notably the collective management of important aspects of a real estate development and the thick layer of rules regarding the use of individual units. It also includes recognition of severe limitations on the exclusionary prerogatives of property owners, insofar as they exhibit unacceptable discriminatory practices (Dagan 2013, 2015). The success of common-interest communities in departing from the preexisting commonsensical understanding of what it means to have a home demonstrates the potential of new property institutions.

VALUES

My discussion of the structure of property implies that the various property institutions are quite stable in their daily operation and can thus (properly) serve both as a premise in people's expectations and as a constraint on the lawmakers' power (Dagan 2015). It also implies that at "property's constitutional moments" (when existing property institutions are changed or eliminated or new institutions are put in place) property law's underlying values are involved, often implicitly, in shaping or reshaping the particular configuration of the property institution at hand. Unlike the frequent portrayal of the (Western) conception of property suggested by both defenders and critics of the status quo, however, property does not serve *only* owners' independence and aggregate utility but also other important values. These other values are relevant when assessing property rights in rural communities, whose members' reliance on access to land is threatened by large-scale transfers of land to which they do not hold formal title.[4] (As one report documents, in many of the recent large-scale land acquisitions in developing countries, "those who are selling or leasing land are not the ones who are actually using it," a situation often generating displacements [Anseeuw et al. 2012, 39, 41].) Appreciating the significance of these values, therefore, is crucial for a property-informed prescription of the appropriate baseline in the developing transnational markets in which these transfers take place.

The leitmotif of the following discussion is that our property values—the very values used to justify many of our existing property institutions—point to substantial if well-circumscribed limits on the owners' right to exclude and to important reasons for recognizing the corresponding rights of nonowners. This point is not only theoretical. In (Western) domestic law, these reasons are often translated into legal rules limiting the owners' right of exclusion. In fact, the right of nonowners to be included and exercise a right of entry is even typical of certain property institutions such as, for example, the law of public accommodations or the fair use doctrine in copyright law (Dagan 2011, chap. 2).[5] To be sure, every property right involves *some* power to exclude others from doing something, but this is a modest truism with hardly any practical implications. Private property is always subject to limitations and obligations, and "the real problems we have to deal with are problems of degree, problems too infinitely intricate for simple panacea solutions" (Cohen 1954, 362, 370–374, 379).

Consider first the most traditional liberal property value, desert for labor, which still enjoys strong popular appeal in contemporary Western societies. Property, in the most charitable rendition of this view, is a reward for productive labor, where productive labor stands for people's efforts, perseverance, and risk taking, as well as the application of their innate intelligence and creativity, despite some daunting philosophical problems in this regard.[6] Laborers merit a reward for purposeful activities directed to useful ends such as the preservation or comfort of our being, because by engaging in value-creating activities, they contribute to the betterment of the human predicament (Buckle 1991, 149–152; Munzer 1990, 255–256, 285–287).

Note that desert theory implies *all* value-enhancing labor is good. Because it is concerned with the intrinsic value of labor, desert does not discriminate between the first and the subsequent labor expanded on a resource or, for that matter, between the labor of the resource's owner and that of another person, such as that of a tenant farmer working on someone else's property (Waldron 1988, 203–204). Modern liberal law does not always go that far, though at times it does, as in cases of adverse possession. Even in less extreme circumstances, however, our property law shows concern for people who invested work in someone else's land. The doctrine is complex, but one approach, which typifies the "Betterment Acts" enacted in most U.S. jurisdictions, gives the owner a choice between paying the value of the improvement and selling the land to the improver at its unimproved value, a rule that seems particularly appropriate for absentee owners who hold the property purely for investment (Dagan 2004, 83).

Similar and perhaps more pointed conclusions emerge from the personhood value of property. Whereas ownership of a fungible property plays a purely instrumental role in an owner's life, holders of constitutive resources are personally attached to their properties, since and insofar as these resources reflect their owners' identities as external projections of their personality (Radin 1982). These differences are morally significant, because perceiving resources as an extension of the self fosters people's moral development by imposing consistency and stability on their resolutions, plans, and projects, thus facilitating a sense of self-discipline, maturity, and responsibility (Waldron 1988, 370–377).

And indeed, (American) law responds to these distinctions largely by according differing degrees of protection to resources (socially) perceived as variously constitutive of their possessor's identity. Thus, the more closely a resource is attached to its holder's identity in their society, the greater the emphasis the law places on negative liberty. By contrast, when resources are viewed as merely valuable assets without direct bearing on their holders' identities, the law's focus shifts to the social standpoint, and adherence to the vindication of owners' exclusivity is correspondingly diminished (Dagan 2004, 216). Indeed, the same property value that is particularly strict about curtailing a nonowner's claim to a constitutive resource, such as someone's home, may be almost indifferent regarding a fungible resource. In some cases, the position of the personhood value of property is almost reversed. When a resource is fungible for its owner but constitutive for another (say, its long-term lessee), the personhood value of property is particularly suspicious of the owner's claim to exclude that particular other (Radin 1986).

The personhood value of property may be significant for the current discussion, because alongside desert for labor, it may serve as a normative foundation for the claims of nonowners to certain rights in land they have improved and on which their personal identity (as well as their communal identity) is constituted (Narula 2013). Moreover, personhood and personal liberty are general, right-based justifications of property. Unlike collective justifications, such as aggregate welfare, they rely on an individual interest, and unlike special, right-based justifications such as desert, they rely on the importance of an individual interest as such rather than on a specific event. These property values, then, entail significant distributive implications: None of them can justify the law enforcing the rights of property owners unless the law simultaneously guarantees necessary as well as constitutive resources to nonowners (Waldron 1988, 115–117, 377–378, 384–386, 423, 429–39, 444–445; 1991).

This claim of nonowners is surely relevant vis-à-vis the government. It requires "an *ongoing* commitment to dispersal of access" and insists that we design our property system so that it dynamically ensures that "lots of people have some" property and that "pockets of illegitimately concentrated power" (i.e., property) do not reemerge (Singer and Beermann 1993, 228, 242–245). But nonowners' claims to access may also be pertinent vis-à-vis private owners. To see why, consider property's role in protecting people's negative liberty. Private property is often justified by reference to its function in protecting people's independence and security through the spread or decentralization of decision-making power (Friedman 1962, 14–16; Barnett 1998, 139–142, 238). But this protective role, rather than universally significant, is particularly important to members of the nonorganized public or of marginal groups with little political influence (Michelman 1987, 1990). The special significance of providing nonowners access to property, and the inverse relation between owners' wealth and power, on one hand, and the importance of safeguarding their right to exclude, on the other, point to categories of cases such as those mentioned earlier, wherein our commitment to personal liberty entails the nonowners' claims to entry rather than the owners' claims to exclusion (Dagan 2011, chap. 2).

I have thus far argued that the conception of property, in its familiar liberal rendition, relies not only on the values of aggregate welfare and personal independence but also on the property values of labor, personhood, and distributive justice. In turn, in different ways and in potentially differing circumstances, these values also support the claims of rural communities whose members face possible large-scale transfers of the land on which they had relied. These nonowners' rights of inclusion, I claim, are not an embarrassing conceptual aberration. Inclusion is indeed less characteristic of property than exclusion, and in the limiting case of inclusion—universal equal access—there is no owner at all. Manifestations of inclusion are still as intrinsic to property as exclusion, because many limitations and qualifications of exclusion, and thus the corresponding rights of nonowners to be included, rest on the very same property values that justify our legal system's support for the pertinent property institution.

Moreover, in addition to its support of fair access and again in sharp contrast to its frequent depictions (or distortions), property is also community-friendly. Property relations participate in the creation of some of our most cooperative interactions. Numerous property rules prescribe the rights and obligations of spouses, partners, coowners, neighbors, and members of local communities. A significant part of property law, as noted, is not about vindicating the rights of autonomous excluders cloaked in Blackstonian armors of sole and despotic dominion, but rather about creating a governance regime for the resource's stakeholders to facilitate the potential economic and social gains of cooperation. These property institutions create an institutional infrastructure that facilitates the long-term cooperation necessary for successful communities. Their sophisticated governance regimes regulate decisions about consumption, investment, management, and allocation. At their core are mechanisms for collective decision making aimed at aligning individual and group goals by aggregating individual preferences or objectives. Such conflict-transforming mechanisms range from democratic participatory institutions, such as simple majority rule, to representative apparatuses, such as a condominium board in a common-interest community (Dagan and Heller 2005).

These features of property may be relevant to rural communities facing large-scale transfers of land, insofar as their informal practices of cooperation in the operation, maintenance, and improvement of the land they rely upon are significant to their constitution as communities (Lehavi

2004). This communal dimension is even stronger when the sites at issue are inherent in the collective personhood of these communities, as evident in the recent discussion about the functions of cultural property for indigenous peoples (Carpenter et al. 2009). Neither claim necessarily implies, however, the entrenchment of the status quo. The informal customary management of commons regimes may unduly privilege insiders at the expense of non–group members and even within the group may particularly benefit powerful leaders (Jaffe 1937; Foster 2012). Corrupt communal structures of this type should be reformed or dismantled rather than entrenched. But insofar as community and personhood are valid, indeed important, property values, claims based on these values in the context of developing transnational markets are endogenous to property; rather than claims against property, these are property claims.

CONFLICTS

Property, I argue, is a loose framework of separate property institutions that regulate diverse resources in different social contexts, each one according to its own distinct balance of property values. I also claim that in shaping a property institution for essential resources, the property values of labor, personhood, and distributive justice support and refine the normative goal of fair access. Moreover, I claim that the community value of property implies that fair access should, in proper cases, rely not only on the rights of individuals but also on the collective rights of their communities. De Schutter and Pistor's goal of sustainability is also covered by existing property theory, because at least in a humanist framework, it relies on another property value—aggregate social welfare. Thus, in a charitable reading, property theory supplies not only the conceptual framework but also the normative underpinnings for this endeavor. This conclusion, as noted, is significant, because it implies that supporters of property should join the cause of securing access to essential resources.

I turn now to the programmatic challenge, starting with the difficulty of accommodating the various values that should inform the new property institution of essential resources. Different property values are not necessarily in conflict. For example, community and welfare are often mutually reinforcing, because interpersonal capital facilitates trust, which leads to economic success, and in turn, to the strengthening of trust and mutual responsibility (Pettit 1995, 209–210). But this is not always the case, and where property values clash, we need to devise a way to accommodate them. Identifying the proper strategy for this task requires some attention to the choice between freestanding pluralism and autonomy-based pluralism (Dagan 2012).

Freestanding- or foundational-value pluralists rely on the observation that human life is replete with irreconcilable competing values and with legitimate wishes that cannot be truly satisfied (Berlin 1969). Worthwhile and potentially incompatible human projects and goods are many, diverse, and qualitatively different. They are governed and evaluated by distinct sets of norms, and monism does violence to these differences (Anderson 1993, 1, 5, 14). Freestanding-value pluralists do concede the difficulty posed by the entailed incommensurability, but they insist that value conflicts can be addressed if we are properly attuned to the values that are internal to and constitutive of the pertinent practice (Anderson 1993, 49). They may admit that in some cases such a contextual normative inquiry may lead to a standoff, but they nonetheless insist that in many others the explicit requirement to apply judgment, which needs to be normatively and contextually justified, entails sharp doctrinal teeth (Singer 2009).

Another and more secure foundation of value pluralism is the modestly perfectionist liberal commitment to autonomy, understood as people's ability to be the authors of their own lives, choosing among worthwhile life plans and being able to pursue their choices (Raz 1986). The rich mosaic of our structurally pluralist domestic property law relies here on the state's obligation to facilitate a sufficiently diverse set of robust frameworks for people to organize their lives (Dagan 2012).[7] Likewise, the different property values that are variously balanced by these divergent property institutions derive from and rely on the ultimate value of individual self-determination. In that personal independence, labor, personhood, community, aggregate welfare, and distributive justice are valuable because they are crucial for people's autonomy, their accommodation should be guided by this ultimate value.

In many domestic property contexts, this prescription simply reinforces the structural pluralist requirement of multiplicity, so people can choose their favorite property institution. Domestically, then, the prescriptions of autonomy-based pluralism tend to converge with those of freestanding pluralism in pointing to the regulative principle of the property institution at hand as the local arbiter for the resolution of value conflicts (Dagan 2012, 1424). Furthermore, both autonomy-based and freestanding pluralism sharpen the commitment of our law to structural pluralism, since they imply that property law should react favorably to innovations based on minority views and utopian theories, insofar as they have the potential to add valuable options for human flourishing that significantly broaden people's choices (Dagan 2012, 1425–1426).

But multiplicity does not always dispel conflicts and is certainly not a panacea insofar as essential resources are concerned. In most cases, acknowledging the role of autonomy as the ultimate commitment from which all property values derive implies that in "vertical conflicts" it must trump. Thus, since economic development is important "precisely because [and thus also only insofar as] it enables human beings to flourish" (Alvarez 2011, 62), if aggregate welfare threatens to undermine people's self-determination, autonomy should take priority (Smith 1995). Autonomy must similarly prevail whenever communitarian demands of loyalty might impede members' voices or their ability to exit (Green 1998). These pristine prescriptions may occasionally seem inappropriate. Sometimes, determining when welfarist or communitarian demands undermine autonomy requires a complex analysis of their overall effect on people's self-determination that also takes into account their positive effects. Other cases are more difficult, because they may involve tragic trade-offs, given the significant welfarist or communitarian price of strict adherence to autonomy. One must recognize that though a rare possibility, the presumption as to autonomy's precedence may be overridden if, and only if, its costs in terms of welfare, community, and the like pass a sufficiently high threshold (Zamir and Medina 2010, 1–8, 79–104).

Either way, the claim that autonomy should be the ultimate value of the property institution of essential resources may alarm progressive readers, given that a large proportion of the people who are to be subject to or affected by this institution do not accept the prescriptions of autonomy. They may find the prioritization of autonomy unacceptable, because it fails to comply with the injunction of equally respecting the dignity of all persons as ends (Nussbaum 2011; Quong 2011). Exploring the validity of this critique of perfectionist liberalism (or rather the thin version of it I endorse) or the sustainability of the alternative position—political liberalism—advocated by the critics surely exceeds the scope of the present inquiry. For my purposes, it will suffice to highlight that by sanctioning (in passing) legal practices that combat practices of (female) subordination and ensure people's ability "to leave one view and opt for another" (Nussbaum 2011, 29, 36), these critics end up subscribing to the modest perfectionist position they purportedly condemn. This inconsistency is not a contingent flaw. One can hardly envisage a plausible meaning of equal respect that downgrades people's right to choose their path or authorizes their systemic subordination. The injunction of respecting all persons equally, which underlies political liberalism's insistence that not all just states of affairs can be legitimately pursued by the state's coercive apparatus (law), requires enabling each individual person to choose, or at least discover, his or her life plan.[8]

Not surprisingly, then, the prescriptions of my autonomy-based approach for the resolution of value conflicts in property broadly converge with the progressive blueprint for accommodating conflicting values when addressing the global land rush that triggers our concern with essential resources.[9] Both prioritize the democratization of the rural poor's access to land over considerations of overall efficiency, and both caution against capture by local elites to the detriment of "female-headed households" and others, "such as newly arrived members of the community" (De Schutter 2011, 528, 532, 538). Revisiting the implications of the property values discussed above and interpreting all property values, including efficiency, as subservient to autonomy further vindicates two additional elements of this blueprint. First, that even where land users lack formal title, their just claims, which are backed by property values, must be recognized and secured before any other measure is adopted (De Schutter 2011, 521, 524, 551). Second, that there should be some preference to small-scale farmers over larger production units,[10] and that insofar as significant land transfers are concerned, there should be limits on the maximum length of land leases so the rights of future generations would not be unduly discounted (De Schutter 2011, 529, 547–548).[11] And yet, one significant exception to this happy convergence remains, a focus on the attitude to competition and markets, to which I now turn.

MARKETS

Competitive market forces are often viewed as a threat to poor rural households, which depend on access to land for farming, gathering wood or water, or grazing cattle. This attitude and the entailed requirement of defensive mechanisms against the market's erosive effects . . . on access to essential resources seem unassailable. The worry is that the poor cannot effectively compete, given their different purchasing power, and that global competition, in particular, undermines their livelihood (see the introduction to this volume).

I want to nonetheless cast doubt on the seemingly inevitable split between competitive markets and guaranteeing the rights of the rural poor (Narula 2013). I argue that the current failings, which are surely unacceptable, are contingent rather than essential to the logic of the market. Indeed, some even result from an abuse of this logic. I further contend that competition, properly designed, can and should be enlisted for securing access to essential resources.

De Schutter and Pistor identify three major problems in the current transnational land markets:[12] (1) they rely on an impoverished conception of property, which is enshrined in prevailing transnational property regimes and prevents the development of more appropriate ("thick") understandings of property; (2) "property deals are made typically not in transparent, liquid markets but in private deals characterized by asymmetries in information and power"; and (3) such large-scale land transfers are often subject to severe problems of capture and unrepresentativeness of local elites and (or) governments, which are "effectively unaccountable to their people" (De Schutter 2011, 528; De Schutter and Pistor 2013). Based on these significant concerns, De Schutter prefers foreign investments that do not involve land transfers. More specifically, he advocates constraining "investment sales" by limiting land marketability and instead encouraging investment in local cooperatives. With proper public assistance (via such measures as "tax incentives [or] preferential treatment in public procurement schemes or in access to loans" [2011, 550]), these cooperatives can secure the preexisting rights of the land's local users and also increase efficiency, given their inherent advantages of economies of scale and risk spreading (De Schutter 2010, 319–323; 2011, 531, 547, 549–551).

As my discussion makes clear, I subscribe to De Schutter and Pistor's view on the inadequacy, indeed the unjustifiability, of the Blackstonian conception of property at the transnational level, and I endorse their hope that a better one will replace it. I also firmly support the claim that private deals characterized by asymmetries of power and information, as well as being subject to severe political economy concerns, are unlikely to allay the normative concerns discussed thus far.[13] Finally, I find the cooperative solution potentially appealing, because "cooperatives that function according to democratic principles, work for their members, distribute costs and benefits equitably, and design and improve clear business plans, can be extremely beneficial to their members" (De Schutter 2011, 550).

The difficulty begins with the observation that this happy scenario is contingent on a correspondingly pleasing internal governance regime and possibly on the public support mentioned earlier as well. I do not argue that these conditions cannot be obtained, but I insist that they are threatened by the same political economy concerns that render property deals problematic in the first place. I do not contend that the threat posed by the cooperative route is necessarily more immanent or severe than that posed by investment sales (though I think we cannot confidently argue in favor of the inverse proposition[14]). Rather, I claim that the choice between these options should not be made by a global social engineer or by the contingent (and not merely coincidental) inertia that tends to perpetuate the Blackstonian model. This crucial decision should be made by the people who will be most affected by it.[15] They are entitled to consider both alternatives and choose whichever is best for them, and a transnational property law committed to an autonomy-based structural pluralism must be designed to ensure that they can effectively make this choice.[16] Finally, a market mechanism can and should be set up for this significant task. If properly calibrated to ensure competition rather than inhibit it, this mechanism could eventually help to overcome or at least alleviate the persistent difficulties caused by considerations of political economy and by asymmetries of power (including purchasing power) and information.

To see how this could be the case, consider the following proposal for structuring transnational development transactions. This preliminary tripartite suggestion is guided by three different insights gleaned from our past and recent experience of land transfers, from the conventional wisdom of antitrust policy, and from a recent institutional innovation developed for the difficult case of domestic land assembly.

The trigger for my first component is Stuart Banner's claim that the (or at least a) dominant factor in the British "conquest by contract" of New Zealand derives from the self-serving construction by the British colonial government of the market for Maori land, especially from 1840 to 1865, when the government was the single purchaser (Banner 2007). By contrast, as Klaus Deininger and Derek Byerlee maintain, relying on some empirical evidence mostly from Peru, "properly designed auctions" generate "very encouraging" results in terms of both "mean payments" and the "positive externalities [generated] by quickly disseminating information on the profitability of agriculture" (Deininger and Byerlee 2011, 110–112). The split between these two scenarios suggests that the problem with many deals in the current global land rush could, at least partly, result from the lack of sufficient buyer competition, as was the case regarding the Maoris. This possibility is supported by recent findings on "wide variation in royalties from land deals in developing contexts," which entails "the lack of corresponding price signals in many affected regions" and thus the possibility open to "some investors [to] exploit this lack of markets and transparency to their advantage" (Anseeuw et al. 2012, 42). Intensifying competition by way of mandatory auctions in large-scale land transfers could thus be part of the solution.[17] The auction mechanism is important not only because it is a means of ensuring buyers pay the right price but also because it allows the incorporation of development conditions that investors must satisfy. Moreover, auctions can and should involve mechanisms for flexible future adjustments that can ensure realization of the investment's expected positive social impact and enable early termination in particularly lengthy leases if circumstances unexpectedly change (Deininger and Byerlee 2011, 111–112). These are significant additional advantages of auctions, despite the difficulties they may generate by ranking not only monetary variables (i.e., the price offered and the amount of the projected investment).[18] But opening up the possibility of nonmonetary variables calls for serious improvement, hence the second component of my proposal, which relies on a conventional wisdom of antitrust.

Antitrust laws foster competition not only by forbidding blunt restraints of trade, such as price fixing, but also by inquiring into the competitive effects of other restrictive practices, including standardizing terms (Sullivan and Grimes 2006, 283; Areeda and Hovenkamp 2010, 380–381). In sharp contrast with this suspicious attitude toward standardization, transnational land markets implicitly accept that potential buyers need not compete over how, or whether, preexisting local users would be integrated or involved in the posttransfer use of the land at hand. Insofar as these people are indeed rightful stakeholders, as I claim they are, this blind spot implies that a vital effect of the investment at hand is in fact not subject to competition, and a key normative injunction in the structural pluralism typical of our property law is disregarded. As a way of dealing with this failure, bidders could be required to submit two options—one for outright purchase of the land and the other for becoming equity owners in a local cooperative, formed along the lines suggested by De Schutter. Alternatively, their proposal could be allowed to include either one or both of these options but would make the entire process contingent on a minimal number of proposals of both types.[19] This prescription rejects the current structure of the global land market, which erases or at least marginalizes the possibility of ending up with such cooperatives. It also rejects, however, De Schutter's a priori preference for such an endgame, because, as noted, this option may also be vulnerable to unacceptable deficiencies. By fostering competition over this element, my proposal seeks to reveal the premium that a competitive process would assign to the involvement of local users. If the selection of the winning bidder is properly structured, which is the task of my proposal's last component, this effect would also generate helpful incentives both to local elites wishing to entrench their status in their communities and to foreign investors who, seeking to gain a competitive edge, would look for cost-beneficial ways of structuring the involvement of preexisting local users.

To see how we can design such a happy selection process, consider Michael Heller and Rick Hills's suggested solution for a somewhat similar problem in domestic settings. To facilitate economic development, states need power to condemn land that is inefficiently fragmented due to the collective-action problem inherent in its assembly. But this power is dangerous and has too often been misused, or even abused, to the detriment of the poor and powerless. Though both the attractive and appalling features of eminent domain seem inextricably connected, Heller and Hills show they can be disentangled if one allows the residents of a neighborhood to collectively decide "by a majority vote, to approve or disapprove the sale of the neighborhood to a developer or municipality seeking to consolidate the land into a single parcel." This procedure gives "neighbors a chance to get a share of the land's assembly value," thus "enlist[ing] them to be supporters of land assembly whenever such an assembly really will have a higher value than the neighborhood that it will replace" (Heller and Hills 2008, 1469–1470).

For this formula to be transplanted to the context discussed here, one need assume that preauction rights are configured so that preexisting land users get a percentage matching their proper stake in the land, given the normative accounting discussed earlier. (This crucial assumption is not easy to implement but is still much simpler than the parallel process of creating a full-blown just-titling system, that is, a system that allocates and records the property rights of all the parties involved, given this "normative accounting.") Giving these land users the authority to determine by majority vote whether to opt for staying put as part of a De Schutter–inspired cooperative or getting higher compensation[20] and leaving their land is an attractive compromise between the frequently meaningless consultation process that currently takes place and the blunt veto power that some authors (e.g., Narula 2013) suggest land users should have.[21] Having this authority also encourages whoever is in charge of this initial allocation process to take the rights of land users seriously; were the financial stakes too low, they would most likely dismiss the alternative of a full-blown sale outright.[22]

If most land users choose the cooperative alternative, it should indeed be adopted. Their willingness to forgo additional compensation to participate instead in a future cooperative endeavor signals their confidence in its success and the endorsement of its expected governance structure. The majority, however, should be allowed to decide otherwise, preferring to receive higher monetary compensation for a full-blown land transfer. Members of local communities should be protected from the unpleasant predicament of having their rights vindicated only through possibly oppressive and unfair communitarian structures. Even when the majority selects the cooperative route, individual members should be able to opt out and receive from the majority the higher monetary compensation that would have been forthcoming had the option of an outright sale been adopted (see, analogically, Heller and Hills 2008, 1470).[23] Admittedly, just like the alternative of allowing only the cooperative option, this mechanism too could be corrupted if it were to be captured by unresponsive government officials or self-interested local elites. The risk, however, would then be confined to one crucial moment, allowing for a reasonably viable demand for (probably international) supervision to ensure its credibility.[24]

CONCLUDING REMARKS

Sympathetic readers may wonder whether this proposal and its conceptual and normative underpinnings are indeed a reinterpretation of our understanding of markets and property, given their stark differences with the denotations of these concepts adopted in developing transnational markets. I insist that they are. Markets are arenas for alienating rights on competitive terms, which means that laws (or conventions) invariably and necessarily construct the rules of competition and the parties' baseline entitlements. Like property, the market is a concept that offers different conceptions (or interpretations), all of which should reflect its ideal of securing the voluntary reassignment of entitlements to benefit all parties involved. In order to reify this ideal and the ideals that make property valuable, we must constantly examine our practices. In the emerging global land market, the plight of land users facing the global land rush makes such reexamination vital, urging the possibility of forcing property and markets to live up to their implicit ideals.

NOTES

Thanks to Eyal Benvenisti, Nestor Davidson, Roy Kreitner, Michael Heller, Doreen Lustig, Katharina Pistor, Ariel Porat, and Leif Wenar for helpful comments, and to Guy Goldstein for research assistance.

1. This by no mean implies that thinking about our subject matter in terms of other human rights (De Schutter 2011) is wrong or redundant. Rather, my claim is that defenders of the right to access to essential resources should supplement rather than supplant their current line of argument with property reasoning.

2. In this sense, the extremity and saliency of the recent wave of transnational land transfers would serve as an important trigger to what may well have been called for in earlier, less extreme or less salient circumstances.

3. The fee tail is an estate that "descends to [the grantor's] lineal descendants . . . generation after generation, and it expires when the original tenant . . . and all of [his] lineal descendants are dead" (Dukeminier et al. 2014, 223).

4. In this respect my account reinforces the claim that informal occupancy should not always be viewed as lawlessness, because it is also a recurring feature of the development of property (Peñalver and Katyal 2010).

5. Other examples of the right to entry include the law of common-interest communities mentioned above, as well as the right to public access to beaches, including privately owned dry-sand portions of beachfront property (Alexander 2009, 801–810); the right to roam over privately owned wilderness or similar sorts of undeveloped land (Lovett 2011); and the compulsory licensing of patents (Adelman 1977).

6. As the text implies, this version of the labor theory of property is different from John Locke's famous account, which was aimed to establish the legitimacy of pre-political robust private property rights. But Locke's account is fraught with difficulties. Notable among them are the tortuous path from the no-spoilage proviso to an endorsement of full-blown money economy; the (implicit) dubious claim that non-owners have no right to complain about appropriations, even if they suffer nonmaterial harms, as long as enough and as good means of subsistence remains; and the feeble contention that, by mixing one's physical labor with an object that belongs to everyone in common, one is able to negate others' rights to that object and establish absolute ownership of it (Waldron 1988, 137–252; Sreenivasan 1995).

7. This reliance assumes, of course, a notion of an effective state that recognizes its obligations to foster its citizens' autonomy.

8. As Leslie Green claims, the position that grounds freedom in self-determination and the view that the value of freedom is founded on authenticity "are not completely distinct," because the former must recognize the significance of the "unchosen features of life" that "friends of authenticity" emphasize as "means to, or constituent parts of, various life plans," whereas the latter must recognize the significance of choice associated with "friends of autonomy," if not "in order to choose one's path in life, then in order to discover it" (Green, forthcoming).

9. I do not raise this convergence as a way of "tempting" progressives to join forces but as an exercise in reflective equilibrium that aims to sharpen theoretical

commitments by confronting them with our normative intuitions about the fairness of some of their concrete implications.

10. Recall that, in its formative era, antitrust was perceived as a cure for the "multiplicity of economic, social, and political evils" of wealth and economic power concentrations (May 1989, 290).

11. Similar duration limitations may also be appropriate for cooperative solutions insofar as they are adopted in such cases as per the mechanism suggested in the following text.

12. Smita Narula further argues that "the market approach" further ignores the baseline issue (Narula 2013). But even the staunchest defenders of the market acknowledge that its working relies on the prescription of baselines. The question of how to set such baselines, then, precedes the controversy over the workings of the market, and I therefore addressed it in previous sections of this chapter.

13. To be sure, these concerns, which threaten to undermine our property values, are not absent from domestic contexts as well. In fact, some of the discussion following relies on measures that attempt to address them in these contexts.

14. De Schutter seems to learn otherwise from the successful Mexican *eijido* system, given that even with full alienability, a large majority chose to remain in the communal system (De Schutter 2010, 322). This outcome, however, may only show to what extent the right to exit is instrumental for both voice and successful governance (Hirschman 1970).

15. I do not deny the more indirect and diffuse effects of such decisions on distant and future groups. In some contexts, their interests can be properly represented by the state apparatus. But this solution may not be satisfactory in some of the contexts considered here; hence my second-best suggestion of setting time limits to whatever property arrangement the proposed procedure yields. See note 11 above and accompanying text.

16. This may well be one of the main pitfalls of the prevailing bilateral investment treaties regime that effectively denies individual societies this choice.

17. A prescription of mandatory auctions need not, and indeed should not, preclude the possibility of investors' initiatives. Rather, it implies that in such cases, "the potential investor is required to present a business plan," and if the "proposed project is considered valuable," others will also be given an opportunity to present competing offers, thus initiating "a public bidding process" (Deininger and Byerlee 2011, 111).

18. Difficult as they might be, multiattribute/multidimensional auctions, notably in the context of U.S. government procurement, involve a robust experience. For the various rating methods applied in such auctions and for the decision process at the Department of Defense, see sect. 15.304 of the *Federal Acquisition Regulations* (General Services Administration, Department of Defense, and National Aeronautics and Space Administration 2005) and chap. 3 of the *Department of Defense Source Selection Procedures* (Under Secretary of Defense 2011), respectively. For a sophisticated economic model developed in this context, see Che (1993).

19. This aspect of my proposal can be improved in at least two, admittedly complicating, ways: (1) allowing bidders to raise other options as well, either by way of alternative governance structures or by offering land users substitute land; and (2)

allowing the community of land users to do the same, so that the options from which they will end up choosing are at least potentially determined bottom-up rather than only top-down.

20. As the text implies, I assume that the various monetary offers would be rated by a professional authority. Even so, difficult questions admittedly remain as per the optimal structuring of the land users' voting procedure in cases of multiple nonmonetary offers.

21. Generally, landowners do not enjoy such veto power under domestic (American) law either, as long as invoking the power of eminent domain is necessary (Merrill 1986). Allowing land users to determine whether to remain put is nonetheless justified within this framework as a way of determining whether a less onerous way of achieving the public purpose might be found.

22. An additional advantage of this way of framing the choice is that "current policies [tend to] play down direct payments for compensation" as opposed to "indirect benefits of investment projects (employment, supply chain opportunities and infrastructure)," which are perceived as "more valuable to affected people." In reality, however, these benefits tend to be "dispersed," "short-term," and too often unjustly distributed (Vermeulen and Cotula 2010, 914).

23. This last aspect raises hard questions requiring further reflection, notably regarding possible conflicts of interest between younger and older members of these local communities.

24. Furthermore, in order to properly engage in market transactions and exercise their market position, these vulnerable and often ill-informed populations would require the support of effective lawyers, financial advisors, and community organizers.

REFERENCES

Adelman, Martin J. 1977. "Property Rights Theory and Patent-Antitrust: The Role of Compulsory Licensing." *New York University Law Review* 52: 977–1012.

Alexander, Gregory S. 2009. "The Social-Obligation Norm in American Property Law." *Cornell Law Review* 94: 745–820.

Alvarez, José. 2011. *The Public International Law Regime Governing International Investments*. The Hague, Netherlands: Hague Academy of International Law.

Anderson, Elizabeth. 1993. *Value in Ethics and Economics*. Cambridge, Mass.: Harvard University Press.

Anseeuw, W., M. Boche, T. Breu, M. Giger, J. Lay, P. Messerli, and K. Nolta. 2012. *Transnational Land Deals for Agriculture in the Global South: Analytical Report Based on the Land Matrix Database*. Bern/Montpellier/Hamburg: CDE/CIRAD/GIGA.

Areeda, Phillip E., and Herbert Hovenkamp. 2010. *Antitrust Law: An Analysis of Antitrust Principles and Their Application*. Vol. 7. 3d ed. Frederick, Md.: Kluwer Law and Business.

Banner, Stuart. 2007. *Possessing the Pacific: Land, Settlers, and Indigenous People from Australia to Alaska*. Cambridge, Mass.: Harvard University Press.

Barnett, Randy E. 1998. *The Structure of Liberty*. New York: Oxford University Press.

Berlin, Isaiah. 1969. *Four Essays on Liberty*. Oxford: Oxford University Press.

Buckle, Stephen. 1991. *Natural Law and the Theory of Property*. Oxford: Oxford University Press.

Carpenter, Kristen A., Sonia K. Katyal, and Angela R. Riley. 2009. "In Defense of Property." *Yale Law Journal* 118: 1022–1124.

Che, Yeon-Koo. 1993. "Design Competition through Multidimensional Auctions." *RAND Journal of Economics* 24: 668–680.

Cohen, Felix S. 1954. "Dialogue on Private Property." *Rutgers Law Review* 9: 357–386.

Dagan, Hanoch. 2004. *The Law and Ethics of Restitution.* Cambridge: Cambridge University Press.

——. 2011. *Property: Values and Institutions.* New York: Oxford University Press.

——. 2012. "Pluralism and Perfectionism in Private Law." *Columbia Law Review* 112: 1409–1446.

——. 2013. "Inside Property." *University of Toronto Law Journal* 63: 1–21.

——. 2015. "Private Law Pluralism and the Rule of Law." In *Private Law and the Rule of Law*, ed. Lisa Austin and Dennis Klimchuk. Oxford: Oxford University Press.

——. 2005. "Conflicts in Property." *Theoretical Inquiries in Law* 6: 197–218.

Dagan, Hanoch and Michael A. Heller. 2001. "The Liberal Commons." *Yale Law Journal* 110: 549–623.

Deininger, Klaus, and Derek Byerlee. 2011. *Rising Global Interest in Farmland: Can It Yield Sustainable and Equitable Benefits?* Washington, D.C.: World Bank.

De Schutter, Olivier. 2010. "The Emerging Human Right to Land." *International Community Law Review* 12: 303–334.

——. 2011. "The Green Rush: The Global Race for Farmland and the Rights of Land Users." *Harvard International Law Journal* 52: 503–560.

De Schutter, Olivier, and Katharina Pistor. 2013. "Governing Access to Essential Resources." Unpublished scoping paper.

Dukeminier, Jesse, James E. Krier, Gregory S. Alexander, Michael H. Schill, and Lior Jacob Strahilevitz. 2014. *Property.* 8th ed. Frederick, Md.: Kluwer Law and Business.

Foster, Sheila R. 2012. "Collective Action and the Urban Commons." *Notre Dame Law Review* 87: 57–134.

Friedman, Milton. 1962. *Capitalism and Freedom.* Chicago: University of Chicago Press.

General Services Administration, Department of Defense, and National Aeronautics and Space Administration. 2005. *Federal Acquisition Regulations.* Washington, D.C.: U.S. Government Printing Office.

Green, Leslie. 1998. "Rights of Exit." *Legal Theory* 4: 165–185.

——. forthcoming. What Is Freedom For? *Oxford Legal Studies Research Paper* 77/2012.

Heller, Michael A., and Roderick Hills Jr. 2008. "Land Assembly Districts." *Harvard Law Review* 121: 1465–1526.

Hirschman, Albert O. 1970. *Exit, Voice, and Loyalty: Responses to Decline in Firms, Organizations, and States.* Cambridge, Mass.: Harvard University Press.

Jaffe, Louis L. 1937. "Law Making by Private Groups." *Harvard Law Review* 51: 201–253.

Lehavi, Amnon. 2004. "Property Rights and Local Public Goods: Toward a Better Future for Urban Communities." *Urban Lawyer* 36: 1–98.

Lovett, John A. 2011. "Progressive Property in Action: The Land Reform (Scotland) Act 2003." *Nebraska Law Review* 89: 739–818.

May, James. 1989. "Antitrust in the Formative Era: Political and Economic Theory in Constitutional and Antitrust Analysis, 1880–1918." *Ohio State Law Journal* 50: 257–396.

Merrill, Thomas W. 1986. "The Economics of Public Use." *Cornell Law Review* 72: 61–116.

Merrill, Thomas W., and Henry E. Smith. 2007. "The Morality of Property." *William & Mary Law Review* 48: 1849–1896.

Michelman, Frank I. 1987. "Possession vs. Distribution in the Constitutional Idea of Property." *Iowa Law Review* 72: 1319–1350.

——. 1990. "Tutelary Jurisprudence and Constitutional Property." In *Liberty, Property, and the Future of Constitutional Development,* ed. Ellen Frankel Paul and Howard Dickman. Albany: State University of New York Press.

Munzer, Stephen R. 1990. *A Theory of Property.* Cambridge: Cambridge University Press.

Narula, Smita. 2013. "The Global Land Rush: Markets, Rights, and the Politics of Food." *Stanford Journal of International Law* 49: 101–175.

Nussbaum, Martha C. 2011. "Perfectionist Liberalism and Political Liberalism." *Philosophy & Public Affairs* 49: 3–45.

Ostrom, Elinor. 1990. *Governing the Commons: The Evolution of Institutions for Collective Action.* Cambridge: Cambridge University Press.

Peñalver, Eduardo Moisés, and Sonia K. Katyal. 2010. *Property Outlaws: How Squatters, Pirates, and Protesters Improves the Law of Ownership.* New Haven, Conn.: Yale University Press.

Penner, J. E. 1997. *The Idea of Property in Law.* Oxford: Oxford University Press.

Pettit, Philip. 1995. "The Cunning of Trust." *Philosophy & Public Affairs* 24: 202–225.

Purdy, Jedediah. 2013. "Some Pluralism About Pluralism: A Comment on Hanoch Dagan's 'Pluralism and Perfectionism in Private Law.'" *Columbia Law Review Sidebar* 113: 9–19.

Quong, Jonathan. 2011. *Liberalism Without Perfection.* New York: Oxford University Press.

Radin, Margaret Jane. 1982. "Property and Personhood." *Stanford Law Review* 34: 957–1016.

——. 1986. "Residential Rent Control." *Philosophy & Public Affairs* 15: 350–380.

Raz, Joseph. 1986. *The Morality of Freedom.* Oxford: Oxford University Press.

Singer, Joseph William. 2009. "Normative Methods for Lawyers." *UCLA Law Review* 56: 899–982.

Singer, Joseph William, and Jack M. Beermann. 1993. "The Social Origins of Property." *Canadian Journal of Law and Jurisprudence* 6: 217–248.

Smith, Stephen A. 1995. "Future Freedom and Freedom of Contract." *Modern Law Review* 59: 167–187.

Sreenivasan, Gopal. 1995. *The Limits of Lockean Right in Property.* New York: Oxford University Press.

Sullivan, Lawrence A., and Warren S. Grimes. 2006. *The Law of Antitrust: An Integrated Handbook.* 2d ed. St. Paul, Minn.: West Group.

Under Secretary of Defense. 2011. *Department of Defense Source Selection Procedures.* Washington, D.C.: Office of the Under Secretary of Defense.

Vermeulen, Sonja, and Lorenzo Cotula. 2010. "Over the Heads of Local People: Consultation, Consent, and Recompense in Large-Scale Land Deals for Biofuels Projects in Africa." *Journal of Peasant Studies* 37: 899–916.

Waldron, Jeremy. 1988. *The Right to Private Property*. Oxford: Oxford University Press.
——. 1991. "Homelessness and the Issue of Freedom." *UCLA Law Review* 39: 295–324.
——. 1996. "Property Law." In *A Companion to Philosophy of Law and Legal Theory*, ed. Dennis Patterson. Malden, Mass.: Blackwell.
Walzer, Michael. 1987. *Interpretation and Social Criticism*. Cambridge, Mass.: Harvard University Press.
Zamir, Eyal, and Barak Medina. 2010. *Law, Economics, and Morality*. New York: Oxford University Press.

CHAPTER 5

MultipliCity

WATER, RULES, AND THE MAKING OF CONNECTIONS IN MUMBAI

Nikhil Anand

INTRODUCTION

Now there is a [state] policy regulation for water that we are bound by. Those structures prior to January 1995 are eligible for basic amenities. We are allowed . . . supposed to give water to them. Those [who have unauthorized structures built] after that date also get water. They make arrangements to take connections, forge ration cards and do such things to get them. . . . In slums our policy is to give water connections to federations of 15 [members]. We bring the connection to them, and their secretary is responsible for bill collection maintenance, bill payment, etc. If the population is at higher elevations, then we provide them with a suction pump and infrastructure at the bottom, and make them responsible for its operation and maintenance. The total revenue of the department is Rs. 1480 crores, of which Rs. 800 crore is the profit.[1] It is the only public utility with such performance. The slum dwellers are good paymasters. The government is not. Central, state governments are difficult. So this is the summary. You have questions?

Early in my fieldwork, I talked with Patkar, a senior hydraulic engineer at the headquarters of Mumbai's water supply department. I asked him to tell me about the city's water system, particularly as it pertained to slum dwellers. Experienced in talking with reporters and researchers about the city's water supply, Patkar gave me a quantitative account of the city's system—its lakes, pipes, scarcities, and topographies. As he started to tell me about the ways in which settlers access water, however, his narrative shifted to incorporate the language of incomplete entitlements and differentiated state policies. This slippage, enacted in the gap between what state technocrats are supposed to do and what they are allowed to do, reveals the flexibility and contingency that settlers are subject to when accessing water in the city. Even though city water rules allow only certain settlers (settled before 1995) to access the system formally, Patkar is aware that nearly all settlers access some municipal water. Patkar takes care to point out that the circumscribed legitimacy of settlers in access-ing water is not based on their inability to pay water bills in Mumbai, nor is it because the city water utility lacks the funds or the expertise to invest in network improvements to the city's settlements. The degree to which settlers (currently comprising 60 percent of Mumbai's popu-lation) can access water depends instead on politically mediated cutoff dates and physically mediated topographies, on pumps and secretaries, and on department policies and the tacit ways in which these can be circumvented.

As he narrated the patterns and normalized exceptions through which settlers accessed water in Mumbai, Patkar's account shuttled quickly among the public, private, and community regimes that all govern Mum-bai's water at different points in its journey from state-controlled dams to people's homes. Water is made a public thing by the collection of rainfall in distant watersheds by the city government and is delivered to hous-ing societies and other neighborhood federations, who are responsible for collecting fees and water rates from their families and consumers and for maintaining the pipes as they go from community co-ops into people's homes. Yet it is not just housing federations but also topography that mediates access to water supply. Therefore, those living in hilly areas are responsible for larger parts of the network (and the pumps, power, and monies they necessitate) than others. As water travels from urban pipes through human bodies, an attention to its governance quickly traces social relations and regimes that are formed through situated encounters of topography, law, and politics. In such a fluid landscape, water troubles attempts at government not only because of the ways in which it travels through diverse legal and technological regimes, but also because it often leaks, percolates, and collects in different locations, despite the politics, laws, and materiality that governs the city.

In recent years there has been an acute sensitivity to the public and private regimes that govern water in cities around the world and the exclusions these affect (Bakker 2007). Indeed as De Schutter and Pistor point out in the introduction to this volume, both public and private governance regimes produce exclusions in matters of water access and a range of other distribution regimes. In Mumbai, for instance, even as residents strongly protest the exclusions and effects of higher prices that frequently accompany privatization projects, the public water authority continues to deny residents of unrecognized settlements the ability to formally apply for water connections. In fact, both water administrators and their reformists have urged an attention not to whether water utilities are governed by corporate or public institutions, but instead to the legal regimes, public obligations, and environmental systems that structure the government of water utilities (see Bakker 2007).

In this chapter I provide an account of the everyday life of water government in Mumbai to help readers think through the questions of access, governance, and essential resources that are the focus of this volume. By drawing attention to the ways in which settlers and other marginal groups make claims on and access water from pipes, politicians, and technocrats of the city, I begin by drawing attention to the history of the Mumbai's water system. Next, I attend to everyday practices through which the system reproduces inequality even as it includes many of those who are marginalized by its rules. Finally, I draw attention to the ways in which the governance regime materialized through the work of hydraulic government in Mumbai enables (or disables) critical processes of voice and reflexivity that are the central concerns of this collection. How does the existing system, with all its difficulties, produce limited and improvised forms of inclusive distribution? What kinds of governance regimes may better achieve these results with water's fluid regimes and materialities? I conclude by drawing attention to the possibility of accessing vital resources in systems of government that are plastic, diffuse, and multiply constituted by different forms of authority.

HISTORIES OF WATER GOVERNMENT IN MUMBAI

From its history as a central node of empire, to its present as the commercial center of India, Mumbai has long been saturated with a continuous and reliable flow of energy and water resources mobilized by the state government. Mumbai's water system was created around the same time as the public systems of New York, London, and Paris (Gandy 2004, 2008). Nevertheless, while the utilities of those cities also initially privileged the upper classes with their services, the public system in Mumbai continues to be restrictive as to whom it serves.

In large part this is due to the legacy of the colonial municipal administration. In the nineteenth century, while designing the water system, Mumbai's planners were constantly limited by the higher authorities in Calcutta and London, who refused to accede to their requirements for a more expansive hydraulic infrastructure (Klein 1986; Dossal 1991). As such, when compared with planners in European cities, administrators in Mumbai were never able to serve a broader "public." Subject to strict colonial evaluations of cost and benefit, they were only able to design water projects for particular populations in Mumbai (Gandy 2008; McFarlane 2008). The legacy of this split persists today and is reproduced through violent and exclusive city rules about who counts as a citizen.

Therefore, although Mumbai's water system is managed by a public water authority—the water department of the Mumbai Municipal Corporation (BMC)—settlers are doubly marginalized in their attempts to access water in the city. They are marginalized both by the city's water rules and the practices of its public officials. First, the city water rules. For much of Mumbai's history, urban settlers who did not live in planned buildings were ineligible to apply for water connections as per the city's water rules. Settlers who are able to prove their residence in a settlement prior to a periodically revised "cutoff date" (currently 1995) can be recognized as living in "declared slums" and can formally access state services (McFarlane 2008). The services that accompany "declaration" are not instantaneous or even wholly assured. The entitlements of declaration, including postal service, water, electricity, toilets, and drainage, are provided very slowly and depend on political and social pressure.[2] While these changes are partial and discretionary, it is important to note that they now entitle those living in recognized tenements a formal procedure by which to access the public system. On the other hand, for those living in undeclared tenements or otherwise ineligible structures, state and municipal rules still preclude their access to water and other public services.

Water quotas are the second site at which settlers are marginalized. Drawing on central government guidelines, Mumbai's water department plans and delivers to settlers approximately half the water they deliver to residents living in planned buildings. In interviews conducted with city engineers, they pointed out that while designing water connections they tried to deliver approximately 150 liters per person daily to those living in "toileted structures"—that is, the apartment buildings of middle-class and wealthy residents. For settlers and others living in "untoileted structures," engineers designed connections to deliver only 90 liters per person per day (lpcd). Even this amount is an overestimate. According to one city engineer with whom I worked, they "do not count" the water needs of unrecognized settlers (who share water connections with recognized settlers) while planning the network. As a result, actual water consumption is often below 90 lpcd for most settlers living in the city's mixed settlements. Therefore, the public system produces inequality in the city at two levels: First, it makes it initially difficult for settlers to qualify for water connections because of its rules, laws, and policies. Second, it allocates less water to qualified settlers through the practices of timing and limiting supply.

THE PRIVATE PUBLIC

In the fall of 2007, I was speaking to Pratibha-*tai*,[3] an activist who has lived most of her life in slums and who has worked on human rights issues for several years, about the World Bank privatization project. I first met her at an NGO campaign meeting, where we spoke of the difficulties that the World Bank's consultants faced in privatizing the water supply. Therefore I was not too surprised to hear her critique the consultants' efforts. But then, much to my surprise, she suddenly interrupted me. "Anyway privatization has already happened," she said. At first I thought she was speaking of the buckets of water that are oftentimes purchased in unrecognized slums. But she was not. She was talking about the metering of water and its consequent charges. I quote:

> Earlier, the BMC never charged for water. Then, in the eighties, they began to charge us half the price, and they [the city councillors] would pay half. Then slowly slowly, they started charging us the whole amount, and said whoever wanted a connection would get one. We thought at least then we will get water, so we didn't resist too much. Earlier, fifteen households needed to come together to apply for a connection.[4] Now they [the BMC] need only four or five households [to approve connections]. . . . But per household the bill was smaller then. Now it's much larger. They also started charging for drainage, and this comes to 40–50% of the bill. . . . Privatization has already happened. . . . Indian people only did privatization before Castalia [the consultants] came.

Very aware of the histories of privatization in Mumbai, Pratibha-*tai* points out that the privatization of the water department has been underway since at least the late 1970s, when the World Bank agreed to finance the department's dam-development projects. For instance, it was during this period that the BMC started billing new connections on a volumetric basis (as opposed to a percentage of their property value) and ring-fenced the water budget from that of the general municipal administration. While seemingly unaware of the longer history of the World Bank's involvement, Pratibha-*tai* also locates agency and complicity for privatization among state department employees themselves, who are willing to meter and bill for water connections.

Pratibha-*tai* was also very aware of the different meanings of the word "private." By first flagging the ways in which slum-dweller groups were "recognized" and given connections by the water department, then describing the installation of water meters, and finally mentioning ongoing efforts to privatize the department's distribution network, Pratibha-*tai* demonstrates an acute understanding of how the term "private" is used in a variety of different ways in the city. It is at once a sign for a particular recognition of households, a technology of delivery, and a form of property (Bakker 2007). While activists say they are against privatization, the different meanings of the word "privatization" have ambivalent and sometimes contradictory meanings for them. For example, many had protested the difficulties of women who had to spend hours waiting and fighting for water at standpost connections. As such, they welcomed the BMC's initiative to give connections to groups of households over a decade ago, even if these connections came with meters. However, activists are now vociferous in their opposition to the proposal that these meters be maintained and read by private companies.

Attention to the everyday practices of Mumbai's water department shows how water services frequently straddle the public and private domains, particularly for settlers who are not always able to put enough pressure on the water department engineers to direct water into their homes. For instance, Pratibha-*tai* me showed the settlement Patkar also described, where (according to Pratibha-*tai*) "people had developed their own system." Because the water department was unwilling to pump water up the hill on which they resided, residents formed associations to collect water at the base of the hill and pump it up themselves. This system delivered water to residents at much higher rates, which were said not only to incorporate the cost of the network but also the electricity needed to power it. In such arrangements, local residents, often tied to politicians, were the water providers, arranging who would get water, how much, and for how long; they would even collect contributions from every house for water supply and undertake maintenance and network extension projects on their own terms (see also Ranganathan [2014] and Cheng [2014] for a description of these processes in Bangalore and Manila, respectively).

As in many other systems of distribution, the profits and viability of private community providers depended on a certain kind of state system—in this case, a system that did not carry water up the hills and to the homes of those living in settlements at high elevations, a system that, in effect, refused to provide for some city residents. When I spoke with water department officials about this, they pointed to the costs that make pumping water extremely expensive. The electricity charges alone would undermine the cost effectiveness, and thereby the viability of the entire system. But topography and technics only matter for some. The willingness of the state to bear the cost of pumping depended on who lived on the hill. City engineers regularly marshal technical and geographic justifications to serve the elite and exclude the poor (Coelho 2005). As Mike Davis (1998) has shown in his work on Los Angeles, the costs of public service provision matter far more when people are poor than if they are wealthy. Throughout its long history, the water department in Mumbai has not hesitated to pump water up to Malabar Hill—home to the city's economically and politically powerful. Thus, contrary to Habermasian notions of the public, it is not only the laws and policies of government that differentiate and divide the public (Chakrabarty 2002; Chatterjee 2004). The public is also divided and differentiated by the situated and prejudiced *practices* of public officials in the field. Through the selective mobilizations of pumps, policies, and pipes, engineers make water flow steadily up the class structure into people's homes.

In Mumbai and other cities, the poor have historically claimed access to water in the city through collective mobilizations (see Coelho 2005; Anand and Rademacher 2011). To this day, city engineers are constantly anxious about protests, and the "law and order problem" that might result when settlers collectively "shout" for water (see also Chatterjee 2004; Coelho 2006).[5] Nevertheless, while mobs, crowds, and other forms of political society remain critical in Mumbai, what I found striking when conducting fieldwork was how residents of certain settlements used other techniques— including those of civil society—to secure water resources. That is, they have now accrued enough political power to compel the city administration to treat them as a deserving public without having to "shout."

For example, adjacent to the settlement on the hill that Pratibha-*tai* showed me were two others, but these were settlements on hills to which the BMC brought water, just like they did for their wealthier counterparts. Drawing on personal favors and rights regimes and working through the registers of civil *and* political society, these settlers successfully established a degree of compromised yet substantive citizenship in the city, at least as far as the provision of water is concerned. It is to these practices of connection making that I now turn.

WATER CONNECTIONS

I had first met Sunita-*tai* and Rajni-*tai* in 2007, when they had come on behalf of their *Mahila Gath* (women's group) to a community meeting organized to protest the World Bank–initiated water privatization project in Mumbai. While they participated actively in the discussions against privatization of the city's distribution infrastructure, Sunita-*tai* and Rajni-*tai* had come to the meeting with a specific grievance. They were having water problems and they needed help. Following the meeting, the community leader had offered his support—a letter written on Asha's letterhead for the city councillor—and also promised to organize a meeting with the councillor. When I met the women again months later, I learnt that the councillor had responded by quickly arranging a new line at his cost. I was not the only one who was impressed. Sunita-*tai* recounted with a smile:

> He even came at 5 o'clock in the morning to check and see in what condition the water was coming! Earlier the pressure was so low, we would have to dig around the pipe and tap it to get water. Now after the councillor's new line, it has become alright.

At one level, Sunita-*tai's* experience indexes a now commonplace route through which settlers redress their different grievances in the settlements. For settlers, access to many of the city's services—schools, hospitals, water—is mediated and facilitated by city councillors, who govern settlements like rajas, dispensing the services of the state to their populations (see also Coelho 2006; Zerah 2008). Yet, Sunita-*tai* was particularly impressed that the councillor came *to* the settlement early in the morning to ensure that the work was done. The councillor's personal visit not only recognized the legitimacy of residents' water complaints; it also revealed the ways in which both settlers and councillors mattered to the management of hydraulic politics. In laying *his* line, the services of the state representative had come *to* the people.

Indeed, the councillor's journey to the settlement indexes a critical shift in Mumbai, largely effected by the extension and power of voting rights in the city. Rather than access engineers hidden in the city's bureaucracy at more distant locations, settlers are able to access the public system through a personal connection with councillors in the settlements. As their democratically elected representatives with influence in matters of Mumbai's administration, councillors are able to pressure water department engineers to grant settlers greater access to the city's water system. With reelection dependent on the ability to respond to the diverse needs of the voters, the moral authority of the city's councillor-rajas is dependent on their ability to make and remake successful water connections (see Appadurai 2002).[6] Though these new connections are discretionary arrangements, they trace a critical pathway through which settlers can have their needs met in the city.

I better understood the dimensions of this everyday yet dramatic shift in a subsequent interview with the *Mahila Gath* in the summer of 2008. I had arrived at the community center of the *Mahila Gath* soaked in the city's humidity. The center was tiled and painted. Outside, a line of taps lined either side of a clean and narrow alley. A fan blew air through the room. It was a nice space, filled with the accoutrements of different urban institutions—posters on malaria provided by the municipal corporation, placards of a political party, and props from an NGO-run anti–domestic violence campaign. While we waited for other *Gath* members to arrive, Sunita-*tai* told me of how the community center was constructed. I was surprised to hear that they had built it with their own funds. Several other centers in the settlement (initially built as reading rooms or gymnasiums, for example) were funded either by political parties or by NGOs, oftentimes with municipal funds. As women came to the meeting, they signed their names in the register, sat down, and began to observe our conversation.

When enough had gathered, Sunita-*tai* began speaking. With practiced poise, she told me that when an NGO came to work in the area in the early 1990s, they helped in the formation of this *Mahila Gath*. At the time, many had trouble with the water supply, and thus, it was quite natural that the first problem they wanted to solve was that of water. In 1993, most women were still purchasing their water from those in the nearby settlement for one rupee a *handa* (a vessel to store water). Because it cost money, they used this water only for drinking and cooking and would take their clothes to the nearby spring to wash. Knowing it was not as clean as city supplies, they only drank this water when there was none in the taps. Thus, before the arrival of state services, they made life possible in the city by paying for some water and drawing on additional sources in the ground. Yet, like other urban residents, they preferred treated city water, not only because it was cleaner, but also because it was more reliable, convenient, and affordable.

Getting municipal water, however, was particularly difficult, because they were new to the city. Their visits to the municipal ward office for a water connection did not bear any results. There, officers told them the settlement was not a declared slum and the municipal corporation could not extend services to them. They then went to the municipal councillor. The councillor told them that because they lived at a high elevation, the line would not work. So they then went with an NGO worker to protest at the head office of the water department—a decision that came at significant personal cost. Together, Sunita-*tai* and the women of the *Mahila Gath* recounted this event to me:

"We spent our little money to go there, even when there was no money in the house. And there we got permission . . . at VT [the head office]. We met the hydrogen [hydraulic] engineer," Rajni-*tai* told me, "and we got the permission and came back to the councillor with it. He was new then. . . . Bringing the permission, even he was surprised. 'You went to VT and got permission!' We told him, we don't want your money, just put in a new water line [for us]. And then he helped us to bring the pipe. We found a plumber, spent 200 rupees each . . . and installed the pipe. From that point, the question of water left us [*panyacha prashna tithéch sutla*]."

As Sunita-*tai* and Rajni-*tai* recounted the story, the group became more animated, interjecting with their memories of this event. They enjoyed remembering the surprise of the councillor. To get water they had to overcome the constraints of legal procedures (of slum recognition), as well as the various practical considerations that precluded their access to water—gravity, money and policy. To get water they had to aggressively mobilize—appearing before city administrators with NGO workers and repeatedly at the offices of councillors and plumbers. They deployed several languages of entitlement: as clients of political parties, resisting protestors organized by civil society NGOs, plumbers' customers, and engineers' citizens. Through such hybrid practices, the women of Sundarnagar reconstituted their water supply. Drawing on the practices of civil *and* political society, they were able to make themselves into a deserving public in the eyes of the city water department, one that was eligible for their biopolitical services.

For many living in the settlements today, the water system is made through multiple, discrete, and everyday relations between residents, councillors, and city engineers, and the plumbers and social workers who connect them. It is a public system of favors, positions, *and* rights, marked by relations of patronage, protest, inequality, and money. In trying to get water, Sunita-*tai* and her companions did not care to distinguish between the NGO, the state, or their various politicians. They sought to obtain a degree of access from whoever could promise it to them. Their success was enabled by the density of institutions they could approach in the city with their claims: NGOs, CBOs, and political parties, as well as public administrators and technocrats. As they told me of how they brought water into the settlement, it became clear how these institutions were drawn on in different ways to bring water home.

While this accomplishment was significant, it was neither complete nor irreversible, since water services for settlers in Mumbai are in a state of constant flux. Annual hydrological cycles, water main leakages, shifting demography, and unanticipated cluster developments constantly compel city engineers to tinker with the water system. Engineers are always rearranging the pipes, pressure, and water timings to cope with changing and growing demand.[7] With these rearrangements, residents in connected settlements like Sundarnagar frequently find that their connections—struggled for and negotiated years before—slowly go dry, and they are required to remake their water connections every few years. As they negotiate with engineers, councillors, and social workers to get water again, their negotiations reproduce the political and technical authority of the city's water experts and patrons. Thus, when water supply decreased in the Sundarnagar in 2008, settlers began to fight and complain about water just as they had fifteen years before. In practices that index belonging as well as the diverse fields of possibility enabled by water, they returned to the spring to collect washing water. Women came to the *Mahila Gath* meetings again to solve these problems, and Sunita-*tai* and Rajni-*tai* remade their social connections with the community worker, the NGO worker, and the city councillor to bring water into their settlements again.

Yet things were not as they were fifteen years ago. Because of their experiences accessing resources in the city, this time the task was a little easier. "We have learnt how to talk in the city," one of them told me. Compromised legal achievements also played a role. Having been in the city for more than fifteen years, their settlement was now also officially recognized by the city administration. Thus they were allowed the extension of state infrastructure. Because of these changes, in 2008 the *Mahila Gath* did not need to mobilize the large number of bodies to go to the city water office, nor did they encounter as much opposition, since they drew on old connections, friends, and councillors to ask for a new pipe. Now included within the rules and relations of the city, this time it was the councillor who came to the settlement with his water pipe.

ON VOICE AND REFLEXIVITY

In the introduction to this volume, De Schutter and Pistor identify a problem in law and politics around the governance of scarce and essential resources. Noting that resources like water and land are necessary to secure the very possibility of life for large numbers of people around the world, they identify structural limitations around not just private property rights to govern such resources but also centralized and communal regimes that often govern their distribution. Indeed, as they point out, with the diverse, unequal, heterogeneous interests that structure our world at a variety of scales, private, public, and communal regimes have all been exclusive and unsustainable in different ways.

As a dynamic system that is constantly in flux, the private and public regimes that govern water supply in Mumbai have diverse and differentiated effects on citizens who live in the city. As a situated accretion of public and private interests, Mumbai's water system also partially materializes the normative goals of reflexivity and voice in governance, but in rather unexpected ways. For example, in some respects the city's public water utility is rather inclusive. It distributes water to more than 15 million urban residents at greatly subsidized rates, even as it generates annual operating surpluses of $100 million a year. Part of the way it is able to do this is by compromising on de facto equity between citizens of the city. For instance, the city water department legally denies water to more than a million settlers who cannot show they inhabited their homes before 1995. The city also delivers less water per capita to settlers than to those living in the city's more affluent high-rises.

At the same time, it is because the system is "public" that it continues to be under the pressure of city councillors. As councillors pressure engineers to extend services to their constituents, often to service their own (private) interests, they have thus far resisted changing the water rules to make water supply accessible to all without their mediation. Instead, they ensure water remains accessible not only by making sure its prices are not increased (at least for settlers) but also by constantly helping settlers get access despite and beyond the practices and rules of city engineers. It is because the public system is liable to the pressure from councillors and a range of other urban experts that settlers have opposed projects that seek to make private companies responsible for water distribution in the city.

Nevertheless, like the water networks of many urban agglomerations, Mumbai's water system is not sustainable. This is not as much because of growing urban populations (which have stabilized, as per the last census), as it is because of the leakages that permeate Mumbai's pipe network (Anand 2015). Part of this leakage is in fact not wastage at all. Denied access to legal connections, many settlers make illegal connections. Yet the aging infrastructure also periodically ruptures, and engineers deal with tens of thousands of leakage reports every year. City engineers in Mumbai, like hydraulic engineers in other cities in the world, are constantly troubled by the materiality and epistemology of leakages; leakages that threaten the viability and sustainability of the city's water system. (see Anand 2015).

FULL HOUSE

As a hydraulic regime saturated with public, communal, and private interests, the water network in Mumbai is full of difficult relations between the politics of technologies and the technologies of politics (Anand 2011). Diverse authorities, materialities, and political claims govern its working in everyday life. As engineers design connections and manage its flows on a daily basis, they are constantly challenged in their ability to rule the system by the obduracy not only of politicians and the shouting public but also by the materiality of the city's water network. Settlers, meanwhile, work hard not just to get a reliable supply of water through the recognition of councillors and social workers, they also struggle to get counted as deserving biopolitical citizens on their own terms, without the help of patrons in the settlements. Finally, people living in agrarian homes beyond the city often find their lives made harder by the ever growing water demands of the city, the increased consumption patterns of urban residents, and the desires of city and federal officials to improve urban infrastructure by expanding and extending its reach.

In such a world of compromised relations, of diverging and differentiated interests, how is it possible to balance the competing governance values of voice and reflexivity in the city? The accreted histories, materials, and politics of Mumbai's infrastructure make it very difficult to change from above or to reform. While structural change is difficult to envision in Mumbai, I would like to explore here the emergent possibilities of reflexivity and voice by examining the relationships between visibility, authority, and the law as they work through Mumbai's water system and shape the everyday practices of hydraulic government in the city.

Inequality is reproduced not only by the rules and laws that govern the system but also because of the prejudiced everyday practices of its authorities. City water rules deny water to any settler who cannot prove he or she has lived at a given address since 1995. Engineers often know of water difficulties in settlements and sometimes leave them be. The reluctance of the city administration to extend water connections is not determined by cost considerations alone. Nor does it have to do with water scarcity. Instead, city administrators are anxious about extending water services to settlers, because they worry about the ways in which these services are often used by settlers to make a legal claim to the house and property these infrastructures serve. Denying settlers the right to apply for urban water is a means of rendering their claims to urban housing invisible.

Subsequently, made invisible and illegal by the city government, settlers practice forms of invisibility of their own—sometimes drawing water from illicit connections beyond the gaze and knowledge of state officials. It is not that the managers of the system are unaware of these invisibilities. Recall Patkar's quote at the start of the paper, when he expresses some knowledge about how settlers who are ineligible are "also getting water." Similarly, engineers are also aware of other invisibilities of the system, including those situated at the sources of Mumbai's water. As agrarian residents are denied water from rivers that are allocated by the state to the city, engineers work hard to ensure their political claims are rendered invisible in discourses about the city and its water scarcity. Such discourses of water scarcity and water emergency produce a series of rules, regimes, and laws that make it very difficult for marginal urban and rural residents to get water reliably. It is because the city has a water shortage, engineers suggest, that they need to control and regulate the exclusions of this urban public hydraulic system. Finally, also deliberately rendered invisible in such renderings of Mumbai's water problems are the physical leakages of water from mains *after* water is drawn to the city. These leakages in fact do produce scarcities of water in the city and sanction regimes of water rationing and exclusive policies and practices of distribution.

Therefore, at one level, reflexivity, here read as being necessary for achieving some degree of fairness, particularly for the politically weaker social groups, is partly achieved by making visible the discordant and often invisible relations that Mumbai's unequal system is built on and through which it is maintained. As settlers and agrarian residents demand their share of the city's water system, they call upon its regimes to recognize and respond to their needs through a variety of public and private strategies. For instance, agrarian residents who live near the city pipes' route do access water, even if they are not counted as urban citizens. City officials are rightly concerned that denying access would compromise the integrity of the water mains passing through these areas.[8]

A final note about authority: Water systems are peculiar in their porosity to diverse material and political claims. They are difficult to govern by a single authority. Whether diffuse and heterogeneous forms of authority are problematic is an ethnographic question worth exploring. As a hydraulic system that is composed of thousands of miles of pipe, as well as city councillors, social workers, hundreds of engineers, and thousands of municipal employees, the public water system in Mumbai provides many locations at which to make vital connections to the city's services. In fact, it is precisely because the system is so big, so "inefficient" (while still being very profitable), and so full of compromised and multiple authorities that settlers are able to connect to the city's water network. In this paper I urge an attention to the possibilities of improvisation, connection, and access that are enabled by the many authorities who govern the city's water.

This is not to say that everything is as it should be in Mumbai, nor is it to say that legal regimes do not matter in the city. Indeed, as I suggested earlier, laws, politics and regulations matter tremendously to Rajni-*tai* and other settlers in Mumbai. There is a lot that can be done with the legal/policy regimes that govern water in the city. For instance, the law that proscribes access for pre-1995 settlers—a law that is peculiar *only* to water services and *only* to Mumbai—is currently being challenged in the state's high court. Other water policies can also be made more inclusive and accommodating of the urban poor in a way that improves not only the equity but also productivity and sustainability of the system. For instance, the norms of supply could be adjusted to provide as much water to settlers as to those living in high rises. The city water department could also undertake the work of providing water lines to the homes of settlers, rather than requiring them to do it at their cost. This would not only have positive equity effects. The city would also receive user fees and the leakages that permeate service lines would be reduced.

Nevertheless, as I argue in this chapter, it is also critical to attend to the practices through which the system is governed. Here, I wish to suggest that the system has come to be *more* inclusive in Mumbai, in part because of the ways in which the authority of engineers and technocrats is being eroded in the city. As city councillors have become increasingly powerful in Mumbai, they also have become a critical pathway for settlers wishing to access urban services despite the laws and governance regimes of the city water department. Seen by engineers and other technocrats of urban government as intruders and obstructions to their work, councillors and their situated interests are not only vital to the workings of Mumbai's water system. They are also a critical (and imperfect) locus at which claims for inclusion and access are made by those who do not have substantive rights to the city.

In *Expectations of Modernity*, anthropologist James Ferguson details household livelihood strategies in rural Zambia in very difficult circumstances. In an account that would resonate in many parts of the world, Ferguson describes how households would send one of their children to work in the city, while others tried to make lives for themselves in their villages. In portraying the households stretched from the country to the city, Ferguson drew on the work of Stephen Jay Gould to characterize this as a "full house" of urban-rural strategies—a set of diverse attachments to the market, work, and the state that serve to reduce risk and make households viable amid uncertain futures of urbanization, the promise of mining, and the difficult conditions of agriculture.

Drawing from Ferguson's work, I see settlers in Mumbai also drawing on a "full house" of strategies to access water's uncertain flow in the city. To access the system, they make diverse kinds of claims—as clients, as citizens, as friends, as customers of roving plumbers, and as members of political society. Belonging to the city in these diverse ways provides different and multiple routes to access water and other aspects of urban life (work, education, health services). While settlers desire access to reliable water connections without these improvisational rituals, their practices recognize that laws, policies, bureaucrats, and regulators may not always work for them. In such a political environment, multiple water regimes constituted by diverse kinds of authority are more likely to yield to their claims. As settlers simultaneously deploy the diverse claims of civil and political society to gain access to water, it is precisely *because* the public water system is so full of joints, employees, pumps, and pressures that settlers can make vital connections to resources that are both scarce and essential.

NOTES

Sections of this paper were previously published by the author as N. Anand, "Pressure: The PoliTechnics of Water Supply," *Cultural Anthropology* 26, no. 4 (2011); and Anand, "Towards an Anthropology of Water in Mumbai," in *The Blackwell Companion to the Anthropology of India*, ed. I. Clarke-Deces (Malden, U.K.: Blackwell, 2011). The author would like to thank the publishers for permission to present revised sections of these selections in this essay.

1. Rs. 5 crore is roughly \$1 million at 2008 rates. These amounts therefore correspond roughly to \$296 million and \$160 million, respectively—a rather healthy revenue and profit for the water department.

2. Achieving declared status therefore involves networks of political patronage as much as it does the exercise of citizenship rights. Further, the "cutoff date" only reifies the divide within Mumbai's settler population between those who can claim state services and those who cannot (McFarlane 2008). In addition, only some informal communities can establish their legitimacy through declaration, so formal services and entitlements are unevenly distributed throughout Mumbai's settler population. Nevertheless, the benefits that accrue as a result of declaration-based policies are real; they mark, as noted earlier, a significant break with the past. Ultimately, declaration is consolidated by politicians with connections to the municipal administration, so securing the entitlements of declaration also depends in part on election cycles.

3. I have changed the names of persons and places I encountered during my fieldwork to protect the identities and confidentiality of my informants.

4. Settlers need to apply for a shared connection as a constituted committee with a given number of members.

5. Recent theorizations of the public in postcolonial cities have called for attention to be given to the different practices of its civil and political formations. In a clear and powerful generalization about the practices of politics, Partha Chatterjee identifies those seen by the state as rights-bearing citizens, as civil society—"elite groups sequestered from popular life within enclaves of civic freedoms and rational law" through the administration of the state bureaucratic apparatus (Chatterjee 2004, 3). He identifies variously marginalized populations as political society—groups that try to use their formal status as citizens and mass mobilizations to compel the state to recognize their citizenship by placing demands on the moral authority of leaders.

6. Councillors do not change the city's water rules to allow all settlers to access municipal water supplies. Instead, they intervene in particular cases of deserving settlers, to argue that they be granted access to the water system regardless of the rules.

7. In the words of one of the city's hydraulic engineers, "There is a water shortage and we have to balance the water. One day we give short supply here, the next day over there."

8. Water leakages, while also critical, have greater difficulties in getting noticed. With pipes frequently underground, leakages are easier to not know about or to ignore. As

reformers and agents of privatization demand an attention to leakages, they sometimes are able to pressure city engineers to do serious work to patch the system. If the leaks were all fixed, not only would less water need to be drawn from the farms and fields of Mumbai's neighbors, there would also be more water in the city pipes for urban residents.

REFERENCES

Anand, Nikhil. 2011. "Pressure: The PoliTechnics of Water Supply in Mumbai." *Cultural Anthropology* 26 (4): 542–564.

———. 2011b. "Towards an Anthropology of Water in Mumbai," in *The Blackwell Companion to the Anthropology of India*, ed. I. Clarke-Deces (Malden, U.K.: Blackwell, 2011: 426–442).

———. 2015. "Leaky States" Water Audits, Ignorance and the Politics of Infrastructure." *Public Culture* 27:2 305–330.

Anand, Nikhil, and Anne Rademacher. 2011. "Housing in the Urban Age: Inequality and Aspiration in Mumbai." *Antipode* 43 (5): 1748–1772.

Appadurai, Arjun. 2002. "Deep democracy: Urban Governmentality and the Horizon of Politics." *Public Culture* 14 (1): 21–47.

Bakker, Karen. 2007. "The 'Commons' Versus the 'Commodity': Alter-globalization, Anti-privatization and the Human Right to Water in the Global South." *Antipode* 39 (3): 430–455.

Chakrabarty, Dipesh. 2002. "Of Garbage, Modernity and the Citizen's Gaze." In *Habitations of Modernity: Essays in the Wake of Subaltern Studies*, ed. D. Chakrabarty, 65–79. Chicago: University of Chicago Press.

Chatterjee, Partha. 2004. *The Politics of the Governed: Reflections on Popular Politics in Most of the World.* New York: Columbia University Press.

Cheng, Deborah. 2014. "Contestations at the Last Mile: The Corporate-Community Delivery of Water in Manila." *Geoforum.*

Coelho, Karen. 2005. "Unstating 'The Public': An Ethnography of Reform in an Urban Water Utility in South India." In *The Aid Effect: Giving and Governing in International Development*, ed. D. Mosse. London: Pluto.

———. 2006. "Tapping In: Leaky Sovereignties and Engineered Dis(Order) in an Urban Water System." *Sarai Reader 6: Turbulence.* Delhi: Sarai.

Davis, Mike. 1998. *Ecology of Fear: Los Angeles and the Imagination of Disaster.* New York: Metropolitan.

Dossal, Mariam. 1991. *Imperial Designs and Indian Realities: the Planning of Bombay City, 1845–1875.* Bombay: Oxford University Press.

Ferguson, James. 1999. *Expectations of Modernity: Myths and Meanings of Urban Life on the Zambian Copperbelt.* Berkeley, Calif.: University of California Press.

Gandy, Matthew. 2004. "Rethinking Urban Metabolism: Water, Space and the Modern City." *City* 8 (3): 363–379.

———. 2008. "Landscapes of Disaster: Water, Modernity, and Urban Fragmentation in Mumbai." *Environment and Planning* A 40: 108–130.

Klein, Ira. 1986. "Urban Development and Death: Bombay City, 1870–1914." *Modern Asian Studies* 20 (4): 725–754.

McFarlane, Colin. 2008. "Governing the Contaminated City: Infrastructure and Sanitation in Post-colonial Bombay." *International Journal of Urban and Regional Research* 32 (2): 415–435.

Ranganathan, Malini. 2014. "Paying for Water, Claiming Citizenship: Political Agency and Water Reforms at the Urban Periphery." *International Journal of Urban and Regional Research* 38 (2): 590–608.

Von Schnitzler, Antina. 2008. "Citizenship Prepaid: Water, Calculability and Techno-Politics in South Africa." *Journal of Southern African Studies* 34 (4): 899–917.

Zerah, Marie-Helene. 2008. "Splintering Urbanism in Mumbai: Contrasting Trends in a Multilayered Society. *Geoforum* 39: 1922–1932.

PART III

Beyond Voice and Reflexivity

CHAPTER 6

Voice, Reflexivity, and Say

GOVERNING ACCESS TO AND CONTROL OF LAND IN CHINA

Eva Pils

SITUATING THE ARGUMENT

The essential resources argument is based on an intuitively appealing conception of human need. Defining essential resources as those "absolutely necessary for the survival of every human being, such as drinking water and basic food, or indispensable for minimum existence in a given society,"[1] De Schutter and Pistor formulate criteria ensuring access to essential goods for all. Such access can be achieved by "governance regimes that embrace as guiding principles voice, defined as the ability to collectively choose the rules by which one wishes to be governed; and reflexivity, which stands for the ability to recognize competing claims as legitimate and the willingness to accommodate them."

In many specific contexts the idea of need underlying the essential resources thesis also seems plausible, not least given the persistent suffering in the world caused by people lacking access to certain resources: "Nobody should be excluded from resources that serve to satisfy basic needs, and the exploitation of the resource today should not jeopardize the ability of the next generation to satisfy its own needs."[2]

The argument, too, that certain economic analyses of the problem at hand, such as the theory of the "tragedy of the commons,"[3] cannot successfully deal with the challenge of securing fair access to certain goods, is persuasive; and certainly, collective autonomy to make rules of governance and mutual understanding (i.e., voice and reflexivity) are generally desirable—even though my actual personal recognition of another's claim on assets in my possession could not be sensibly *required* to justify a taking of those assets from me, for example, through expropriation.

I focus here on whether the requirements of voice and reflexivity, and the underlying definition of essential goods, give appropriate and sufficiently clear guidance from the perspective of the social problem I have chosen to address. My discussion points to problems with treating land solely as a resource. From this particular perspective, a good conception of just access to land must take legitimate interests in protection from arbitrary interference with housing and property into account. If exclusion must not lead to grave injustice, the same is true of forcible redistribution, the goal (or at least the intended consequence) of expropriations and evictions. Current occupants of land and housing must not be treated like figures on a chessboard, easily moved around by other decision makers. The problem of governing access to and control over land and housing must be understood as also being one of distribution of resources but not only as such.

On this basis, it is useful to be critically aware of the implicit consequentialism of the essential resources thesis, as well as of its commitment to a definition of human need. First as to the consequentialist underpinnings of the essential resources thesis, it is a thesis reminiscent of the global theory of responsibility associated with philosophers such as Peter Singer, who advances the possibility of negative responsibility:[4] If there are sufficient resources to satisfy basic needs yet some people fail to get them, anyone who would have been able to prevent this result has responsibility for the suffering of those excluded.[5] There are well-known arguments generally critical of utilitarian and consequentialist theory.[6] The point here is merely to say that in devising rules and practices for governing resources, an exclusive focus on the distributive consequences of one or another regime may program us to overlook injustices in the process of redistribution.

An exclusive focus on distributive consequences can also reinforce a tendency to think of the good in question as a resource of value to impersonal users, abstracting from the good's multiple potential legitimate purposes and ways of being important. Since land, in particular, is significant in many different ways, some of which are related to its location and history while others are not, its relevance to survival may differ from user to user, relative to a given society,[7] further complicating its assessment as a resource. The Chinese example in particular cautions against treating land entirely as a resource whose value is to be determined with reference only to purposes or functions it could serve for anyone indiscriminately, obliterating the history (and location) that may have made it especially significant to particular individuals or communities.

A good regime of governance for land, which of course *can* be (also) a resource, should therefore not exclusively aim at achieving fairness of access to a subtractive resource, because this definition does not allow us to take all the iniquities of takings into appropriate consideration. If this argument is correct, the requirements of voice and reflexivity must be critically examined with regard to what they can do to address the problem of more complex rights violations. Although much narrower in scope, this examination draws on the wider criticisms of consequentialist and welfare-utilitarian theory and of economic efficiency–based assessments of development (Arnott and Salomon 2014).

A second, related concern is that making sense of the idea of (basic) needs, which essential resources are expected to satisfy, is difficult, because it is difficult to measure and compare needs. The above, two-pronged definition on the one hand suggests that essential resources are those necessary for survival—however, survival on the very lowest terms of mere subsistence, say, of having adequate food and drinking water, is in many places less of a problem than survival on slightly more generous terms.[8] The second prong of the above definition, on the other hand, implicitly defines need as relative to the conditions in a particular society. However, if human need is relative not merely to the condition of being human but relative to particular human societies, why not address the question of what is due to the members of a particular society by use of a more explicitly and manageably relative moral concept such as that of equality?[9] Such a broader moral concept might better serve the need to deal with understanding and addressing different kinds of injustice in property regimes, including that of arbitrary expropriation. It could serve as a reminder that no evaluative requirement can be understood in isolation from other values of political morality.

In sum, despite its intuitive appeal and importance in addressing a pressing global concern, the essential resources thesis may have undesirable implications that are not immediately evident as long as it is only examined in the context of certain, evidently shocking practices of exclusion. It must be asked whether the requirements of collective voice and reflexivity adequately capture what is required to protect people from injustices, or whether further or different requirements should be articulated. Saying as much is not to say that the principles of voice and reflexivity must be rejected; rather, it may be good to consider whether a nonconsequentialist account can give these principles a more persuasive foundation that also addresses their inherent limitations.

The discussion in the following examines general features of the Chinese land-tenure system and of Chinese eviction and expropriation practices, which, as I show, also center on welfare and utility considerations, with these concerns in mind. The argument here therefore in some ways reverses the perspective from which the essential resources thesis was formulated. It considers how this thesis, in some ways directed against exclusion, plays out when it is not the excluded but the would-be excluders who are in a socially, politically, and legally weak and persecuted position, on the assumption that a reasonable legal system must take both types of social group into consideration.

THE CURRENT REGIME GOVERNING ACCESS
TO AND CONTROL OVER LAND

It is necessary, to understand the background against which current discussions of the landgrab and eviction problem in China take place, to take a very brief look at basic features of the extant land-tenure system, the rules governing takings and evictions, and the way in which these rules have come into being. Prior to the reforms introduced by the Chinese Communist Party, the Chinese state recognized private landownership. The land reforms introduced by the party from the 1930s onward began with expropriations of rural landowners deemed to be better off and redistribution of land to poorer or politically privileged households. The forcible creation of very big rural collectives, however, culminated in the great famine of 1958–1959, which resulted from policies and measures described in recent research.[10] Scholars have argued that this famine, during which between 20 and 40 million excess deaths are supposed to have occurred, was man-made: that it was the consequence of centralized control over land use combined with disastrous agricultural policies and repressive withholding of agricultural output (especially grain) destined for urban consumption or export.

In urban areas, by contrast, the institution of private landownership was not abolished, despite strident political rhetoric against it, the introduction of compulsory government lease schemes and individual expropriations, control of all economic activity under the planned economy, and the breakdown of the legal system in the last decade under Mao (Pils 2014).

The post-Mao Constitution of 1982, last revised in 2004, said in its Preamble that China would "remain in the primary stage of socialism for a long time to come."[11] This was a signal meant to justify the introduction of reforms, in particular the recognition of private property rights and a private market of sorts in land. However, it did not mean privatization of landownership. On the contrary, the state wrote not only a principle of "socialist public ownership" of all land into the reform-era Constitution of 1982, but also specified that rural and suburban land was to be collectively owned, whereas urban land was to be state owned. The 1982 Constitution's stipulation that all urban land was owned by the state effectively expropriated those who had privately owned urban land until then (Hua Xinmin 2011; Zhou Qiren 2012).

On the basis of these changes, new rules in the 1980s (especially the 1988 constitutional amendment and Land Administration Law) created rights of use or "usufruct" rights (*yongyi wuquan* 用益物权) in land. Such rights allowed farming families to produce for private profit. Maintaining collective landownership, it yet freed farming households from many restraints of the planned-economy era (even though prices and production continued to be regulated for some time), and it allocated a "residential plot" land-use right to each family belonging to a rural collective. As a consequence of these reforms, rural incomes rose rapidly, especially in the early 1980s and until the (early) 1990s. While reallocation of use rights in collectively owned plots was initially possible, reforms since the 1980s have created more stable rural land-use rights, making the system less flexible but also more predictable and reliable. In the neoliberal analysis of research institutions such as Landesa and that of the World Bank, this amounts to creating stronger individual rights and encouraging farmers to have the confidence to invest in their land (Landesa n.d.). Of course *yongyi wuquan* were limited to the right to use and draw gains from the land, but this hardly mattered in the just-mentioned economic analysis. And such a definition could not limit how people defined their actual relationship with the land; even less how actual takings affected them.

In urban areas, a new right of land use for construction purposes was created; and the state, represented by urban governments, was therefore able to grant or allot such urban land-use rights to individuals for the purpose of urban (residential or industrial) property development. The urban right of use has become the basic building block of China's real estate market (Randolph 2007). To make land available for urban construction purposes, the state created mechanisms for expropriating (*zhengshou*) collectively owned (rural or suburban) land and turning it into state-owned land. Urban land can be "reclaimed" or "resumed" (*shouhui*) as it is deemed to be already in state ownership, and buildings on it can be expropriated for the same purpose.

A property developer normally turns to the state for the legal acquisition of new rights of use for construction. The state remains owner of urban construction land, but urban rights of use can be privately held and freely circulated on the urban real estate market, and buildings on the land can be privately owned.[12] Laws and regulations from the 1980s onward, including the 2007 Property Rights Law and the 2011 State Council Regulation on Expropriation of Buildings on State-Owned Land, introduced procedures that the state must follow to expropriate rural and suburban landowning collectives or private homeowners in urban areas.

This system has resulted in ample opportunities for coercive redistribution of land for purposes such as urban construction (urbanization) and infrastructure projects such as dams etc. Urbanization, which has already caused one of the biggest migrations in human history, is set to continue (with some 250 million more Chinese citizens expected to have moved from rural to urban areas by 2025) and is considered the cause of much social unrest,[13] the scale of which is significant (Johnson 2013a, 2013b). The mechanisms of expropriation and forced transfers of rural land-use rights are also used for the purpose of creating large agribusinesses. As a further result, the state has become a chief recipient of revenue generated through fees for land-use rights in the context of "property development" while dispossessing and dislocating many citizens.

The rules on expropriation and demolitions read superficially similar to those of liberal legal systems centered in private property rights: Expropriation and urban demolition decisions are subject to strict requirements of "public interest" and compensation,[14] in some cases including resettlement.[15] But these rules function differently, if at all, in a system that does not allow private land transfers, as the Chinese system does in many settings, so expropriation and demolition are the only ways of changing land use. The legal rules are further weakened by systemic incentives for corruption amongst a predatory complex of land and real estate administrations working in collusion with the private real estate industry (Zhu Jiangnan 2012), and it has given rise to extensive circumvention of the rules, especially to the creation of what is widely referred to as "minor property rights" or *xiaochanquan*. These are informal "rights" in land that are not (generally) recognized by the state but that are traded on a gray-zone (and hence also corrupt) urban real estate market (Pils 2009).

The discussion in the following sections considers the further implications of this property regime for the essential-resources thesis. In the
first two sections, I discuss the causal relationship between the existing regime and poverty and the causal relationship between the existing
regime and waste (or "sustainability" of land use) to assess the system's
ability to deal with access to and control over land as a problem of
resource distribution. These sections primarily discuss the type of welfare
considerations addressed by the essential resources thesis. They point
to numerous problems with the land-tenure system's role in reducing
poverty and ensuring sustainability of land use but also attribute these
problems to wider governance issues in China. The section following
these turns to what I term "eviction injustices"—the iniquities of rules
and practices in eviction contexts.

GROWTH AND POVERTY CONCERNS

Great progress in the effort to overcome poverty, especially in the
early 1980s, was widely attributed to the rural land reforms of that era.
Nevertheless, after this initial success, income gaps between rural and
urban areas began to widen, and basic subsistence remains a challenge for
the many Chinese citizens who are deemed to live in "poverty" in accordance with domestic and international standards (S.C. 2011).[16] According
to China's government records, 99 million people still lived beneath the
poverty line as of March 2013 (Liu Chang and He Dan 2013). A significant proportion of the poor are rural residents or migrants with a rural
residence status. Poverty has many different causes, but in different ways,
it can be causally connected to the system for land rights. The discussion
here merely points to some obviously relevant, possible causal connections, without attempting to be complete. It suggests that the existing
property system has produced desirable (e.g., overall economic growth)
and undesirable consequences (e.g., relative impoverishment of rural residents—that economic growth, enabled in part by the land-tenure system,
has come at a cost to some.

First, there is the issue of the rural-urban divide, described earlier
as an aspect of different regimes for urban and rural land. Due to the
household-registration system, membership in rural collectives is in effect
compulsory for many; and due to the interrelated rules of the property
regime system, rural residents can find themselves "tied" to the land and
the conditions of poverty in their location. As members of landowning

collectives they are deemed to get not only food but also social security from legal entitlement to land use. If migrant workers become jobless or ill, for example, they are not entitled to social welfare in the cities to which they have migrated. Rather, the state's expectation is that they will return to their home villages and a safe workplace as farmers, because they have retained membership in the rural collectives from which they originated. In their places of household registration, they are also entitled to social services, but the level of welfare is generally far below that of urban areas.

While collective landownership may afford a safety net, this net can also become a trap. It can tie rural residents legally to land that is unproductive. As long as they are so tied, they are limited to the economic options their place of household registration offers. There are many places in China where, due to a variety of factors— environmental degradation; pollution of land, air, and water; and infrastructure—it is extremely difficult to continue growing food and drawing water from the land. In the south of the province of Ningxia, for example, agriculture is plainly almost impossible due to desertification, and malnutrition clearly leads to stunted growth in children and adults.[17] In precisely those places, on the other hand, there is little other work to be found. As a result, those who can leave to try to find work in the cities (leading to the phenomenon of "hollow villages," *kongxincun*), but as rural migrants they are severely discriminated against and face a lack of welfare provisions in urban locations. For these "rural residents" the property regime and household-registration system is a source of economic hardship. It works as a safety net only if one accepts the prior determination that rural residents are not entitled to the same welfare as urban residents.

The problem described here is closely related to a fiction that underlies the land system designed by the party-state: the fiction, namely, that collectives whose size, property (resources), and membership are determined by party-state rules provide adequate resources for the collectives' members. The party-state also postulates that there is a certain "red line" demarcating a minimum amount of arable land that China as a nation must have, without having offered an adequate explanation as to why the red line is set where it is or, indeed, why China might not resort to alternative ways of procuring food.[18] As the demand for food rises and consumption patterns change, China is increasingly using resources such as land in other countries, yet this has not led to any changes in the basic property system locking an unknown number of rural families into relative poverty.

Second, similar problems affect those parts of the rural population who are locked into collective landownership in areas where natural resources are so polluted that they represent health hazards. The legal reasons for why rural residents find themselves tied to such land are the same as discussed earlier. In these cases the issue is not so much access to any land or water as it is access to *safe* food and water satisfying minimum standards, but in terms of their effect the problems are similar to those previously discussed.

According to a study published in May 2013, of the 1.86 trillion *mu* (Chinese acres) of farming land in China, 1.3 trillion are deemed to have "medium" or "low" productivity; and "70% of farmland is polluted due to overuse of fertilizer and pesticides or industrial effluent pollution and similar reasons, affecting the nation's food safety" (Bai et al. 2013). The issue of environmental pollution even more starkly illustrates that future-generation members of rural collectives depend for their subsistence and well-being on decisions made by the present-day generation and that the actual members of rural collectives lack the (political) power to protect land against degradation. Pollution affects communities whose members are tied to polluted land and water resources via the collective ownership system in especially harsh ways, as the existence of "cancer villages"[19] and the prevalence of lead poisoning in certain areas (Human Rights Watch 2011) well illustrates, and it reaches far into rural areas where there is little industry but a lot of pollution.[20]

While being tied to collectives whose land is inadequate or polluted can be described as a consequence of a dual-track land-tenure system that features compulsory rural collectives, it would hardly be fair to attribute all of these problems to the land-tenure system; in fact, they are related to a number of wider flaws in the legal-political system, including the lack of judicial oversight of administrative decisions and the repression of calls for transparency and fairness as "factors of social instability."

A third aspect of the land-tenure system that affects the material welfare of the poor and can lead to impoverishment are land and building expropriations for other purposes, including that of gaining available land for new urban construction. This problem is directly related to the "eviction injustices" discussed later in this chapter. Between 1991 and 2005, some three million rural residents a year were thought to have been affected by land takings and demolitions, an estimated total of 50–60 million as of 2007 (Yu Jianrong 2009).[21] After 2007 no numbers on rural takings became publicly available, and no information, not even an estimate, has become available on the number of urban residents affected by evictions and building demolition;[22] although in 2010 the official media quoted a government official as saying that "more than half of China's existing residential structures . . . will be demolished and rebuilt in the coming 20 years."[23]

The prevalence of such evictions is causally connected to the existing property regime, which gives extensive control to the state both as current owner of urban and potential expropriator of rural and suburban land. Expropriation and eviction do lead to destitution in some cases: for example, when no compensation is paid; or when protesting citizens are driven to seek justice in urban centers, where they tend to become socially and economically impoverished, in addition to being persecuted by the government. However, not all citizens affected by expropriations or evictions are clearly left worse off economically, let alone destitute. Important though the problem of becoming impoverished through expropriation is, the problem with expropriation and demolition appears to lie more centrally in what are later discussed as wider eviction injustices.

PRODUCTIVITY AND SUSTAINABILITY CONCERNS

Even though it may be argued that the party-state's extensive control of land use has enabled China's real estate boom and thus helped its economic growth, it is also apparent that the rigidity of rural land tenure and the wide powers given to the party-state can affect productivity and sustainability adversely and are likely to produce some undesirable consequences, at least in the longer term.

First, the productivity ("economic gains that enhance welfare") of agriculture on the current, household-oriented model is a matter of concern. Issues arise in the context of land lying untilled by absentee "farmers" (*nongmin*) who have gone to the cities to work. Bai and colleagues estimate that

> between 230 and 260 million rural residents [i.e., people with rural household registration] are currently working in the cities and that the village population is shrinking even as the amount of rural construction land is rising; this leads to a large amount of rural land lying waste. We estimate the proportion of rural wasteland currently reaches 1.85–2.85 million hectares, equaling one-fourth to one-third of the total of land currently available for urban use. (Bai et al. 2013)

In addition, a rather large area of good-quality farmland has been expropriated and built on. The just-cited report puts the amount of such land at 2.42 million hectares over the past ten years (Bai et al. 2013; Ruan 2013).

According to some researchers and institutions, productivity is also affected by the weakness of rights of use currently held by farmers (Landesa Rural Development Institute n.d.).

An added productivity concern, albeit one only indirectly affecting the availability of farmland, is that of construction meeting investors' but not potential users' demands and therefore enhancing welfare only marginally.[24] Possibly the systems for expropriation and eviction themselves also lead to low productivity so far as the use of land for construction purposes is concerned, for example, when land is taken and developers sit on it to wait until prices go up (the state tries to control such conduct).

While some believe that strengthening individual household–based rural land-use rights helps to boost productivity, others argue that larger-scale agriculture would serve this goal better. In recent years, the party-state has apparently expressed preference for this approach as part of a wider campaign to modernize the Chinese countryside. The "New Countryside" as it is envisioned and propagated by the authorities will have tall residential buildings with modern appliances, and it will be economically efficient through the establishment of large agribusinesses, thus concentrating the use of land both for agriculture and housing (Liu 2013); it appeals to those primarily seeking economic efficiency, such as Premier Li Keqiang (Li Xueren 2013).

Scholars have argued, critically, that the concentration of farmland in the hands of large agribusinesses undermines the original purpose of the current system for rural land (ensuring each household's basic welfare) and leads to eviction injustices similar to those discussed later (Liu 2013) and that abuses of the New Countryside policy in the form of building luxury homes occur.[25] To the extent that these criticisms are borne out by facts on the ground, they illustrate competition between different goals and suggest that productivity increase at the cost of individual rural households is not necessarily desirable.[26]

Third, sustainability (environmental and resource preservation) concerns arise from environmental pollution issues, as already mentioned. Closely related additional concerns arise from overuse of land for particular purposes, for instance, for urban construction purposes in areas whose natural environment does not support an urban population density—Beijing, for example, is too arid to support its current population, which leads to the redirecting of water from the surrounding Hebei Province (Chen Tian 2013).

In addition, large infrastructure projects such as giant dams have raised a plethora of concerns not only with the difficulties they have caused to evictees (discussed later) but also regarding the environmental consequences of such projects. These problems have been discussed at length with regard to the Three Gorges Dam, for example, and reports suggest that not only long-term critics but also officials and authorities responsible for the project are now willing to concede that it has resulted in problems with sediments, greater risks of flooding, and a reduction of biodiversity (Watts 2011).

It is difficult to assess the seriousness of these issues in a quantitative way, not only due to lack of expertise, but also because it is difficult to access information regarding environmental pollution in China. Environmental issues involve questions of accountability as well as—from a Chinese government perspective—social stability,. Publicly available reports on environmental issues are often vague and reticent, reflecting a system with an extensive, labyrinthine, and widely criticized State Secrets Law, which until recently treated even meteorological survey data as state secrets (Ren Zihui 2007; Human Rights Watch 2011), and according to which reports on soil pollution remain so classified (Jing 2013). In the context of intense suppression of environmental and land rights activism, even the dissemination of legal regulations to rural pollution victims can trigger retaliation from officials, as Chinese researchers report.[27] What can be said with confidence is that the pollution and contamination of land and water is a problem widely understood to diminish sustainability and productivity, in particular of farmland.

The severe pollution issues China is experiencing at present are likely aggravated by the presence of a powerful authoritarian state that not only wields control over land but is also characterized by political power concentration at all local and central levels of the state administration, rendering efficient environmental impact assessment and similar mechanisms introduced to prevent further pollution difficult, and generally hampering efforts to hold polluters accountable. Lee Liu moreover argues that the rural-urban divide privileges urban areas over rural ones and leads to a diversion, as it were, of urban pollution into the countryside (e.g., cancer villages; Liu 2010). In addition, the ease with which the government can take land contributes to the phenomenon of mammoth infrastructure projects with adverse environmental impact.

In sum, the rigidity of the rural-urban divide enforced through the land-tenure and household-registration systems is widely held responsible for the fact that so much farmland remains uncultivated, resulting in low productivity, and there is a debate about whether enhancing power concentration through the creation of agribusinesses or enhancing individual household–based land rights would spur productivity. At the same time, wide powers wielded by the party-state with regard to land have enabled or at least failed to prevent unsustainable (e.g., polluting) kinds of land use. It could be argued that the comprehensive power of the party-state over land and, more widely, its authoritarian exercise of political power should also be factors allowing the authorities to address unproductive or unsustainable land use, for instance by changing the performance criteria whereby officials are assessed, and lack of productivity, for instance by reallocating land rights to large agribusinesses. However, the success of such policy changes would depend at least in part on the degree to which officials' incentives do, in fact, consist in official performance criteria, as opposed to rent seeking and various other forms of corruption (Zhu 2012). More generally, a public discussion of the goals of productivity and sustainability can hardly get off the ground when information is withheld and popular criticism is suppressed.

LANDGRAB AND EVICTION INJUSTICES

To assess the questions mentioned at the outset, namely whether the essential resources thesis and the requirements of voice and reflexivity work well in the context of evictions and landgrabs in China, it is necessary first to take stock of these injustices. The grievances produced by this system are vast and serve to throw a light on the many different ways in which, depending on social and political circumstances, control over land is important. It was observed earlier that material dispossession can lead to impoverishment and material disadvantage that can be considerable, and that is certainly among the grievances evictions and expropriations produce. But land takings and housing demolitions do not invariably deprive people of essential goods needed for survival, even though both access to land as a food resource and access to housing are often not secured. The problems evictees face are not limited to access to goods, even if these were defined generously along International Labor Organization terms as including, for example, *security* of shelter and/or land tenure. A brief survey of the grievances typical in these contexts shows that not all of them can be captured in economic terms.

The problems discussed in the following sections are: first, evictions not in the public interest; second, compensation, when denied or inadequate; third, the problems of coerciveness; and fourth, violence. Economic analysis can help us, up to a point, to understand the first two problems. I argue here that the more broadly conceived injustice of a denial of say is related to the tendency to *reduce* analysis to the first two mentioned issues, ignoring or dismissing the third and fourth ones as merely incidental complications occurring in some cases.

On the first point, to understand when an eviction or expropriation is "for a public interest purpose," it is important to remember that Chinese law uses similar words as those articulated originally in liberal property regime contexts but largely prohibits private transactions that make state expropriation an exception in those regimes (due to socialist public ownership and its attendant limitations on transferability). At the same time, the state actively encourages development, and therefore generally takes the view that "public" interest must be understood so broadly as to become virtually meaningless. A major property developer once commented that "[there is] no such thing as demolition and relocation that is not in the public interest. As long as it is [for the purpose of] urban construction, it is in the public interest."[28]

And, as pointed out earlier, attempts to restrict expropriations by explicitly excluding certain scenarios from public interest have been largely unsuccessful in practice.

While according to this mainstream interpretation the public interest restriction has no restrictive effects and therefore appears next to meaningless, it is important to see that the argument advanced here is not unreasonable and may be correct from the perspective of economic aggregate-welfare analysis. At least, we can observe that property development has generally contributed to gross domestic product (GDP) growth. How could this not be in the public interest, understood on purely economic terms?

This general welfare perspective also explains the official approach to the second question, namely that of how to compensate those affected by evictions and/or expropriations. Compensation is generally viewed as a matter of weighing individual, private interest (of evictees) against the supposed public interest (in eviction and expropriation). There is, consequently, some debate about appropriate standards for compensation. According to current legal rules, rural residents are compensated not for the market value land will have once it becomes part of urban real estate but instead for lost putative agricultural output (even in cases where land is no longer used as farmland);[29] while in urban areas, compensation is for the market value of the buildings but not the land taken from urban residents. In both cases it falls (often) far short of future market value of the land; the Landesa Institute has concluded in a long-term study that, on average, market value was forty times the amount of compensation actually paid. This computation did not take into account the 40 percent of cases in which no compensation at all was paid (Landesa Rural Development Institute n.d.). More in-depth individual cases studies confirm this impression in anecdotal ways;[30] they also suggest that the denial of compensation and uses of violence are reactions to citizens' attempt to protect their rights in these cases.

What is remarkable about the officially accepted, mainstream way of discussing the compensation issue is that by focusing on a balancing exercise between private and public "interest" (*liyi*), it can submerge and suppress other grievances. Thus, having rendered "public interest" restrictions ineffective, official discourse generally directs attention away from the fact that in addition to posing problems of assessing any conflicting material interests on sides (evictors and evictees), evictions and expropriations are coercive and may involve violence. The eviction or expropriation is treated as though it were a transaction between consenting individuals, where only the "price" at which land is acquired is at issue, and as though a compulsory acquisition of land is justified as long as that price is right. Mainstream discourse can then easily criticize those who resist and ask for more (compensation) for their greed and selfishness, since their demands can be juxtaposed with an abstract public interest in evicting and/or expropriating them and contrasted with the silent majority of evictees' compliance. By suppressing awareness of the coercive nature of evictions and expropriations, mainstream discourse maintains a focus on problems that can be understood in accordance with cost-benefit analysis.

The coerciveness that distinguishes expropriations from private transactions is in many concrete cases rendered a more serious issue by violence fostered by the party-state. In many cases, for example, "consent" declarations by evictees are obtained under duress, through violence or threats of violence, which can occur from the point when the government reaches out to rural or urban households to "negotiate" compensation and resettlement with them. Because the government is required to secure "agreements" before the process of clearing the land in question to prepare it for construction, there is a positive incentive to put evictees under pressure to sign.[31] In cases of refusal to sign, orders to evict and demolish forcefully can be made—evictees do not really have a meaningful option to refuse—and the process of implementing such orders can involve further violence (Amnesty International 2012).

Compounding these problems, access to justice is frequently denied. In a climate of intimidation, only the very determined will try to seek the protection of the law against an eviction decision, either via the court litigation system or the system for petitioning the party-state, known as "letters and visits." But both the courts and the "letters and visits" system often fail people when they complain about the illegalities of landgrabs or demolition orders. The courts use a number of techniques, sometimes in combination, to refuse to admit complaints (*bu yu shouli*) in administrative or civil litigation.[32] Even when they take a case, they normally narrow down the scope of their review and address only the issue of compensation but not that of the legality of an expropriation or demolition, and litigation may only in exceptional cases stay execution orders for demolition, so that "your house may be gone by the time you've won your case," as one lawyer put it (Pils 2014).[33] Once a decision awarding more compensation has been won, it may still be difficult to enforce.

Partly because access to justice through the courts is so difficult, citizens often use the court and petitioning systems concurrently. Petitioning, however, puts them at further risk of retaliation, which can again include state-centered violence as well as forceful "deportation" back to one's hometown and extralegal detention in special facilities for petitioners. In the course of petitioning, individual human lives can become entirely unhinged.

The experience of people facing landgrabs and forced evictions (again, not all those affected would describe themselves as victims) suggests that the value of having access to goods essential to survival cannot easily be separated from numerous other goods. Rather, a just property rights system must give consideration to the process of taking property away from a particular individual or group. These processes can be harmful to property rights or security of tenure as an aspect of the human right to housing, for example, but they can also be harmful to a plethora of other rights and legitimate interests, including life and liberty. A property system like the Chinese one, which is set up to rely on large-scale expropriations for goals as varied as urban construction, dam projects, reforestation, and large-scale farming, must be understood as one crucial cause of these further eviction injustices. Experiences of such injustices lead to reactions that would make no sense if their victims were focused exclusively on their property holdings or vested interest in housing. Nothing illustrates this more forcefully than the suffering of evictee protestors, especially those such as suicide protesters, who risk liberty and life to resist. In their cases, the problems of landgrabs and evictions can become so serious that they lead to the destruction of human lives.

In conversation, a liberal scholar once vehemently rejected my suggestion that people who resorted to extreme forms of protest were defending their "dignity" (*renge zunyan*), because in his view, ordinary people in China did not "yet" have such a concept. "What they will think is just: 'I have no way of going on living [*wo wufa huoxiaqu*].'"[34]

This mental state may be responsible for the suicides that have occurred in eviction contexts.[35] They challenge (albeit indirectly) the interest-oriented view preferred by the authorities, as discussed in the next section, and in doing so they illustrate that not only scarce material goods but also imponderable goods and considerations are material to survival.

In sum, in the state-driven discourse about eviction, welfare interests, or *liyi*, play a prominent role. According to official views, all eviction conflicts are defined as being about welfare interests, and it follows, from a state perspective, that all such conflicts can in principle be solved with money or material compensation of the evicted. But in fact, cost-benefit analyses of the consequences of evictions fail to encompass the rights violations occurring in the context of demolition, forced eviction, and expropriation. There is no moral neutrality in the process and purposes of an expropriation, and hence one cannot determine whether it was unjust merely by, for example, comparing property holdings before and after the expropriation. Any welfare argument is at base a consequentialist argument, and its limitations lie in the fact that concern for what produces more welfare, however measured, is not necessarily conducive to treating a person with respect—it is not always the same as concern for persons; and as Rawls argued in his criticism of utilitarianism, it may fail to take into account the difference among persons (Rawls 1970). The state-led discourse about evictions not only fails to capture some eviction injustices through its inability to comprehend them as anything other than economic losses; it would also implausibly suggest that any protest against evictions and landgrabs was in essence a fight for better compensation, with disregard for any other concerns and demands expressed by protestors.

Therefore, more comprehensive (and abstract) concepts accommodating different kinds of potential rights violations must be involved in assessing property regimes. It is important to recognize the dependency of the good that lies in land on other goods, which include the protection of basic rights and of access to justice.

RECONSIDERING THE REQUIREMENTS OF JUSTICE IN PROPERTY REGIMES: "SAY" AND RIGHTS

After Tang Fuzhen, standing on the roof of her house and facing what she regarded as the unlawful, unjustified, and violent demolition of her home by a demolition team physically attacking members of her family, committed suicide by self-immolation in 2009 (Cohen 2010), officials concerned in her case complained that she had failed to take a correct moral stance. Reportedly, one said that she had "put personal interests above the public interest" (Yu Jianrong 2014; Pils and Svensson 2014).[36]

The officially propagated view reflected in such comments is not only broadly welfare-utilitarian (grounded in the argument that expropriations and demolitions are necessary to support construction that in turn supports GDP growth) but also authoritarian (grounded in the view that the state, or the party and state, have the authority to make rules as they see fit). Such attitudes find expression not only in criticisms of recalcitrant individuals like Tang Fuzhen, but also in legislation and other rules, "normative documents" and "red-letterhead documents," and collective exhortations of the public. Official billboards at eviction sites, for example, will typically read, "Support the National Construction Project," "Thoroughly Implement the Scientific Development Perspective, Build a World City with Chinese Characteristics!," "Advance in Solidarity, Revive China, Love the Motherland, Build the Motherland!," and so on.

The case of Tang Fuzhen captured the public imagination, not least because it exposed what was inappropriate about the state-led discourse. Tang Fuzhen was by no means the first or last such suicide protester against evictions; there have been dozens of reported cases (Amnesty International 2012), and there may have been more cases that went unreported.[37] It was her case, however, that triggered a national debate. It illustrated that, when evictees protest, they do not in fact merely seek better compensation for their land or homes. Not all of their complaints, nor indeed all of their adverse experiences, can be captured by an assessment of their economic losses. Rather, much of what they protest against is the lack of individual and substantive "say" in the decisions the state makes over their land, homes, and lives.

While it is of course not possible to assess the distribution of views about evictions and expropriations across the Chinese nation,[38] anecdotal evidence suggests that criticism of eviction injustices has in recent years implicitly or explicitly emphasized the interconnectedness between rights immediately protecting welfare interests in eviction contexts and broader constitutional and human rights. Popular views of eviction conflicts are reflected in the banners, graffiti, and other protest slogans of evictees: "Defend Our Homes! Return Our Land! No Violence! Down with Corruption!,"[39] "Uphold and Protect the Constitution, Defend Human Rights," "Give Me My Land Back, Protect My Home," "Severely Punish Violent Thugs; Safeguard Citizens' Lives and Property," "The Wind and Rain May Enter but the Emperor May Not" (Pils 2010). Graffiti in demolition zones have compared evictees' experiences to "foreign invasion" and compared the perpetrators of eviction injustices to fascist regimes.[40] A "Citizen Broadcast" similarly featured a group of citizens holding up two banners and chanting the slogans "Lawful Private Property Is Sacrosanct and Must Not Be Violated! Return My Home! Rebuild My Home!" (He Yang 2010).[41]

From the perspective of some of these popular views, the government's decisions and its claim to control over land and buildings underpinning such decisions violate their rights of ownership, understood in a broad and nonpositivistic way, as well as other individual rights. Since the idea of private property rights captures with great simplicity the classical liberal demand that the state must respect the rights and interests of individual citizens and the idea of protection of economically and socially weak against arbitrary power exercise, private property is an especially popular concept used in protest action.

In the cities, some argue that the 1982 Constitution unfairly took away landownership that had been left untouched throughout China's socialist era, and transferred it to the state (Hua Xinmin 2011; Zhou Qiren 2012; Pils 2014). References to "thuggery" and "robbery" and "foreign invasion" not only criticize the violence that often accompanies expropriation and eviction processes but also make an underlying claim about the rightful allocation of homes destroyed or land taken.

In the countryside, from the perspective of rural evictee activists, the state has expropriated many collectives without regard to its own rules, which are supposed to protect against land takings. Some also perceive the state as having violated a social pact that gave rural residents security of their land holdings under socialism or as having destroyed traditional land rights with which it had no right to interfere. Periodically, such views find expression. For example, in a number of peasant landownership declarations that emerged toward the end of 2007, villagers asserted comprehensive rights of ownership in excess of the letter of current Chinese law.[42] In Wukan Village in Guangdong Province, where protests erupted in late 2011 and early 2012, villagers vocally demanded "their" land back, although this resulted neither in a return of "their" land nor in a genuine amelioration of village self-rule (democracy) under the village autonomy system (Pomfret 2013). Apart from such explicit declarations and demands, there are also entrenched practices that implicitly reject the hold the party-state claims to have on "their" land, such as the gray-zone "minor property rights" transactions mentioned earlier.

Evictees also protest dispossession and violations of housing rights by use of the ubiquitous phrase "No Home To Return To."[43] As they become more aware of international housing rights standards, they add these standards and the vocabulary associated with them to their repertoire, for instance in actions taken on World Habitat Day.[44] Going beyond individual cases and experiences, they address the more complex flaws of the system and organize collective protests, such as "surround-and-observe" actions (given this description since unlicensed "demonstrations" are illegal, and licenses for protests such as these unheard of), which often take place near government or court buildings, and sometimes organize in-courtroom actions, such as the shouting of slogans.[45]

Claims that the state must recognize a more comprehensive right of private landownership than currently articulated under Chinese law, implicit arrogations of such a right by informal (illegal) private land transfers (in the transfer of "minor property rights"), and wider activism making explicit the connection between private rights of access to and control over material resources and other rights, including civil and political rights. These claims show why it is important to recognize that individuals must have a degree of "say" in the affairs that closely affect them, and that they must have some minimum control over their lives. As an eviction rights lawyer commented, "These issues do not merely concern *liyi*, they do not merely have to do with money. They directly concern the right to speak [*huayuquan*]."[46]

The anecdotal evidence on the ground, only briefly surveyed here, suggests, moreover, that merely the ability to influence collective decisions over land would not be adequate to protect such control, to give individuals a sufficient amount of "say" in their lives. While there is no intention here of disputing that collective interest may justify (land) takings and evictions, any such justification is premised on the principle that, absent such overriding and (according to a principle of voice) collectively articulated concerns, individuals are rightfully in control of their property and entitled to be protected from arbitrary acts by the state affecting their right to housing (which includes security of tenure). And the mere fact that a particular legal regime purports to recognize private property and housing rights does not ensure protection as long as other vital rights are unprotected, including, of course, the right of the individual to speak up against decisions made in the name of a collective entity. While this may seem so uncontroversial as not to be worth mentioning in many systems, it is important to emphasize such a principle of "say" in the Chinese legal system, and this particular system may serve as an example of what can happen when the state systematically denies certain (large) segments of the population the protection of their individual private property rights, arguing that asserting private rights would in these contexts be selfish.

It is therefore necessary to complement the requirements of voice and reflexivity in the sense that, while these principles hold, individual rights must in principle also be respected. Any required limitations of the right of (private) property owners to exclude, for example, must be understood in this light. They must recognize that, in principle, those affected by redistribution of their homes or land to others must have a say in this process and that public interest restrictions on expropriation can only make sense in the context of a property system committed to a principle of protecting private property rights. Conversely, the adequacy of a regime (or set of legal rules and institutions) governing expropriations and evictions is not ensured simply by ensuring adequate compensation for takings. Their many vilifications and glorifications notwithstanding, private property rights, like housing rights, capture important aspects of individual freedom and dignity for those who have built lives relying on the security they afford, even though there is nothing in the present discussion suggesting that such rights are absolute. On the contrary, their boundaries can only be sensibly determined by taking other principles and legitimate goals into appropriate account.

CONCLUSION

This discussion urges three principal conclusions. First, political contention about land use, including in particular the problem of evictions, suggests that in many contexts land should not be thought of in a tabula rasa sort of way, as a resource to be distributed in accordance with measurable goals, no matter what would be required to redistribute access to and control over it. This conclusion requires us to respect individual rights and dignity as an integral aspect of legitimate property regimes. In reminding us that private rights can serve the important goals of empowering potential victims of power abuse, it amounts to an argument *for* exclusion, but not on neoliberal terms; rather, it would empower people facing evictions to resist these measures even if their eviction would apparently serve economic growth. It would acknowledge some functional similarity between the right to exclude of property owners and individual housing rights ("security of tenure"), and it would not serve as a general argument against forced redistribution of resources or taxation.

Second, in making rules to govern access to and control over resources, we are required to pay attention to nonmaterial goals such as freedom[47] and other nonconsequentialist types of consideration affecting what arrangements we should make for access to essential goods. As decisions about rules governing land are political in nature, the political nature of property-related decisions should prompt us to pay attention to all political values that should be pursued by a political system; these are not limited to the values most closely associated with property but include, for instance, civil and political rights. The problem is one of appropriately weighting the different kinds of *competing* principles, but these goals are amenable to "practical concordance."[48]

Third, on the basis of the discussion of eviction and landgrab injustices, "voice" and "reflexivity" need to be complemented by a principle of "say." This principle can be described by reference to central moral-legal rights, such as the classic liberal foundation of private property rights, but it must not be misinterpreted as a right against redistribution. Understood correctly it includes a right of limited economic freedom and against arbitrary (or predatory) takings and the right to housing, as recognized, for example, in the Universal Declaration of Human Rights. These rights and the civil and political rights central to their defense by no means justify disregard for collective goals or the exclusion of others in all cases, but recognizing their possible independent weight is important when dealing with situations in which the collective principle of "voice" would be ineffective in articulating the requirements of justice.

NOTES

I would like to thank the participants of the June 2013 conference on "Governing Access to Essential Resources" at Columbia Law School for their comments on an early draft of this paper; Margot Salomon, Kirsten Ainley, and Ryan Jablonski for their comments during a presentation at the London School of Economics Laboratory for Advanced Research on the Global Economy Supper Club on 11 June 2014; and the class 2014/15 of the Institute of Transnational Legal Studies at King's College London for their comments on 4 November 2014.

1. Olivier De Schutter and Katharina Pistor offer this definition in their introduction to this volume. Essential resources (goods) are also defined by their consumption being subtractive (it results in there being less of them) and exclusion from them (e.g., by private owners) being feasible and possibly economically efficient. The position developed here agrees with the essential resources thesis's critical argument that properties of certain goods cannot dictate the rules governing access to them. This, as the authors point out, would seem to be the mistake underlying theories that treat goods as private *because* they are subtractive and excludable. For the project on Governing Essential Resources, see http://web.law.columbia.edu/global-legal-transformation/justice-allocation-scarce-resources#Governing Access to Essential Resources.

2. The paper De Schutter and Pistor may mean (only) that if someone happens to be already in control of a good that is essential to someone else's survival, and they (actively) prevent this other person from gaining access to the essential good they control, they act immorally. Perhaps for the purposes of the paper the difference between these two positions is not in focus.

3. De Schutter and Pistor discuss this briefly, criticizing the identification of this theory with Adam Smith's and John Locke's respective theories.

4. "If it is in our power to prevent something bad from happening, without thereby sacrificing anything of comparable moral importance, we ought, morally, to do it" (Singer 1972).

5. Even so, one must account for the fact that in the real world we always start with some sort of de facto distribution of control over goods, including many essential goods (cf. Murphy and Nagel 2004), arguing that pretax income and property should not be seen as what people are morally entitled to.

6. Rawls famously criticized utilitarianism for its inability to take seriously the difference between persons (Rawls 1970).

7. So far as the reality of land redistribution in China is concerned, there appear to be no contemporary examples for land takings to give access to others so that these others will not starve.

8. The goods just mentioned are directly related to land use; the availability of a number of further goods (say, education) can be indirectly related to it, for example, where agriculture is the exclusive basis of income. If we attach preferential value to the function land has with regard to food and water to ensure barest physical survival (say, not starving), we may fail to understand the real problems a property regime leads to

"on the ground." One can easily imagine specific situations in which land could be taken away from people for reasons other than to secure others' survival.

9. It would have to be acknowledged that in specific situations, even a fair and equal distribution of resources might leave people with less than what is essential, a fact which a discussion based on a concept of "need" may unhelpfully obscure.

10. Yang Jisheng, *Tombstone: The Untold Story of Mao's Great Famine*, translated by Stacy Mosher, Guo Jian, and Allen Lane, New York: Penguin, 2012; Frank Dikoetter, *Mao's Great Famine: The History of China's Most Devastating Catastrophe, 1958–1962*, New York: Walker, 2011; Zhou Xun, T*he Great Famine in China, 1958–1962: A Documentary History*, New Haven, Conn.: Yale University Press, 2012

11. Preamble, Constitution of the People's Republic of China. The Preamble quoted Mao Zedong here, but Mao had never elaborated on the phrase.

12. Scholars argue about whether the urban land-use rights acquired in this process come close to fee simple absolute rights over land. Donald C. Clarke discusses this in "China's Stealth Urban Land Revolution," *American Journal of Comparative Law* 62:323–366 (2014).

13. Renewed acknowledgments of the fact that landgrabs and demolitions are a prime cause of social unrest or "mass incidents" are issued periodically (see Huang 2012; Hou 2014).

14. It is important to note that the 2011 regulation no longer contemplates compensation or resettlement arrangements for residents who are merely tenants. 国有土地上房屋征收与补偿条例 [State council regulation on expropriation of and compensation for buildings on state-owned land], 2011, www.gov.cn/zwgk/2011–01/21/content_1790111.htm.

15. Like the Fifth Amendment and unlike the Declaration of the Rights of Man and the Citizen, the PRC Constitution does not prescribe prior compensation.

16. To quote, "over the past 12 months, China's rural population considered to be in poverty declined to about 99 million from 122 million—the first time the country has started to consider those with a yearly net income of less than 2,300 yuan as 'destitute'" (Chang and Dan 2013).

17. Personal observation in 2005, 2008, and 2010 in Tongxin County, Ningxia Autonomous Region.

18. Bai Chong'en, et al. (2013) published a draft for discussion at a gathering of a group known as "China Forum 40" on 27 May 2013. This draft paper is explicitly critical of the "red-line" approach. Discussion group member (coauthor) Xu Lin is head of the National Development and Reform Commission Planning Department (see http://baike.baidu.com/view/1353085.htm#sub6150060), and this text may be considered to contain useful data.

19. Lee Liu argues that cancer villages are connected to "model city" developments. He mentions the property regime as a factor that renders "the poor . . . unable to leave the poisoned land" (Liu 2010).

20. In the previously mentioned arid areas in Ningxia, for example, groundwater is called "bitter" and widely thought to be the cause of a high prevalence of cancer. Personal observation in 2005, 2008, and 2010 in Tongxin County.

21. Yu Jianrong estimated in 2007 that 50–60 million had been affected by then and that about half could not find new jobs and lacked social security and were therefore at risk of becoming destitute (Yu Jianrong 2009).

22. China Social Law Net, citing information from the Ministry for Human Resources and Social Security, notes that some 59 million rural residents affected by land takings have been put on social welfare payments in "pilot projects" that, as of July 2010, "covered" 23 percent of the entire country, presumably referring to the total population or the total number of people similarly in need. 人社部：累计2500多万被征地农民纳入基本保障 [Ministry for Human Resources and Social Security: Over 25 m peasants have been included in social welfare program], 23 July 2010, www.cslnet.cn/show_tit.aspx?id=949&r=8472912.

23. This official in August 2010 was quoted saying that China "annually sees more construction than any other country." In recent years, the official said, China had had "up to 2 billion square meters of development annually" and "around 40 percent every year [had been] created by the demolition of older buildings" (Yanfeng 2010).

24. This argument runs into the general difficulty with understanding and defining welfare. Perhaps even when no one gets to move in, the construction activity and increase in wealth generated through current urban construction does enhance welfare overall (Chiang [2014] mentions an estimated number of 49 m vacant homes).

25. Author's own case study on the outskirts of Beijing in 2010. Residents showed photos of official events announcing the establishment of New Countryside villages from a few years ago and real estate developer brochures of high-end luxury villas, some of which had already been built, in the same spot.

26. In urban areas, some public discussion also links the property system to the existence of a real estate bubble: It has been observed that the system encourages officials to take land at "prices" (expropriation or eviction compensation standards) they can effectively set themselves. However, bubbles also occur under entirely different property regimes.

27. Yang Sujuan and at a public seminar in January 2013

28. Yang Ming (杨明), chairman of Beijing Huayuan Group Ren Zhiqiang, says: "There is no such thing as demolition and relocation that is not in the public interest. As long as it is [for the purpose of] urban construction, it is in the public interest [北京华远集团董事长任志强：不存在非公共利益拆迁 只要是城建都是公共利益]," *Oriental Outlook Weekly* (瞭望东方周刊), http://finance.ifeng.com/opinion/zjgc/20100210/1822226.shtml.

29. Efforts are underway to reform compensation standards at the time of this writing. They have not yet led to legislative changes.

30. In a case (expropriation decision announced in 2002) in Zigong, Sichuan, the ratio was ca. 70:1, whereas in a more recent case (decision announced in 2009) in Hangzhou, the ratio was ca. 23:1 (Pils 2006, 2010).

31. The laws, of course, do not allow, and indeed many rules prohibit, the fear tactics and measures commonly used to get residents to move out; explicit prohibitions reflect the fact that demolition zones are zones of coercion and danger. See State council regulation cited in note 13.

32. Both are used in practice.

33. Instructions from the Supreme People's Court to lower courts suggest that courts try to avoid getting involved altogether. 最高人民法院关于违法的建筑物、构筑物、设施等强制拆除问题的批复[SPC answer regarding the forced demolition of dangerous buildings, structures and facilities], 2 April 2013, www.court.gov.cn/qwfb/sfjs/201304/t20130402_182970.htm; "中国法院不再受理行政机关的强拆申请案引发热议" [SPC decision no longer to accept administrative authorities' applications for forceful demolition orders triggers heated debate], Radio Free Asia, www.rfa.org/mandarin/yataibaodao/renquanfazhi/cq-04032013105224.html.

34. #77 2013–1.

35. It has been argued that China has a tradition of suicide protests (舍身取义), and with regard to Tibetan suicide by self-immolation, it has been argued that this is a form of self-empowerment, not mere despair. These motivations could coexist (Lee and Kleinmann 2000).

36. Yu attributes such attitudes, inter alia, to the tendency to contrast evictee protesters in a dehumanizing, "them versus us" way.

37. For example, in conversation, a rights lawyer mentioned two unreported cases of deaths attributable to forced evictions in one month in Beijing alone. #6 2014–1. Another lawyer drew attention to the large number of "hidden cases" of eviction violence at a seminar: "苏州城镇化与拆迁研讨会—范木根等案分析" [Seminar on urbanization and demolition and relocation in Suzhou—an analysis of the case of Fan Mugen and other cases], 19 January 2014 in Beijing; "阵容庞大：范木根自卫杀人案和维稳拆迁研讨会/视频" [Great turnout: Seminar on the self-defense homicide case of Fan Mugen and stability-preservation style demolition and relocation], 22 February 2014, http://news.boxun.com/news/gb/china/2014/02/201402220159.shtml#.UzxWtLmPI5p.

38. This attempt to sum up some of the lessons from eviction processes (eviction injustices) draws on evidence from individual cases of protests by communities facing evictions, and it does not attempt to assess the popular mood in a quantitative way. Doing so would be difficult, partly due to the politically repressive environment.

39. Pictures from August 2009 and July 2010 on file with author.

40. Pictures from July 2009 on file with author.

41. Citizen Radio (公民博报), "私有财产神圣不可侵" [Private property is sacrosanct and must not be violated], 28 May 2013, http://v.youku.com/v_show/id_XNTYzOTIwOTQ4.html. This report is said to have been produced at an eviction site in Changzhou (Jiangsu Province).

42. Letter entitled "黑龙江72村4万农民宣布拥有土地所有权向全国的公告—南岗村, 富锦市" [40,000 peasants from 72 villages in Fujin City, Heilongjiang, declare their ownership of land to the entire nation], 9 December 2007, www.peacehall.com/news/gb/china/2007/12/200712091236.shtml. This and the other 2007 declarations mentioned here are discussed in "Peasants' Struggle for Land in China" (Pils 2009).

43. This phrase is used, for example, in *Emergency Shelter* (Yang 2010).

44. The text of a protest poster used for this action runs, "I want a home / A home where the wind may enter, the rain may enter, but no mafia 'emperor' may enter /

9.6 million square kilometres of land / Yet year after year I cannot find a home that belongs to me!" It was used on 4 October 2010, in a World Habitat Day action in Beijing. Document on file with the author.

45. Author conversation, July 2011.

46. # 2014–1. This lawyer continued to comment that "the government uses violent demolition and relocation, because that helps them raise GDP. It's a very simple logic."

47. Addressing Locke, Sen, and Nussbaum, "Essential Resources" argues that "it follows that property regimes are not just an expression of freedom but both a product and determinant of access to resources and abilities."

48. "We recognize that at times these goals conflict with one another and that it is impossible to maximize one without infringing on at least one of the other two: trade-offs may be required. . . . [The concept of practical concordance] holds that some norms are so important that they cannot be trumped by others or balanced out but also takes into account the decreasing marginal utility of protecting any single interest" ("Essential Resources").

REFERENCES

Amnesty International. 2012. "Standing Their Ground: Thousands Face Violent Evictions in China." www.amnesty.org/en/library/info/ASA17/001/2012/en.

Arnott, Colin, and Margot E. Salomon. 2014. "Better Development Decision-Making: Applying International Human Rights Law to Neoclassical Economics." *Nordic Journal of Human Rights* 32: 44–74. http://dx.doi.org/10.1080/18918131.2013.878892

Bai Chong'en, Cai Hongbin, Huang Haizhou, Li Bo, Ma Jun, Wei Jianing, Wu Ge, Xu Lin, Yuan Li, Zhou Chengjun, and Zhou Hanhua 白重恩、蔡洪滨、黄海洲、李波、马骏、魏加宁、伍戈、徐林、袁力、周诚君、周汉华，"土地制度改革与新型城镇化" [Chinese land reform and a new form of urbanization]. 27 May 2013, www.yicai.com/news/2013/05/2734345.html.

Chen, Tian. 2013. "Beijing's Limits to Growth Detailed." *Global Times*, 21 March. www.globaltimes.cn/content/769548.shtml.

Chiang, Langi. 2014. "Flood of Empty Homes Exceeds Needs of First-Time Buyers in China." *South China Morning Post*, 11 June.

Cohen, Roger. 2010. "A Woman Burns," *New York Times*, 25 January. www.nytimes.com/2010/01/26/opinion/26iht-edcohen.html?pagewanted=all.

He, Yang. 2010. *Emergency Shelter.* Independent documentary film.

Hou, Liqiang. 2014. "Rule of Law Bluebook Exposes Causes of Mass Incidents." *China Daily*, 16 April. http://language.chinadaily.com.cn/article-211716-1.html.

Hua, Xinmin. 2011. "Chaqian lawyer comment: private ownership of land has never disappeared" [华新民拆迁律师点评：土地私有产权从来就没有消失过]. *QQ.com*, 4 July. http://news.qq.com/a/20110701/000579.htm

Huang, Cary. 2012. "Land Grabs are Main Cause of Social Unrest, Experts Say" [揭示群体性事件诱]. *South China Morning Post*, 20 December.

Human Rights Watch. 2011. "My Children Have Been Poisoned: A Public Health Crisis in Four Chinese Provinces." 15 June. www.hrw.org/reports/2011/06/15 /my-children-have-been-poisoned-0.

Johnson, Ian. 2013a. "Leaving the Land: China's Great Uprooting." *New York Times,* 15 June.

——. 2013b. "Leaving the Land: Pitfalls Abound in China's Push from Farm to City." *New York Times,* 13 July.

Landesa Rural Development Institute. n.d. "Our Progress." www.landesa.org/where -we-work/china (accessed 7 June 2013).

——. 2011. "China's Farmers Benefitting from Land Tenure Reform." February. www .landesa.org/where-we-work/china/research-report-2010-findings-17-province -china-survey.

Lee, Sing, and Arthur Kleinmann. 2010. "Suicide as Resistance in Chinese Society." In *Chinese Society: Change, Conflict and Resistance,* ed. Elizabeth Perry and Mark Selden, 221–228. Routledge, Abingdon,

Li, Jing. 2013. "Report on Mainland China's Soil Pollution a 'State Secret.'" *South China Morning Post,* 26 February. www.scmp.com/news/china/article/1158602 /report-mainland-soil-pollution-state-secret.

Li, Lianjiang, and Kevin J. O'Brien. 2004 "Suing the Local State: Administrative Litigation in Rural China." *China Journal* 51 (January): 75–96.

Li, Xueren. 2013. "Premier Underlines Developing Scale Farming." *China.org.cn,* 31 March. www.china.org.cn/china/2013–03/31/content_28408103.htm

Liu, Chang and He, Dan. 2013. "China to Increase Efforts to Alleviate Poverty." *China Daily,* 25 March. www.chinadaily.com.cn/china/2013–03/25/content_16341128 .htm.

Liu, Kan. 2013. "Upheaval in Chinese Villages: A Case Study of Rural Land Expropriation for 'Large-Scale' Commercial Farming in Rural China." *Land Deal Politics Initiative* 18 (February).

Liu, Lee. 2010. "Made in China: Cancer Villages" *Environment* (March/April). www .environmentmagazine.org/Archives/Back%20Issues/March-April%202010 /made-in-china-full.html.

Murphy, Liam B., and Thomas Nagel. 2004. *The Myth of Ownership: Taxes and Justice.* Oxford: Oxford University Press.

Pils, Eva. 2006. "Land Disputes, Rights Assertion and Social Unrest: A Case from Sichuan." *Columbia Journal of Asian Law* 19: 235–292

——. 2009. "Peasants' Struggle for Land in China." In *Marginalized Communities and Access to Justice,* ed. Yash Ghai and Jill Cottrell, 136–160. Routledge, Abingdon

——. 2010 "Waste No Land: Property, Dignity and Growth in Urbanizing China." *Asian-Pacific Law & Policy Journal* 11 (2): 1–48.

——. 2014. "Contending Conceptions of Ownership in Urbanizing China." In *Resolving Land Disputes in East Asia,* ed. Fu Hualing and John Gillespie, 115–172. Cambridge University Press, Cambridge.

Pils, Eva and Marina Svensson. 2014. "Yu Jianrong: From Concerned Scholar to Advocate for the Marginalized." *Contemporary Chinese Thought* 46: 1.

Pomfret, James. 2013. "Freedom Fizzles Out in China's Rebel Town of Wukan." *Reuters*, 28 February. www.reuters.com/article/2013/02/28/us-china-wukan-idUSBRE91R1J020130228.

Qian, Yanfeng. 2010. "'Most Homes' to Be Demolished in 20 Years." *China Daily*, 7 August. www.chinadaily.com.cn/china/2010–08/07/content_11113982.htm.

Randolph, Patrick. 2007. "The New Chinese Basic Law of Property: A Real Estate Practitioner's Perspective." http://lawprofessors.typepad.com/china_law_prof_blog/files/basicpropertylaw_comments.pdf.

Rawls, John. 1970. "Chapter 1 ('Justice as Fairness'), pp. 3–53." *A Theory of Justice*. Cambridge, Mass.: Belknap.

Ren, Zihui. 2007. "Chinese Regime Classifies Meteorological Information as State Secrets." *Epoch Times*, 6 February. www.theepochtimes.com/news/7–2-6/51328.html.

Ruan, Victoria. 2013. "Debts Weigh Down New Push for Urban Reform." *South China Morning Post*, 6 June.

Singer, Peter. 1972. "Famine, Affluence, and Morality." *Philosophy & Public Affairs* 1: 229–231.

S.C. 2011. "Life at the Bottom of the Middle Kingdom." *Economist*, 2 December. www.economist.com/blogs/freeexchange/2011/12/chinas-poverty-line.

Watts, Jonathan. 2011. "China Warns of 'Urgent Problems' Facing Three Gorges Dam." *Guardian*, 20 May. www.guardian.co.uk/world/2011/may/20/three-gorges-dam-china-warning.

Yu, Jianrong. 2009. *Subaltern Politics: Dialogues and Lectures* [底层政治—对话与演讲]. Hong Kong: China Cultural Publishing House.

——. 2014. "Do China's Tang Fuzhens Regret Self-Immolation?" Trans. Stacy Mosher. *Contemporary Chinese Thought* 46: 1.

Zhou, Qiren. 2012. "The Mystery of the Nationalization of Urban Land" [城市土地国有化之谜]. *Urban and Rural China Review* [城乡中国系列评论之二十六], 26. http://zhouqiren.org/archives/1329.html.

Zhu, Jiangnan. 2012 "The Shadow of the Skyscrapers: Real Estate Corruption in China." *Journal of Contemporary China* 21 (74): 243–260.

CHAPTER 7

Tenure Security and Exclusion Processes in Peri-urban Areas and Rural Hinterlands of West African Cities

Alain Durand-Lasserve

In most developing countries in Latin America, Asia, and Africa, a large proportion of the urban population lives in "informal" settlements.[1] Except for street dwellers and people living in temporary camps following disasters and armed conflicts, most people have a shelter, but they have no or limited access to essential resources such as safe water and no security of tenure.[2] This situation discourages households from investing in improvements to their homes and neighborhoods. Slums—the generic term used to classify informal, illegal, or unplanned settlements—are the invisible "zones of silence" on tenure security (UN-Habitat 2006). While tenure insecurity is only one criterion that characterizes what the United Nations defines as slums (UN-Habitat 2003), the urban poor tend to be frequently exposed to various forms of eviction or displacement. Furthermore, rapidly increasing land prices in cities contribute to the spatial expansion of informal settlements in their periphery (Huchzermeyer and Karam 2006).

The correlation between poverty, tenure insecurity, and vulnerability has been described and analyzed extensively in developing cities over the last two decades. To a large extent, the map of urban poverty in developing countries overlaps that of slums. Tenure insecurity is the combined result of poverty—to which it contributes—and of rules and laws with which only the wealthier segment of the population can comply. Access to land with secure tenure that can be traded in formal markets is usually out of reach for low- and middle-income households, who have little choice but to rely exclusively on informal land markets.

Given the magnitude of urban poverty and its impact on economic development and social stability, much attention has been paid to sub-Saharan Africa by aid and development agencies and programs (UN-Habitat, UN Development Program), international financial institutions (the World Bank and African Development Bank), regional institutions (African Union, Economic Commission for Africa 2011a, 2011b, 2011c; European Union 2004), and bilateral aid agencies (GIZ— German Cooperation, French Cooperation, Millennium Challenge Corporation). Many national and local governments have embarked on slum-upgrading programs and tenure formalization in cities.[3] But the driving forces behind the formation of informal urban settlements have frequently been neglected, and proposed solutions have often created new problems.

This chapter focuses mainly on francophone West African countries (hereafter "the subregion"), which are part of sub-Saharan Africa.[4] It proposes a methodological framework that allows for a better understanding of why a vast majority of households cannot obtain secure tenure. It takes into account the various factors impacting the relationship between modes of access to land, security of tenure, and exclusion processes in both peri-urban areas and the rural hinterlands of West African cities. Different attempts to improve access to land and security of tenure are discussed in the final part of this chapter. Many of these attempts have failed or have achieved limited results, because they were based upon segmented and static analysis of local situations and focused exclusively on formal market mechanisms for allocating land without questioning the legitimacy and feasibility of rules aimed at regulating it in the context where these policies were implemented.

The proposed methodology helps analyze the functioning and dynamics of land allocation and land markets while identifying problems that might compromise the design of inclusive land policies. It thereby contributes to the goals of this volume, namely to identity institutions and practices that help achieve the normative goals associated with essential resource governance: a modicum of voice afforded to all affected constituencies.

Since the focus of the chapter is provision of land for housing and not provision of housing, the rental sector—which accounts for up to 50 percent of households in West African cities—will not be addressed as such. Still, land delivery has an impact on tenants in informal settlements, who typically have no lease and are therefore doubly exposed to insecurity. They are also extremely vulnerable to upgrading and improvement programs, which inevitably result in changes in land values and rents.

The sources used in this analysis include desk studies on tenure issues and formalization policies carried out in urban areas in sub-Saharan countries, as well as recent research and evaluation fieldwork in which the author has recently been involved.[5] This text is therefore the result of fieldwork, especially of interviews with a wide range of stakeholders: residents, allottees, buyers and sellers of land, managers of intermediaries (property companies), surveyors, notaries, brokers, land administration staff, commune councillors, and decision makers at government levels. In the analysis of modes of access to land, particular attention has been paid to the relationship between rules enacted by the state and the actual practices placed in their political, social, economic, and cultural contexts.

DEFINITIONS AND METHODOLOGICAL FRAMEWORK

From a theoretical and practical point of view, any meaningful discussion about access to land with secure tenure and exclusion processes in cities requires the identification of: (1) the relationship between land-tenure status (the basis on which land or property is held or owned) and security on one hand, and property rights on the other;[6] (2) the supply of and access to land through allocations or market by the different land-delivery channels; (3) the interactions of these channels, which permit us to understand the competition between different modes of access; and (4) the other factors that impact the land-delivery system.

Payne (2004) and Durand-Lasserve (2006) provide conceptual and methodological frameworks for classifying the full range of tenure categories, the degree of associated security,[7] and the property rights. Their classification is presented in figure 7.1, which covers all possible situations encountered in developing cities. Improving the understanding of the relationships between land tenure, property rights, and security of tenure requires a typology that is not only based on the hard facts in a formal, legal sense, obtained through reading legal documents or census data, but also addresses less statistically measurable issues, such as perception of security of tenure, as this has a major influence on investment and other decisions affecting land markets. More generally, social attitudes toward land vary considerably from one context to another. Information on such issues cannot be readily obtained; direct evidence is required from households themselves and this, in turn, requires primary research at whatever level is possible (Payne et al. 2012).

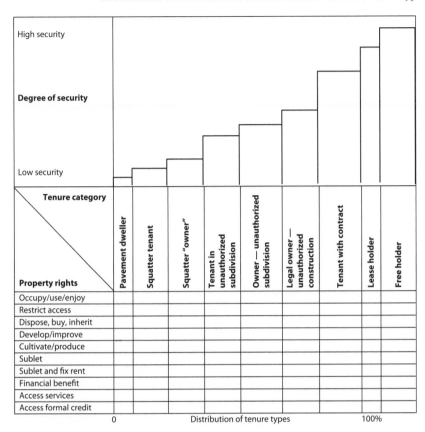

Figure 7.1   Notional matrix of land tenure and property rights.

Note: As men and women do not typically share equal access to property rights, figure 7.1 leaves space for one to notate gender-based inequity. Similarly, a different system of notation can be employed to record other variables.

Source: Payne and Durand-Lasserve, 2012.

This typology makes a clear distinction between tenure status and property rights. For example, it is possible for one person to enjoy zero probability of removal without due process but to have no ability to sell or mortgage his or her property. Another individual may suffer a low but nonzero probability of summary eviction but may be free to sell, upgrade, or sublet his or her property—albeit at a price discounted for the risk. Although the first person is "secure" and the second is not, the degree of the second person's property rights could, in fact, be greater (Payne et al. 2012).

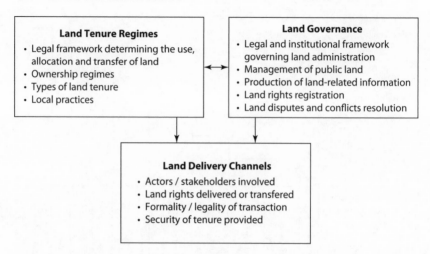

Figure 7.2   Land-tenure regimes, land governance, and land-delivery channels.

The notion of a land-delivery channel is helpful in understanding the different modes of access to land for housing, land-tenure improvement mechanisms, and land transactions. Two variables that interact with each other must be taken into account: land-tenure regimes and land governance, which concerns the processes by which decisions are made and implemented regarding access and use of land and the way conflicting interests can be reconciled. Figure 7.2 represents links between land-delivery channels, land-tenure regimes, and land governance.

Land-delivery channels refer to all the stages in the process whereby land (1) is characterized by a particular tenure status when first sold or allocated as essentially residential; (2) can be the subject of improvement in that status; and (3) is sold on the markets before or after tenure improvement. The concept of the land-delivery channel complements that of land market, which refers only to land transactions at a given point in time, irrespective of the initial tenure status or stage of the improvement process at which the transaction takes place (Durand-Lasserve, Durand-Lasserve, and Selod 2014).

Knowing not only the initial tenure status and the possibilities of improvement but also the market segments on which land can be sold helps us to understand the interrelations between the different land-delivery channels that appear in the land-delivery system.

Interrelated factors affect the context in which the land-delivery system operates. Nine major factors can be identified: (1) history; (2) global

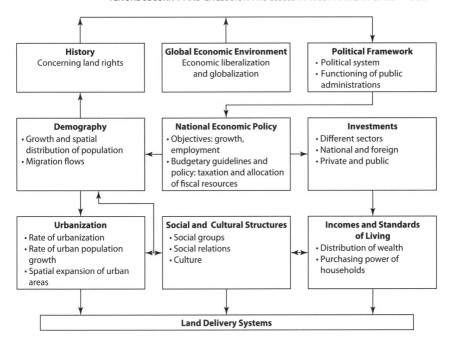

Figure 7.3   Factors impacting land-delivery systems and their interactions.

economic context; (3) political framework and governance; (4) national economic policy; (5) investments according to sectors of activity; (6) employment, incomes and standards of living; (7) social structures and culture; (8) demography; and (9) urbanization. Figure 7.3 presents these factors and their interactions.

With an understanding of this context, drivers of changes in land-delivery systems can be identified, and the situation that prevails in sub-Saharan African cities today can be analyzed. From an operational perspective, this analysis may allow governments to identify factors over which they have some control as compared with others over which they have little or no influence.

HIGH LEVEL OF TENURE INSECURITY IN URBAN AND PERI-URBAN AREAS IN WEST AFRICAN CITIES

The proposed methodological framework provides a better understanding of unequal access to land and to secure tenure for different social groups and why tenure insecurity is quantitatively so important in West African cities, all of which are currently confronted with high urbanization rates. The interplay of the following factors is crucial: (1) the prevalence of poverty,[8] (2) legal pluralism, (3) the coexistence of three interrelated land-delivery channels, and (4) speculative investments in land that go along with a high degree of fraud and corruption in land administrations.

Sub-Saharan Africa has not completed its demographic transition. Its population of 900 million inhabitants (as of 2013) will likely increase to more than 1.1 billion in 2020 and 2 billion by 2050, approximately one-fifth of the projected global population.[9] In 2013, 40 percent of the population was urbanized; that proportion will rise to more than half by 2030 and will approach 60 percent by 2050. The annual rate of growth of the urban population in sub-Saharan Africa was 3.8 percent between 2000 and 2005. It is expected to be 4.5 percent in West Africa between 2010 and 2030 (Godin 2010).

In comparison with other cities in the world, those in sub-Saharan Africa have the highest percentage of people affected by insecure tenure (UN-Habitat 2012a). In 2010, 61.7 percent of the urban population of the region (and higher yet in West African countries) lived in informal settlements with no infrastructure, as compared with 32.5 percent in all developing countries (United Nations 2014). Recent data suggest a slow decline in the growth rate, but the number of inhabitants at the regional level is still rising.

In urban and peri-urban environments, demand for land is driven not only by housing needs but also by land speculation and the fact that land is treated as a store of value in countries that lack small saving schemes and social security systems. Moreover, owning land is an inflation-proof investment, inasmuch as its price will increase more quickly than average income in the long term.

Tenure regimes in the subregion are characterized by legal pluralism, that is, the coexistence of multiple legal systems and rights, such as customary rights, with "positive" or "modern" law enacted by the state. The legal and administrative framework of land management remains to a large extent a legacy of the colonial period. Postindependence national governments have inherited the land prerogatives of the colonial power with some adaptations to their respective situations through various national acts and land codes (Ouedraogo 2011). Similar basic principles apply to most countries in the subregion: (1) the state remains the eminent owner of the national land, which can be allocated only after it has been registered under its name (*immatriculation*);[10] (2) the state allocates land using a Torrens system—the "top-down" administrative creation of private landownership following the "purging" of customary land rights[11]—and then establishes a "civil register" of land in the form of the *livre foncier* (Comby and Gerber 2007; Ouedraogo 2011), where landownership titles (*titres fonciers*, or TFs) and their transactions are centrally registered; (3) transactions of titled land (land with ownership rights) take place within the framework of the civil code; and (4) use rights and their transactions are recorded in registers, usually kept at local levels.[12]

Experts unanimously agree that this system is a failure. All countries of the subregion proved unable to deliver and register land titles at scale. The existing registration system cannot be instituted everywhere and can hardly be updated. A century after it was introduced, less than 5 percent of all land is reported as registered in sub-Saharan Africa[13]—this figure includes state-owned land.[14] Its coexistence with customary rights and precarious titles gives rise to competing land markets with different levels of legitimacy, legality, tenure security, and prices. Moreover, it opens doors to corruption in land administration and—for this very reason—can hardly be reformed or improved. The urban poor are extremely vulnerable in this context.

This system contrasts strongly with customary land "ownership," which refers to the communal possession of rights to use and allocate agricultural and grazing land by a group sharing the same cultural identity. This customary land "ownership" existed before colonization. It is still predominant in rural areas, peri-urban areas of cities and, to a lesser extent, in urbanized areas. A single person usually administers on behalf of the group. Decisions—made in principle on a consensual basis—must comply with the cultural tradition of the community concerned. The extent of any rights to use the land depends on the agreement made between the customary community and the person receiving the rights. Within the group, social institutions defend or protect these rights against other claims regarding the land.

Recent empirical observations in the periphery of African cities suggest that the transfer of customary land is governed by a combination of informal practices, reinterpreted customary norms, and market economy rules (Rakodi and Leduka 2004; Durand-Lasserve 2005; Werhmann 2008).

Recognition of customary rights in the subregion applies more in rural areas than in urban or peri-urban areas. The right of customary holders to subdivide and sell land is recognized in Togo and to a lesser extent in Benin. Even when they are formally recognized, customary rights do not give their holders the same transfer or development rights as those attached to ownership or precarious titles. To have their rights administratively recognized, customary holders are often forced to relinquish large parts of their land. In return, rights to their land are converted to use rights, with a provisional permit, and in a later stage, possibly to ownership rights.

Current trends toward the recognition of customary land rights, along with the implementation of decentralized land policies, can be observed in West and Central African countries (African Union, African Development Bank, and Economic Commission for Africa 2011b). However, these trends are counterbalanced by a resistance to change from subregional institutions and central governments and stakeholders in the formal private land market, who view customary rights as obstacles to secure investments.

Regardless of the level of recognition, customary land is transacted, albeit under conditions of insecurity and at prices that are always lower than prices for comparable land in formal markets. This legal pluralism implies substantial diversity in tenure status—and tenure status determines the price of land. The occupier of a plot of land may have a full-ownership title or only a precarious title. Alternatively, he or she may not have a title but rather a sale agreement or certificate that can be authenticated by local authorities. In addition, an occupier may hold an administrative permit that allows one to apply for precarious title. The occupier of the plot can also claim a customary right. A quantitative survey on land markets in Bamako (Durand-Lasserve, Durand-Lasserve, and Selod 2014) shows that plots with ownership titles are worth up to 5.7 times the price of similar plots with only customary rights attached. The difference can increase to a magnitude of 8 in well-located peri-urban rural communes.[15] Research conducted by the author in the peri-urban areas of Cotonou, Dakar (Senegal), and Lome (Togo) between 2011 and 2013 provides very similar numbers.

Three land-delivery channels can be identified in West African cities: (1) the customary channel, wherein the first or original transfer involves customary land; (2) the public channel through which allocations or sales are initially made by public and para-public authorities; and (3) the formal private channel through which land and plots with ownership titles are initially sold with legally registered deeds by property developers, cooperatives, or individuals. This is illustrated in figure 7.4, which is based on

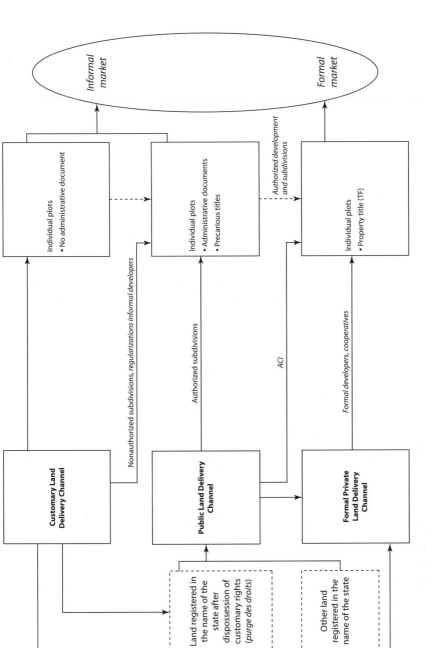

Figure 7.4 The land-delivery system.

the city of Bamako, Mali, but applies with some adjustments to all cities of the subregion (Durand-Lasserve, Durand-Lasserve, and Selod 2014).

As can be seen, linkages between the three land-delivery channels constitute the land-delivery system. Land is initially provided through two delivery channels: the customary one, which predominates in peri-urban areas, where land use is being transformed from agricultural to residential, a transformation now gradually extending to the rural hinterland of Bamako; and the public and para-public delivery channel. These two channels feed into the formal private channel, which delivers serviced plots with ownership titles at much higher prices. Plots in these three channels may be the subject of successive transactions in land markets, and their degree of informality varies according to tenure, legality, and registration of the transactions. Legal and nonlegal practices are found in both land allocations and market transactions. Even in the public channel, legal procedures are not always followed. Transactions involving land obtained from the customary and public channels by private individuals or small property developers are usually carried out in informal land markets. Because the development of the formal market is severely hindered by complex procedures, very high costs of formalization, and risks of disputes over titles, informal land markets are tolerated if not encouraged by city administrations throughout the subregion.

An analysis in terms of land-delivery channels shows that in all cities of the subregion, four main modes of accessing land can be identified, with various levels of tenure security and land prices and some variation from one country to another but very comparable trends and dynamics over time. The first mode involves the acquisition of a piece of land on the formal market, directly from its owner, from a property developer, or through a land agency that may have bought it earlier in the customary or public channel and may have subsequently obtained ownership title. This mode of access is more common in urban areas where land has been titled than in peri-urban areas and the rural hinterlands of cities where other forms of tenure are still dominant. Available data suggest that it is relatively rare and accounts for only 13 percent of land owned by households in the Bamako district (as of 2009) and 4.2 percent in Cotonou, Benin (as of 2002). However, one can observe that titled land is increasingly being made available around cities, where private property developers are currently buying large amounts of customarily held land, managing to obtain ownership titles, subdividing the land, and selling titled plots outright to urban buyers. Similar practices are common throughout the subregion, with slight differences due to the status of national domain land and of the level of recognition of customary ownership. For example, in the periphery of the Bamako district, the average number of ownership titles delivered monthly on land purchased from customary owners by urban-based buyers has increased drastically over the last few years, from 627 per month between 2005 and 2012,[16] to 1,160 per month in 2013, to 2,000 per month between January and April 2014.[17] This increase is linked with the massive and sometimes fraudulent purchases of customary land on the outskirts of Bamako by urban buyers with the support of some officials in charge of land administration during the governance crisis that has accompanied the political transition in Mali.

The second mode of access to land is through a public land subdivision scheme carried out by the state or local authorities (*lotissement étatique* or *lotissement municipal*). Until the early 2000s, this form of access to land was quite common in all urban and peri-urban areas of cities in the subregion. Public land is allocated or sold at below market price, usually to respond to the demands of political clienteles. It is usually delivered with a precarious title. In this case, tenure can, in principle, be upgraded at a later stage to full-ownership title.

Public land-delivery channels usually target the middle classes. According to data from the African Development Bank (2011),[18] in 2010 the middle class represented a small percentage of the population of West African countries.[19] This kind of government allocation of land is now in decline: Public land reserves have been progressively exhausted on the peripheries of cities. Liberalization and privatization of land markets have made the direct provision of land for housing by governments more difficult.

The third mode of access is acquisition of a plot of land from a customary owner who has subdivided his land (customary subdivision) and sold it out on what we can call the customary land market. A land sale agreement is made with customary owners and signed in front of witnesses. The transaction is authenticated or stamped by local authorities (usually the village council or mayor). Recognition of a customary land subdivision by the central or local government allows the buyer of a plot to apply for a precarious title. At a later stage, the buyer can apply for an ownership title if the subdivision has been authorized.

The fourth mode involves buying a piece of land on the informal noncustomary market. A wide range of secondary, informal land markets derive from customary and public land-delivery channels. They concern land with a low level of tenure security. Transactions are not registered and are rarely recorded. They are accessible to low-income households, but market pressures on peri-urban land and increases in prices tend to exclude the poorest households.

The third and fourth modes of access to land characterize informal settlements. Although they allow low-income households (and to a lesser extent middle-income households) to gain access to plots, security of tenure is by no means guaranteed. Moreover, prices are still relatively high, because these informal markets also attract speculators. As a result, the poorest households have no choice but to find rental accommodations in informal settlements, with no security of tenure and precarious tenancy rights.[20] The sustained growth in land prices, high transaction costs, and time-consuming tenure-upgrading procedures, together with the involvement of a large number of stakeholders and the multiplicity of tenure systems, combine to significantly reduce affordability and make secure access to land very difficult for the urban poor.

While large-scale foreign investments in agricultural land have given rise to an extensive literature over the last decade, speculative investments in urban and peri-urban areas and in the rural hinterlands of cities have rarely been analyzed, much less with a comparative perspective. These investments are the main cause of price increases in land markets. The speculators are mostly national urban-based elites and, to a lesser extent, members of the middle class. Two speculative strategies are commonly used, usually together. The first is to buy land and wait for a price increase, which usually accompanies urbanization. This phenomenon has been observed in particular in Abomey-Calavi and around Porto-Novo in Benin (Grisoni-Niaki 2000; Balagoun 2009; Agossou 2011). The second strategy is to improve tenure status; land prices increase sharply when tenure is upgraded. This is confirmed by the author's own research and observations in West African cities over the last ten years.

There are two main practices to generate added value that derives from tenure upgrading: one used primarily by elites and the other by the emerging middle class. In the case of Bamako, the former can be summarized as follows. Customary land is bought in rural communes in the peri-urban area of the city and in its rural hinterland. The certificate of sale signed by the customary seller and the buyer is authenticated by the mayor (*attestation de vente authentifiée*). By proposing an agricultural development project, it is possible to obtain a precarious title (*concession rurale*), which may be transformed into an ownership title after registration (*immatriculation*) of the land in the name of the state.[21] The land can later be subdivided into smaller plots, which can be sold with ownership title (*lotissement privé formel*), thereby enhancing the land's market value, since land sold with an ownership title can be sold at five to eight times the price of a similar plot with only customary rights.

The middle class typically employs more diverse channels. First, buyers may acquire customary land and simply wait for regularization of tenure and then sell the land to others. Second, they may upgrade a precarious title into an ownership title and then sell the land at a much higher price than the purchasing price for customary land. The gains associated with tenure upgrading are contingent on several factors: the duration of the upgrading process; the cost of land; extra costs incurred through corruption (euphemistically called "payment without receipts"); evolving rules governing the application for obtaining a precarious or an ownership title; and market demand for land. Last but not least, betting on regularization and legalization of title is risky. Because the volume of applications for tenure upgrading far exceeds the processing capacity of land administration institutions, and because of the pervasiveness of fraud and corruption, applications are processed in a highly selective fashion. In general, priority seems to be given to applicants with privileged access to information, substantial financial resources, preferential access to the judiciary, and/or preferential access to administrative and political power ("government land clienteles"). For members of these constituencies, the advantages of land conversion clearly outweigh the risks involved in these transactions. Surprisingly, this phenomenon, which is common and well known to all stakeholders in all cities of the region, is usually ignored by experts, aid agencies, and development agencies.

Based on recent observations made by the author in Benin, Mali, Rwanda, and Togo, it seems fair to say that land speculation is a self-perpetuating process as long as land values increase over time and speculative behavior contributes to the market pressure on land. The process is fueled by the common practice of reinvesting returns derived from land sales into land markets, especially when high demand drives land prices up. There is also anecdotal evidence in Mali, Benin, and Togo of laundering money from illegal activities by channeling it into land and property development.

Inequitable access to land has costly long-term social, economic, and environmental implications. Over the last thirty years the gap between average income and the market price of land has been increasing around the globe in urban and peri-urban areas. Rising land prices exclude large sections of the urban population from legal and affordable land with secure tenure as well as housing, thereby forcing many people into informal settlements (Payne and Durand-Lasserve 2012). The poorest households are excluded from access to land and are predominantly tenants in these settlements. As a result, urban segregation and social cleavages are increasing (Bertrand 1998; Grisoni-Niaki 2000).

The state not only sets the rules and procedures to be followed in formal land market; it may also undertake or supervise tenure-regularization projects in informal settlements, yet it rarely has the required means to do so. As a result, these projects are frequently diverted from their objectives: While the poor have access to land with insecure tenure and can hardly improve it, the rich buy land on the customary or informal markets, manage to formalize and subdivide it, and sell plots at high profit on the formal land market.

Inequalities also contribute to the uncontrolled spatial expansion of the city, with relatively low occupation density in the city center and perpetuation and expansion of informal settlements on the outer ring of peri-urban areas—informal settlements with no security of tenure and limited access to services and infrastructure. This contributes to conflicts between households, communities, local authorities, the state, land administration institutions, politicians, and holders of customary rights. These conflicts can be especially frequent in peri-urban areas, where the market pressure on land is strongest. In all countries of the subregion, land-related conflicts represent 70 percent to 90 percent of cases in civil courts, despite the intervention of community-based jurisdictions, the function of which is to prevent or resolve land disputes at the local level.

POLICY RESPONSES TO INSECURE TENURE

For the last twenty-five years, land policies promoted by foreign and international development agencies under Western influence have emphasized the development of formal land markets, land titling, and the registration of real property (Buckley and Kalarickal 2006; Deininger, Selod, and Burns 2011). The World Bank was an early supporter of systematic land-titling programs in urban areas and began funding a major program in Peru in 1998. In subsequent years land titling became one of the major policies promoted by the World Bank and major bilateral aid agencies (Deininger and Feder 2008). It was expanded to developing countries in sub-Saharan Africa with the support of bilateral aid agencies, such as the Millennium Challenge Corporation (MCC) in Benin and the UK Department for International Development (DFID) in Rwanda, with mixed results.

Despite their influence on the international discourse on land policy issues (World Bank 1993), international financial institutions and other aid agencies did not enjoy much leverage over the tenure policies of national governments. The latter consider land to be a matter of national sovereignty. They have therefore resisted insistent demands from international finance institutions and aid agencies to reconsider default state ownership in all untitled land and have instituted land reforms and new land codes aimed at weakening this principle. Still, recent institutional and legal changes observed in the subregion suggest that governments are adopting a more pragmatic approach (Rochegude and Plançon 2010). While there are still considerable differences of opinion between, on one side, international finance institutions and aid and development agencies and, on the other side, national governments concerning the state's prerogative over land and its eminent domain rights, tenure-regularization issues are less controversial. The policy emphasis is therefore placed more clearly on legal framework reform, support for private land markets, and greater flexibility in handling land tenure. Legal reforms include, among others, new land codes combined with policies aimed at decentralizing control over land (Rochegude and Plançon 2010), including devolving the state's land prerogative to local governments and the recognition of customary land uses as land rights in sub-Saharan Africa, especially in rural areas, where there is less pressure on land markets than in urban or peri-urban areas.

The primary stated purpose of titling is to provide real rights (ownership rights, surface rights, or a long-term lease) to landholders whose tenure is informal. Many justifications have been put forward in favor of land titling over the last two decades (for a summary see Payne, Durand-Lasserve, and Rakodi 2009), including but not limited to:

- securing land occupation and combating evictions;
- preventing tenure conflicts;
- improving the position of the poor by transforming the assets they possess into "living capital," that is, into assets that can be alienated and mortgaged (de Soto 2000);
- securing investments and facilitating access to credit;
- stimulating and unifying land markets;
- facilitating operations to develop and service land; and
- increasing tax revenue (land and property tax) of the state and local authorities.

Potential contradictions of these different objectives are rarely discussed. For example, securing investments in land, which requires ownership rights, does not necessarily improve land tenure for those living in informal settlements whose tenure could be secured by other means. Ownership rights delivered in land-titling programs typically are not accessible to all parties and often go hand in hand with the development of a formal land market. Titling may therefore result in the appropriation of land by more affluent urban households, thereby accentuating exclusionary dynamics, which can be seen as a logical outcome of market forces. It is possible, in principle, to minimize or prevent exclusion by controlling the process by which appropriation takes place. That, however, requires political will and sound knowledge of the procedures and practices through which ownership titles are delivered and land is allocated and transacted. The case of Benin, discussed in detail later, illustrates the difficulties of implementing titling programs in the subregion.

Titling programs may cover a whole country—as was the ambition of the National Land Regularization Programme implemented in Rwanda between 2008 and 2013[22]—or a region within a country. Titling can also be implemented on an experimental basis in a test area before being rolled out at the regional or national level. This was the case in an operation launched in 2006 by the MCC in Benin, where Cotonou and several other cities were singled out for pilot projects. The goal was to convert 60,000 precarious titles (*permis d'habiter*—residence permits) into an equal number of ownership titles (TFs). This objective was revised down to 30,000 in 2008, only two years into the project, and then again in 2011 to 15,000, as problems with implementation began accumulating. All in all, the project involved 28 areas spread over 20 urban communes in Benin.

MCC provided funding for the establishment of the National Property Title Commission (Commission nationale d'appui à l'obtention des titres fonciers—CNAO-TF). It also subsidized the bulk of the cost of converting precarious titles into individual ownership titles, a task that normally would be the full responsibility of the State Property Department of the Ministry of Finance.[23] Only a small portion of the actual cost of titling—between 10 and 18 percent, depending on cases—was charged to beneficiaries.

The titling project had several objectives, one of which was to facilitate access to bank credit. It was implemented when the Organization for the Harmonization of Business Law in Africa—which includes seventeen mostly Francophone West African and Central African countries—adopted a new act regulating conditions for access to mortgaged credit.[24] According to this act, only ownership titles (freehold titles or other real rights) can be mortgaged. This legal provision provided a strong incentive for governments to implement land-titling policies. Titling was supposed to boost investment and contribute to economic development while helping to combat poverty. Another objective was to contribute to the smooth operation of the land market through unquestionable ownership rights to ensure "effective, fair allocation of land."

The first step in implementing this ambitious plan was to select the areas where the pilot projects would be carried out. In a subset of these areas, the state had earlier divided land into publicly designated subdivisions (*lotissement étatique*) and had given the plot holders the opportunity to obtain precarious titles (*permis d'habiter*). This procedure made it relatively simple to allocate individual ownership titles. However, in most areas the land had originally been subdivided and sold by customary holders (customary land subdivision). By paying various fees and complying with lengthy procedures, every occupant could obtain a precarious title after the government legalized the subdivision of land. Before individual ownership titles could be granted in those cases, it was essential to clearly delineate the area and to grant general ownership title to a land association (*association d'intérêt foncier*—AIF). AIFs were established in each area, and landholders were designated as "presumed owners" of the plots. Landholders could then submit requests for individual ownership title to the AIF. Applications were processed by land surveyors and notaries under the responsibility of CNAO-TF. The ownership title, however, was delivered by the State Property Department of the Ministry of Finance.

The entire process turned out to be much more complicated than expected. Most occupants who had access to land through the customary channel and informal markets lacked even precarious title and had only a simple sale agreement (*convention de vente*). Subsequent transfers had not been registered, and land disputes proved to be more numerous than anticipated. Occupants who were reluctant to follow a process that kept traditional representatives at a distance did not fully support the top-down titling program. Their involuntary exclusion from the titling process resulted from the program's assumption that they were represented by their elected mayors: This did not correspond to their perception of governance at municipal level. Furthermore, some potential beneficiaries were sidelined or not even kept informed about the process by municipal authorities and local elites under various pretexts (poverty, illiteracy).

At the end of the program in January 2012, despite the fact that several thousand applications had been filed, only 130 *titres fonciers* (TFs) out of an expected 30,000 had actually been issued. The CNAO-TF continued its work, and by the end of the third quarter of 2013, around 1,500 TFs had been issued. These difficulties could have been mitigated if the interests that were at stake with respect to creating and allocating ownership titles, the various modes of access to land, and the key role of informal land markets had been properly assessed, and if the interactions among the various channels of the land-delivery system had been better understood. Last but not least, cultural factors were largely ignored in favor of a more ideological approach.

These land-titling policies usually go along with policies that support the development of private land markets. The latter include the creation of housing finance institutions, the establishment of formal housing development companies, and the creation of various forms of public-private partnerships: land development agencies (e.g., *Agence de cession immobilière* in Mali) or various incentives for real estate companies. To make these policies acceptable to the broader public, these interventions are frequently portrayed as meeting the demand for social housing (*logements sociaux*), when in fact these companies target upper-middle-income and high-income groups.

Speculative strategies by urban-based elites in peri-urban areas, which go along with the development of the private form of land markets, are spreading into the rural hinterlands of cities. New forms of tenure insecurity arise, especially for low-income households when the land they bought from customary owners is subsequently claimed by affluent people, who can provide an authentic or forged ownership title. This frequently results in households' displacements in what can be called market-driven displacement. These displacements are rarely recorded as evictions, either because they do not require the use of force or because some form of compensation is paid to the "displaced" or "removed" households, irrespective of whether the payment is fair and equitable. There are no data on the scale of such displacements or evictions, but it is reasonable to assume that their number worldwide is much higher than the number of forced evictions (Durand-Lasserve 2006).

The globalization of economic relations and the development strategies of international finance institutions impose formal legal institutions and mechanisms without taking account of local historical and cultural factors, like the legacy of customary tenure on one hand and the introduction of state and private ownership during colonization on the other. Socioeconomic factors (see fig. 7.3) are also rarely considered. Social inequalities tend to be ignored in the statements of international finance institutions, suggesting that formal land market and individual landownership could enable everyone to access housing. This discourse downplays the impact of intense competition for access to land by a diverse group of potential buyers and their asymmetric power, income, financial resources, and access to information.

Finally, development agencies and regional organizations are now promoting more flexible approaches to tenure informality than had been adopted in the early 2000s (Max, Diop, and Simmoneau 2013). These may take the form of more inclusive land policies, tenure regularization or other policies to improve security of tenure (UN-Habitat 2004, 2012b), and the design and implementation of new land tools. Such land tools, especially those involving information about land and recording and registration systems, are adapted to a diversity of land-tenure forms and land-delivery channels.

Regional institutions' initiatives in the land sector (African Union, African Development Bank, and Economic Commission for Africa 2011a, 2011b, 2011c), as well as national initiatives, including the national conferences on land (*états généraux du foncier*) organized by governments that have accompanied the democratic shift in West Africa in the 1990s and early 2000s, increasingly include civil society organizations in framing national land policies. These initiatives have contributed to the progressive recognition of the diversity of land rights—notably customary communities' rights—and people's voice regarding secure access to land. However, national conferences have only a limited reach: Their organization and stakeholders' consultation processes remain under the strict control of the states, which retain the discretion to the claims included in the debate. The integration of customary land rights or claims is incorporated in the debates. In contrast, land informality in cities, which, as discussed in this chapter, concerns the vast majority of the population in urban and suburban areas, is only rarely discussed, if at all. Background documents and proceedings of national conferences suggest that the terms of the debate are deeply influenced by the elite's vested interests in urban land. In short, for the most pressing issues voice is excluded, leaving little room for reflexivity in addressing competing claims for urban and peri-urban land.

The same weakness is apparent in the Land Administration and Governance Framework, which was initiated worldwide by the World Bank in 2010 and includes most West African countries: Only formal tenure is taken into account, which excludes the majority of the population in most countries from consideration.

Generally speaking, tenure regularization—other than land titling initiated by governments—amounts to the issuance of a precarious title or the creation of expectations for full-ownership title with respect to land that originally was part of the customary or other informal markets. Security of tenure—the main claim of the population—rather than access to full landownership is the core concern. The process is usually accompanied by redevelopment and the physical upgrading of selected informal settlements.

Available evidence suggests that in most cases eligible households benefited from on-site tenure regularization, but in some cases residents had to be displaced and resettled in other areas. Either way, they received an administrative document issued by the local authorities, which enabled them—upon payment of fees and taxes—to obtain a precarious title. However, such a title does not guarantee security of occupation in the long term, because in principle the plot can be taken back by the commune or the state if it is not developed within a stipulated time frame. Whether this is enforced depends on the local or national political context. An administrative document or precarious title only provides its holder with secure tenure as long as no other person claims ownership of the land by producing documents or other proofs of title for the same plot issued earlier. In case of eviction or dispossession, for example, for the purpose of infrastructure projects, landholders or occupants with precarious title or weak proof of possession will not be afforded voice to determine if and how they should be compensated. The rules governing expropriation do not apply to nonowners. Compensation then depends on unilateral government decision, especially when households facing dispossession are not sufficiently organized to express their preferences. In these cases, compensation is limited to investments made on the land, not the land itself, and displaced households rarely obtain compensation corresponding to the replacement value of their shelter.

Mali provides well-documented illustrations of tenure regularization of land purchased on customary or informal land markets in the periphery and rural hinterland of Bamako (Durand-Lasserve, Durand-Lasserve, and Selod 2014). Customary land can be sold in two different ways. In the first instance, the customary landholder will ask a private surveyor to subdivide his land (customary subdivision), and the plots will be sold on the customary market. Buyers have no more proof of "ownership" than an *attestation de vente*, generally stamped or authenticated by the mayor's office in the relevant commune. Subsequently, the land may be transferred or sold again. In the second instance, the *préfet*[25] will take the initiative to subdivide customary land—notwithstanding the fact that the law does not authorize this. Oftentimes, this subdivision is justified by the resettlement of households displaced on the occasion of the upgrading and restructuring project in an urban settlement. As a general rule, 20 percent of the subdivided land will go to the surveyor; 40 percent to the *préfet*, who will sell plots with an administrative document called a *bulletin* or allocate them to displaced households; and only 40 percent goes to the customary holders, who will also receive a *bulletin*.

Once the land has been occupied and developed, frequently at the request of the concerned inhabitants and sometimes at their expense, the mayor's office can regularize and physically upgrade the settlement by building streets. This often requires displacing some occupants. The original customary subdivision becomes a *lotissement municipal*, which ensures better security of tenure but is not necessarily authorized by the state. The commune then issues a *bulletin* with the number of the plot together with a map drawn up by the surveyor but without the allottee's name. The bearer of this document can apply for a precarious title *(concession rurale d'habitation* or *concession urbaine d'habitation)*, which involves paying "local development taxes"; typically, receipts will be issued for only a small share of the sums paid. Payment without receipts is one of the mechanisms that fuel corruption circuits within local and central government land administrations.

These procedures fall short of providing full ownership and provide only precarious titles. Many households consider an administrative document (*bulletin*) or a precarious title an adequate level of tenure security. However, because of massive fraud and high levels of corruption surrounding the issuance of precarious or ownership titles, a household's right can be challenged by people who claim title to the same land.

Tenure regularization is often presented by authorities and perceived by beneficiary households as a step toward landownership. However, most stakeholders find it difficult to fully comply with the legal and regulatory requirements for receiving a precarious title (which can later be converted into an ownership title) because of the length, complexity, and cost of regularization procedures. Other difficulties include corruption, fraud, trouble in accessing up-to-date land information, the limited processing capacity of land administration, and the often poor state of maintenance of land-related registers. As a result, the prospect of obtaining a more secure title is not necessarily a sufficient incentive to initiate the regularization process.

A further obstacle to tenure regularization in land is resistance against reforming the government institutions responsible for land administration. Officials in land administrations and surveyors, who occupy a key position and retain disproportionate power in the processes for access to land, have every interest in maintaining the complex procedures they alone understand, thus also maintaining a position of dependency for the citizens applying for regularization. As Balagoun (2009) has put it, land administrations "are committed to maintaining the current system to the extent that, by multiplying administrative acts concerning the ownership and use of land, it multiplies the opportunities to collect taxes, tax stamps, etc." These administrations exert considerable power over elites and decision makers, including ministers and members of parliament who benefit from preferential access to land and are unwilling to support any attempt to improve land governance and transparency. In all cities in the subregion, a considerable share of urban households' housing expenditures is confiscated or diverted by a few hundred actors involved in land administration, especially those working in tenure upgrading and regularization. The plurality of legal regimes, predominance of informality, coexistence of several land markets with different pricing systems, and inadequacies of land governance contribute to the very high level of corruption and fraud within land administrations.

Tenure regularization can reduce both the number and intensity of disputes. However, it can also be the source of new disputes, especially when the resulting allocation of land rights is considered illegitimate. Moreover, tenure regularization can also contribute to the improvement and acceleration of procedure for compensating occupants in cases of displacement or expropriation by public authorities. Regularization may weaken the land prerogatives of the state while giving it the legal means to acquire land when needed for urban development projects. Yet when the amount of compensation is unilaterally set by the public authority and paid long after expropriation has taken place, this practice disadvantages landholders.

CONCLUSION

This chapter has argued that the obstacles faced by the urban poor in accessing land with secure tenure must be studied within a methodological framework that takes account of the diversity of situations on the ground. The framework developed in this chapter helps identify the land-delivery channels and the modes of access to land for housing in West African urban and peri-urban areas. It emphasizes the relationship between rules and procedures laid down by the state on the one hand and social practices on the other. The vast majority of households cannot comply with the conditions fixed by the state and instead relies on informal markets, which do not comply with rigid state rules governing land transactions.

This pattern is particularly pertinent in West Africa, where legal pluralism is a core feature of land and tenure regimes. It helps explain why in most cities of the subregion 70 to 80 percent of the urban population lives in informal settlements without secure tenure and with very limited or no basic services.

As discussed, three main land-delivery channels feed urban land markets. The customary channel supplies a large part of the land available on the informal market, which is accessible to low-income households. It also provides—with tacit state support—urban elites and private land development companies with land, as this land has the potential to be fully formalized. These constituencies have the means to purchase agricultural land around cities, obtain ownership title, and—following subdivision— convert this land into building land. The plots will then be sold at very high prices on formal land markets, with individual ownership titles providing maximum security of tenure to those able to afford them. Bribes paid to members of the land administration combined with long and opaque procedures encourage such practices. This suggests that private land developers benefit both from the informal market and the formal market, where they sell lots at a price higher than the purchase price.

The public land-delivery channel allows for the sale or allocation of lots in public housing developments. Once precarious titles are obtained, these plots can be channeled into the land market. This channel also contributes to the supply of land for developers and for the formal market. This can take the form of public-private partnerships for projects usually presented as "social housing" (*logements sociaux*), which in fact are targeted at the middle class. The state also provides land for private developers directly. In this case, the land will be subdivided and the plots sold out on the formal market.

Private land developers operate at the intersection of all land-delivery channels and take advantage of both the state rules that apply to the formal market and social practices by which low-income households can access land without secure tenure in the informal market. Scarcity of land for housing is thus to a large extent the result of politics and institutional choice. Legal rules with which the majority of the urban population cannot comply contribute to scarcity.

Increasing land scarcity and competition reduce opportunities for the poor to access secure land for themselves. As informal land is channeled into formal land markets, the poor are priced out of the market and effectively excluded from secure title.

Low-income households may upgrade their tenure but rarely enjoy complete security tenure, given the cost and preferential access to power it requires. In the long, drawn-out process from informal possession to full protected ownership rights they are tempted to sell their plot on the informal market. Obtaining precarious title is an important step toward tenure regularization. However, this policy can backfire and weaken the situation of households that cannot provide proof to assert their rights. Moreover, low-income households may not benefit from an on-site regularization and may be relocated far away from their initial location. Access to landownership is often presented as the means for the poor to improve their standard of living. Yet the practices that result from property rights reforms serve mainly the interests of formal land developers, the elites, and the middle class.

Land-titling policies advocated by international organizations claim to provide access for all to secure tenure by reducing its access cost. They also advocate compliance with the formal rules and procedures, or the rule of law, as a means for creating a level playing field in the form of a unified land market. In the best-case scenario, all stakeholders should have access to fully protected property rights irrespective of income, social relations, or political power. Unfortunately, these policies fail to take into account the social and political conditions of the countries of West Africa, including the importance of patron-client relationships and social networks. There are no shared legal or procedural standards and no common norms on which a unified governance regime could be based. Policies that focus on titling and development of a formal market have therefore largely failed. It is necessary to devise a more appropriate strategy attuned to the complexity of access to land for housing in West African cities, in contexts characterized by fragmented societies, extreme poverty, and basic survival strategies by poorest households on one hand, and reluctance of political powers to recognize and accommodate competing claims on the other. This chapter has attempted to demonstrate the need for such a framework and the issues such a framework will need to address.

NOTES

1. "Informal," used in reference to a settlement or a neighborhood, means that the occupants do not comply with the norms set by governments with regard to tenure status, occupancy rights, planning, and construction.

2. UN-Habitat (2004) defines security of tenure as "an agreement between an individual or group to land and residential property, which is governed and regulated by a legal and administrative framework (the legal framework includes both customary and statutory systems). . . . A person or household can be said to have secure tenure when they are protected from involuntary removal from their land or residence by the state, except in exceptional circumstances, and then only by means of a known and agreed legal procedure, which must itself be objective, equally applicable, contestable and independent" (30–31). To take into account the perception of tenure security by people and communities, UN-Habitat expands the definition of tenure security by incorporating a degree of confidence that land users will not be arbitrarily deprived of the rights they enjoy over land and the economic benefits that flow from it.

3. Legal and institutional frameworks and social practices with regard to land delivery and access to urban land in West African cities are very similar to those found in Francophone Central African cities.

4. In its most commonly accepted meaning, formalization of land rights refers to the incorporation of a set of practices and rules within the framework of "positive law," that is, the law of the state. Accordingly, formalization of land rights aims to give them an identifiable legal form, either by transcribing statements or deeds or by establishing and recording facts. It encompasses tenure regularization, in addition to land titling.

5. Contribution on land markets in West and Central Africa for the "State of the African Cities" (UN-Habitat 2010); research on the social and economic impacts of land titling (Payne, Durand-Lasserve, and Rakodi 2009); evaluations of tenure regularization programmes in Rwanda and Benin carried out by the author between 2010 and 2013; a World Bank research project on the land delivery channels and system in Bamako in 2013–2014 (Durand-Lasserve, Durand-Lasserve, and Selod 2014); a study on security of tenure policies (Payne and Durand-Lasserve 2012); and a report prepared in 2013–2014 for the French Development Agency and the Ministry of Foreign Affairs on formalization of land rights and obligations.

6. As the term is used here, a "property right" is the authority to determine how a resource is used. It has a broader meaning than "ownership right," which is the

legal right to the possession of a piece of land. It refers to article 544 of the French Civil Code, which defines it as "the right of enjoying and disposing of things in the most absolute manner, provided they are not used in a way prohibited by the laws or statutes."

7. Security of tenure also depends on other factors such as (1) social recognition: a household whose plot is in a village, or neighborhood or settlement where everyone knows the occupants can expect some solidarity from the neighbors if their occupation is called into question; (2) registration of transfers, particularly in cases of inheritance; (3) mobilization, often organized by associations of communities threatened with eviction; (4) relations with the administration and political authorities, particularly political parties; or (5) land prices, as the high value of certain land can result in an attempt at land-grabbing. In addition, the validity of documents and property titles, including ownership titles, is often challenged and gives rise to many conflicts (Durand-Lasserve, Durand-Lasserve, and Selod 2014).

8. The percentage of national population living in poverty, that is, with less than US$1.25 per day, ranges between 50 percent (Mali) and 70 percent (Guinea) in all countries of the subregion, except in Togo, Senegal, and the Ivory Coast (African Development Bank 2011. A larger share of the poor appears indeed to be living in urban areas nowadays—hence the phrase "urbanization of poverty"—even though overall poverty has come down substantially (Christiaensen, De Weerdt, and Yasuyuki 2013).

9. World population 2012 as reported by the UN Department of Economic and Social Affairs, Population Division (United Nations 2014).

10. This general principle is being eroded along with the decline of the state monopoly on land and does not apply in some countries of the subregion, such as Benin.

11. Procedure by which the state cancels a community's customary rights to their land. This administrative practice allows the state to take ownership of customary land. It is legally justified by the presumption of state ownership of all land within its territory for which a title has not been issued.

12. Use rights holders can develop and build the land. Use rights can, in principle, be converted into ownership rights after the holder has fulfilled a series of conditions, passed through complex regularization procedures, and paid taxes and fees. A use right is evidenced by a title usually qualified as "precarious." They are referred to by various names depending on the country: *concession rurale, concession urbaine ou rurale à usage d'habitation, permis d'occuper, permis d'habiter,* and *lettre d'attribution.*

13. Registration procedures concern only ownership titles.

14. In Mali, according to the 2009 census, 8.5 percent of households (with no distinction made between urban and rural households) said they owned their land with an ownership title. In Benin, according to the 2002 census, the percentage was 1.9 percent.

15. A "commune" is a local authority governed by a mayor. It corresponds to the term "municipality" in English.

16. Djiré 2013.

17. Data collected by the author.

18. The African Development Bank defines members of African middle classes (without "floating class") as individuals with US$4–20 per capita daily consumption.

19. Middle class by percentages by country: 3.2 percent in Burkina Faso, 4.3 percent in Guinea, 8.1 percent in Mali, 8.8 percent in Togo, 11.8 percent in Senegal, and 18.9 percent in the Ivory Coast.

20. In Abidjan, 75 percent of the population were tenants in 1994.

21. Legally, the land is considered to belong to the state and not the customary owners from whom it was purchased, and it is the state that sells its property.

22. This program is based on the delivery of ownership or leasehold titles and must be considered as a systematic titling program.

23. *Direction des Domaines de l'Enregistrement et du Timbre.*

24. *Acte uniforme portant organisation des sûretés dans les Pays de membres de l'Organisation pour l'Harmonisation en Afrique du Droit des Affaires.* The new act was adopted on 15 December 2010. It canceled and replaced the previous act adopted on 17 April 1997.

25. The *préfet* is the central government representative at the administrative entity (*Cercle*) within which the *commune* is located.

REFERENCES

African Development Bank. 2011. "The Middle of the Pyramid: Dynamics of the Middle Class in Africa." *Market Brief,* 20 April.

African Union, African Development Bank, and Economic Commission for Africa. 2011a. *Land Policy in Africa: A Framework of Action to Secure Land Rights, Enhance Productivity and Secure Livelihoods.* Addis Ababa, Ethiopia.

——. 2011b. *Land Policy in Africa. West Africa Regional Assessment.* Addis Ababa, Ethiopia.

——. 2011c. *Land Policy in Central, Eastern, Northern, Southern & Western Africa. Synthesis Report.* Addis Ababa, Ethiopia.

Agossou, N. 2011. "Paradoxes de l'étalement urbain à Porto-Novo: Dynamique démographique et économique vs dynamique foncière." *Les Cahiers d'Outre-Mer.* October–December: 467–484.

Balagoun, P. A. 2009. *Conséquences des pratiques des acteurs fonciers sur l'attractivité et la compétitivité de la Commune d'Abomey-Calavi (République du Bénin).* 3ème journées de recherches en sciences sociales. Montpellier, France: INRA, SFER, CIRAD.

Bertrand, M. 1998. "Marchés fonciers en transition. Le cas de Bamako, Mali." *Annales de Géographie* 602: 381–409.

Buckley, R. M., and J. Kalarickal. 2006. "Land Market Issues: The Mystery of Capital Revisited. Urban Land Policy—Is Titling the Answer?" In *Thirty Years of World Bank Shelter Lending: Directions in Development Infrastructure,* ed. R. M. Buckley and J. Kalarickal, chap. 3. Washington, D.C.: World Bank.

Christiaensen, L., J. De Weerdt, and Todo Yasuyuki. 2013. "Urbanization and Poverty Reduction—The Role of Rural Diversification and Secondary Towns." Policy Research Working Paper 6422. Washington, D.C.: World Bank Africa Region Office of the Chief Economist.

Comby, J., and Gerber, C. (2007). Sécuriser la propriété foncière sans cadastre. Paper presented at the World Bank Urban Research Symposium on May 14–16 2007.

A revised version of the paper is available under the title: "Reconnaître et sécuriser la propriété coutumière moderne." http://www.comby-foncier.com/prop-cout -moderne.pdf.

Deininger, K., and G. Feder. 2008. "Land Registration, Economic Development, and Poverty Reduction." In *Proceedings of the 2008 Land Policy Conference. Property Rights and Land Policies*, ed. K. Ingram and Yu-Hung Hong, 257–295. Boston, Mass.: Lincoln Institute of Land Policy.

Deininger, K., H. Selod, and A. Burns. 2011. *The Land Governance Assessment Framework: Identifying and Monitoring Good Practices in the Land Sector*. Washington, D.C.: World Bank.

De Soto, H. 2000. *The Mystery of Capital: Why Capitalism Triumphs in the West and Fails Everywhere Else*. New York: Basic.

Djiré, M. 2013. "La ruée sur les terres péri-urbaines -un sujet supplémentaire d'inquiétude pour la gouvernance foncière au Mali." Communication préparèe pour la Conférence Annuelle de la Banque Mondiale sur le Foncier et la Pauvreté, March 2014, Washington, D.C.

Durand-Lasserve, A. 2005. "Land for Housing the Poor in African Cities. Are Neo-customary Processes an Effective Alternative to Formal Systems?" In *Urban Futures: Economic Growth and Poverty Reduction*, ed. N. Hamdi, 160–174. London: ITDG.

——. 2006. "Market-driven Evictions and Displacements: Implications for the Perpetuation of Informal Settlements in Developing Cities." In *Informal Settlements. A Perpetual Challenge?*, ed. M. Huchzermeyer and A. Karam, 202–227. Cape Town, South Africa: University of Cape Town Press.

Durand-Lasserve, A., M. Durand-Lasserve, and H. Selod. 2014. *Land Delivery Systems in West African Cities: The Example of Bamako*. Joint publication of the French Development Agency and the World Bank. Washington, D.C.: World Bank.

Durand-Lasserve, A., and L. Royston, eds. 2002. *Holding Their Ground: Secure Land Tenure for the Urban in Developing Countries*. London: Earthscan.

European Union. 2004. Task Force on Land Tenure Policy Guidelines for Support to Land Policy Design and Land Policy Reform Processes in Developing Countries.

Godin, L. 2010. Besoins d'investissements des villes africaines d'ici 2030. Agence Française de Développement et Cities Alliance, June 2010. A Contribution to the Joint Program Cities Alliance and French Development Agency "Financing African Cities." Paris.

Grisoni-Niaki, J. C. 2000. "Dynamiques foncières et immobilières. Explosion urbaine et développement local à Cotonou." *Annale de la Recherche Urbaine* 86: 119–125

Huchzermeyer, M., and A. Karam, eds. 2006. *Informal Settlements. A Perpetual Challenge?* Cape Town, South Africa: University of Cape Town Press.

Max, M., D. Diop, and C. Simmoneau. 2013. *Repenser les moyens d'une sécurisation foncière urbaine. Le cas de l'Afrique francophone*. Montréal: Éditions Trames.

Ouedraogo, H. 2011. *Mythes et impasses de l'immatriculation foncière et approches alternatives*. Fiches pédagogiques. Paris, France: Comité Technique Foncier et Développement.

Payne, G. 2004. Land tenure and property rights: an introduction. *Habitat International* 28: 167–179).

Payne, G., and A. Durand-Lasserve. 2012. "Holding On: Security of Tenure—Types, Policies, Practices and Challenges." A Research Paper Prepared for the Special Rapporteur on Adequate Housing as a Component of the Right to an Adequate Standard of Living, and on the Right to Non-Discrimination in this Context, Raquel Rolnik, to Inform Her Study on Security of Tenure. http://newgpa.org.uk/wp-content/uploads/2015/04/Holding-on-Security-of-Tenure-Final-2012.pdf.

Payne, G., and C. Rakodi. 2009. "Social and Economic Impacts of Land Titling Programmes in Urban and Peri-urban Areas: A Short Review of the Literature." In *Urban Land Markets. Improving land Management for Successful Urbanization*, ed. Lall, Freire, Yuen, Rajack, Helluin, 133–162. Washington, D.C.: Springer/World Bank.

Rakodi, C., and C. Leduka. 2004. *Informal Land Delivery Process and Access to Land for the Poor: A Comparative Study of Six African Cities*. Birmingham, U.K.: University of Birmingham.

Rochegude, A., and C. Plançon. 2010. *Décentralisation, acteurs locaux et foncier en Afrique. Mise en perspective juridique des textes sur la décentralisation et le foncier*. Paris, France: Comité Technique Foncier et Développement, Agence Française de Développement, Minstère des Affaires étrangères.

United Nations. 2014. "Economic and Social Council Report of the United Nations Human Settlements Programme on Human Settlements Statistics." Note by the Secretary-General. Statistical Commission Forty-fifth Session, item 4 (b) of the provisional agenda: items for information: human settlement statistics. 4–7 March 2014.

UN-Habitat. 2003. *Global Report on Human Settlements 2003: The Challenge of Slums*. London: Earthscan.

———. 2004. "Global Campaign For Secure Tenure: A Tool for Advocating the Provision of Adequate Shelter for the Urban Poor." Concept Paper 2nd Edition. Nairobi, Kenya.

———. 2006. "Owners Without Titles: Security of Tenure in Cities of the Developing World." Chap. 2.5 in *State of the World Cities Report 2006–2007*. Nairobi, Kenya.

———. 2010. *The State of African Cities 2010. Governance, Inequalities and Urban Land Markets*. Nairobi, Kenya.

———. 2012a. *State of the World Cities Report, 2012–2013*. Nairobi, Kenya.

———. 2012b. *Handling Land. Innovative Tools for Land Governance and Secure Tenure*. Nairobi, Kenya.

Werhmann, B. 2008. "The Dynamics of Peri-urban Land Markets in Sub-Saharan Africa: Adhering to the Virtue of Common Property vs. Quest for Individual Gain." *Erdkunde* 62 (1): 75–88.

World Bank. 1993. "Housing: Enabling Markets to Work." A World Bank Policy Paper. Washington, D.C.: World Bank.

CHAPTER 8

Redirecting Regulation?

LAND TITLING AND CAMBODIA'S POST-NEOLIBERAL CONJUNCTURE

Michael B. Dwyer

Recent debates about "global land-grabbing," although varied and wide-ranging, have brought clearly into focus the precarious junction at which neoliberalism as a development project currently sits. The transnational farmland deals that have proliferated over the last half decade seem to fit the definition of "innovative new solutions" demanded by the head of the UN Food and Agriculture Organization (FAO) in early summer 2008 as global leaders and food security experts looked down the barrel of rising commodity prices and growing unrest in food-importing countries (Lacey 2008). Calling for "joint-venture agreements between, on the one hand, those countries that have the financial resources and on the other, those that possess land, water and human resources" (Diouf 2008, 8), the FAO director general was merely putting a neoliberal spin on a long-standing narrative of increased production and yield. But there was a problem as well. Even if countries like China, India, and the United Arab Emirates were simply pushing the doctrine of comparative advantage— "outsourcing's third wave" as the *Economist* (2009) put it—to its next logical step, the kinds of deals being proposed made it clear that the global landscape of development cooperation was shifting. ZTE Corp.'s plan to develop millions of hectares of biofuel in the Democratic Republic of the Congo; large-scale Saudi and Indian investments in Ethiopia; traditional U.S. allies like South Korea and Egypt turning away from commodities markets and toward the direct procurement of foreign farmland: These were signs that the global food regime was being questioned by some of its most important participants. Even as neoliberalism's ideology of transnationalized, market-led development was being reinforced and expanded, its geopolitical center was beginning to dissolve.

After three decades of frustration and limited impact, it is perhaps not surprising that southern governments were turning to other sources—and even other models—of development (Nyíri 2009; Ban and Blyth 2013). South-south development partnerships had of course been happening for some time, but the scale of the phenomenon, alongside the growing clout of the so-called BRICS (Brazil, Russia, India, China and South Africa) nations' more widely added political heft, was distinctly new. Murmurs of a "Beijing Consensus," however ill-defined, signified that some at least were seeing a distinct challenge to the hegemony that the United States and its allies had struggled to maintain in the field of development for half a century. In Laos and Cambodia, where I work, it seemed telling that two World Bank land-titling projects closed ignominiously in 2009— ironically, just as the bank (along with the FAO, the International Fund for Agricultural Development, and the UN Conference on Trade and Development) was beginning to propose land titling as a key solution to the "landgrab" problem (FAO et al. 2010; Dwyer 2013).

This chapter examines the case of Cambodia for what it can reveal about the governing of essential resources at what I will argue is best viewed as a post-neoliberal conjuncture. The end of the World Bank land-titling project gave way to a few years of casting about in the Cambodian land administration sector and coalesced in 2012 in a radically different approach to land titling: a rural titling campaign rolled out in the year leading up to a major national election that was (surprisingly to many) contested in ways the country had not seen in years. Looking at the shift in land titling—in particular, in the geography and apparent rationale that post-2012 titling pursued—highlights at once an important regulatory moment that emerged alongside popular frustration with the allocation of large areas of arable land to industrial developers, as well as the profound limits that a reorientation of land titling faces if other types of regulation are not embraced as well. This situation highlights the possibilities of looking beyond not just the neoliberal development model but also beyond the limits of the vision inherent in the current approach. Such is the combination of possibilities and entrenched limits that I will elaborate as Cambodia's post-neoliberal conjuncture. The case, I suggest, has wider applicability as well.

In their introduction, De Schutter and Pistor provide a theoretical argument for why property regimes—even if they can be reoriented in more equitable ways—are unlikely to be sufficient to the needs of ethically governing the distribution of essential resources. Using the hegemony of market-led resource allocation as their point of departure, De Schutter and Pistor argue that more generalized regulatory regimes—institutions that are socially "thick" and responsive to the needs of society's weakest members—are needed to produce and maintain "a political and social context that allows for contestation of norms and institutional arrangements . . . where bargaining powers are not too uneven." In the case of Cambodia's recent titling campaign, we see hints of both the "voice" and "reflexivity" (by those at the bottom and the top, respectively) that De Schutter and Pistor argue is necessary. But as the case study in this chapter demonstrates, these hints have yet to blossom into an adequate response. This no doubt reflects the extreme power imbalances in contemporary Cambodian society, especially in the hinterland areas, the target of land concessions and the new titling campaign. Nevertheless, the ongoing commitments to titling and concessions as sufficient mechanisms to calibrate the Polanyian "double movement" between economic development and social protection (Polanyi 1944) highlight the lasting influence of neoliberal thought. If the post-neoliberal moment is to be truly seized, a more practically adequate set of regulatory efforts is needed.

The first part of this chapter presents the reorientation of land titling in the wider context of Cambodia's property formalization and development efforts of the last two decades. The second part reflects critically on the implications of the explicitly protective shift in the deployment of land titles and elaborates the need for more adequate forms of regulation. The third and final section offers a few conclusions on the importance of the case more generally.

BEYOND DE SOTO: THE REORIENTATION OF LAND TITLING IN CAMBODIA

Cambodia's property formalization efforts emerged from the larger context of the country's imbrication in, and gradual extraction from, the regional geopolitics of the Cold War. Following the extensive displacements of the Khmer Rouge period (1975–1979), smallholder farming resumed during the 1980s after the country was invaded and stabilized by Vietnam. Despite an official policy of collective farming, the new government recognized quickly that the horrors of the Khmer Rouge made this policy untenable and allowed smallholder agriculture to reemerge. Although the agricultural landscape was far different than it had been prior to 1975, due to both the wholesale displacement caused by the Khmer Rouge's radical collectivization effort and, during the 1980s, lingering violence and insecurity in much of the country, small-holder entitlements nonetheless reemerged gradually and locally during the 1980s (Chandler 1993; Gottesman 2003). In 1989, in preparation for the Vietnamese military withdrawal from the country, the government allowed farmers to apply for land certificates that would verify their rights to the land under their control. These documents—receipts for applications for title—meant little in the strict legal sense (they did not convey formal property rights) but nonetheless formed the first generation of property documents in postwar Cambodia.

During the 1990s, as smallholder agriculture continued to develop and expand, the lingering conflict between the remnants of the Khmer Rouge (operating from bases in the mountains near and along the Thai-Cambodia border) and the UN-supported Cambodian government gave rise to a substantial economy of timber extraction. This was deeply infused into Thailand's efforts to capitalize on the post–Cold War transition by turning "battlefields into marketplaces," often through the establishment of resource-extractive regimes with its neighbors, also including Laos and Myanmar (Innes-Brown and Valencia 1993; Hirsch 2001). In Cambodia, the mid-1990s' emergence of a large-scale network of logging concessions amid a wider context of insecurity and ongoing militarization created a rapacious logging economy amid a social and political atmosphere that was "neither war nor peace" (Le Billon 2000, 786). While the later part of the decade brought an eventual settlement to the military conflict, it also left a concession-oriented economy in which elite patronage formed a key mechanism for the "management" of state resources—a situation that articulated conveniently with neoliberal rhetoric of privatization—amid an extensive landscape of logged-out "state lands" that would later be targeted for large-scale agricultural concessions (Hughes 2007; Un and So 2009; Cock 2010).

These twin processes of smallholder agriculture and concession-based development were the terrain on which a second generation of property formalization emerged. These efforts—land titling and economic land concessions (the latter given the term "economic" to distinguish them from the logging concessions that preceded them)—produced a radically bifurcated geography of formal property rights during the period between the late 1990s and late 2000s (fig. 8.1). While the details of this process are beyond the scope of this chapter, the essential points are that land titling was largely aimed at individual households and, more importantly, tended toward areas where population density was high and tenure already fairly secure (fig. 8.1, shaded areas). This approach, while questionable from the perspective of tenure enhancement, was justified on other grounds, including handing out as many titles as possible—a goal geared toward the provision of loan collateral (see de Soto 2000)—and the need to build institutional capacity bit by bit (Ballard 2010; Biddulph 2010). As land conflicts proliferated elsewhere, however—largely due to the parallel geography of enclosure through the granting of large economic land concessions (fig. 8.1, areas outlined in bold)—this approach increasingly came under fire from activists, NGOs, and scholars who favored the prioritization of tenure improvements (ibid. Grimsditch and Henderson 2009; So 2009; Adler and So 2012). During the latter half of the 2000s, as concessions and their problems continued and lack of title became an increasingly prominent rallying point (e.g., Grimsditch and Henderson 2009; Bugalski and Pred 2010), Cambodia's land situation fit—and in some ways anticipated—key pieces of the wider "global landgrab" debate.

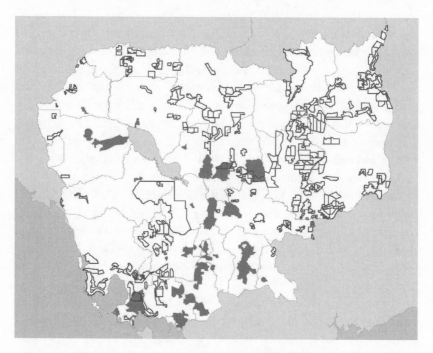

Figure 8.1   Economic land concessions (outlined in bold) and areas targeted by systematic land titling (shaded) prior to 2009. See text for caveats.

A radically different geography of land titling has emerged in the last two years via the "student volunteer" program described below and represented—in a highly approximate manner, as elaborated shortly—in figure 8.2. This reorientation begins, however, with two other land programs launched (at least on paper and in the public imagination, if markedly less so on the ground) by the rewriting of Cambodia's Land Law in 2001. The 2001 Land Law,[1] a major milestone in Cambodia's postconflict development efforts, included provisions for not only individual titles and economic land concessions but also for "social" land concessions and communal land titles. These latter two interventions aimed to address the land-tenure needs of landless people and indigenous communities, respectively. Given these ends, they were oriented largely toward the hinterland rural spaces, the former toward areas across the country where vacant lands were believed to exist, the latter toward the northeastern part of the country where indigenous communities (as that term has taken root in Cambodian popular discourse and law; see Baird 2011) were most likely to live. For a variety of reasons—often glossed as "bureaucratic" but raising a series of additional questions given the speed at which economic land concessions (also heavily bureaucratic) have been rolled out—the amount of land distributed as social land concessions or titled as indigenous communal lands has been miniscule. Describing the former, the head of the German land-sector assistance program wrote in 2012: "We can say today that the legally based distribution of state land to the landless and land poor has virtually failed" (Müller 2012, 3). Given that the number of communal titles distributed thus far is in the single digits,[2] this statement more or less applies to the latter as well.

An important exception to this anemic result is the "national" component of the social land concession program, so called because it is administered by the central government, in particular by the military, in contrast to the foreign donor program, which worked with provincial governments. This program has handed out what is by most counts more land than the donor version of the program—the German advisor quoted above put it at "a few thousand" families (Müller 2012)—but numbers are difficult to come by. One key dimension of the social land concession and indigenous titling programs, despite their uneven rollout and the opacity of the former's "national" component, is the model of distributing state land rather than formalizing existing property rights. Whereas the earlier round of titling was geared toward certifying existing rights (namely, the "rights of possession" defined by the 2001 Land Law), the recent reorientation

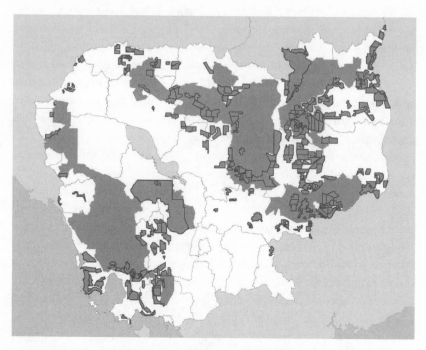

Figure 8.2   Economic land concessions (outlined in bold) and areas targeted by systematic land titling (shaded) since mid-2012. See text for caveats.

of "titling" to rural areas (fig. 8.2) is more in line with the model of state land distribution described above.

In mid-2012, Prime Minister Hun Sen announced a new initiative aimed at handing out titles in areas that were "once covered by forest, canceled economic land concessions, [and] existing land concessions being disputed by local villagers" (*Cambodia Daily* 2013b). Conducted by widely publicized "student volunteers" equipped with GPS units and camouflage uniforms (*Phnom Penh Post* 2012b), the campaign is a key piece of what the prime minister calls his "leopard skin strategy"—an effort to maintain smallholder farming within the wider network of economic land concessions (Müller 2012, 10; *Phnom Penh Post* 2012a). The precise geography of the new initiative is thus far quite opaque—figure 8.2 was made by shading in areas that are either former forest concessions, current or previous economic land concessions, or both, and was simply intended to illustrate that the types of land being targeted by the new initiative exhibit a significantly different national geography than the areas targeted previously.

The rollout of the new ("Order 01") initiative has been extremely rapid. Roughly six months after the program's launch, the prime minister announced that it had given out more than 125,000 titles that were issued to 74,066 families and covered more than 214,000 hectares of land (*Cambodia Daily* 2013b).[3] Despite their lack of geographic specificity, these numbers yield an important statistic: Compared with the 1 percent cited above, 214,000 hectares is closer to 10 percent of the area under economic land concessions (see *Cambodia Daily* 2013a). Compared with the miniscule results of earlier hinterland-oriented land distribution efforts, the new campaign is impacting—albeit in ways that are not entirely clear—more than an order of magnitude more land and far more than the "few thousand" households mentioned above. Indeed, one of the key dilemmas facing indigenous communities in the northeast is whether to take the new titles on offer immediately—an action that is said to disqualify them from receiving a communal title later—or to continue waiting for what many consider a safer, more expansive, and less divisive form of land tenure (*Cambodia Daily* 2012a, 2013c).

DISCUSSION

Two larger points are important for the purposes of this chapter. The first is that the spatial reorientation in land titling described above appears very much to be in a Polanyian mode of responding to a growing social crisis over the commodification—and specifically the illegitimate enclosure—of one of Cambodia's most essential resources: farmland. Hun Sen is famous for playing both sides of the landgrab issue, handing out concessions in the name of development (and in support of key political relationships) but also warning that in light of the violence of the country's past, the Cambodian peasantry cannot be pushed too far without engendering the real possibility of revolt. With the elections of July 2013 on the horizon, elections that were subsequently interpreted to hinge in important ways on land issues (Un 2013), many observers interpreted the new titling campaign as merely the latest in a long line of keen political moves designed to dampen the impacts of rapacious resource exploitation in time for upcoming elections (cf. Un and So 2011).

The critical side of this point, however, is not whether the campaign is "merely" a ploy to win votes but the degree to which it constitutes an adequate check on the depredations of capital and associated state power (cf. Polanyi 1944). Here the question is partly an open one, in that the concession polygons shown in figures 8.1 and 8.2 are not "fully formed" in terms of their on-the-ground enclosures. Although the population is comparatively light, at least four hundred villages sit either partially or entirely inside concession areas (fig. 8.3). And because of how concession polygons tend to be produced—*before* rather than after companies finish surveying the areas provisionally allocated to their projects—the polygons in figures 8.1, 8.2, and 8.3 do not represent land that has been alienated already but land where enclosure is still in the making (Dwyer et al. forthcoming). To the extent that titles arrive in time, they may help. Nonetheless, the heavier burden must come down on the other side, in the sense of titles being both too little *and* too late. The lateness is the more obvious dimension: Most (and perhaps all) of the concessions shown in the figures were issued before the titling campaign described above began. In contrast, the title-based regulatory approach outlined by the FAO and others in their 2010 paper on "Principles for Responsible Agricultural Investment That Respects Rights, Livelihoods and

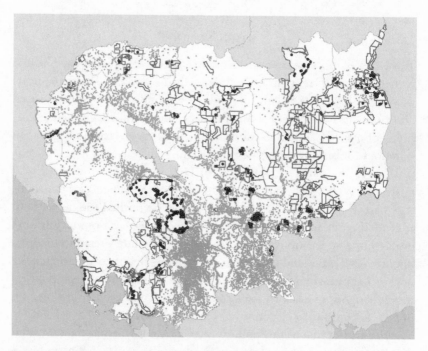

Figure 8.3 Economic land concessions and official village locations. Villages are divided into those whose surveyed point locations are inside (dark points) and outside (light points) concession areas.

Resources" has titles arriving *before* the concessions (FAO et al. 2010, 3). Indeed, if property rights in the areas in question were strong, the "land-grab" problem would by most definitions not exist.[4]

But titles are also too little, and it is here that the post-neoliberal label is perhaps most useful in the legacy sense of the term. The fascination with property formalization as a form of development intervention began (at least in its current guise) with de Soto's theory of the "double life" that formalization permits land to take on (de Soto 2000). As this securitization-oriented use of property has receded in importance compared with the ten-ure dimension, titling has nonetheless remained in place as a pillar of much thinking about how to fix the problem. The "Principles for RAI" paper, for example, begins by advocating the creation of "countrywide systematic identification and registration of rights" as the first step in realizing its first principle: the protection of existing property rights (FAO et al. 2010, 3; see also Dwyer 2013). This prioritizing of formalization as regulation is common elsewhere as well and points to a suspicion of the state that is common to both neoliberalism and many on the Left. As I suggest below, such a narrow view of regulation demands in many instances to be rethought.

The second point about the Cambodian case is essentially geopolitical. The great irony of Cambodia's current land-titling campaign is that it is following the basic geographical approach suggested in the RAI paper, but it is doing so just as the influence of the World Bank and other Western development actors seems to be waning. The RAI paper advocates titling land "countrywide" but concedes that "countries with limited resources may do well to initially focus efforts on areas with high agro-ecological and infrastructure potential and expand from there" (FAO et al. 2010, 2). In shifting its spatial target from the de Soto-esque geography shown in figure 8.1 to what I have called the Polanyian geography shown in figure 8.2, the Cambodian government is coming fairly close to prioritizing "areas with high agro-ecological and infrastructure potential" in its land-titling efforts. (The significant limit, as noted already, is that this is not being done "initially" but is occurring instead after more than 2 million hectares of concessions have been granted.) Remarkably, this shift comes more than two years after the end of the World Bank–funded Land Man-agement and Administration Project (LMAP), the titling program respon-sible for the titling geography in figure 8.1, which ended—notably—after a conflict between systematic titling and a state-backed landgrab in central Phnom Penh escalated into a World Bank Inspection Panel investigation and subsequent fight between the bank and the government (Bugalski and Pred 2010; Dwyer 2013). Two years later, an even more pronounced (although not nearly as dramatic) decline in Western influence seems to be occurring again. The same issue that led to the end of the LMAP project—the exclusion of citizens from the due process of title adjudication—was, according to an early 2012 paper by the head of the German land assistance program, on the immediate horizon for a new round of collaborative problem solving in the land administration sector. This included various "milestones," progress on which continuing German aid would be contingent (Müller 2012, 12). The intended timing of this project (Müller 2012) coincided to the month with the launch of the new titling campaign, and forced German Technical Assistance (GIZ) and the Technical University of Munich to cancel a summer school program that had been running for the previous few years.[5] After decades of influence, Western governments may be finally relegated to providing the "technical assistance" they have long offered—this time in content as well as in name.

CONCLUSION

This state of affairs may not be all bad. While the specific technology of titling is almost certain to be inadequate for the job it is being asked to do, the larger point is that the question of regulation has reemerged as significant, often in very public and even dire ways. Many of the proposed regulatory answers that do move beyond the technology of property formalization turn out both thin and narrow. Third-party certification, for instance, has difficulties following up on its stated commitments, as well as its narrow coverage of industries as a whole. Nevertheless, there are good reasons to believe that other regulatory solutions are becoming increasingly politically possible. Two interlocking arenas for ongoing engagement are clear.

The first is public pressure of a transnational sort. The scrutiny of international scholars, especially those who are able to treat the cases and regions comparatively, is extremely helpful, because it provides those who are pushing for more equitable forms of regulation and accountability at home with powerful allies far away. Creating and supporting additional fora (like the one that produced this book) that reach out into the networks of local scholars with access to policy makers at all levels would be a helpful way to continue to push these ideas and discussions forward. Similarly, getting the notion of practical concordance (i.e., the need to balance conflicting goals without compromising any) into conversation with the concept of the "triple bottom line" (stressing economic, social, and environmental outcomes) would help push both conversations forward. Perhaps most simply but importantly, reconnecting governance to the concept of accountable regulation in the rich sense of that term rather than in the thin sense illustrated above, would open up a whole field of questions that in many cases are far from current policy agendas or at best lurking around their edges.

Second, the explicitly geopolitical dimensions of essential resource governance may not be such a bad thing. One of the appeals of de Soto's proposition, after all, was that it let the global north off the hook, so to speak, both in calling global wealth redistribution politically dead and by conjuring a solution to underdevelopment by discovering untapped wealth beneath the feet of the southern poor. As emerging powers like China, India, and Brazil commit significant state resources to transnational "soft power" endeavors, they are beginning to put their money where neoliberal development would not: in long-term investment that, problematic as it may be, would not attract sufficient capital under the neoliberal model. The neoliberal model, of course, never operated in purely economic terms; it was, as widely noted, predicated on American power and as thus sometimes required politically motivated spending. But in many areas—Southeast Asia and sub-Saharan Africa, for instance, as contrasted with the Middle East and Central Asia—this type of spending has been in short supply. As politics emerges as a more normal piece of the picture, it not only becomes less of a dirty word. It is also an indication that the geopolitical stakes of southern development (and underdevelopment) are rising again as a global concern. And if Americans are worrying about what is happening in Cambodia again (or Laos or Mozambique), that is probably a good thing.

NOTES

Note on data sources: The figures in this chapter were created by the author using publicly available data and additional data graciously provided by the Cambodian League for the Promotion and Defense of Human Rights. More details are available in Dwyer (2013) and upon request.

1. Law no. 197/C, 30 September 2001.
2. *Cambodia Daily* (2012b), supplemented by the author's interviews, February 2013; see also Baird 2013.
3. For reference, the shaded area shown in figure 8.2 is on the order of 8 million hectares; the shaded area is thus only a rough proxy for the target area not the area actually titled (which is much smaller).

4. For variations on this theme of timing, see also the chapters by Vakulabharanam and Dagan in this volume. Dagan argues that property rights, if handled correctly, should protect weaker parties precisely by ensuring that their rights are recorded before any transfer or reallocation of assets occurs. Vakulabharanam presents an account similar to mine but involving titling in areas targeted for mining projects in India.

5. Technische Universität München, Master's Programme and Doctoral Studies Land Management and Land Tenure home page, entry for 3 September 2012, www .landentwicklung-muenchen.de/master (accessed late 2012).

REFERENCES

Adler, Daniel, and Sokbunthoeun So. 2012. "Reflections on Legal Pluralism in Cambodia: Towards Equity in Development when the Law Is Not the Law." In *Legal Pluralism and Development Policy: Dialogues for Success*, ed. Caroline Sage, Brian Tamanaha, and Michael Woolcock, 83–92. Cambridge: Cambridge University Press.

Baird, Ian G. 2011. "The Construction of 'Indigenous Peoples' in Cambodia." In *Alterities in Asia: Reflections on Identity and Regionalism*, ed. L. Yew, 155–176. London: Routledge.

———. 2013. "'Indigenous Peoples' and Land: Comparing Communal Land Titling and Its Implications in Cambodia and Laos." *Asia Pacific Viewpoint* 54 (3): 269–281.

Ballard, Brett. 2010. "Land Titling in Cambodia: Procedural and Administrative Exclusions." Paper presented at the RCSD International Conference on Revisiting Agrarian Transformations in Southeast Asia: Empirical, Theoretical and Applied Perspectives, Chiang Mai, Thailand, 13–15 May 2010. http://rcsd.soc.cmu.ac.th /InterConf/paper/paperpdf1_497.pdf.

Ban, Cornel, and Mark Blyth. 2013. "The BRICs and the Washington Consensus: An Introduction." *Review of International Political Economy* 20 (2): 241–255.

Biddulph, Robin 2010. *Geographies of Evasion: The Development Industry and Property Rights Interventions in Early 21st Century Cambodia*. PhD diss., University of Gothenburg.

Bugalski, Natalie, and David Pred. 2010. "Formalizing Inequality: Land Titling in Cambodia." Land Research Action Network. http://www.landaction.org/spip .php?article7

Cambodia Daily. 2012a. "Ethnic Minorities Risk More Than Just Land." 6 December.

———. 2012b. "Canadian Aid for Communal Land Titles to End in March." 13 December.

———. 2013a. "Arrests of Land Rights Activists Doubled in 2012." 24 January.

———. 2013b. "Hun Sen to Cease Delivering Land Titles." 29 January.

———. 2013c. "National Program Dropped Communal Titles." 6 February.

Chandler, David. 1993. *The Tragedy of Cambodian History: Politics, War, and Revolution Since 1945*. New Haven, Conn.: Yale University Press.

Cock, Andrew R. 2010. "External Actors and the Relative Autonomy of the Ruling Elite in post-UNTAC Cambodia." *Journal of Southeast Asian Studies* 41: 241–265.

De Soto, Hernando 2000. *The Mystery of Capital*. New York: Basic.

Diouf, Jacques. 2008. "The Food Crisis and the Wrong Solutions." *Global Perspectives*, October.

Dwyer, Michael B. 2013. "The Formalization Fix? Land Titling, State Land Concessions, and the Politics of Geographical Transparency in Contemporary Cambodia." LDPI Working Paper 37. Ithaca N.Y.: Land Deal Politics Initiative.

Dwyer, Michael B, Sokbunthoeun So, and Emily Polack. "Property Rights and 'Better-Practice' Concessions: Lessons from Cambodia's Leopard Skin Landscape." *Revue Internationale de Politique de Développement/International Development Policy*, forthcoming.

Economist. 2009. "Outsourcing's Third Wave." 21 May.

FAO, International Fund for Agricultural Development, United Nations Conference on Trade and Development, and the World Band Group. 2010. "Principles for Responsible Agricultural Investment that Respects Rights, Livelihoods and Resources." Available at: http://siteresources.worldbank.org/INTARD /214574-1111138388661/22453321/Principles_Extended.pdf.

Gottesman, Evan 2003. *Cambodia After the Khmer Rouge: Inside the Politics of Nation Building*. New Haven, Conn.: Yale University Press.

Grimsditch, Mark, and Nick Henderson. 2009. "Untitled: Tenure Insecurity and Inequality in the Cambodian Land Sector." Bridges Across Borders Southeast Asia, Centre on Housing Rights and Evictions, and Jesuit Refugee Service, Phnom Penh and Geneva.

Hirsch, Philip. 2001. "Globalisation, Regionalization and Local Voices: The Asian Development Bank and Re-scaled Politics of Environment in the Mekong Region." *Singapore Journal of Tropical Geography* 22: 237–251.

Hughes, Caroline 2007. "Transnational Networks, International Organizations and Political Participation in Cambodia: Human Rights, Labour Rights and Common Rights." *Democratization* 14: 834–852.

Innes-Brown, M., and M. J. Valencia. 1993. "Thailand's Resource Diplomacy in Indochina and Myanmar." *Contemporary Southeast Asia* 14: 332–351.

Lacey, Marc. 2008. "Across Globe, Empty Bellies Bring Rising Anger." *New York Times*, 18 April.

Le Billon, Philippe. 2000. "The Political Ecology of Transition in Cambodia 1989–1999: War, Peace and Forest Exploitation." *Development and Change* 31: 785–805.

Müller, Franz-Volker. 2012. "Commune-based Land Allocation for Poverty Reduction in Cambodia: Achievements and Lessons Learned from the Project: Land Allocation for Social and Economic Development (LASED)." Paper prepared for presentation at the Annual World Bank Conference on Land and Poverty, Washington, D.C., 23–26 April.

Nyíri, Pal. 2009. Extraterritoriality: Foreign Concessions: The Past and Future of a Form of Shared Sovereignty. Inaugural oration at Amsterdam's Free University, 19 November. http://www.espacestemps.net/document7952.html.

Phnom Penh Post. 2012a. "Largest teak nursery in Cambodia." 4 July.

——. 2012b. "PM's land titling scheme full of ambiguity." 6 July.

Polanyi, Karl. 1944 [2001]. *The Great Transformation*. Boston: Beacon.

So, Sokbunthoeun. 2009. *Political Economy of Land Registration in Cambodia*. PhD diss., Northern Illinois University.

Un, Kheang. 2013. "The Cambodian People Have Spoken." *New York Times*, 9 August.
Un, Kheang, and Sokbunthoeun So. 2009. "Politics of Natural Resource Use in Cambodia." *Asian Affairs* 36: 123–138.
——. 2011. "Land Rights in Cambodia: How Neopatrimonial Politics Restricts Land Policy Reform." *Pacific Affairs* 84: 289–308.

CHAPTER 9

_____

Erosion of Essential Resources in Neoliberal India

A BOTTOM-UP VIEW

Vamsi Vakulabharanam

The idea of essential resources (such as the means to produce a basic live-lihood) as different from other goods (private, public, or common-pool resources) does not arise so much from the unique internal nature of these goods (e.g., their inherent attributes, such as excludability or subtractabil-ity). Rather, the difference results from the fact that these resources are indispensable to the basic survival of the people who use them. They need to be governed differently than other goods, because we associate a value of moral repugnance to the withdrawal of these goods from the poor.[1] This chapter seeks to address whether it is possible to imagine a skeletal governance structure or regime for essential goods that could span mul-tiple spatial levels, including the local, provincial, national, and global.

In this paper, I work with the concrete experience of two South Indian states—Andhra Pradesh (AP) and Telangana.[2] Through the case study of AP's tribal economy and the peasant economy of Telan-gana, I discuss how the erosion of access to essential goods has gath-ered momentum in the past few decades. From this description, I present broader reflections on the question of devising appropriate governance structures for essential goods.

GRANITE QUARRYING IN THE PEASANT ECONOMY OF KARIMNAGAR

The Indian mining department makes a distinction between major and minor minerals. In the case of minor minerals quarried in plots of less than five hectares, exemption is given from environmental clearance and a public hearing in the area where mining is anticipated. Granite mining gets categorized as a minor mineral, which according to the law is currently exempted from environmental clearance and public hearing (Department of Mines and Geology, Andhra Pradesh; see www .aponline.gov.in.).

To mine granite, an aspiring miner first needs to apply to the Department of Mines and Geology, at which point there is involvement with local government at two levels. At the first level, a "no objection certificate" must be issued by either the local bureaucracy (block or *mandal*) or an agricultural committee at the block level. Due to persistent local activism in the Karimnagar area, local forest officials need to be consulted as well. At a second level, the villages under whose jurisdiction the granite hillocks fall need to provide their consent. At the village level, the local elected body of representatives (typically the village president or *sarpanch*) must grant its approval for the proposed mining activity. The rent share of the mining department (a royalty paid by the mining party) amounts to about 5 to 10 percent of the total revenue from mining; the local government does not receive any share of the rent (sourced from field research with the local mining officials in Karimnagar, Telangana, in 2012).

The political economy of granite quarrying is an important factor in the erosion of essential resources. In terms of its size and profitability granite mining is quite lucrative for those who hold critical control rights as leaseholders (owners) or regulators (Maringanti et al. 2012). Granite is extracted from the hillocks that dot the Telangana landscape, especially in the Karimnagar district. It is estimated that the size of this economy is anywhere between US$150 to 300 million per year (Maringanti et al. 2012). The profit margins approach 600 percent per annum on the total capital outlay (fixed and variable). After initial processing, much of the granite is exported by sea to China. Chinese buyers process and sell it in various markets across the world such as the United States, Japan, Singapore, and Indonesia, as well as in the Chinese domestic market (including for use in the Olympic Bird's Nest stadium in Beijing).

In a field exercise that my colleagues and I conducted in 2012, the mining officials informed us that more than 90 percent of the mining leaseholders are from the local state, Telangana (which has a population of over 40 million). They are either wealthy businessmen who have ventured into mining or local politicians who have considerable clout in the region. Part of the capital for the leasehold comes from public and private banks and part of it comes from the private savings of the leaseholders. The workers are typically migrants who work long hours for low wages. In field conversations with the employers we could glean that the migrants were hired partly for lower wages and partly because migrants tend to be less concerned about the deterioration of local livelihoods due to mining processes.

The leaseholders frequently pay bribes (a small portion of the total profit) to the local bureaucrats and the village-level leaders to obtain the requisite approvals. In contrast, the majority of the villagers does not obtain employment in the quarries or do any revenue from the proceeds. At first glance, they do not lose much either, since granite is quarried from the hillocks surrounding the villages. There is virtually no agricultural land on these hillocks the villagers own (from field research in Karimnagar, Telangana, 2012).

However, the negative externalities of quarrying contribute directly to the erosion of essential resources for locals. First, the blasting of the hillocks and the use of explosives in the process damages the housing structures of all those who live near the hillocks. Village settlements are usually ordered in such a way that housing for the poor (typically Dalits or the so-called untouchables, who are largely agricultural workers) is constructed away from the center of the village and closer to the hillocks. Second, waste runs into the local bodies of water, such as lakes or ponds or rivers, and thereby pollutes the water resources used by the villagers. Polluted water in turn results in various health issues and negatively impacts the livelihoods of fisherfolk in the village. Irrigation is also affected, since the contaminated water cannot be used for crop cultivation. Moreover, with the destruction of the hillocks, the drainage systems of ecosystems in the region are seriously damaged, undermining the ability of the soil to retain water. Third, quarrying affects wildlife habitats on the hillocks and causes wildlife (such as bears) to roam closer to the villages. These hillocks also sometimes house old temples that are considered sacred by the villagers. The temples are frequently destroyed in the mining process, which challenges the cultural life and identity of the villagers. Furthermore, the destruction of bodies of water, drainage systems, and natural habitats affects rainfall patterns and the continuation of people's livelihood in the region. The reach of the deleterious effects of mining is so great as to be felt by goats, custard apple groves, honeybees, and wells (from field research in Karimnagar, Telangana, 2012).

BAUXITE MINING IN THE TRIBAL ECONOMY OF
VISAKHAPATNAM

Unlike the somewhat weak legal structure safeguarding the peasant common-property resources, there are multiple constitutional and legal safeguards to protect tribal rights. The constitutional provisions aimed at safeguarding the rights of tribals and their livelihoods include article 342 of the Indian Constitution (on the notification of scheduled tribes), article 46 on the Directive Principles of State Policy (on ensuring economic and educational interests), and article 244 and the fifth schedule (on autonomy of the tribal groups). Further safeguards are included in the 1996 Panchayat Extension to Scheduled Areas Act (on the self-governance of tribal communities and their power to manage natural resources). Similar safeguards can be found at the state level, including the AP Scheduled Area Land Transfer Regulation Act (1 of 1959) as amended by Regulation II of 1970, which is aimed at protecting tribal lands. These legal safeguards notwithstanding, leases were being granted to nontribals. In response to this, Samata—an NGO working for tribal people in 1997—filed a public interest litigation in the Indian Supreme Court that highlighted the encroachment by nontribal actors on tribal lands (Samata 2003). The Indian Supreme Court ruled in favor of the tribals. The ruling stated that granting mining leases to private companies in the tribal (scheduled) areas was illegal. The judgment also stated that only tribal cooperatives or the state-owned Andhra Pradesh Mining Development Corporation (APMDC) could, with permission from the local community body, undertake mining in these areas. In 2006, a new law came into effect: the Scheduled Tribes and Other Traditional Forest Dwellers (Recognition of Forest Rights) Act, 2006 (hereafter FRA 2006). This legislation strengthened the protection of tribal land rights by stipulating that the safeguarding of forest-dwellers' rights and the conservation of forests are not mutually conflicting goals. This act also applies to the scheduled areas in India and exists alongside the other legislative acts that protect the rights of tribal people. Importantly, the rights over the forest lands include individual as well communal rights (see Prasad et al. 2012).[3]

The Araku region in the Visakhapatnam district of AP is considered a scheduled—or specially protected—area according to Schedule V of the Indian Constitution. This implies that nontribals are not allowed to occupy land that falls under the scheduled area. There are 3,564 tribal hamlets encompassing multiple vulnerable tribal groups in the Araku region alone.

Currently, tribal livelihoods in this region are based primarily on three sources: food cultivation, harvesting forest fruits, and planting of selected cash crops (i.e., coffee). The cultivation of food grains (coarse as well as fine grains such as rice) rests on the continued existence of commons in the surrounding forests. Food grains are usually cultivated on hill slopes with rotating cultivation. In times when grain fields lie fallow, tribals depend on harvesting to a greater extent in the commonly owned forest lands. Tribals also rely heavily on the forest for collecting food and minor forest produce, such as tamarind, pepper, and forest gum, all of which are then sold in the nearby markets. A state-supported tribal cooperative called the Girijan Cooperative Corporation (GCC)[4] buys these goods (mainly tamarind) from the tribals for a fair price. GCC was established to prevent the exploitation of tribals by the local moneylending communities. The local moneylending communities tend to be buyers too, and they charge high interest rates and pay below-market prices. In addition, the Integrated Tribal Development Agency (ITDA) has supported tribals in planting coffee seeds in small plantations that are owned by individual tribal families. During the initial years of planting, the ITDA even offered subsidies in food-grain consumption and so forth. Finally, some tribal families have also begun to cultivate other cash crops, such as cashew and turmeric (from field research in Araku, AP, 2012).

Tribals have relative autonomy with regard to their food-grain cultivation and collection of minor forest produce. When it comes to cash crops, however, tribals interact with nontribals as intermediaries. Nontribals have a strong presence in the region, mainly as merchants and moneylenders. These intermediaries profit heavily through credit-product market interlinking. In the coffee plantations, moneylenders provide loans while demanding a crop collateral. Their greater bargaining power allows them to extract very high interest rates (36 to 60 percent) in addition to any profits made from selling the produce. These interactions with the outside world notwithstanding, the integrity of the tribes has been maintained, mostly because of interventions by governmental agencies such as the GCC and the ITDA. However, this balance is now being challenged by attempts to introduce bauxite mining (Prasad et al. 2012).

In light of the previously cited Supreme Court Samata ruling, the state faced an uphill battle in introducing bauxite mining in tribal areas. However, the AP state government has found openings in the ruling to push for mining in the Araku region, especially since 2005. As mentioned, the Samata judgment allows for the state mining development corporation

(APMDC) to mine in the scheduled areas. The AP government has there-fore pushed for bauxite mining through this vehicle. Formally, mining would be carried out by APMDC on behalf of private companies. In return, APMDC would get about 1.25 times of the seigniorage fee paid to the mining corporation as rent and 0.5 percent of the annual turnover of the companies. The mining expenses will be borne by the private compa-nies (from field research in Araku, 2012).

The AP state has already entered into agreements with two major firms. One is an Indian firm, Jindal South West Holdings Limited,[5] and the other a multinational firm, ANRAK.[6] The state signed memoranda of understanding with these two firms in 2005 and 2007, respectively. APMDC still needs to obtain consent from the tribal village councils and the tribal advisory council. Although consent is still pending, a seaport has already been exclusively assigned for the mining purposes of the multina-tional firm. Efforts are afoot to construct aluminum refinery plants adja-cent to the Schedule V areas of Araku; these plants will become functional as soon as the mines becomes operational (Suchitra 2012). In all of Araku region, the state has plans to mine twenty-seven hills across a vast territory that will affect thousands of tribals. The AP state government is clearly act-ing in the interests of the private companies against a vast majority of the local people. This "mining face" of public governance contrasts with the "tribal face" of the government agencies, GCC and ITDA.

Another major challenge to the protective legal framework for trib-als is the implementation of the previously mentioned FRA 2006. The state of AP has deliberately delayed distributing individual or commu-nity land titles in this region, anticipating the bauxite-mining processes. About 160,000 hectares of Araku land belong to the tribals according to the surveys done by forest officials. However, according to the tribals, only 16,000 hectares have been assigned individual land titles so far.[7] In a field exercise conducted in 2012, it was found that the land adjoining the bauxite reserves had been exempted from legal titling despite legiti-mate claims by forest dwellers (Prasad et al. 2012). Tribal communities for the most part have filed claims for individual rather than communal titles. While tribal communities use common lands quite extensively in the forests, not all these commons have been claimed under community rights,[8] even though the FRA 2006 allows for it. There is also the practice of incorrectly assigning common land to ad hoc joint forest-management committees instead of to the tribal communities themselves (Reddy et al. 2011). While tribals have common property rights over the hills under which the bauxite reserves fall, these areas would fall under the community rights under FRA 2006. The strategic failure to distribute the titles in the areas adjoining bauxite reserves is a clear violation of the sprit of FRA 2006. As it currently stands, even tribals who have obtained individual titles will be affected through negative externalities discussed later in this chapter.

The conflict over bauxite mining has to be placed in the broader political economy that is unfolding in the region. On the supply side, the entire Araku region contains a wide variety of minerals—bauxite, laterite, calcite, limestone, mica, china clay, and precious red and white stones. According to surveys done by the Geological Survey of India, AP accounts for about 21 percent of the total bauxite reserves in the whole country. More than 90 percent of this is located in the Araku region and other forest regions of the Visakhapatnam district (*District Census Handbook* 1967).

On the demand side, due to the growth and rising demand from the aviation industry, the use of aluminum has increased tremendously across the world in the last few decades. The demand from Indian industry is relatively marginal as of now; instead, multinational companies have begun to exert a lot of pressure on the Indian government to grant leases to mine bauxite. The rising demand puts pressure on existing governance regimes for tribals and fosters the erosion of essential resources of tribal communities through different paths. First, the rivers that pass through the Araku region will be severely disrupted and contaminated due to opencast mining. This in turn will affect the livelihood of tribal communities in all the aspects described earlier: crop cultivation, minor forest produce collection, and coffee plantations will all suffer. Second, essential resources of the larger population surrounding the Araku region will be affected, especially the water supply of the city of Visakhapatnam and other towns in the region (Suchitra 2012). Third, since bauxite mining is typically opencast it will require the clearing of a large forest cover, with negative implications for the ecological balance in the region. Fourth, mining will affect the biodiversity for which the region is famous. Fifth, it will leave huge amounts of radioactive mud in the conversion process from bauxite to alumina. Current practice suggests that much of this will be dumped in open ponds and lakes, further contaminating bodies of water. Sixth, in our field investigation, we found health affects (respiratory and skin diseases) have already been noticed in areas where laterite mining has begun. From the above six points, I conclude that the negative implications/externalities are going to be significant.

Two broad inferences can be drawn from these two case studies for governing essential resources. Property rights regimes, whether those based on individuals or communities, have failed in both cases to safeguard essential resources for peasant and tribal communities in these two regions of AP and Telangana. Second, although tribal areas have much stronger legal protection, they have still witnessed the rapid erosion of essential resources.

Attempting to understand the various processes that cause the erosion of essential resources must therefore go beyond the local political economy and the specific property rights regimes assigned to peasant and tribal areas and the broader legal structures defined by Indian constitutional law. This is the question addressed in the remainder of this chapter.

EXPLAINING THE EROSION OF ESSENTIAL RESOURCES IN INDIA

A number of explanations can be advanced for explaining the erosion of essential resources in contemporary India, ranging from the inadequacy of property rights to broader explanations related to the transformation of economic and social relations in the context of global capitalism.

As discussed in the previous section, property rights explanations have a number of shortcomings. Individual property rights have been titled, albeit imperfectly. In the case of the peasant economy, titling was accomplished in the colonial period itself, and property rights have been delineated for a long time (Guha 1963). This has not stopped granite quarries on land that is supposed to be under the jurisdiction of village governments. In the case of the tribal economy in Araku, land titling is currently an ongoing process and is likely to gather pace in the coming years. Land titling per se, can be improved in the latter case, but even if this happens, it is hard to prevent the state and the mining department from mining in these areas, since the hillocks where opencast mining will take place fall under common property rights that are ambiguously defined. Moreover, titling is often offered as panacea for all the problems of the poor by the World Bank and other multilateral agencies (Mitchell 2005). Yet titling has often increased rather than controlled the erosion of essential resources, as title holders are unable to protect their titles against economic or legal pressures, and many are strategically excluded from titling.

Revisiting the governing commons literature may be useful to see if it can help explain the rapid erosion of essential resources. A lot of work done on forests—viewed as common-pool resources—through the pioneering framework of Elinor Ostrom (e.g., see Ostrom 1999; Gibson, Mckean, and Ostrom 2000) has focused on self-governance aspects of communities as the basis for successful conservation of these forests. This explanation may not be adequate, however, for explaining two cases of Karimnagar and Araku discussed in this chapter. In both regions, notwithstanding their very different populations and political economies, the forces of erosion seem to be arising from the Indian state, especially the government of AP, and from private capital (local or multinational). There is certainly room for improving the governance of the commons in both regions, but this is different from explaining the erosion of access to essential resources faced by peasants and tribals in both regions.

One reason for the weakness of common-pool resource management is the way in which it has been institutionalized in the Indian context. The primary logic of the current legal infrastructure is obtaining consent of the local governing body, which assumes that this body functions democratically. As suggested earlier, democratic processes are often undermined by bribes and the bargaining power of economic interests. In some cases an environmental assessment is required (e.g., mining major minerals such as bauxite), whereas for others exemptions are granted (e.g., granite quarrying on small plots of land). Compensation for expropriated use is often not available, since some activities do not result in overt displacement, and even where compensation has been promised, it has resulted either in unfair compensation or none at all (e.g., Drèze, Samson, and Singh 1997).

Moving beyond an institutional critique that focuses on property rights, I suggest that a political economy perspective produces important insights into the erosion of essential resources. In the case of Karimnagar, multiple quarry owners backed by the state and its mining division caused the erosion. In the Araku case, large private companies backed by the power of the state threaten the existence of commons and essential resources of the tribals. In both cases, invoking David Harvey's idea of "accumulation by dispossession" and the three mechanisms of dispossession he identifies offers new insights (Harvey 2003). First, dispossession operates through the acquisition of lands from small producers such as peasants, tribal people, artisans, and the urban poor in the name of special economic zones and other development projects. Second, public sector enterprises transfer their ownership rights to private players at below-market value. Third, and this is most apparent in the cases discussed in this chapter, commons are appropriated with ease, because the laws governing them are weak, not enforced, or tampered with by local and regional politicians.

There are important legal differences in how essential resources are governed in the two cases discussed. The tribal economy is much better protected in law, including constitutional law, compared with the peasant economy. Nonetheless, in both cases erosion is occurring amid weak resistance. While the erosion of essential resources happens at a rapid pace through accumulation by dispossession, the state government in this region has unleashed over the past ten years a host of populist packages, such as cheap provisioning of food grains, subsidized housing, or making private health care available to the poor (Vakulabharanam and Motiram 2014). This combination of primitive accumulation and populism (which is fiscally unsustainable) seems to have co-opted the population into these processes and has largely blunted resistance.

GLOBAL DYNAMICS AND DEPENDENCIES: OSCILLATIONS IN THE REGIMES OF CAPITALISM?

Why do processes of primitive accumulation come to the fore once in a while in capitalist economies? Economies seem to go through what has been termed in the literature as different regimes of accumulation. For instance, in the last 150 years or so, the global capitalist system has gone through oscillations between regimes produced through profitability crises and regimes produced through effective demand crises. The profitability crisis of the long depression (1873–1896) produced the regime between 1900 and 1929 (interspersed by World War I). The Great Depression (1929–1939) produced the post–World War II regime, wherein economies across the world witnessed increased intervention by the state, which acted as a stimulator of aggregate demand. Post-1970s, markets and primitive accumulation seem to have played a more central role, in response to the profitability crisis of the 1970s. Post-2008, the neoliberal regime of the post-1970s period seems to have gone through one round of major crisis, and various economies are still grappling with this crisis today. There seems to be an oscillation between profitability crises and aggregate-demand crises, with profitability crises typically producing regimes that have engaged in intensified primitive accumulation processes (see Vakulabharanam 2014) and witnessed higher levels of inequality. Aggregate-demand crises seem to produce some amount of progressive redistribution (such as after the Great Depression), and these "great trans-formations" seem to be a regular feature in capitalism.

The neoliberal period has witnessed governments acting on behalf of elites in appropriating the individual or common properties of the poor (farmland or other productive assets). The effect may very well be a long-term perpetuation of poverty, since a large number of the poor have lost control over their already meager productive properties (or essential goods) at a rapid pace.

When a regime change occurs, the strategies and learning pro-cesses that have been relevant in protecting essential goods for the poor become irrelevant. Therefore, it is important to keep in mind the struc-tural changes and crises that capitalist societies undergo, while thinking through the effective design of policies that govern essential goods. Is it possible to devise governance regimes for essential goods that transcend these regime changes?

DISCUSSION AND CONCLUSIONS

Governance regimes at the local level for essential goods need to take into account various factors that operate at different levels of articulation in the global capitalist structures and dynamics. A key factor is that capital-ist systems undergo institutional transformations. If, through painstaking efforts, an institutional configuration is created to protect essential goods, these institutions could get entirely overwritten or substantially weakened after a deep crisis. One familiar power structure that constantly reappears is what is called accumulation by dispossession. This is the structure that periodically causes a violent dissolution or weakening of the institutions that were created to safeguard essential goods. It is therefore important to ask the question: Is it possible to create a robust institutional framework within the available array of capitalist institutions?

The conclusion from this paper to the above question is negative. However, can we imagine a different set of institutions that are robust and independent from the oscillations of capitalism? This would require a whole other exercise to work out a detailed framework. I conclude with a gesture toward an answer without offering a fully worked-out answer. Part of the imagination around a solution ought to lie in the better mod-eling of essential goods with the involvement of institutions at the local, regional, provincial, national, and international levels. This should act as an institutional bulwark against the very working and oscillations of capital. Through concerted popular struggles, a different legal basis needs to be created that emphasizes equity and sustainability criteria (as the top two criteria) in preventing the erosion of essential goods. There are also deeper systemic processes that affect the entire global community and go beyond the considerations of the immediate local (such as the cumulative factors accounting for global climate change) that need to be taken into account. Another important part lies in the imagination of a production structure for essential goods that lies outside the functioning of capital. What this implies is that cooperative or other forms of production of essential goods need to be put in place that reduce the dependence of the majority of the poor on the changing dynamics of capital. These spaces may need to be richly endowed with the local specificities but need not remain highly localized and fragmented. They could be connected through alternative networks that link the local to all the other levels of articulation and span the entire globe. What needs to be imagined is a network of cooperatives that help one another in the form of credit, knowledge, and institutional experience with equity and sustainability.

NOTES

1. See also Olivier De Schutter and Katharina Pistor's introduction in this volume.

2. The Telangana state was formed by dividing the united state of Andhra Pradesh in June 2014. The residual portion of united Andhra Pradesh has now been named Andhra Pradesh (see Vakulabharanam and Motiram 2014).

3. In the years before FRA 2006 was tabled, there was an interesting debate between middle-class conservationists and advocates of tribal rights (see Rangarajan 2005).

4. *Girijan* literally means *hill people*, in this case, the tribals.

5. Jindal is an Indian company that was allotted land by the AP state. It will set up a refinery to produce alumina for exports.

6. ANRAK is a joint venture of the government of Ras al-Khaimah from the United Arab Emirates and AP-based Pennar Cements for setting up an aluminum plant in Visakhapatnam. ANRAK is supposed to produce alumina for export with an investment exceeding US$2 billion.

7. The information on tribal claims is available from the tribal department of AP.

8. *Community rights* and *common property rights* are used interchangeably in this chapter.

REFERENCES

District Census Handbook. 1967. Visakhapatnam, Hyderabad: Superintendent of Census Operations, Government of Andhra Pradesh.

Drèze J., M. Samson, and S. Singh. 1997. *The Dam and the Nation: Displacement and Resettlement in the Narmada Valley*. Delhi: Oxford University Press.

Gibson, Clark, Margaret McKean, and Elinor Ostrom, eds. 2000. *People and Forests: Communities, Institutions, and Governance*. Cambridge, Mass.: MIT Press.

Guha, Ranajit. 1963. *A Rule of Property for Bengal: An Essay on the Idea of Permanent Settlement*. Paris: Mouton.

Harvey, David. 2003. *The New Imperialism*. Oxford: Oxford University Press.

Maringanti, A., V. Vakulabharanam, S. Motiram, and S. Surepalli. 2012. "Tragedy of the Commons I: Granite Quarrying in Telangana." *Economic and Political Weekly* 47 (42): 10–13.

Mitchell, T. P. 2005. "The Work of Economics: How a Discipline Makes Its World." *European Journal of Sociology* 46 (2): 297–320.

Ostrom, Elinor. 1999. "Self-Governance and Forest Resources." Occasional Paper 20, CIFOR, Bogor, Indonesia.

Prasad, P., V. Vakulabharanam, K. Laxminarayana, and S. Kilaru. 2012. "Tragedy of the Commons II: Mining in Tribal Habitats of Araku Valley." *Economic and Political Weekly* 47 (42): 14–17.

Rangarajan, Mahesh. 2005. "Fire in the Forest." *Economic and Political Weekly* 40 (47): 4888–4890.

Reddy, M. Gopinath, Anil K. Kumar, Trinadha Rao, and Oliver Springate-Baginski. 2011. "Issues Related to Implementation of the Forest Rights Act in Andhra Pradesh." *Economic and Political Weekly* 46 (18): 73–81.

Samata. 2003. *Surviving Minefield—An Adivasi Triumph. A Landmark Supreme Court Judgment Restoring the Rights of Tribals (Samata vs. the state of A.P. & others)*. Hyderabad: Samata.

Suchitra, M. 2012. "Cheated for Bauxite." *Down to Earth*. Accessed 1 September 2012, www.downtoearth.org.in/content/cheated-bauxite.

Vakulabharanam, V. 2014. "Economic Turbulence in Capitalism: Twentieth Century and Beyond." In *Marxism: With and Beyond Marx*, ed. A. Bagchi and A. Chatterjee, 115–135. New York: Taylor and Francis.

Vakulabharanam, V., and S. Motiram. 2014. "The Dissolution of 'United' Andhra Pradesh: Insights from Growth and Distribution Process, 1956–2010." *Economic and Political Weekly* 49 (21): 59–70.

CHAPTER 10

Comparing Water Access Regimes Under Conditions of Scarcity

THE TALE OF TWO COMMUNITIES IN THE UNITED STATES

Michael Cox

In their introduction to this volume, Olivier De Schutter and Katharina Pistor describe and critique the dominant discourse regarding the role of property rights in governance, including environmental governance. This discourse divides economic goods and regimes into three well-known categories, and this division is usually accompanied by the argument that each type of good (private, public, common) is best governed by a particular property regime. These arguments generally play the role of "just-so stories" (Wilson 2007) about how particular types of policies are supposedly ideal for different types of goods or environmental problems. This term was adapted by Stephen Jay Gould (1978) in reference to evolutionary explanations of human behavior. A just-so story is essentially a hypothesis told in the form of a highly plausible narrative, which is frequently taken as fact rather than as something to be tested.

This perspective implies a very basic type of matching process, whereby characteristics of the object of governance—in this case economic goods—are matched with the governance arrangements that best fit them. One could refer to this matching process as a diagnostic analysis, which "seeks to disaggregate environmental issues, identifying elements of individual problems that are significant from a problem-solving perspective and reaching conclusions about design features needed to address each of the elements identified" (Young 2002, 176). Essentially, a diagnostic approach attempts to "fit" institutional prescriptions to problems that they have a good chance of ameliorating. While the basic logic and taxonomies just mentioned are useful, they are incomplete as a basis for a diagnostic approach to environmental governance analysis, which is still underdeveloped. As De Schutter and Pistor suggest, the matching process as it is most commonly represented leaves out several critical elements that are important to consider when examining the governance of what they call essential resources. One such element De Schutter and Pistor mention is path dependence.

My goal for this chapter is to move beyond just-so stories and further develop a diagnostic methodology by examining the role of path dependence in natural resource management, and specifically to examine the role that property rights can play in path-dependent dynamics. Understanding this role will enable us to productively shift the discourse of property rights toward a more rigorous diagnostic approach. After discussing some background and the concept of path dependence, I will develop this discussion through two brief case studies that demonstrate the role of property rights in path-dependent natural resource management.

TAKING PATH DEPENDENCE SERIOUSLY: ANALYTICAL IMPLICATIONS

An emphasis on path dependence (North 1990; Arthur 1994; Cowan and Gunby 1996; Heinmiller 2009) signifies a departure from the traditional discourse, which focuses primarily on maximizing efficiency, that is, allocative or Pareto efficiency, and the like (Weimer and Veining 2005). Path dependency has been seen as controversial in some circles, as it implies that current conditions in an economy may not be efficient or optimal but may in large part be a reflection of historical contingencies and distributions of interest and power (see Liebowitz and Margolis 1995). The perspective of path dependence is likely to value adaptability more than efficiency as a primary policy goal, or at least to value them in equal measure. There are many examples of the presence of a trade-off between maximizing a system for a particular goal and maintaining a level of adaptability in that system. In general, as uncertainty increases, we may weigh adaptability more than optimality or productivity.

Path dependence is present in a system when past events curtail current options for that system. *Lock-in* (Marshall 2005) is a closely related concept, and has historically been used to express how an economic system can become "locked-in" to the use of a particular (and potentially inferior) technology because of historical self-reinforcing dynamics.

Indeed, much of the literature on path dependence and lock-in was developed from a technological perspective (see Arthur 1989, 1994).

North (1990) adapted Arthur's discussion to argue that institutional arrangements display similar path-dependent properties. Pierson (2004) later applied these ideas to the sphere of politics. In more environmentally specific treatments, Heinmiller (2009) explores sources of path dependence in water institutions such as the Colorado River Compact, Araral (2005) describes the path dependence of irrigation aid in the Philippines, and Unruh (2000) has applied these concepts to explain how the persistence of a particular techno-institutional complex (TIC) has made it difficult to switch from a carbon-based economy. He states that such "complexes are composed of large technological systems and the public and private institutions that govern their diffusion and use. TIC's emerge through synergistic coevolution initiated by technological increasing returns and perpetuated by the emergence of dominant technological, organizational and institutional designs" (Unruh 2000, 826). The concept of a dominant design as the centerpiece of a TIC to which other elements adapt has historically been mostly applied to technologies, examples being the QWERTY keyboard and the internal combustion engine. I would also suggest that certain institutional dominant designs, such as the rule of prior appropriation in the U.S. Southwest to determine property rights, also exist and have spurred similar dynamics.

There are several well-identified sources of path dependence and lock-in. The ones I will discuss here include:

1. Network effects or techno-institutional complementarities
2. Vested interests
3. Sunk costs
4. Economies of scale
5. Transaction costs

Network effects, also known as coordination effects, essentially occur when two elements in a TIC are complementary to each other, such that the value or functionality of one is dependent on the presence of the other. A complementary relationship between two different types of elements is referred to as an *indirect network effect*, whereas a *direct network effect* would occur between two identical types of elements (such as between two cellular phones). Categories of elements can be taken from the literature on various types of capital, including:

1. Natural capital (soil, forests)
2. Physical capital (physical infrastructure, technology)
3. Human capital (knowledge, skills)

Any type of complementarity between elements of these broad types leads to some measure of path dependence, because it means that any element that is part of a network of such interdependency cannot be simply replaced without sacrificing the functionality of the larger network. Thus, changing one element may involve replacing the entire network of elements, which incurs high "switching costs," to use the popular jargon. Further, to switch from a dominant design can be extremely difficult, as elements of physical and human capital may have developed to adapt and reinforce the dominance of this design.

The second element is vested interests. A TIC serves particular interests, specifically of those actors who have adapted their own human capital to the existing elements. These actors, to the extent that they are self-interested, will act to preserve the status quo or potentially to even further entrench the system along a particular path to further their own interests. There is a particularly direct relationship between property rights and vested interests, since property rights regimes tend to advantage those actors who have the strongest rights.[1]

A third element is *sunk costs*, which are costs that cannot be recovered. Within the context of this discussion, the most important example of this is the costs incurred in the construction of large amounts of physical capital. Once in place, much physical capital is highly durable and cannot be replaced without sacrificing the costs that were incurred in its construction. This durability exacerbates the path dependence created by techno-institutional complementarities, even when a change in a non-infrastructural element would require the replacement of highly durable physical capital. Additionally, there is substantial evidence that human beings value sunk costs and are hesitant to depart from a path that has incurred them (Kahneman and Tversky 1979).

Fourth, economies of scale are probably the most widely known of those items on this list. Within the context of economic production they refer to declining average costs of producing a particular unit as more units are produced, due to the fact that fixed costs may not increase with increased production.

Finally, transaction costs are well known within the institutional literature as the costs of forming, monitoring, and enforcing agreements. Marshall (2005, 65) describes a basic typology of transaction costs that I will employ here. First, transition costs are transaction costs incurred in making an institutional or technological change. The higher these costs, the more path dependence is present. Marshall describes two types of transition costs. *Institutional transition costs* are the costs of "deciding upon and implementing an institutional change," which include "research and institutional design," as well as "negotiation, bargaining and decision making." Similarly, *technological transition costs* are those incurred in developing and implementing a novel set of technologies. These costs are incurred in the present.

An additional type of transaction costs are Marshall's "lock-in" costs. These are essentially costs that are created in the future based on institutional or technological change in the current period. By making institutional and technological decisions now, we may be locking ourselves into a current path if we impose onerous transition costs on ourselves in the future. They essentially reflect the extent to which current decisions lock a system into a certain way of doing things.

The distinction between transition and lock-in costs can be usefully applied to construct two basic sets of diagnostic questions that we might ask when we are considering making a property rights–based prescription. The first concerns how well the prescription fits with the current path a system is on. The second regards what effects the prescription will have on the future state of the system, specifically, how much additional path dependence will be produced as a result of the implementation of the prescription. This leads to two diagnostic questions we can ask of any particular intervention:

1. How does this prescription interact with the current path the system is on, based on the elements identified above? Would these interactions be likely to produce a positive result?
2. To what extent, and how, would the implementation of this prescription set the system down a heavily path-dependent trajectory?

Each of these initial questions leads to a set of sub-questions that are specific to the elements of path dependence. In the next section I will explore two case studies that demonstrate the importance of asking these questions. But before moving on, it is important to discuss the implications of the path-dependent view for environmental policy and institutional analysis.

The first point regards a dominant discourse in economics that has tended to view path dependence as something to generally be avoided and something inimical to common (and quite narrow) notions of economic efficiency. One common argument stipulates that, since transaction costs can impede the functioning of markets and market transactions, they are something to be minimized so that trading can ensue and allocative efficiency can be maximized (Colby 1990). This exact argument has been applied in the case studies I will describe with respect to water and water markets, where high transaction costs are seen as a barrier to transferring water from supposedly "low-value" agricultural uses to "high-value" urban uses.

I do not find the standard argument convincing, because I do not find the notion of allocative efficiency to be an unproblematic or "scientifically neutral" policy goal, given that it strongly weighs the preferences of those with the needed political clout and financial resources to express their interests in well-functioning markets. I have no problem with the goal as such, but I do not see it as value neutral, which the language of efficiency strongly implies, nor do I see it as one that should be preferred over many others that we might specify. In any case, I do not think that path dependence is something that can be avoided. If we like the path we are on, then we presumably want to *encourage* at least some measure of path dependence.

There is another way in which the emphasis on path dependence departs from standard economic analysis. Within the discipline of environmental economics (and applied/welfare economics generally), a diagnosis begins by imagining an ideal situation, usually the perfectly competitive market. The diagnosis then proceeds by analyzing the extent to which a particular situation departs from this ideal, and these departures are seen as evidence that one type of policy intervention or another might be appropriate for approximating the ideal.

In contrast, a diagnostic that recognizes path dependence turns this approach on its head. It proceeds in an inductive fashion from a particular social and ecological context and considers how it might be adapted to achieve a particular goal, keeping in mind the constraints inherent in the existing path. This approach is analogous to differences between "hard energy paths" and "soft energy paths" or a chemical analysis that starts off with observing the constraint of the "adjacent possible," which in a chemical context is all the possible products that a set of reactants could produce (Kauffman 2002). Simply put, recognizing path dependence means that we cannot start with an idealized abstraction, because we may not be able to obtain something that could meaningfully approximate such an ideal. To a large extent we have to deal with what we have and make marginal steps from there. With this discussion in mind we now turn to the case two studies.

PROPERTY RIGHTS AND LOCK-IN:
TIME VERSUS QUANTITY-BASED RIGHTS

In this section I describe two empirical examples of the role property rights can play in path dependence: (1) as a part of an institutional prescription itself, and (2) to set the stage for later development as a historical event to which a modern institutional prescription must adapt itself. The cases demonstrate these roles in the water-management sector of the southwestern United States. The first describes the acequia irrigation communities in the Taos valley of northern New Mexico, while the second explores the effects of the regime of prior appropriation on irrigators in the San Luis valley of southern Colorado.

Colorado and New Mexico, like many other states in the union, formally follow the doctrine of prior appropriation in their water-management practices. Prior appropriation is a "first in time, first in right" regime, meaning that whoever first applies water to a "beneficial use" establishes the right and the priority of use over other subsequent users. In times of water shortage in a drainage basin, senior appropriators—those with the earliest and thus more highly prioritized diversion dates—are supposed to be the first provided their allocated rate of flow. Only once their rights have been fulfilled do more junior rights holders receive water. In situations in which the senior diversion is furthest downstream, a "call" is placed on the river, and all junior upstream users must allow water to flow by to the senior. While the guiding principle is the same across these two states, it is important to note that Colorado is much more diligent in its enforcement of the doctrine. Calls on the river are commonplace in much of Colorado but relatively rare in New Mexico.

ACEQUIAS IN NEW MEXICO:
TIME-BASED AND PROPORTIONAL RIGHTS

An *acequia* is a community of irrigating farmers. The acequia farmers in New Mexico and in parts of southern Colorado are the descendants of the Spanish colonists who moved north along the Rio Grande from Mexico beginning around 1600. These colonists brought with them several Spanish irrigation traditions, most importantly the communal-management regime (Rivera 1998). Water within each acequia is managed communally, and compliance with community obligations is required for an individual to maintain his or her individual water rights. Thus, within each acequia, private-level rights are subject to communal rules and norms.

The great majority of the existent acequias are in New Mexico, specifically in its northern half, which is more mountainous and therefore receives more water. Taos valley is in Taos County, one of the northernmost counties in New Mexico. Taos valley, as well as the San Luis valley, is shown in figure 10.1. The orange line in this figure delineates the border between Colorado to the north and New Mexico to the south.

Taos valley is 2,070 meters above sea level and encompasses approximately 400 square kilometers. The acequia-irrigated area in the valley is approximately 40 square kilometers. The valley is bordered to the east and southeast by the Sangre de Cristo mountain range, which supplies most of the available water through snowmelt. Annual precipitation in the valley averages around 30 centimeters per year. The snowmelt water flows westward across the valley until it evaporates, percolates into the ground, or flows into the Rio Grande gorge.

Each acequia has a well-defined system of governance, led by a mayordomo and three commissioners. The mayordomo decides how water is distributed within his or her acequia and monitors for infractions. He or she also oversees the annual canal or "ditch" cleanings each spring. The commissioners serve several administrative, legislative, and judicial roles. They are frequently called on to arbitrate disputes and support the mayordomo in enforcing ditch rules.

The Taos acequias have been influenced by external government throughout their history. The most influential government agency is now the New Mexico Office of the State Engineer (OSE). This agency is required to regulate all of the water in the state of New Mexico in accordance with the doctrine of prior appropriation, which amounts to running adjudications in each basin to document each individual water right and the priority date assigned to it. This perspective on water rights is quite contrary to that adopted by the acequias, which emphasizes the equality of different communities' water rights, themselves being normally expressed in units of time or proportions instead of specific amounts or rates. Since 1969 the OSE has been conducting a water rights adjudication case in Taos to implement its management and property regime.

The attempted application of the prior appropriation regime to the acequia communities has been problematic, in large part because it represents a radical departure from the techno-institutional path on which acequias themselves had already been set several hundred years prior.

A critical aspect of this path is the use of time-based water rights, as opposed to quantity-based water rights. Within each acequia, water rights are expressed in units of time. Between acequias, the pattern tends more to use of proportional rights (although sometimes in units of time as well), dividing up whatever is available between acequias via physical structures.

The effective implementation of time-based rights within each acequia requires numerous adaptations that form a network of complementarities. In the acequias' case, these include the following additional elements:

1. Low levels of economic resources (historically)
2. Small community size (socially and geographically)
3. A large degree of spatial clustering
4. A decentralized monitoring system

These factors and the set of complementarities they entail are not an exhaustive list of the interdependent factors that have enabled the acequias to persist over time (see Cox 2013a). They do, however, interact particularly strongly with each other in that it would be difficult to affect one without affecting the rest. This is precisely what leads to path dependence as defined earlier. It also means that any policy intervention that affects any one of these factors could lead to problems by disrupting the network.

Rights to water in the acequias are expressed in units of time. Farmers either call their mayordomo when they want water or attend regular meetings at which they receive their allotted time to irrigate. In both cases the mayordomo maintains a list of who has the right to irrigate at what time. It is a rotation-based distribution system, and users are given water rights in proportion to their land rights. This time-based system is an important adaptation to the low level of resources that the acequias have historically had to deal with, since time-based rights are easier to monitor than quantity-based rights, at least with low levels of technology. The reason is that effectively enforcing quantity-based rights in the water sector would require installing stream gauges on every water user's main offtakes, which is something that the acequias (and the New Mexico OSE for that matter) have not had the resources to systematically implement. Time-based rights only require observing when water is flowing through a particular ditch.

In addition to this, the acequias' time-based rights help facilitate a low-cost decentralized monitoring system that helps them minimize the transaction costs involved in implementing their system. Because of the time-based system, members are incentivized to monitor one another when it is their turn to irrigate in the rotation. Thus they do not require external incentives to monitor conformance with the management system. Farmers who are geographically proximate to one another tend to indirectly monitor the actions of their neighbors (see another example of this in Trawick 2001). In Taos this process is referred to as "walking the ditch," whereby a farmer who is not receiving water during his or her turn in the rotation will walk upstream along the irrigation main ditch to see who is taking it out of turn and preventing it from reaching his or her headgate.

Decentralized monitoring is also enabled by the fact that acequia farmers have traditionally lived on the private parcels of land they irrigate, which are small in size and spatially clustered. These parcels all cluster near the river or a main canal and are contiguous within an acequia. Because of small size and proximity, it is not overly difficult for members to detect and confront those who might be taking water out of turn. The detection of rule breakers in turn effectuates sanctions.

For allocation of water among different acequias, the main pattern that can be observed is for several communities to divide the available water via a diversion that physically splits the water from an intake into particular proportions. Whatever water leaves the river and enters the intake is automatically divided up. These structures, along with the rest of the irrigation infrastructure (individual headgates, earthen canals) represent both a complementarity and a durable sunk investment for the acequias.

In addition, there are vested interests within the acequias to maintain this system. This has been amply demonstrated by the extent to which the acequias have fought the imposition of the regime of prior appropriation by the OSE. The dispute over this imposition played out via a state-run water adjudication suit known as the Abeyta case. The length of the Abeyta case (started in 1969, provisionally concluded in 2011–2012) also signifies the extensive institutional transition costs involved in shifting from an existing path.

Nonetheless, as discussed by Cox (2013b), it is important to mention that the acequias have in fact made a rather substantial shift from their historical path in the modern period. They faced a complex set of social and economic disturbances to which they were not well adapted. In the acequias current state, much of their historical techno-institutional path is at risk, and their future is in doubt. This is seen by many of the acequia members as a very negative situation, a point that underlies the previous observation that in many cases path dependence may be seen as desirable if it maintains a collectively desired state of affairs.

PRIOR APPROPRIATION IN COLORADO:
QUANTITY-BASED RIGHTS

The regime of prior appropriation has been more thoroughly imple-mented in Colorado than in New Mexico. In a way it has acted as a sort of institutional "dominant design": a blueprint for constructing a particu-lar system, which once implemented, becomes the regime to which other institutions and technologies must adapt themselves. Because of this his-torical process of adaptation, there are many existing complementarities of human and physical capital throughout the state. Large interests are now vested in the institutional status quo; as a result, the transaction costs involved in shifting away from the regime would be enormous. These facts certainly apply to the San Luis valley (SLV).

The SLV is located in south-central Colorado (see fig. 10.1) and has a population of approximately 45,000 mostly rural residents. It is much larger than the Taos valley and is similarly bordered by the Sangre de Cristo mountain range to the east, with the San Juan Mountains to the west. The mountain valley floor sits at around 2,300 meters above sea level and spans roughly 2,000 square kilometers. The valley receives little rain, with just 15–25 centimeters falling annually. As in Taos, agriculture in the arid region depends heavily on water from the nearby mountains for irrigation. There are two aquifers, one that is shallow and "unconfined" and a second that is confined and believed to be largely disconnected from surface flows.

As part of a larger project exploring adaptation to changing snowmelt regimes in the Southwest, Cody et al. (2013) describe the evolving path dependence in the SLV. My discussion of this case is mostly based on my involvement in that project and the narrative that Cody and colleagues present. Unlike in the Taos valley, the regime of prior appropriation has a history of strong enforcement in the SLV. Water rights are denominated in rates of flow, specifically, cubic feet per second. Each ditch company and every other type of water user in the valley has a water right assigned to it, and this has a particular priority date that establishes the hierarchy of rights in the valley. There is an extensive system of monitoring and enforcement, led by specialized state employees, that quantitatively moni-tors water use and ensures that in times of shortage senior water rights holders receive their water before junior water rights holders do. There are therefore extensive complementarities between property rights and human and physical capital built into the regime. This human capital is again

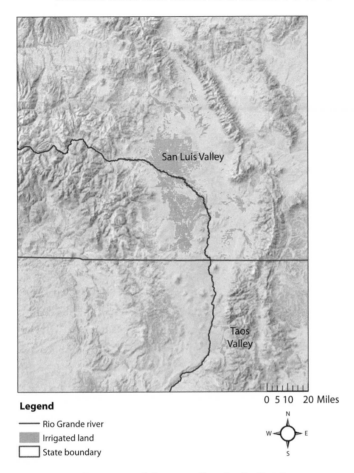

Figure 10.1   Locations of the two valleys in the Southwest.

associated with vested interests in the status quo. In parts of the valley that are installing wireless telemetry systems to increase the efficacy of water-use monitoring, these complementarities are likely to increase.

The SLV has experienced several significant droughts, one of which occurred in the early 1950s. Cody and coworkers present evidence indicating that the doctrine of prior appropriation incentivized individual-level, as opposed to collective, responses to this drought. This individual response was to construct private groundwater wells and to pump water from the shallow aquifer in the valley. The reason that the regime of prior appropriation may have encouraged individual-level responses is that senior rights holders had little incentive to coordinate with junior rights holders to reduce surface-water abstractions, since the amount of water they received was guaranteed and not dependent on fulfilling any social obligations. The junior rights holders were thus left with little recourse but to adapt individually, that is, to suffer through droughts or abandon their farms.

Digging wells and center-pivot sprinkler systems introduced new technologies into an already comparatively technology-heavy governance regime. This gave rise to new techno-institutional complementarities and also strengthened a second element of path dependence: durable sunk costs. It also allowed for agricultural expansion by existing as well as by new users, thereby further strengthening vested interests in the system. To some extent, this adaptation also introduced economies of scale, since each center-pivot system, an irrigation technology in which sprinklers rotate around a central pivot generally located over a private well, incurs a fixed cost and can cover a set area, incentivizing farmers to use a quantity of water that can irrigate this entire area.

In part because of this earlier adaptation to preexisting property regimes, the response to another series of droughts in the 2000s was again to resort to groundwater, but in increased amounts. Because of the severity of the drought, this time it had dire consequences for the state of the unconfined aquifer, which declined precipitously as a result. An interesting twist in the last decade has been an attempt among some members of the valley to impose strong restrictions on groundwater use through the development of a groundwater subdistrict. This can be interpreted as a response of vested interests in the valley and their realization that the current path, in particular its indirect dependence on groundwater, had become untenable. It remains to be seen, however, whether this response is too little too late, or whether the users in the valley can adapt from the individualized path that results in rapid resource depletion, which they have set themselves on since the 1950s (or much earlier, if we count the advent of prior appropriation). Many of the farmers interviewed in the valley indicated that they doubted whether the charges imposed for groundwater pumping would be sufficient to deter overuse of the aquifer system.

CONCLUSION

The two cases exemplify two very different property rights regimes with ramifications for other attributes of the systems as presented in table 10.1.

Table 10.1   Comparison of the two cases

	Taos Valley	San Luis Valley
State	New Mexico	Colorado
Regime	Mostly time based	Mostly quantity based
Institutional basis	Community based	State run
Lock-in	Lower	Higher
Monitoring technology	Minimal	Extensive
Groundwater development	Minimal	Extensive
Economies of scale	Lower	Higher
Productivity	Lower	Higher
Vested interests	Lower	Higher
Complementarities	Lower	Higher
Transaction costs	Lower	Higher
Sunk costs	Lower	Higher
Sustainability	Higher	Lower
Equity	Higher	Lower
Vulnerability to water markets	Higher	Lower

Compared with Taos, the SLV is much more locked in to a particular path, as qualitatively measured by each of the subelements of path dependence identified earlier. While Taos has nontrivial amounts of these elements, each exerts a much greater presence in the SLV system. The SLV has more technology implemented in monitoring and groundwater extraction, and some of this takes advantage of economies of scale. This in turn makes it more productive and creates strong economic interests in favor of the status quo. There is therefore a strong set of complementarities in the SLV that are less present in the Taos case.

The SLV system is also less sustainable than the Taos system, at least as measured by total and per capita consumption of groundwater. The Taos acequias make some use of groundwater, but they do not have an extensive system of wells, and as a result, there is of yet no evidence of overextraction. The Taos system is also more equitable as measured by the heterogeneity of water rights among communities. The picture would look a bit hazier, however, if intracommunity water allocation was taken into account, as documents produced as a part of the Abeyta case show a fairly high amount of heterogeneity in the amount of water rights held by individual users. Finally, if we look at the last row in the table, the SLV system has proven to be much less vulnerable to the pressures of external water markets than the Taos acequias. This is due to the strength of the vested interests in the SLV and the political will and power they hold, which also relates to their productivity and economic strength. Water markets have, however, proven to be an important disturbance to the Taos acequias.

Overall, this simple comparative analysis reinforces the idea that judging the performance of a particular institutional property regime is multidimensional and quite complex. At best we can hope for synergies among the outcomes that we value, but in some cases we may face trade-offs between important outcomes (such as adaptability and productivity, as stressed in this chapter).

Based on the analysis in this chapter, an interesting question to ask is: Which of these two property rights regimes is better suited to adapt technologically and institutionally to new challenges? Acheson and Wilson (1996) in their comparison of community-based and bureaucracy-managed fisheries make perhaps the strongest argument in favor of the adaptive advantages of what they refer to as "parametric management." This is a generalization of time-based rights that include any rights that stipulate *how* a resource is to be extracted rather than *how much* is to be extracted.[2] In addition to determining for how much time someone can use a resource, parametric management prescribes permitted technologies and where within a resource system extractive activities can take place. Acheson and Wilson (1996) contrast this with "numerical management," which prescribes how much of a resource is extracted.

Parametric management seems, at least superficially, to be consonant with the argument developed in this chapter that we should concern ourselves less with achieving a particular outcome and instead focus more on the capacity to adapt to continually developing circumstances. Furthermore, numerical systems tend to be more cost intensive. To effectively implement a numerical management regime, more environmental information will be needed in many cases than for a parametric regime. This environmental information requires additional levels of technology; greater technological intensity is likely to create additional lock-in via techno-institutional complementarities.

Still, it may be that numerical management has advantages in achieving greater adaptation, provided the required technology is available at reasonable costs. With the information provided by such technologies we may in fact be able to adapt to changing conditions more effectively. Many systems have shown to be more effective in managing scarce resources when technology helps establish a common understanding regarding the condition of the resource. Finally, quantity-based rights that are specified in proportions to the total amount available, while still numerical in formal terms, may be more adaptable and require less technology, as long as it is possible to establish the total amount available and the proportions for different users. For fisheries this is enormously difficult, while for the acequias and for water regimes it may be less so.

As can be seen, the answer to the above question is not clear-cut. Regardless of these comparisons, the notion of path dependence has two strong implications for our ability to make useful institutional prescriptions. The first implication is that every systems is constrained by history and cannot easily vault from a current path into an entirely different configuration or state. It follows that any prescription based on a diagnosis of the current state of affairs is inherently limited. Given path dependence, it makes little sense to prescribe a particular change in the system without acknowledging the limitations to such a change imposed by past choices and events. This is a lesson that the New Mexico OSE has been confronting since it began to impose its own property rights regime onto the acequias.

Thus, current practices (institutions, technologies) can become self-reinforcing. In the Southwest the regime of prior appropriation has value merely because of the enormous amount of adaptation that has occurred since it was implemented. To depart from it now would incur substantial costs throughout the state of Colorado. Many scholars studying community-based systems are accustomed to thinking about the inherent value of local customs and resource-management practices such as those of the acequias, but in the context of strong complementarities this inherent value is potentially generalizable to more complex systems.

There is another conclusion that follows from the above analysis, which has been discussed at length among scholars interested in resilience, adaptive management, and other similar processes: An intervention aimed at solving a problem must take into account the possibility that this intervention will create future lock-ins. Unfortunately, this has been historically underemphasized, as dominant institutional designs have frequently been imposed without much consideration of the vested interests and complementarities they would encourage. The perspective of path dependence indicates that, rather than insisting on the imposition of such dominant designs, any prescription of new institutions or related policies must take into account our limited ability to predict future events and thus must be seen as part of a process of ongoing experimentation, as opposed to a one-off optimization effort. Path dependence also has implications for academic research, to which I now turn.

The discussion above suggests that future research should be directed toward understanding what institutional conditions encourage lock-in or adaptability. We are perhaps fundamentally limited in our ability to predict how current decisions create future lock-in conditions, or by what scientists studying complexity and chaos refer to as "sensitivity to initial conditions." This phenomenon describes the extent to which small changes in the parameters of a model can self-reinforce over time to lead to widely divergent outcomes. While usually applied to purely physical systems, the same observation has been made with respect to social systems, in which "specific patterns of timing and sequence matter; starting from similar conditions a range of social outcomes is often possible; large consequences may result from relatively 'small' or contingent events" (Pierson 2004, 18).

One response to this problem could be to say that we simply need more data, specifically longitudinal and panel data to document patterns over time. Statistical explorations of serial autocorrelation are perhaps the most well-established way within the social sciences of examining how the past influences the future. But statistical correlations will not capture the complex ways in which systems develop over time along one path or another. This is because their ability to detect path dependence depends on this dependence being quantitatively measurable along a particular dimension, and it is not at all clear that this is always (or usually) the case. Moreover, obtaining high-quality longitudinal data relevant to the study of human-environment interactions is frequently prohibitively expensive.

Alternatively, the case study approach has also been championed as one way to examine change over time (see George and Bennett 2005). In particular, the idea of "process tracing" has been put forward as an "analytic tool for drawing descriptive and causal inferences from diagnostic pieces of evidence—often understood as part of a temporal sequence of events or phenomena" (Collier 2011, 824). Bennett and Elman (2006) argue that within-case process tracing–based methods offer unique advantages in their ability to unpack causal complexity and the historical contingencies involved in path dependence.

There is certainly merit in these ideas, and it is likely that both statistical and small-n comparative analysis along with within-case process-tracing methods have a role to play. A historical weakness of case study methods and the particular method of process tracing has been a lack of detailed protocols and standardization that would enable the comparison of multiple applications. Recent developments, however, indicate that a systematic review of process-tracing methods is feasible (Beach and Pedersen 2013).

In any case, I would argue that in order to address the diagnostic questions posed earlier with respect to property rights and to understand how current decisions can affect our ability to adapt in the future, we have to look at how past decisions have affected our ability to adapt in the present. The task may be somewhat similar to scholars studying the evolution of particular species. In each situation, we are faced with a tremendous challenge in trying to predict how current events will affect future processes (such as the future evolution of a species). In describing how institutional analysis ought to be done, Hodgson (1998, 168) draws a direct comparison between examining institutions and biological evolution. He states:

> These ideas facilitate a strong impetus toward specific and historically located approaches to analysis. In this respect there is an affinity between institutionalism and biology. Evolutionary biology has a few laws or general principles by which origin and development can be explained. Analysis of the evolution of a specific organism requires detailed data concerning the organism and its environment, and also specific explanations relevant to the species under consideration. Evolutionary biology requires both specific and general theories.

I agree with the sentiment expressed here. The complexity involved in institutional development and path dependence requires that we maintain a certain level of specificity (which imposes limitations on generalizability) in our examination of these processes. However, to do so in a scientifically rigorous fashion requires that we use a consistent set of "general principles" (such as the concepts outlined earlier) that describe sources of path dependence. A balance between specificity and generality must be struck in order to compare the complex historical contingencies present across similar sets of cases.

NOTES

I gratefully acknowledge support for this work from the National Science Foundation through grant number 1115009.

1. See Hanoch Dagan in this volume for an analysis of different property rights regimes, including some that seek to balance interests of different constituencies.

2. For an elaboration on this point see also Edella Schlager in this volume.

REFERENCES

Acheson, J. M., and Wilson, J. A. 1996. "Order Out of Chaos: The Case for Parametric Fisheries Management." *American Anthropologist* 98 (3): 579–594.

Araral, E. 2005. "Bureaucratic Incentives, Path Dependence, and Foreign Aid: An Empirical Institutional Analysis of Irrigation in the Philippines." *Policy Sciences* 38 (2/3): 131–157.

Arthur, B. 1994. *Increasing Returns and Path Dependence in the Economy.* Ann Arbor: University of Michigan Press.

Arthur, B. W. 1989. "Competing Technologies, Increasing Returns, and Lock-In by Historical Events." *Economic Journal* 97: 642–665.

Beach, D., and R. B. Pedersen. 2013. *Process-Tracing Methods: Foundations and Guidelines.* Ann Arbor: University of Michigan Press.

Bennett, A., and C. Elman. 2006. "Complex Causal Relations and Case Study Methods: The Example of Path Dependence." *Political Analysis* 14: 250–267.

Cody, K., S. M. Smith, M. Cox, and K. Andersson. 2013. "Emergence of Collective Action in a Groundwater Commons: Irrigators in the San Luis Valley of Colorado." In *Society and Natural Resources.* http://www.tandfonline.com/doi/abs/10.1080/08941920.2014.970736#.VQtWWo7F_wy.

Colby, Bonnie G. 1990. "Transactions Costs and Efficiency in Western Water Allocation." *American Journal of Agricultural Economics* 72 (5): 1184–1192.

Collier, D. 2011. "Understanding Process Tracing." *PS: Political Science and Politics* 44 (4): 823–830.

Cowan, Robin, and Philip Gunby. 1996. "Sprayed to Death: Path Dependence, Lock-In and Pest Control Strategies." *Economic Journal* 106 (436): 521–542.

Cox, M. 2013a. "Applying a Social-Ecological System Framework to the Study of the Taos Acequia Irrigation System." *Human Ecology* 42 (2): 311–324.

Cox, M. 2013b. "Modern Disturbances to a Long-lasting Community-based Resource Management System: the Taos Valley Acequias." *Global Environmental Change* 24: 213–222.

George, A. L., and A. Bennett. 2005. *Case Studies and Theory Development in the Social Sciences.* Cambridge, Mass.: MIT Press.

Gould, S. J. 1978. "Sociobiology: The Art of Storytelling." *New Scientist* 80: 530–533.

Heinmiller, B. T. 2009. "Path Dependency and Collective Action in Common Pool Governance." *International Journal of the Commons* 3 (1): 131–147.

Hodgson, G. 1998. "The Approach of Institutional Economics." *Journal of Economic Literature* 36 (1): 166–192.

Kahneman, D., and A. Tversky. 1979. "Prospect Theory: An Analysis of Decision Under Risk." *Econometrica* 47: 263–291.

Kauffman, S. 2002. *Investigations.* New York: Oxford University Press.

Liebowitz, S. J., and S. E. Margolis. 1995. "Path Dependence, Lock-In, and History." *Journal of Law, Economics and Organization* 11 (1): 205–206.

Marshall, G. 2005. *Economics for Collaborative Environmental Management.* Sterling, Va.: Earthscan.

North, D. 1990. "A Transaction Cost Theory of Politics." *Journal of Theoretical Politics* 2 (4): 355–367.

Pierson, P. 2004. *Politics in Time: History, Institutions, and Social Analysis.* Princeton, N.J.: Princeton University Press.

Rivera, J. 1998. *Acequia Culture: Water, Land, and Community in the Southwest.* Albuquerque: University of New Mexico Press.

Trawick, P. 2001. "Successfully Governing the Commons: Principles of Social Organization in an Andean Irrigation System." *Human Ecology* 29 (1): 1–25.

Unruh, G. C. 2000. "Understanding Carbon Lock-In." *Energy Policy* 28: 817–830.

Weimer, David, and Aidan Vining. 2005. *Policy Analysis: Concepts and Practice.* 4th ed. Upper Saddle River, N.J.: Prentice Hall.

Wilson, D. S. 2007. *Evolution for Everyone: How Darwin's Theory Can Change the Way We Think About Our Lives.* New York: Delacorte.

Young, O. 2002. *The Institutional Dimensions of Environmental Change: Fit, Interplay, and Scale.* Cambridge, Mass.: MIT Press.

PART IV

Governing Essential Resources in Action

CHAPTER 11

Go with the Flow

LESSONS FROM WATER MANAGEMENT AND WATER MARKETS

FOR ESSENTIAL RESOURCES

Vanessa Casado-Pérez

All governance regimes involve trade-offs, but discussions about designing an optimal framework too often revolve around faulty generalizations about markets, oversimplifying existing regimes that are poorly suited to the task. Given the current scarcity crisis threatening the subsistence of many of the world's poor, as the introduction by Olivier De Schutter and Katharina Pistor describes, we face an acute need to establish a framework to allocate resources required to sustain life. This chapter draws on experiences with water markets to complement this volume's normative analysis of the values of voice and reflexivity that should guide the allocation and management of those resources. It argues that certain lessons can be learned from current practices of water management in Spain and other developed economies, particularly from the use of well-regulated water markets to organize allocation of scarce water resources. Even when property rights and markets are portrayed as politically neutral, they may in practice be skewed against those with little purchasing power. However, the reality is even more complicated: The nonneutrality of markets and property rights can also be used to eliminate the outsized influence of purchasing power, to accommodate and balance competing claims—embodied in the idea of reflexivity—and to give voice, that is, to grant decision powers to those who hold a right.

In contrast to food, land, or even electricity, which can also be characterized as essential resources and for which Western societies more or less readily accept markets, the market has not typically been deemed a proper mechanism to mainly allocate water (Anderson and Snyder 1997, 49), at least not for initial allocations. Urban water is mostly under government control. Even in the United States, where markets are ubiquitous, there are more public water utilities than in many European countries. Only 15 percent of the U.S. population is served by private water companies (Gleick et al. 2002, 23). In the same vein, in Italy, a referendum to privatize public water utilities was voted down in 2011. A quite populist political platform based on only five points, one of them "public water," performed surprisingly well in the 2013 election. Moreover, in many jurisdictions, such as California, water is inherently public property, even as use rights are private. These regimes differ sharply from how most societies treat land, where private, fenced plots are often the norm. Depending on relevant social practices and legal rules, water-use rights are typically allocated by prior appropriation, by permits, or by holding title to the riparian land, not by buying the rights or bidding at an auction. Moreover, all those allocation means are subject to public interest standards that translate into constraints on property rights and into rights to broader participation in water management. Therefore, water represents a useful example for other markets, like land or food, where the market has been central.

The introduction to this volume reviews the shortcomings of each type of property regime. This chapter suggests that no single, pure regime can adequately allocate essential resources, by demonstrating how different types of goods and governing regimes have successfully coexisted in water. It also argues that property rights and markets should be part of any allocation regime. This chapter does not argue for a sharp definition of property rights or for unconstrained water markets. Individual property rights in water are tempered by principles other than individual profit, and well-managed markets can serve not only efficiency but other values. Property rights in water and water markets can be constrained by other principles, such as equity, self-determination, and regard for others. These are the principles that De Schutter and Pistor argue should guide the governance of essential resources.

Property rights, whether in the form of permits or otherwise, help delineate private from public interests. For example, the lack of clearly delineated water-use rights for groundwater has frequently resulted in the overexploitation of aquifers, as the analysis of the San Luis valley in California shows (see Michael Cox in this volume). By contrast, property rights constrain rights holders. Such rights can be defined to ensure that each small landowner has access to some water, rather than granting full ownership rights on a first-come, first-served basis or to those with the greatest economic power to exploit them. If groundwater is regulated, principles such as beneficial or reasonable use could be applied. In the case of water, dynamic efficiency requires the flexible allocation of existing property rights to adapt to changing circumstances, and this is where water markets have been used successfully. Many jurisdictions have introduced market tools to reallocate water initially allocated by public agencies. Markets are not guided only by efficiency; other rules keep markets in check and demonstrate that markets can incorporate public interest concerns, including sustainability and community values.

The second section of this chapter describes the constraints that have been used in water management, which include limits on water markets and on the mechanisms of water transfer. It shows that water markets are not stand-alone mechanisms but part of a wider management system that includes administrative agencies and local communities and reflects the simultaneous presence of private, public, and common goods in the water realm. The third section demonstrates that water markets, if properly regulated, are not necessarily in conflict with access to water to cover basic needs. The fourth section describes the role of communities in water management and discusses the interaction of markets with communities, defined both narrowly (e.g., irrigators) and more broadly (e.g., society). Finally, the fifth section concludes by arguing that property rights and well-regulated markets should be considered critical components of the management of water and other essential resources.

CONSTRAINED EFFICIENCY IN WATER MARKETS

Water markets typically do not operate as free markets but have mechanisms in place to prevent undesirable effects from unconstrained commerce. Water markets in Chile present a partial exception, as its system was influenced by heavily libertarian economic theories that advocated a free water market. The Chilean experience has been widely criticized, because it concentrated power in the hands of nonconsumptive users, mainly hydropower companies (Bauer 1997, 1998, 2004).

However, such free markets are not the rule. In many jurisdictions, there are limits to speculation (Zellmer 2008), a worry that pervades most markets and is accented when it comes to essential resources. First, there is typically an obligation to use the water rights that have been granted. Further, if a water right is transferred, the transferee has to use it; otherwise the initial rights holder loses the right (Cal. Water Code §§484.a and 1015). Second, in some jurisdictions, there is a limit on how much

water can be held by agents who are not rights holders. This can be justified in noneconomic terms but also on efficiency grounds to avoid market
power concentration. For example, in the state of Victoria in Australia, the
percentage of shares that can be owned without a water-use license or registration is limited (the so called 10 percent non-water-use limit; Son and
Waye 2010, 451). The underlying idea is that water is so central to human
life that it is socially unacceptable to hoard it or profit from it as others go
thirsty. Third, in many jurisdictions, the price for water can be capped or
fixed, even though this can undermine economic efficiency. These caps are
designed to prevent private parties from selling or leasing water at a price
higher than the subsidized price they paid themselves. In Spain, for example, a price cap can be imposed on the price for water leased among private
parties (article 69.3 Spanish Consolidated Water Act, *Texto Refundido de la
Ley de Aguas* – R.C.L. No. 1 (B.O.E. 2001, 176), hereinafter CWA). Similarly, where water banks—clearinghouses with an administrative agency
as broker—exist, buying and selling prices are usually fixed (Gray 2008,
55–56), often quite explicitly for the purpose of preventing undue profit
(Anderson and Hill 1997, 8). In another such example, California's State
Water Project has turn-back pools that create a sort of internal market.
Specifically, state water contractors—agencies that receive water based on
contracts with the Department of Water Resources—can resell their water
surplus, but only at a lower price lower than they paid, which means that
they merely reduce their losses (Hanak 2003, 18).

Further restrictions include rankings of water uses and restrictions
on alienating water for purposes that are incompatible with the ranking.
In Spain, for example, ranking is used for initial allocation and for per-
missible transfers of water rights; domestic use ranks above agriculture,
followed by industry (articles 60 and 67 Spanish CWA). If there are two
competing applications, the use rights are granted to the higher-ranked
one. Further, water users can only transfer their permits to rights holders
whose use is ranked equal to or higher than their own. Thus, as a general
rule, a farmer cannot transfer his or her water to a manufacturing company. This ensures that the social value placed on different water uses is
incorporated not only in initial but also in secondary allocations of water.

Managed water markets can also achieve environmental sustainability
using a variety of mechanisms, including by refusing to authorize transactions that damage the environment, taxing water transactions and devoting
those funds to environmental restoration, and allowing the purchase of con-
sumptive rights and their conversion to instream flow, nonconsumptive uses.

A well-known example of a water market illustrates how markets can be constrained to serve other values beyond efficiency. California's 1991 Water Bank[1] is widely considered to have handled the 1991 drought crisis successfully, even though it only allocated 5 percent of the water used in California. It only operated during the crisis, it fixed prices to prevent excessive profits, and it required potential buyers to conserve water before acquiring more on the market. Similarly, other types of markets suggest that other values in addition to efficiency can be pursued through markets. Transactions between neighboring farmers are very common and also contribute to a more efficient allocation. Such transactions strengthen the sense of community among water users. They also approximate efficiency by allowing farmers to make the most of their water while helping other agricultural users who would otherwise lose crops: A farmer entitled to water who does not need it can transfer that resource, which would otherwise go unused. These transfers may be barters of goods, rights to water the following year, or monetary transactions. In sum, water markets can serve additional values in addition to efficiency.

ON THE COMPATIBILITY OF WATER MARKETS AND HUMAN RIGHTS

It has been argued that there is a basic human right to water or that water is conceived as a merit good, according to which every individual has right to a certain amount of water. Current estimates put the amount of water each person needs access to at approximately 100 liters per day (Gleick 1996, 83–92),[2] a quantifiable amount that could be built into water markets. Individual needs even at this level represent only a tiny part of water use in a given economy and could be provided publicly or privately, via many different mechanisms, including markets.

This chapter focuses on water markets as transfer mechanisms between rights holders and attempts to show that managed water markets should not be associated with the same stigma carried by policy interventions commonly sponsored by international organizations in the developing world, such as privatization (Binswanger and Rosegrant 1994; Easter et al. 1994). One such negative example can be seen in the case of Cochacamba in Bolivia, which under the auspices of the World Bank was required to turn over its public water provision to an international corporation and to pass the costs of infrastructure on to consumers (Glennon 2005, 1890).

In contrast, appropriately designed markets can help ensure access to water for all. For example, a public standpipe system had worse outcomes on water quality, quantity, convenience, and price of water in Mozambique than a market-based system, which allowed users who were connected to the water distribution infrastructure to resell water to those who were not (Zuin et al. 2014). Resellers did not make huge profits; instead, they sought to meet subsistence needs, solidify relationships, and reap other community-oriented benefits (Zuin et al. 2014, 284–286). In many Western societies, by contrast, water providers are public, and consumers hardly ever fully cover infrastructure costs, because subsidies abound (Gómez-Limón and Martin-Ortega 2011, 78). Markets for water do exist in these countries, but they are not unregulated.

As mentioned earlier, water markets can be regulated to ensure that water is not exclusively allocated to whoever will pay the highest price to the exclusion of the rest. Mechanisms that are already employed in different countries around the globe to ensure the compatibility of efficiency and access include:

- Use priorities and interventions, including the suspension of water markets in times of drought
- Bans on irrigating lawns, filling swimming pools, and washing cars with a hose when water is scarce, while ensuring water for basic needs
- Fixed rates for the minimum volume needed per household, adjusted for the number of members, making basic water affordable to all
- Penalties for uses that are less pressing; revenues obtained from them cross-subsidize basic needs (Chohin-Kuper and Strosser 2008, 16; Mullin 2009)
- Direct government subsidies to ensure basic individual needs are met; for example, voucher systems for basic allocations to ensure access to the poorest

Subsidies may trump concerns that water markets threaten access by poor households to water. Those fears arise because urban water suppliers may pass onto consumers the high prices they pay on the market. However, subsidies should be tailored and should not translate into overtly cheap water. Overtly cheap water may result in overuse by some, while excluding others who may obtain more value for water or need it for basic survival. An alternative or an additional measure for subsidizing the amount to cover basic needs is to endow a user's connectivity to the grid, the most expensive part of a water system (Gee 2004, 39). If the water infrastructure were subsidized, water could be allocated to different users through a price, perhaps by charging more for those uses above the basic needs.

THE ROLE OF COMMUNITIES IN WATER MANAGEMENT

As a result of economies of scale in water infrastructure, communities, rather than individual farms, often hold water-use rights, and communities are responsible for interacting with public agencies. Aggregating their interests into irrigation organizations, instead of interacting individually with the administrative agencies, may provide an advantage to farmers. Those organizations may also have economies of scope because they have direct or indirect power to manage related resources, such as land, which may ensure better coordination. Local communities may adopt specialized institutional forms, such as irrigation districts, or use existing political structures, such as counties.

Ostrom (1990) contested the tragedy of the commons, showing that homogenous groups, under certain conditions, succeed in managing some common-pool resources. She offered a number of examples of irrigation communities with practices that included markets. The irrigation community in the Tibi Dam in Alicante (Spain) produced and made public important data—including water storage, water delivered in the previous rotation, or price and quantities of water sold in the previous rotation—that helped farmers make choices before the auction of water deliveries (Ostrom 1990, 79). Even if today's water management challenges involve more heterogeneity than the society in Ostrom's example, the role played by local communities and their irrigation organizations cannot be disregarded; witness the success of California's West Basin, which Ostrom studied in her doctoral dissertation (Ostrom 1990, 133). Property rights and markets are not incompatible with a polycentric system of governance, as this section explains.

Typically, these communities are embedded in larger management units, defined by jurisdictions, as is the case in the United States, where water management is usually decided at the state level (Thompson et al. 2013, 14), or by ecological considerations, where the river basin determines the scope of the governance regime (Brajer et al. 1989, 495–497). In Europe, for instance, ecological principles were imposed by the Water Framework Directive (Council and Parliament European Water Framework Directive 2000/60; 13, O.J. (L 327) 1 (EC)). Assuming that some autonomy is granted to communities to arrange their affairs locally—which may not map neatly onto the relevant environmental units—there still should be some higher-level rules that coordinate management along ecological lines. These communities serve both as delegates to the larger water agencies and as representatives of their member-farmers. Some even play a role representing the community at large, not only irrigators; under some systems, all inhabitants in a particular area are members of the water district. The structure of these communities usually is designed to give voice to members, who shape the community's internal regulations. However, in some instances, highly influential members may get a better deal and outvote the less powerful. Given the heterogeneity of communities, communal governance structures should depend on the specifics of each case.

Ostrom and Schlager (1992) identify five "rights" in the bundle of property rights: access, withdrawal, management, exclusion, and alienation. If communal regimes by themselves are sometimes insufficient and pure private property rights lead to a tragedy of the commons, then a management system may profit from dividing these different "rights" among different decision makers at all levels of government. For instance, the local irrigation community may hold management and exclusion rights, but an individual farmer may be the one with a right to use or withdraw. In water management, structures are commonly nested, and powers are divided among different decision makers who represent competing claims for the resource. For example, some irrigation communities in California have veto power over water transfers by individual members to outsiders (Thompson 1993). In addition, the right of an irrigation community may be tempered by the broader powers of an administrative agency such as the Bureau of Reclamation, which manages the Central Valley Project. The division of rights among decision makers risks an anticommons tragedy (Heller 1998; Bretsen and Hill 2009). However, some coordination and transaction costs may simply be a necessary price to pay as part of a scheme that integrates all the competing interests to water, a resource that is a mix of public, communal, and private.

Communities tend to be trusted, familiar institutions. That means institutional regimes that govern water will gain through integrating them while respecting their autonomy. This is particularly useful in the mechanisms water markets have for review and compensation, which account for the effects of transactions on those who are not part of them.

Water sales can have an impact on the rural community from which the water is sold. But as one moves from the theoretical definition of externality to the level of political reality, it becomes more difficult to discern what should count as an external effect and whether it should be compensated. Effects on communities are much more ambiguous and contested than direct externalities imposed on other rights holders or the environment. When critics of water markets warn of the potential effects on third parties, they usually include the negative effects on rural communities from which the water originates: unemployment for farmworkers (direct effects), fewer business transactions for farm suppliers (indirect effects), and broader effects on the rural communities in general (spillover effects). In addition, if transfers outside the jurisdiction are allowed, it is important to have a system to ensure that the fixed costs of infrastructure are fairly allocated and that the buyer shoulders part of them (Meyers and Posner 1971, 22). Otherwise, the economic viability of the region might be threatened, as costs would be shouldered by a smaller number of parties.

Many economists refuse to take into account some of these external effects, which they term "pecuniary," because they see them as simple market interdependencies. They equate them with changes in price concurrent with the reallocation, which may have equity implications but not real economic effects. For them, water is no different from any other resource, such as the reallocation of a manufacturing factory from one village to another village located in a different region. However, even among economists, some argue that water is different in terms of its effects on third parties. They argue that, in contrast to other goods, when water is reallocated there are no offsets: Water flows away, but no compensatory jobs are created in the area (Griffin 2005, 230). Under this conception, the effects of a water transfer on the agricultural community should be taken into account. This is especially the case if a water reallocation is caused not by more efficient water use, but instead because fields are left idle, resulting in lower production and lower labor and machinery inputs. In fact, the Model Water Transfer Act for California (Gray et al. 1996, 9) only explicitly considered the costs imposed on communities by water reallocation in transactions in which water comes from land fallowing. Even in the case of fallowing, the first lands left idle are often those that produced low-value-added crops. A review of studies regarding the effects of fallowing between 6 and 25 percent of farmland in an area suggests that fallowing affects usually less than 1 percent of the economic activity of the region (Hanak 2003, 81).

Even if the effects are small, there are straightforward ways for a market to take them into account. First, some transactions may not be permitted in order to avoid those effects. A direct cap could be stipulated on the amount of water that can be transferred outside the district, or approval could be required for transfers. A cap may ensure that the effects are not huge. Twenty-two out of California's 58 counties require approval for transfers of groundwater outside the jurisdiction (Hanak 2003, 29).

Second, the community may be allowed to participate in the review of the transaction before an administrative agency evaluating the effects of the transaction. In California, agencies must consider community externalities—framed as the impacts on the county where water originates—in the review of the infrastructure used for transferring water (a different review than the step authorizing the transfer; Cal. Water Code § 1810). Likewise, another provision of the California Water Code offers a sort of backdoor protection: Suppliers may not sell water freed as a result of fallowing in excess of 20 percent of the water supplied (Cal. Water Code § 1745.05 b), unless the agency decides otherwise following a public hearing that allows participation from community members. A public hearing promotes a broader voice without barring suppliers' individual goals. Another way to achieve a similar outcome, while relying more on the market, would be to grant a community the right of first refusal before a transfer. Such a right is granted in Spain to the river basin organizations (article 68.3 Spanish CWA) but could also be given to the local community.

Third, the internal regulations of an institution may require approval at the community level before an individual farmer can sell the right. Doing so may be justified to preserve communal interests, but it may also block transfers inappropriately and favor certain users against others, especially if the voting system is skewed. For example, a small farmer willing to sell water to an outsider may be prevented by the community from entering into the transaction if votes at the community level are weighted according to acreage. In that instance, larger landowners would likely have an incentive to ensure that they can buy that water cheaply, at a lower price than if they had to acquire it on the open market. In California, market transactions are usually blocked when communities give a vote to all landowners, not only those with irrigation rights (Thompson 1993, 734). Hence, the discretion of the irrigation community should not be unlimited. To balance regional, local, and individual claims, voice in the form of some participation, alongside a mandate to an agency to consider local effects, could be more respectful of individual rights than simply giving a community an outright veto.

Fourth, if external effects exist and need to be compensated, one mechanism would be a designated mitigation fund created by taxing the transactions. Howitt et al. (2007) acknowledge the controversies regarding the definition of pecuniary externalities but accept that it is politically necessary to take them into account; they suggest such mitigation funds could be a temporary measure, designed to encourage a shift toward efficient behavior (Howitt et al. 2007, 92). A transitional remedy might train workers to shift to other business sectors in the area or could take the form of general assistance measures directed at improving a region's broader economy. The community should be granted governance over the investment of those funds. In California's Butte County, a fee (5 percent, which amounted to $3.75 per acre-foot sold) was established in 2001 to compensate for the local effects of transactions (Hanak 2003, 96).

In voice and in voting, a balance should be struck between empowering the local community and empowering the individual farmer. Mechanisms that have been successfully used in water markets could apply to any essential resource being transferred outside the local community. Granting certain powers or rights to the community, whatever institutional form those take, is a means of tempering individual property rights and respecting community concerns.

CONCLUSIONS

This chapter has used examples from water management, particularly examples related to the governance of water markets, as a potentially fruitful source of inspiration for managing essential resources. Markets are not the primary or only way in which water is managed, but they play an important role.

Water is an essential resource with unique features. This uniqueness has been enshrined in law to a higher degree than for food and land, even though no one doubts that those are also essential. The social conception of water has contributed to the coexistence of values that might otherwise seem at odds, striking a balance between individual claims, communal needs, and more general values, such as sustainability. This apparent conflict has been mitigated through well-regulated markets with constrained property rights.

Water management is particularly challenging, because it entails the management of private, common-pool, and public goods. As a result, pure regimes such as private property, common property, or centralized property, rarely exist. Instead, most water-management systems employ a mix of methods that combines all three systems to respond to scarcity challenges and the special values associated with water. This means that the right balance will be highly context specific. Still, in any context, this chapter has suggested that property rights and constrained markets can play an important role in that management structure.

Different claimants—individuals or not—can, for instance, be assigned different sticks in the bundle of property rights. Alternatively, those property rights could be constrained according to other values, including equity. Property rights can allocate resources in a way that upholds reflexivity and voice. Water property rights ensure reflexivity by incorporating limits on those rights based on values other than efficiency; they enhance voice by giving a rights holder the opportunity to participate in the nested organizational structure that manages water.

Too often outlier experiences, such as that of Chile, are seen as representative and give a bad name to property rights and markets in water and essential resource management. In reality, rules that establish water markets often reflect our equity, communitarian, and sustainability concerns, in addition to efficiency.

Water management is imperfect, but it has faced and responded to the challenge of balancing competing goals. It should therefore offer guidance for allocating other essential resources. An approach designed to ensure voice and reflexivity can benefit from a governance system that mixes government, communities, and markets, and from a property regime that mixes private, public, and common rights.

NOTES

1. One intuitional form of water markets is a water bank, which works as a public clearinghouse sponsored by a public agency. Some are established to work solely during crisis periods, but others are permanent.

2. The basic minimum is around 20 liters, but between 50 and 100 liters per person is a good target standard. See European Water Initiative, "Water and Sanitation as Human Rights," www.euwi.net/files/FAQ_Right_to_water-sanitation_0.pdf.

REFERENCES

Anderson, Terry L., and Peter J. Hill, eds. 1997. *Water Marketing. The Next Generation.* Lanham, Md.: Rowman and Littlefield.

Anderson, Terry L., and Pamela Snyder. 1997. *Water Markets. Priming the Invisible Pump,* Washington, D.C.: Cato Institute.

Bauer, Carl J. 1997. "Bringing Water Markets Down to Earth: The Political Economy of Water Rights in Chile, 1976–95." *World Development* 29 (5): 639–656.

———. 1998. "Slippery Property Rights: Multiple Water Uses and the Neoliberal Model in Chile." *Natural Resources Journal* 38 (1): 109–155.

———. 2004. *Siren Song: Chilean Water Law As a Model for International Reform*. London: Routledge.

Binswanger, Hans P., and Mark W. Rosegrant. 1994. "Markets in Tradable Water Rights: Potential for Efficiency Gains in Developing Country Water Resource Allocation." *World Development* 22: 1613–1625.

Brajer, Victor, Al Church, Ronald Cummings, and Phillip Ronald. 1989. "The Strengths and Weaknesses of Water Markets as They Affect Water Scarcity and Sovereignty Interests in the West." *Natural Resources Journal* 29: 489–509.

Bretsen, Stephen N., and Peter J. Hill. 2009. "Water Markets as a Tragedy of the Anticommons." *William and Mary Environmental Law and Policy Review* 33: 723–784.

Chohin-Kuper, Anne, and Pierre Strosser. 2008. "Water Pricing in Europe and Around the Mediterranean Sea: Issues and Options." Paper presented at the Fourth EWA Brussels Conference: European Water Management and the Economic Aspects of the Water Framework Directive. Brussels (Belgium), November 4th, 2008. www.ewaonline.de/portale/ewa/ewa.nsf/C125723B0047EC38/90E45AEC74 290744C1257563003484E7/$FILE/EWA2008_Chohin_Strosser_conf.pdf.

Easter, K.William, Guy Le Moigne, Walter J. Ochs & Sandra Giltner, eds. 1994. "Water Policy and Water Markets," World Bank Technical Paper 249.Gee, Alexander. 2004. "Competition and the Water Sector." *Antitrust* 2: 38–40.

Gleick, Peter. 1996. "Basic Water Requirements for Human Activities: Meeting Basic Needs." *Water International* 21: 83–92.

Gleick, Peter, Gary Wolff, Elizabeth L. Chalecki, and Rachel Reyes. 2002. *The New Economy of Water: The Risks and Benefits of Globalization and Privatization of Fresh Water*. Oakland, Calif.: Pacific Institute.

Glennon, Robert. 2005. "Water Scarcity, Marketing, and Privatization." *Texas Law Review* 83 (7): 1873–1902.

Gómez-Limón, José A., and Julia Martin-Ortega. 2011. "Agua, economía y territorio: nuevos enfoques de la Directiva Marco del Agua para la gestión del recurso." *Estudios de Economía Aplicada* 29 (1): 65–93.

Gray, Brian E. 2008. "The Market and the Community: Lessons from California's Drought Water Bank." *Hastings West-North West Journal of Environmental Law and Policy* 14: 1453–1462.

Gray, Brian E, Richard E. Howitt, Lawrence J. MacDonnell, Barton H. Thompson Jr., and Henry J. Vaux Jr. 1996. "A Model Water Transfer Act for California." *Hastings West-North West Journal of Environmental Law and Policy* 4: 3–22.

Griffin, Ronald. 2005. *Water Resource Economics*. Cambridge Mass.: MIT Press.

Hanak, Ellen. 2003. *Who Should Be Allowed to Sell Water in California? Third-Party Issues and the Water Market*. San Francisco: Public Policy Institute of California.

Heller, Michael. 1998. "The Tragedy of the Anticommons: Property in the Transition from Marx to Markets." *Harvard Law Review* 111: 621–688.

Howitt, Richard E., Erin Mastrangelo, James J. Murphy, Ariel Dinar, Vernon L. Smith, and Stephen J. Rassenti. 2006. "Mechanisms for Addressing Third-Party Impacts Resulting from Voluntary Water Transfers." In *Using Experimental Methods in Environmental and Resource Economics*, J. List, ed. 91–112. Northampton Mass.: Elgar.

Meyers, Charles J., and Richard A. Posner. 1971. "Toward an Improved Market in Water Resources." Legal Study No. 4, U.S. National Water Commission, Washington, D.C.

Mullin, Megan. 2009. *Governing the Tap*. Cambridge, Mass.: MIT Press.

Ostrom, Elinor. 1990. *Governing the Commons*. Cambridge, Cambridge University Press.

——, and Edella Schlager. 1992. "Property Rights Regimes and Natural Resources: A Conceptual Analysis." *Land Economics* 68: 249.

Son, Christina, and Vicki Waye. 2010. "Regulating the Australian Water Market." *Journal of Environmental Law* 22: 431–459.

Thompson, Barton H., Jr. 1993. "Institutional Perspectives on Water Policy and Markets." *California Law Review* 81 (3): 671–764.

Thompson, Barton H. Jr, John D. Leshy, and Robert H. Abrams. 2013. *Legal Control of Water Resources*. 5th edition, St. Paul, Minn.: West.

Zellmer, Sandra. 2008. "The Anti-speculation Doctrine and Its Implications for Collaborative Water Management." *Nevada Law Journal* 8 (3): 994–1030.

Zuin Valentina, Leonard Ortolano, and Jennifer Davis. 2014. "The Entrepreneurship Myth in Small-Scale Service Provision: Water Resale in Maputo, Mozambique." *Journal of Water, Sanitation and Hygiene for Development* 4 (2): 281–292.

CHAPTER 12

───

Ecology

WATER GOVERNANCE'S MISSING LINK

Scott McKenzie

Water is a scarce and essential natural resource. Estimates suggest that as much as 80 percent of the world's population suffers from water insecurity (Vörösmarty et al. 2010). This shortage has pushed interest in improving water governance to remedy the tragedy of exclusion as discussed by Katharina Pistor and Oliver De Schutter.

Water governance includes values, norms, and laws (Rogers and Hall 2003, 4). In most cases, governance has a distinctly human design, such as improved irrigation for agricultural fields, pipes and waterworks for drinking water, or dams for generating energy. Furthermore, a significant amount of academic scholarship, NGO advocacy, and policy think-tank work focuses on human aspects, such as revisions to privatization, identifying benchmarks to cooperation, or designing new antipollution technology. This is for good reason; as outlined in the introduction, many of the causes of scarcity are human-made. However, these steps often overlook how water's ecological role can inform the governance picture by taking advantage of naturally occurring systems and cycles instead of fighting against them.

This chapter explores how water's ecological role can be used to improve both specific pieces of governance and the wider picture to positively transform allocation of this essential resource. I will discuss intersections of the ecological role of water and governance, including (1) the human right to water, which implicates measurements of how much water citizens need; (2) basin management, which provides an ecological unit of scale for cooperation and management; and (3) water reuse as a natural function of water in the environment, which informs the water-use and disposal processes. These examples and case studies serve two purposes. First, they show the benefits of basing governance on these ecological roles of water. Second, they argue that the ecological role of water needs to be incorporated on a broader governance scale.

The Pistor and De Schutter framework points out that classic governance focuses on understanding resources according to their nature— meaning their basic qualities. These contribute to the types of governance regimes (common pool, private, etc.) associated with these resources. These qualities also play a guiding role in how free-market forces shape and restrict access to these resources. Pistor and De Schutter propose a more context-specific understanding of particularly scarce and essential resources. The purpose of this chapter is to investigate those natures by way of an ecological lens, which, like the proposed framework, is highly dependent on context. Here, governance is reconceptualized within the proposed framework by placing a focus on nature—now taking the meaning of forces that influence the world. The areas that this chapters focuses on—the human right to water, basin management, and water reuse—become alternatives that promote both sustainability and equality.

This chapter is divided into two parts. The first section discusses the relationship between water's ecological role and its governance, highlighting many of the same considerations as Pistor and De Schutter's examination of the roots of scarcity. The second section examines the previously referenced examples to see where the environment can provide guidance to explicate syncing governance of this scarce essential resource with natural systems in light of Pistor and De Schutter's observations for how water can be more equitably and sustainably allocated.

WATER'S ECOLOGY AND GOVERNANCE

Water governance attracts attention from academics, policy makers, and citizens who want to improve the management and use of this resource. The processes and institutions involved in governance should achieve a range of normative values, including equality and sustainability. However, many existing approaches to water governance ignore the ecological role of water. This comes at a great cost. More than one billion of the world's citizens lack access to clean water. Two billion humans are affected by water shortages, and 2.4 billion people do not have access to adequate sanitation (Corcoran 2010). The tragedy of exclusion is real and can be quantified.

Water governance covers a wide range of policies and institutions. Governance includes "political, social, economic and administrative systems that are in place to develop and manage water resources, and the delivery of water role, at different levels of society" (Rogers and Hall 2003, 7). Governance can also be thought of as both a process that includes debate and discussion about ends and means or a "tool kit" that focuses on specific problems (Castro 2007). Suggestions for improving water governance cover a wide range of ideas, including "dialogue, participation, negotiation, networking and partnership" (Tropp 2007). Experts have created a number of classifications to conceptualize water governance. This chapter will use the three classifications for water governance developed by Rogers and Hall. These classifications are constitutional, organizational, and operational. *Constitutional* governance includes policy and laws (these may or may not be specifically part of a state constitution), *organizational* governance deals with coordination and administration, and *operational* governance looks at use (Rogers and Hall 2003). Each of these areas is examined in the next section through the lens of water's ecological role.

This chapter uses the term *ecological role* to propose an important factor in governance. In this chapter the definition of water's ecological role will be applied broadly and includes water's properties and the way it functions and circulates though the ecosystem. Ecology and the natural environment have been the subject of extensive study since the early days of science but do not always guide governance. It is important not to confuse water's ecological role with ecological services, though due to the diversity of literature in this subject there certainly could be conceptual overlap. An example often given of ecosystem services is the provision of clean drinking water. In this case the "service" is framed as a good obtained from the environment (Millennium Ecosystem Assessment 2005). Consideration of water's ecological role is different, because it does not look for outcomes from the environment but rather considers how the environment should shape the governance picture. The ecological focus suggested here threads the needle between the universal and local. Many suggestions for governance best practices focus on universal issues such as public participation (Huitema et al. 2009). However, governance also involves local implementation. Looking at the ecological role recognizes that while there are universal aspects to water, these can vary in their local expression.

Polluted rivers, inadequate irrigation, and unaffordable drinking supplies make water appear to be suffering from a physical shortage, poor governance, or both. While there are vast amounts of saltwater in the oceans, globally only 2.5 percent is freshwater—potable by thirsty humanity. Much of this freshwater is locked up in glaciers and permafrost, leaving a much smaller amount readily available for our drinking, sanitation, cleaning, agriculture, or industry (Oki and Kanae 2006). This scarcity is compounded by water's uneven distribution around the world, increasing the extreme water stress faced in parts of the globe (Pimentel et al. 1999). Experts predict an even greater percentage of the population will be affected by water shortages in the future. Models show that water use is expanding as a result of factors such as population growth and increases in the global standard of living (Meadows 2004). This is the absolute scarcity discussed by Pistor and De Schutter.

Some researchers have suggested that physical scarcity is a scapegoat for more subtle problems that stem from "injustice and inequality" ("Santa Cruz Declaration on the Global Water Crisis" 2014). This aligns with issues of voice and reflexivity that were brought up by Pistor and De Schutter. While these voices acknowledge that physical shortages exist, they believe a number of issues, including poverty, pollution from resource extraction, land-grabbing, and a lack of transparency at many levels of governance, are responsible for the shortages many people face. Improved policy dialogues that incorporate all affected stakeholders, including frequently overlooked groups such as women and the impoverished, have been suggested to combat water provision problems.

Water governance's social and environmental parts are impossible to separate (Hoekstra 2010). However, ecology is often treated apart from the water governance framework and considered an issue that needs to be overcome or subdued. This separates human wants and environmental realities into two categories. Water governance is often driven by and constructed toward human wants while fighting against nature (e.g., excessive building of dams on a river or overextraction of groundwater for irrigation). By contrast, nature has a reality that exists outside "economic or political status and . . . cannot be manipulated" (Hoekstra 2000). This division can also be framed as an extension of the science-policy interface. Water's ecology is a function of science, which is a factual understanding of the natural and social world that follows systematic evidence-based methodology. By contrast, governance and policy are intentional but political in nature and dynamic (Althaus, Bridgman, and Davis 2013). Efforts at harmonization are not new. Bringing these two sides together was discussed as part of the 1992 UN Conference on Environment and Development in Rio de

Janeiro and was a strong element in the resulting Agenda 21 action plan (Falkenmark 2001).

When governance completely rejects the ecological, it relies on human ingenuity to subdue the natural world. The Great Man-Made River in Libya is a striking example. Former leader Muammar al-Qaddafi started the main construction and excavation on the project to bring water from deep in the desert to the country's main cities. This "Eighth Wonder of the World" involved digging of wells hundreds of meters deep in the Nubian Sandstone Aquifer. The water was transported via an elaborate system of underground tunnels and storage tanks to the major cities over a 1,000 kilometers away. Tripoli and agricultural areas like the Jeffara Plain rely on this unsustainable extraction of fossil water. Water from the Nubian Sandstone Aquifer is as much as 38,000 years old and recharges slowly. Estimates vary for how long this supply will last, but no one questions that the country will face hardship when these aquifers are empty (Salem 1992). The Great Man-Made River ignores sustainable use of the aquifer and treats ecological concerns as being surmountable with planning and finance.

These suggestions for water's ecology and governance do not advocate that science is infallible. Science has internal biases connected to the place and production of knowledge (Livingstone 2010). For example, water is often described with universal facts, such as the constant hydrological cycle. However, this does not accurately describe some water, such as in polar regions or the desert (Linton 2008). Similarly, suggestions to adopt governance scaled on the ecosystem have at times been rife with political biases (Cohen and Bakker 2014). Bringing water's ecological role and governance closer together uses the current understanding of science in as apolitical way as possible to improve contemporary governance.

The next section will explore Rogers and Hall's three classifications for water governance—constitutional, organizational, and operational—both as independent areas where the ecological role of water could improve governance and for the greater proposition that the ecological role of water needs to be considered more broadly in the governance debate. These examples and case studies underscore the ecological role of water as a useful starting point for governance, because it connects natural systems and processes with governance goals and objectives instead of ignoring or fighting against them. When this connection happens, governance is better able to fulfill normative values such as sustainability and equality.

ECOLOGY AND GOVERNANCE IN PRACTICE

This section moves from the insight generated by Pistor and De Schutter's framework for scarce essential resources and provides more insight into a discussion that shows how the ecological role works to make governance better able to reach normative goals such as sustainability and equality. Each example and case study explains in detail how the ecological role of water can be incorporated to address ongoing governance questions. Areas where concerns have occurred are considered and solutions are discussed as an example of how and why the ecological role of water works.

CONSTITUTIONAL GOVERNANCE—CONNECTING RIGHTS AND LIFE'S BASIC REQUIREMENTS

Water is a critical component for all life, including human life. In the Rogers and Hall governance classification, the human right to water is a constitutional aspect that serves to link water's ecological role in maintaining life to governance that requires citizens be provided with water. This right is an acknowledgment that all humans require a consistent supply of clean water to live (Bulto 2011). While Pistor and De Schutter identify that legal rules can result in scarcity, the human right to water is increasingly invoked at the national and international level through legislation, resolutions, and court cases to promote basic living standards and equality.

This human right gives all citizens a guarantee that their state will supply water that complies with quantity, quality, location, and affordability requirements (Linton 2012). The right to water is rooted in an acknowledgment that this resource plays an essential role in maintaining human health in a variety of ways, including hygiene, food preparation, and sanitation (Gleick 1998). Although not as established as other human rights, the right to water is often used as both a governance standard and a legal tool.

The right to water is increasingly included in state constitutions and is now recognized at the international level (Bluemel 2004). Many states have already incorporated the human right to water in their constitutions. These include Kenya, Ecuador, Paraguay, Argentina, Bolivia, Brazil, California (U.S.), the Democratic Republic of the Congo, Ecuador, India, Nicaragua, Tunisia, Uganda, and Uruguay (WaterAid 2014). Similarly, this right has been featured in international declarations and treaties, including the 1977 UN Mar del Plata Water Conference, the Geneva Convention, the Convention on the Rights of the Child, and the Convention to Eliminate All Forms of Discrimination Against Women. Most recently the UN General Assembly passed Resolution 64/292 in support of the right to water.

The right to water has also become a tool of activists for influencing policy and fighting against negative aspects of water privatization (Bakker 2007). In many places, water infrastructure or supply rights have been sold to private investors. There is a hope that this will result in increased funding for modernization while minimizing waste. However, costs to consumers often skyrocket beyond what they are capable of paying. The right to water can be used as a legal tool to protect access to affordable water for all people.

Sufficient quantity, or how much water humans need to live, helps define water's ecological role in this human right. General Comment 15 to the International Covenant on Economic, Social and Cultural Rights is the clearest expression of this parameter and states that each person has a right to an amount that will maintain human life (Bulto 2011). While the concept of sufficient quantity is not difficult to understand, a misinterpretation can easily separate water's governance from ecology.

The South African court case *Mazibuko v. City of Johannesburg* is one well-cited example of sufficient quantity. In South Africa, the human right to water was included in the country's 1996 constitution. However, this instrument does not define the quantity. The applicants challenged Johannesburg's water policy, which provided 6 kiloliters per household per month. The applicants could not afford to pay for additional water and turned to the human right to water to establish that the state needed to provide a greater quantity for their basic needs. At its root, this became a question of economic equality.

The applicants had initial success. Judge Tsoka of the Johannesburg High Court found for the applicants and ordered each person be supplied with 50 liters per day. The judge relied on international guidelines and testimony from an international expert to understand and define the ecological requirement for the amount of water needed by a person for life (Danchin 2010). The Supreme Court of Appeal lowered the quantity requirement to 42 liters per person per day (Williams 2010). Instead of relying on international experts, the court heard expert testimony from a local engineer who was familiar with the township and its environment. This provided an even more refined understanding of the connection between this universal value and the local implementation.

Ultimately, these findings were overturned by the Constitutional Court, which found for the city. This court used a reasonableness standard to evaluate the implementation of the human right to water. Under this analysis, the state only needed to prove that it was taking measures toward helping citizens realize the right the right. This court's finding took a different direction from the lower courts by breaking the connection between water's ecological role in maintaining life and governance.

The ecological role of water informs governance by suggesting the amount of water needed to sustain human life in a flexible manner. The appellate court came closest to connecting this ecological role with governance, because while it noted the specific amount of water needed for life may change based on location, it still resulted in a requirement for a fixed quantity of water. This court allowed the right to be evaluated based on its context and reinforced its connection to the ecological role. In contrast, the Constitutional Court shows the right to water can be easily disconnected from its ecological role in maintaining life.

When the quantity requirement is connected to the ecological role of water, governance better fulfills goals such as equality. As the applicants in Mazibuko noted, when people do not have the financial means to pay for water they will face increasing health and sanitation hardships. A reasonableness standard does little to help these groups of people. Using the ecological role of water as a standard for the amount of water needed helps to protect the meaning and purpose of the human right to water and furthers the normative goals of governance.

ORGANIZATIONAL GOVERNANCE—MANAGEMENT BY ECOLOGICAL BOUNDARIES

Water basins can be ecological units that function as boundaries for management—even if they are enormously large and branch in myriad directions. Basin management focuses on cooperative plans that utilize a water resource as a whole and serve as a connection between the organizational level of governance and water's ecological role in boundary setting. This goal is often accomplished through agreements that outline shared principles, create systems for conflict resolution, and establish organizations responsible for the direction of the basin. As Pistor and De Schutter point out, there is urgent need for institutional arrangements that foster the achievement of these particular normative goals. To this end, basin management acknowledges a natural unit for stronger polycentric governance in basins, which can result in increased political cooperation and a more normative goals including waters sustainable use.

Basin management involves "jointly developing and managing the water basin as a unit without regard to international borders; sharing of the benefits of that development and management according to some agreed-upon formula; a procedure for investigating and resolving the inevitable disputes constructively" (Kliot, Shmueli, and Shamir 2001, 244). These steps help states transcend the real and difficult issue of national level protectionism and move toward consensus for the management of their shared resource (Teclaff 1990). The main challenge is reconciling the ecological unit of the basin with political boundaries.

Basin management has a strong history of political support and implementation (Finger, Tamiotti, and Allouche 2006). United Nations Secretary-General Dag Hammarskjöld supported the principle in 1956. The International Law Association concurred in 1961 that a river basin should be managed as a cohesive whole and that basin states should create an organization for basin administration. In 2014 the UN Convention on the Law of Non-Navigable Uses of International Watercourses, which includes many basin-management principles, went into force after decades of development. Globally, 145 countries are part of 263 international river basins and an unknown number of aquifers (Giordano and Wolf 2003). Many basins around the world show aspects of collective management. Examples include: the Amazon Cooperation Treaty Organization (Bolivia, Brazil, Colombia, Ecuador, Guyana, Peru, Suriname, and Venezuela), the Niger Basin Authority (Benin, Burkina Faso, Cameroon, and the Ivory Coast), and the International Commission for the Protection of the Rhine (Germany, France, Luxembourg, the Netherlands, and Switzerland) (Eckstein 2014).

Basin-wide management in any of its forms occurs on two levels: political and administrative (Kliot, Shmueli, and Shamir 2001). The political level involves legal instruments, including international treaties such as the Convention on the Protection of the Rhine or the Treaty for Amazonian Cooperation. Day-to-day implemententation such as data gathering and longer-term planning, including development projects, is coordinated by transboundary organizations. These organizations should include representation from the many different stakeholders in the basin and help build trust and confidence between partner states (Giordano and Wolf 2003). There are many different models of basin-wide management. Some include only surface waters, while others include groundwater resources.

Some only focus on one aspect, for example, hydropower, while others include a more integrative approach that combines water use for agriculture, people, and the environment.

Basin-wide management works because it provides a unit of governance that connects a collection of states that share a common resource. While the basin boundaries set the unit for management, there are a number of other sources of governance, including state laws and local ordinances, that provide strength and support. Basin-wide management creates a natural hub for polycentric governance. In the past, most governance has taken place in monocentric models. In monocentric models the state is at the center of governance. Polycentric governance recognizes multiple overlapping centers of governance at different hierarchical levels (Ostrom, Tiebout, and Warren 1961). Polycentric governance is advantageous, because it is "more resilient and better able to cope with change and uncertainty" (Huitema et al. 2009, 3). Both the flexible nature of basin-wide schemes and polycentric governance reinforce how the universal concept of using the basins boundaries can reflect the needs and realities in each local implementation.

Basin management brings rewards for all stakeholders beyond what they could achieve on their own, because coordinated actions have a higher rater of return (Krutilla 1967). For example, stakeholders can work together to jointly maximize hydropower production. The United States and Canada show that working together helps them maintain energy during periods of low water while minimizing impact to aquatic species. Basin management also improves the exchange of information and increases trust between basin members. This underscores how basin management reduces the potential for conflict between states competing for a shared scarce resource. Even when total political agreement may not be reached, there are steps such as bilateral treaties that can prepare the basin for eventual agreement (Waterbury 1997).

The Nile is one basin that is increasingly coming under stress from a lack of coordinated management. The basin covers 3,349,000 square kilometers and touches the territory of eleven states: Burundi, Ethiopia, Kenya, Rwanda, Tanzania, Uganda, Eritrea, Sudan, South Sudan, Egypt, and the Democratic Republic of the Congo. The massive size of this geographic unit complicates the political process of forging basin management. Egypt has relied on outdated treaties to secure the lion's share of the Nile's water and stifle development by other basin states. Egypt protects this imbalance, because 97 percent of its freshwater comes from the Nile and a vast majority its population lives along the narrow verdant strip that borders the river's banks (Frenken 1997). Other basin states now want to begin development on the Nile. The Grand Ethiopian Renaissance Dam is one answer to underutilization of water resources and low socioeconomic status (Salman 2013).

Starting in 1999, many Nile basin states took steps to create the Cooperative Framework Agreement (CFA). The CFA includes formal goals and rules for the governance of the Nile basin and establishes a management organization to carry out day-to-day work developing and sharing the Nile's resources. The CFA has been signed by several basin states but has not yet been ratified by the number needed to go into force. In contrast to this broad support, Egypt has steadfastly opposed these attempts at basin management (Mekonnen 2010).

In the status quo, Egypt and Ethiopia are pursuing development strategies that give little or no consideration to other states. In Egypt's case, it has slowed development in other states. In Ethiopia's, downstream states are in fear of a supply disruption, while environmental questions loom about the construction of a large dam. However, the CFA and the Nile basin also show how management at the basin level works to further governance goals such as sustainable development. Political cooperation has been fostered through the process of developing the CFA, and states have worked together though this process to begin joint development and have reaped more sustainable economic and environmental rewards from their cooperation (Mekonnen 2010).

A basin-wide approach to the Nile is feasible, even in this highly politicized environment, when kept in perspective. As suggested earlier, there are a number of gradient steps that states can take before they achieve full agreement on the allocation of all water in the basin. This could include agreement on technical projects such as a hydropower dam, harmonizing environmental regulations, or even bilateral or subtreaty regimes (Waterbury 1997). These steps would allow other pieces of polycentric governance to continue, including at both the state and local levels. While such lesser steps may lack the grand vision or the high level of economic and environmental payoffs that could come though full basin-wide management, they are certainly better than the current situation of each state taking unilateral action.

Governance at the organizational level incorporates water's ecology when it takes the basin boundaries as a unit for management. As the Nile case shows, stakeholders' failure to come to agreement on basin manage-ment encourages disjointed development and risks political discord. This hurts governance's ability to achieve goals such as sustainability. Basin management creates a foundation for the polycentric governance of water at the exact scale the water covers.

OPERATIONAL GOVERNANCE—REUSE FOLLOWING THE HYDROLOGICAL CYCLE

Water governance often discusses water scarcity and shortages. One way to address this lack is to make more water available through reuse schemes. Reuse takes its cue, but not by necessity its implementation, from the hydrological cycle and the way it recycles water in the environ-ment. Reuse is at the operational category of water governance and con-nects different consumers ranging from drinking water users, industry, and agriculture with a simple property of water. While waste can be a large element of the scarcity equation, reuse works because it links the ecological property of water being recycled and used again with gover-nance to promote a more sustainable water supply.

Water is a resource in motion. The hydrological cycle describes the way that water flows though the ecosystem. Water falls from the atmo-sphere to the earth in the form of precipitation such as rain or snow. It flows through rivers and streams and into lakes and aquifers, often ending in the ocean. On land, water can be used multiple times by plants and animals, including humans (Oki and Kanae 2006). The hydrological cycle is completed when water evaporates from land, bodies of freshwater, or the oceans and returns to the atmosphere. In the hydrological cycle water is reused both in the microscale by different plants and animals and in the macroscale (Chahine 1992).

Water reuse is promoted because it makes more water available. Studies have found that water remains in the atmosphere for perhaps eight or nine days before returning to Earth as precipitation. However, precipitation often comes far from where water is needed. Given the time and effort required to move water from where it falls to where it is used, reuse is a far more attractive option (Rogers 2006). Two broad types of reuse exist. The first, indirect, describes how coriparian cities use water from a common river and reuse naturally occurs between upstream utilization and downstream consumption. The second type of reuse, direct, is active recycling of water from a city for use again in that same area (Dishman, Sherrard, and Rebhun 1989). Schemes that promote reuse can reduce the cost of water and help guard higher-quality water supplies (Al-Hamaiedeh and Bino 2010). In addition, reuse reduces the environmental impact of water infrastructure (Wade-Miller 2006).

Water-reuse schemes recognize that different types of water have different uses. For example, high-quality water should be reserved for an important use such as human consumption. Low-quality water, including water with higher levels of biological pollution can be designated for irrigation (Campisano and Modica 2010). Water-reuse schemes often reflect these classifications by taking water from a high-quality use, recycling it, and using it for a lower-quality use. Reuse water has been identified as being good for "agricultural and landscape irrigation, industrial applications, environmental applications (surface water replenishment, and groundwater recharge), recreational activities, urban cleaning, firefighting, [and] construction" (Meneses, Pasqualino, and Castells 2010, 267). Some reuse projects take wastewater and convert it to use for irrigation, while others use water for industry. Some projects use membranes to purify water, while others incorporate wetlands (Bixio et al. 2006). Because reuse is so closely linked to the local implementation, each project takes this universal property of water and applies it to a specific area.

Public acceptability and a lack of guidance are major reasons governance does not implement schemes that take advantage of this natural property. For many people there are lingering concerns that reuse water may be dirty or dangerous, and some people are repulsed by a "yuck factor" (Ching 2010). Studies have suggested that reuse projects have better results when they incorporate public participation by including different stakeholders and using their knowledge and expertise in the decision-making processes (Huitema et al. 2009). Additionally, states and local authorities often lack rules and regulations for implementing reuse. This leaves policy makers without a road map to help guide reuse projects. Reflecting these issues, only a small percent of available water is reused. In the United States reuse only accounts for 7.4 percent of the total wastewater (Wade-Miller 2006). Surveys in other countries suggest few have significantly implemented water-reuse projects (Meneses, Pasqualino, and Castells 2010). However, there are projections that reuse could increase due to water scarcity, greater public acceptance, and improved regulations.

Australia is one country that is addressing water reuse, focusing particularly on domestic and storm water (Dillon 2000). Many factors are pushing Australia toward increased reuse, including an expanding population, citizen calls for environmental protection, more urbanization, higher industrial and agricultural demands, and maintaining high-quality water for better applications (Po, Nancarrow, and Kaercher 2003). Australia has set ambitious targets for reuse. For example, the Western State Water Strategy aimed to recycle 20 percent of Perth's wastewater (Anderson, Bradley, and Radcliffe 2008). Previously, water was generally seen as a single-use product. However, reused water is now seen as providing a consistent year-round supply at the same quality level.

There are many examples of reuse in Australia. Residents in one area were given recycled water for toilet flushing and plant watering (Po, Nancarrow, and Kaercher 2003). Other projects have focused on reusing water for industrial-scale gardens and agriculture. One of the marquee reuse projects has been operating since 2001 at Sydney Olympic Park, where storm water and wastewater are reused for irrigation at the venue itself and for homes in the surrounding community. This water is purified with microfiltration and reverse osmosis. The project saves Sydney 2,300 cubic meters of water per day (Anderson, Bradley, and Radcliffe 2008). Environmental protection stays paramount; most water-reuse projects underwent required environmental impact assessments to ensure they were sustainable and did not have long-term negative environmental impacts.

Australia's water governance has a significant impact on the promotion of reuse. Australia has addressed the social side of reuse to improve buy-in, acceptance, and support from the public for these projects. There has been significant pushback on some reuse projects. In one case a local government was changed because of negative public reaction to the initiating of a reuse scheme. Other reuse schemes were derailed by citizen activism with media and Internet sites (Po, Nancarrow, and Kaercher 2003). Australia has improved social acceptance for reused water through education and managing citizen knowledge (Stenekes et al. 2006). Similarly, Australia addressed the regulations for reuse. Before reuse was a significant policy issue, there were no clearly defined user rights and responsibilities (Po, Nancarrow, and Kaercher 2003). Now there are guidelines for reuse in the National Water Quality Management Strategy (Dillon 2000). These guidelines separate water into four categories and set standards for each. Australia has fostered the expansion of water reuse by addressing these problems.

As Australia shows, mimicking the hydrological cycle though reuse makes governance work by increasing the amount of water available where it is needed, thus promoting sustainability. The additional factors pushing increasing water use by states around the world are causing a squeeze on the resource, because the amount of freshwater on Earth is relatively fixed. While reuse is not a panacea, the operational part of governance does represent one way to address current and future water shortages by expanding the supply.

Reuse schemes speed up the natural processes by which water is constantly recycled in the ecosystem and through the hydrological cycle. This helps states achieve a major goal of governance by ensuring a supply of water in the area where it is needed and extends the current supplies of water promoting the normative goal of sustainability.

CONCLUDING REMARKS

There can be little doubt that the world is facing a period of extreme water stress. The infinitesimal fraction of clean water available for human use will increasingly be contested at the local, state, regional, basin, and international levels. There is certainly the need to seek out information and answers about how to expand the space where voice and reflexivity can guide access to these resources. The purpose of this piece was to question some assumptions surrounding the governance and the nature of these resources to promote a "thicker" regime. The ecological role is not a single issue but a range of factors that can occur at governance's constitutional, organizational, and operational levels. The pieces of the water governance picture that were discussed here—the human right to water, basin management, and water reuse—work because they harness the strength of naturally occurring events.

Water's ecological role pervades all aspects of governance. As shown here, at the constitutional level, the ecological role can be implicated though the human right to guaranteed quantities of water sufficient to ensure life. This looks to the amount of water needed to sustain life as the measure for how much water should be supplied by any government. At the organizational level, water's ecological role provides boundaries that serve as units for governance and management at the basin scale. These units transcend state political boundaries, but a polycentric basin-wide approach does not need to involve a total loss of autonomy to improve the sustainable management of these resources. At the operational level, the reuse of water mimics the hydrological cycle. This increases the amount of water available for consumption by an increasingly thirsty humanity in the locations where the demand is high, instead of relying on erratic precipitation or limited groundwater supplies.

These examples and case studies highlight how water's ecological role can be incorporated in governance to better achieve normative goals such as equality and sustainability. When governance takes the ecological role as a starting place, natural cycles and patterns are internalized and leveraged instead of rejected. The result is governance at all scales that exhibits broader sustainability and equality. This chapter has discussed applying the principle of governance reflecting the ecology role in the case of water. There is reason to believe that this concept could be applied to the governance of other resources such as energy or biodiversity.

Water governance, encompassing the political, social, economic, and administrative systems that regulate and supply water to the consumer, plays a critical role in fulfilling normative values such as equality and sustainability. Recognizing that governance needs to be rooted in the natural contours of the resources will improve governance's ability to achieve normative goals for this scarce and essential resource.

REFERENCES

Al-Hamaiedeh, H., and M. Bino. 2010. "Effect of Treated Grey Water Reuse in Irrigation on Soil and Plants." *Desalination* 256 (1): 115–119.

Althaus, Catherine, Peter Bridgman, and Glyn Davis. 2013. *The Australian Policy Handbook*. Sydney: Allen & Unwin.

Anderson, John, Jim Bradley, and John Radcliffe. 2008. "Water Reuse in Australia and New Zealand." In *Water Reuse: An International Survey of Current Practice, Issues and Needs*, ed. Blanca Jiménez and Takashi Asano, 105–121. London, U.K.: IWA.

Bakker, Karen. 2007. "The 'Commons' Versus the 'Commodity': Alter-globalization, Anti-privatization and the Human Right to Water in the Global South." *Antipode* 39 (3): 430–455.

Bixio, D., C. Thoeye, J. De Koning, D. Joksimovic, D. Savic, T. Wintgens, and T. Melin. 2006. "Wastewater Reuse in Europe." *Desalination* 187 (1): 89–101.

Bluemel, Erik B. 2004. "The Implications of Formulating a Human Right to Water." *Ecology LQ* 31: 957.

Bulto, Takele Soboka. 2011. "The Emergence of the Human Right to Water in International Human Rights Law: Invention or Discovery?" *Melbourne Journal of International Law* 12 (2): 1–25.

Campisano, A., and C. Modica. 2010. "Experimental Investigation on Water Saving by the Reuse of Washbasin Grey Water for Toilet Flushing." *Urban Water Journal* 7 (1): 17–24.

Castro, José Esteban. 2007. "Water Governance in the Twentieth-First Century." *Ambiente & Sociedade* 10 (2): 97–118.

Chahine, Moustafa T. 1992. "The Hydrological Cycle and Its Influence on Climate." *Nature* 359 (6394): 373–380.

Ching, Leong. 2010. "Eliminating 'Yuck': A Simple Exposition of Media and Social Change in Water Reuse Policies." *International Journal of Water Resources Development* 26 (1): 111–124.

Cohen, Alice, and Karen Bakker. 2014. "The Eco-Scalar Fix: Rescaling Environmental Governance and the Politics of Ecological Boundaries in Alberta, Canada." *Environment and Planning D: Society and Space* 32 (1): 128–146.

Corcoran, Emily. 2010. *Sick Water?: The Central Role of Wastewater Management in Sustainable Development: A Rapid Response Assessment.* The Hague: UN Environmental Program.

Danchin, P. 2010. "A Human Right to Water? The South African Constitutional Court's Decision in the Mazibuko Case." *European Journal of International Law,* www.ejiltalk.org/a-human-right-to-water-the-south-african-constitutional -court%e2%80%99s-decision-in-the-mazibuko-case.

Dillon, Peter. 2000. "Water Reuse in Australia: Current Status, Projections and Research." In *Proceedings of Water Recycling*, ed. Peter Dillon, 99–104. Adelaide: Australia 2000.

Dishman, C. Michael, Joseph H. Sherrard, and Menahem Rebhun. 1989. "Gaining Support for Direct Potable Water Reuse." *Journal of Professional Issues in Engineering* 115 (2): 154–161.

Eckstein, Gabriel. 2014. "Transboundary Water Management Organizations." *International Water Law Project,* http://internationalwaterlaw.org/institutions /transboundary_wmos.html.

Falkenmark, Malin. 2001. "The Greatest Water Problem: The Inability to Link Environmental Security, Water Security and Food Security." *International Journal of Water Resources Development* 17 (4): 539–554.

Finger, Matthias, Ludivine Tamiotti, and Jeremy Allouche. 2006. *The Multi-Governance of Water: Four Case Studies.* Albany, N.Y.: SUNY Press.

Frenken, Karen. 1997. *Irrigation Potential in Africa: A Basin Approach.* 4. FAO Land and Water Bulletin. Rome, Italy: Land and Water Development Division, Food and Agricultural Organization.

Giordano, Meredith A., and Aaron T. Wolf. 2003. "Sharing Waters: Post-Rio International Water Management." *Natural Resources Forum* 27: 163–171.

Gleick, P. H. 1998. "The Human Right to Water." *Water Policy* 1 (5): 487–503.

Hoekstra, Arjen Y. 2000. "Appreciation of Water: Four Perspectives." *Water Policy* 1 (6): 605–622.

——. 2010. "The Global Dimension of Water Governance: Why the River Basin Approach Is No Longer Sufficient and Why Cooperative Action at Global Level Is Needed." *Water* 3 (1): 21–46.

Huitema, Dave, Erik Mostert, Wouter Egas, Sabine Moellenkamp, Claudia Pahl-Wostl, and Resul Yalcin. 2009. "Adaptive Water Governance: Assessing the Institutional Prescriptions of Adaptive (Co-)Management from a Governance Perspective and Defining a Research Agenda." *Ecology and Society* 14 (1): 26.

Kliot, Nurit, D. Shmueli, and U. Shamir. 2001. "Institutions for Management of Transboundary Water Resources: Their Nature, Characteristics and Shortcomings." *Water Policy* 3 (3): 229–255.

Krutilla, John. 1967. *The Columbia River Treaty: The Economics of an International River Basin Development*. Baltimore, Md.: Johns Hopkins University Press.

Linton, Jamie. 2008. "Is the Hydrologic Cycle Sustainable? A Historical–Geographical Critique of a Modern Concept." *Annals of the Association of American Geographers* 98 (3): 630–649.

——. 2012. "The Human Right to What? Water, Rights, Humans, and the Relation of Things." *The Right to Water: Politics, Governance and Social Struggles*, ed. Farhana Sultana and Alex Loftus, 45–60. London: Earthscan.

Livingstone, David. 2010. *Putting Science in Its Place: Geographies of Scientific Knowledge*. Chicago: University of Chicago Press.

Meadows, Donella H. 2004. *Limits to Growth: The 30-Year Update*. White River Junction, Vt.: Chelsea Green.

Mekonnen, D. Z. 2010. "The Nile Basin Cooperative Framework Agreement Negotiations and the Adoption of a 'Water Security' Paradigm: Flight into Obscurity or a Logical Cul-de-Sac?" *European Journal of International Law* 21 (2): 421.

Meneses, Montse, Jorgelina C. Pasqualino, and Francesc Castells. 2010. "Environmental Assessment of Urban Wastewater Reuse: Treatment Alternatives and Applications." *Chemosphere* 81 (2): 266–272.

Millennium Ecosystem Assessment. 2005. *Ecosystems and Human Well-Being*. Vol. 5. Washington, D.C.: Island Press.

Oki, Taikan, and Shinjiro Kanae. 2006. "Global Hydrological Cycles and World Water Resources." *Science* 313 (5790): 1068–1072.

Ostrom, Vincent, Charles M. Tiebout, and Robert Warren. 1961. "The Organization of Government in Metropolitan Areas: A Theoretical Inquiry." *American Political Science Review* 55 (4): 831–842.

Pimentel, David, O. Bailey, P. Kim, E. Mullaney, J. Calabrese, and L. Walman. 1999. "Will Limits of the Earth's Resources Control Human Numbers?" *Environment, Development and Sustainability* 1 (1): 19–39.

Po, Murni, Blair E. Nancarrow, and Juliane D. Kaercher. 2003. *Literature Review of Factors Influencing Public Perceptions of Water Reuse*. 54/03. Technical Report. Acton, Australia: CSIRO Land and Water.

Rogers, Peter. 2006. "Water Governance, Water Security and Water Sustainability." In *Water Crisis: Myth or Reality*, ed. Peter Rogers, Ramon Llamas, and Luis Martinez-Cortina, 3–36. New York: Taylor & Francis.

Rogers, Peter, and Alan W. Hall. 2003. *Effective Water Governance*. 7. Global Water Partnership Technical Committee Background Papers. Stockholm Sweden: Global Water Partnership.

Salem, Omar M. 1992. "The Great Manmade River Project: A Partial Solution to Libya's Future Water Supply." *International Journal of Water Resources Development* 8 (4): 270–278.

Salman, Salman M. A. 2013. "The Nile Basin Cooperative Framework Agreement: A Peacefully Unfolding African Spring?" *Water International* 38 (1): 17–29.

"Santa Cruz Declaration on the Global Water Crisis." 2014. *Water International* 39 (2): 246–261.

Stenekes, Nyree, Hal K. Colebatch, T. David Waite, and Nick J. Ashbolt. 2006. "Risk and Governance in Water Recycling Public Acceptance Revisited." *Science, Technology & Human Values* 31 (2): 107–134.

Teclaff, Ludwik A. 1990. "The River Basin Concept and Global Climate Change." *Pace Environmental Law Review* 8: 355.

Tropp, Hakan. 2007. "Water Governance: Trends and Needs for New Capacity Development." *Water Policy* 9: 19–30.

Vörösmarty, Charles J., P. B. McIntyre, Mark O. Gessner, David Dudgeon, and A. Prusevich. 2010. "Global Threats to Human Water Security and River Biodiversity." *Nature* 467 (7315): 555–561.

Wade-Miller, G. 2006. "Integrated Concepts in Water Reuse: Managing Global Water Needs." *Desalination* 187 (1): 65–75.

WaterAid. 2014. *Rights to Water and Sanitation* website, www.righttowater.info.

Waterbury, John. 1997. "Between Unilateralism and Comprehensive Accords: Modest Steps Toward Cooperation in International River Basins." *International Journal of Water Resources Development* 13 (3): 279–290.

Williams, Lucy A. 2010. "The Justiciability of Water Rights: Mazibuko v. City of Johannesburg." *Willamette Journal of International Law and Dispute Resolution* 18 (2): 211–255.

CHAPTER 13

Water Scarcity in Morocco

VOICE, NARRATIVE, AND ESSENTIAL RESOURCE GOVERNANCE

John Hursh

This chapter discusses water scarcity in Morocco, including its causes and its extent, the key developmental and environmental challenges that water scarcity creates, and the effects of water scarcity on Morocco's rural population—particularly in relation to agricultural production and rural livelihoods. The second part of this chapter investigates the ideas of voice and narrative as they relate to essential resource governance. Finally, this chapter concludes by examining how individuals and communities may reclaim their voice to govern essential resources through the reappropriation of local institutions. To do so, it evaluates the responsiveness of water user associations (WUAs) to local needs, finding that while generally disappointing, locally adapted WUAs help individuals and communities reclaim voice, reshape narrative, and improve local governance.

BACKGROUND

Water scarcity has long created developmental and environmental challenges in Morocco. Featuring predominantly arid and semiarid climates, Morocco receives very little rainfall and experiences erratic precipitation that affects snow accumulation, corresponding snowmelt, and groundwater availability (Diao et al. 2008, 119). These conditions have contributed to numerous droughts, including ten severe droughts between 1900 and 2000 (Diao et al. 2008). In what is already a water-scarce country, the ongoing reduction of available surface water and groundwater further stresses Morocco's water resources (Food and Agricultural Organization [FAO] 2005; USAID 2014). Moreover, the frequency of droughts is increasing. For example, Morocco endured a significant drought almost every other year throughout the 1990s (Diao et al. 2008, 119). Despite these already difficult conditions, Morocco will likely experience even greater water scarcity in upcoming years, as environmental models predict both reduced precipitation and rising temperatures (Paeth et al. 2009, 121).[1]

While Moroccans have long dealt with water scarcity, climate change and increased water demand exacerbate the challenges that water scarcity creates. Current government policies also amplify these difficulties. For example, regional development plans emphasize expanding the water-intensive sectors of irrigated agriculture (*Plan Maroc Vert*) and luxury tourism (*Plan Azur*) despite the strain these activities exert on water resources (Tekken and Kropp 2012, 961). Likewise, while the Moroccan government and private sector have invested heavily in developing Morocco's water resources, the water available from surface-water sources, such as snowmelt in the Atlas Mountains, is nearing its physical limits (Diao et al. 2008, 119).[2] At the same time, the majority of rural Moroccans lack access to potable water (Davis 2006, 91).

The agricultural sector places the greatest strain on the country's water resources, consuming at least 80 percent of water annually (He et al. 2006, 322).[3] Irrigated agriculture in particular contributes to water scarcity by driving an unsustainable water demand through an increasingly large amount of irrigated farmland.[4] This issue is compounded by a reliance on reservoir dams already made less efficient by sediment trapping (Snoussi et al. 2007, 591) and siltation (FAO 2005; Richards 2008, 15).[5] Irrigated agriculture also contributes to environmental problems, such as salinization, which is the most serious water-quality issue in Morocco (FAO 2005). Salinization can decrease the productivity of irrigated soils by more than 50 percent in only twenty years (Schilling et al. 2012, 21), and some areas already demonstrate large amounts of salinized soils.[6]

While irrigated agriculture dominates water consumption, the majority of Moroccan farmers, particularly the poor and landless, practice rain-fed agriculture, which characterizes more than 90 percent of Morocco's arable land (Schilling et al. 2012, 20).[7] Of course, precipitation is essential to rain-fed agriculture, and ecological projections suggest decreased agricultural productivity and reduced yields under current conditions (Schilling et al. 2012, 16; Tekken and Kropp 2012, 975).[8] Further, deciding to grow crops that require more water—such as wheat rather than barley—and depleted groundwater increase the vulnerability of the rain-fed sector (Schilling et al. 2012, 24).

Worsening socioeconomic conditions at least partially attributable to water scarcity have forced rural Moroccans to embrace adaptive livelihood strategies, including diversifying employment and migration (Obeid 2006, 5). Rural-to-urban migration is one of the most common strategies and deserves special consideration, given the number of Moroccans who undertake this activity and the socioeconomic and environmental outcomes it entails. Since as early as 1980, 100,000 Moroccans have left the countryside each year to seek employment in cities and towns (Swearingen 1987a, 162). Once rural Moroccans reach urban centers, they often find themselves enduring substandard living conditions in informal settlements (Richards 2008, 15). Already densely populated, Moroccan cities lack sufficient human resources and employment opportunities to address current levels of migration. Consequently, urban poverty grows alongside this migration. Rural-to-urban migration also contributes to poor environmental outcomes by disrupting peri-urban irrigation schemes (FAO 2005) and contributing to unsustainable urban and coastal demand for water (Diao et al. 2008, 119; Schilling et al. 2012, 16; Tekken and Kropp 2012, 973). While rural-to-urban migration is neither new nor unique to Morocco, recent research strongly suggests that environmental conditions now drive the decision to leave the Moroccan countryside.[9] This notable finding underscores the need to include environmental considerations within broader policies aimed to increase human well-being and improve socioeconomic conditions, including essential resource governance.

Moroccan government policies cannot end water scarcity or reverse climate change, but they can help ease the negative outcomes that water scarcity creates and climate change exacerbates. Government policies championing intensive irrigation or luxury tourism while failing to aid Morocco's rain-fed agricultural sector aggravate existing environmental problems while also contributing to the pronounced economic inequality within Morocco. Moreover, by failing to adjust its water-management practices to account for climate change and population growth, Morocco will almost certainly encounter increasingly severe problems stemming from water scarcity, including serious deteriorations in living conditions and even resource conflict (Schilling et al. 2012, 18–20; Tekken and Kropp 2012, 974).

Addressing water scarcity requires innovative solutions that account for local ecological conditions and socioeconomic realities. One such example is collecting water from dew, which can provide a useful supplementary water source for coastal communities in southwest Morocco

(Lekouch et al. 2011, 2264). This supply-side solution is cost effective because the water source requires only light sterilization to be potable (Lekouch et al. 2011). Developing successful demand-side solutions to reduce water use or improve water-use efficiency will be more difficult. For rain-fed agriculture, shifting planting patterns and crop types can reduce the impact of water scarcity and climate change, but monitoring irrigation practices and soil conditions remains time-consuming and costly (Schilling et al. 2012, 24). Likewise, while policy recommendations to manage water demand rather than chase water supply are hardly new to Morocco (Lahlou and Colyer 2000, 1011), the political influence of key economic interests, such as the agricultural and tourism sectors, suggest that Moroccan legislators will continue to pursue less promising supply-side solutions (Tekken and Kropp 2012, 974). Finally, while technological improvements, such as dual-use rainfall techniques and using treated wastewater in agriculture can help alleviate water scarcity by improving water-use efficiency (Richards 2008, 13; Bauwens 2009), these improvements provide at best a partial solution.

GOVERNING ESSENTIAL RESOURCES: VOICE AND NARRATIVE

In their introductory chapter to this volume, Olivier De Schutter and Katharina Pistor define voice as "the normative proposition that people should have a say in the rules by which they are governed, —especially when it comes to governing access to resources critical for their survival." They note that when properly understood, voice allows "*all* members of a group, community, or society to claim their share in resources essential to their survival." Thus, with respect to essential resources, voice claims foremost that individuals have the right to design the rules that govern their access to and use of these resources, but this definition also insists that this right extends to all members of a group, community, or society. Accordingly, voice features strong rights of self-determination and self-governance as well as a requisite right of inclusiveness that guarantees all individuals the right to participate. Of course, no group, community, or society practices voice as equitably as described above, and disagreements between local users and broader communities over resource use and resource governance are common. These disagreements often arise from who can and cannot express voice when determining the use and governance of resources. Within Morocco, such disagreements typically concern water and land and frequently pit the *makhzen*—a group of political and economic elites that ostensibly serve as advisors to the monarchy—against the Moroccan citizenry.

The influence of the *makhzen* is a well-recognized aspect of Moroccan society (Daadaoui 2011). Moreover, the development of this group's influence helps to explain current inequalities in resource use and resource governance in Morocco. Following independence in 1956, King Mohammed V solidified his political power by securing the support of wealthy rural elites or "notables" who controlled large amounts of land and natural resources. Charrad describes this relationship as a "coalition between palace and tribe," where Mohammed gained the support of rural elites in exchange for a guarantee of nonintervention in rural affairs (Charrad 2001, 153). King Hassan II assumed the throne in 1961 and began to enact a variety of laws and policies that exerted even greater government control over land and natural resources.[10] Hassan's government often justified this increased intervention on environmental and economic necessity, yet these interventions did not match ecological realities or the needs of local populations that relied on these resources for subsistence and livelihoods. Instead, Hassan's development policies further enriched political and economic elites, including rural notables who were often members of the *makhzen*. By the mid-1980s, Hassan had become an authoritarian ruler "presiding over a clientelist political machine and operating in association with a small and privileged national bourgeoisie" despite—or perhaps because of—"crushing poverty" and a "large and growing gap between the rich and the poor" (Tessler 1987, 221).

While rural notables and the *makhzen* grew wealthier, rural poverty, landlessness, and the spread of informal urban settlements (*bidonvilles*) also increased. King Mohammed VI assumed the throne in 1999, and although his government has made more of an effort to use and govern resources more equitably, these and other issues stemming from unjust resource use and acquisition remain unresolved in contemporary Morocco. At the same time, powerful economic interests and political elites continue to have a disproportionate say in determining the rules that govern resources. Consequently, the voice of the rural population—especially the rural poor—often goes unheard. Furthermore, Moroccan women face even greater challenges to exert their voice, as gender discrimination and patriarchal interpretations of Islamic law weaken their claim to essential resources, particularly land (Joseph 1996, 14–15; Obeid 2006, 15).

If voice describes the ability of individuals to create the rules that govern their use of resources, narrative perhaps best captures how individuals create the conditions to allow the voice of some and deny the voice of others. In this sense, narrative is the process that individuals and groups use to justify including or excluding others from resource use and resource governance. In Morocco, government officials, political and economic elites, and religious leaders rely on specific narratives to engender the social values and legal rules necessary to justify an inequitable use of resources, thereby muting voice. For example, the Moroccan government has continually invoked an environmental narrative that attributes land degradation to traditional agricultural and pastoral practices, even though ecological studies and environmental data do not support these claims (Davis 2006, 92–96). Likewise, religious leaders have applied discriminatory social norms and patriarchal interpretations of Islamic law to frustrate women's ability to participate in social and economic life (Salime 2011, 1–4) despite clearly contradicting the Islamic legal principle of gender equality.[11] As these examples illustrate, understanding the relationship between narrative and voice is critical for assessing how legal and policy outcomes affect the use and governance of essential resources.

A key aspect of the narrative-voice relationship is how narrative shapes voice in knowledge production. By privileging some historical accounts and certain bases of knowledge—while rejecting others—narrative constructs voice by deciding whose history and what knowledge matters. When politically mobilized, narrative can significantly influence the legal and policy discussions that inform voice and order the governance of essential resources. Postcolonial and critical legal scholars have demonstrated how such narratives enable the voice of some and silence the voice of others. They have also shown the power of narrative to obscure legal and policy outcomes. Here, the neoliberal development narrative that insists on a facially equal international economic regime despite further entrenching material inequality amassed during imperial and colonial plunder is most instructive (Mattei and Nader 2008, 10–34).[12] This narrative obscures current socioeconomic conditions by presenting the material inequality stemming from colonial practices as a neutral explanation for poverty in the global South, while also diverting attention from the historical biases of the international economic system (Thomas 1999, 6).

Narrative can also have a lasting effect on how societies legitimize unequal access to essential resources. Within North Africa, colonial actors invented an environmental history that blamed indigenous North

Africans for the region's supposed environmental and agricultural woes (Davis 2007, 2). Colonial actors employed this declensionist narrative of environmental decline to justify the implementation of laws and policies that resulted in widespread land dispossession and resource expropriation (Davis 2007, 6). Importantly, this narrative did not end with colonial independence but persists within the postcolonial state. Governments, international organizations, and major donor agencies all relied on this narrative to advance neoliberal policy despite a lack of reliable supporting data (Davis 2006, 94). Moreover, domestic economic and political elites seized on this narrative to further economic self-interest and political gain.

The Moroccan government relied on this narrative to enact laws and policies that followed colonial approaches to land use and resource governance. For example—and contrary to government assertions—the 1980s agricultural crisis that traded short-term agricultural profits based on citrus fruit exports for long-term food insecurity and the need to import basic cereals was not due to natural causes but to specific governmental policies that incentivized these outcomes (Swearingen 1987a, 159–63). The misuse of water, including an ineffective and monolithic irrigation model and the ill-advised construction of numerous dams, significantly contributed to this crisis (Swearingen 1987a, 160–61). Moreover, government officials largely ignored the rain-fed agricultural sector, even though it accounted for roughly 70 percent of Morocco's cultivated land and over 90 percent of its farmers (Swearingen 1987a, 162). By adopting policies advanced by the declensionist narrative, Moroccan policy makers failed to break with the colonial past and effectively allowed rural notables to recolonize the Moroccan countryside by appropriating colonial farms and expanding an outdated and unsustainable irrigation model (Swearingen 1987a, 163–66).

RECLAIMING VOICE

As the previous section demonstrates, legal and policy outcomes that allow only a small minority to benefit from essential resources undermine the voice of individuals and marginalize communities. Narrative contributes to these exclusionary outcomes by creating the conditions that allow for suppressing or even silencing voice. Institutionally, continually denying voice can result in a democratic deficit in which governing institutions do not reflect the will of citizens. Elite capture of key institutions is both a contributing factor and resulting outcome of this deficit.

This situation certainly holds true in much of the Middle East and North Africa, where many of these states have not succeeded in building democratic institutions or strong civil societies following colonial independence (Alkadry 2002, 740, 747–748). These shortcomings are at least partly attributable to colonial actors who destroyed existing sociopolitical and economic institutions, leaving a governance void now exemplified by ineffective legislative bodies and authoritarian leaders backed by elites or the military (Alkadry 2002, 745–746). Of course, democratic deficits and ineffectual institutions are not limited to postcolonial states or the global South.[13] Nonetheless, the distorted socioeconomic and political conditions that resulted from colonial practices present especially difficult challenges for building and maintaining responsive governments and inclusive institutions in postcolonial states.

This concluding section examines how individuals and communities can reclaim their voice to essential resource governance through the reappropriation of local institutions. While weak or extractive institutions undermine voice, strong and inclusive institutions embolden voice, allowing individuals and communities to use and govern essential resources more equitably. Within Morocco, the local adaptation of WUAs offers one such example. Although certainly not a panacea, a subset of WUAs have shown a surprising capacity to adapt to local needs. This adaptive process illustrates how individuals can reshape institutions to address local concerns while also improving essential resource governance.

WUAs are common throughout North Africa and the Middle East.[14] While the overall assessment of WUAs remains mixed, these institutions have led to improved resource governance in some countries. Within Egypt WUAs have demonstrated improved irrigation operation and maintenance, less water pollution, and more efficient water use, while in Yemen WUAs have improved irrigation services (World Bank 2007, 47).

The Moroccan government created its WUAs in the early 1990s. Officially, the Moroccan legislature created WUAs in 1992 by enacting Law No. 2–84 (FAO 2005). However, the government has favored WUAs as the preferred policy option for improving coordination between farmers and irrigation officials since the mid-1980s (Faysse et al. 2010, 50). Once established, irrigation authorities planned three activities for WUAs: facilitating communication between farmers and irrigation officials, maintaining irrigation canals, and collecting fees on behalf of the irrigation authority (Faysse et al. 2010, 56). The creation of WUAs was consistent with the Moroccan government's partial withdrawal from the agricultural sector

(Faysse et al. 2010, 54). This withdrawal followed a larger trend of decentralization and lessened state intervention in the 1990s. For water resource management, Morocco's 1995 Water Law (Law No. 10–95) provided the clearest articulation of this trend by decentralizing the management of water resources to basin-level agencies and introducing a consultative process that encouraged water users and public authorities to work together to develop plans for water use, distribution, and development (USAID 2010, 12).

WUAs are the most localized water-management institution in Morocco. At the other end of the management spectrum, the Ministry of Energy, Mines, Water, and the Environment oversees state water-management policy, while the Ministry of Agriculture, Rural Development, and Fisheries is responsible for irrigation water (USAID 2010, 13). Regionally, the Catchment Basin Authorities are the most important water-management institution, as they create master development and use plans and issue water-use permits (Salman and Bradlow 2006, 91). There are nine large-scale irrigation schemes within Morocco, with a number of WUAs in each scheme (Faysse et al. 2010, 49). WUA activity varies widely across the different schemes. For example, a 2007–2008 study of five large-scale irrigation schemes showed that three irrigation schemes (Doukkala, Gharb, and Loukkos) contained 106 WUAs, none of which functioned, while the Tadla irrigation scheme contained 36 WUAs, all of which were active (Faysse et al. 2010, 55).

WUAs rely on a group assertion of control rights to manage resources. State-sanctioned WUAs, such as those in Morocco, feature a management assignment, which is generally a portion of a catchment area, as well as a responsibility to reduce negative off-site effects (Mitchell 2006, 184). WUAs encourage the devolution of resource management to local communities by allowing individuals within these communities to operate and maintain irrigation systems (World Bank 2007, 47). WUAs also encourage participatory resource management by fostering stakeholder consultation between government officials, local communities, and the private sector (World Bank 2007, 53). Finally, WUAs advance local governance by featuring an elected governing board that follows established, transparent procedures (World Bank 2007, 47).

Within Morocco, there is broad recognition that addressing complex water resource challenges requires coalition building that involves all stakeholders (Faysse et al. 2012, 127). The participatory function of WUAs meets this need. WUAs also offer the Moroccan government an opportunity to demonstrate its commitment to respecting the voice of small-scale farmers. Empirical research shows that strong state involvement within the water-management sector reduces the willingness of farmers to engage with or participate in WUAs. Indeed, one case study showed that stakeholders embraced participatory programs in which a decentralized government provided confidence that their negotiated outcomes would be respected and implemented (Carr et al. 2012, 1). These findings reflect the experience of small-scale Moroccan farmers—not yet entirely incorporated in broader policy discussions—for whom decentralization and diminished state intervention have only gradually begun (Faysse et al. 2010, 54). But, by respecting the autonomy of WUAs, the Moroccan government can begin to regain the trust of small-scale farmers, whose voice has long been excluded from resource management and policy deliberations.

WUAs have the potential to increase the voice of local communities in essential resource governance. However, in practice, numerous obstacles undermine their effectiveness and thereby hinder the realization of this potential. In Morocco, many WUAs have proved unsuccessful due to an inability to secure financial resources and a lack of political commitment (Faysse et al. 2010, 50). A lack of financial resources prevents WUAs from completing important activities such as distributing water or maintaining irrigation canals, while a lack of political commitment results in uncollected association fees and rarely held general assemblies (Faysse et al. 2010, 56). Thus, despite their focus on participatory governance, WUAs have often failed to increase voice.

WUAs are also subject to elite capture, which of course subverts voice. Empirical research conducted in former socialist states shows that powerful individuals may use WUAs to formalize existing power asymmetries (Theesfeld 2011, 91). This is a valid concern for Moroccan policymakers, as rural notables have previously succeeded in capturing local institutions, such as farmers' organizations (Faysse et al. 2010, 62). Likewise, rural development associations organized around traditional *khattara* irrigation systems have led to the reinforcement of local power structures (Oshima 2008, 41). Reinforcing these power asymmetries is problematic for a number of reasons, but perhaps none more so than perpetuating patriarchal biases even as donor agencies call for greater female representation in WUA governance (USAID 2010, 2).

The failure of WUAs to increase voice reflects decades of development policy that ignored small-scale farmers or enacted development policies on their behalf, but without seeking their input or considering their preferences. Indeed, the Moroccan government largely organized WUAs around irrigation scheme design without taking into account local community social structures (Faysse et al. 2010, 57). At the same time, research shows that many Moroccan officials did not express genuine political commitment to transferring irrigation authority to local entities, which of course undermines the very purpose of WUAs and participatory resource governance (Faysse et al. 2010). As a result, it is unsurprising that Moroccan farmers tend to view WUAs with considerable apathy and that the majority of WUAs remain dormant (Faysse et al. 2010, 57, 63).

Clearly, most Moroccan WUAs have not realized their potential to increase voice. However, despite this general outcome, a subset of WUAs have performed very well and helped communities to reclaim their voice in essential resource governance. Specifically, WUAs that local communities have appropriated for local socioeconomic needs and ecological conditions have proven active and effective. This outcome shows that WUAs remain a valuable option for addressing water scarcity, provided local communities can wrest control of these institutions from government officials and local elites. Here, local adaptation does not require a radical break from government officials involved in resource management. Indeed, local communities will need to work with government officials, particularly irrigation authorities, to manage water resources most effectively. Nonetheless, local communities must have the autonomy to manage WUAs without undue government interference or excessive influence from local elites for these institutions to reach their participatory potential. Only under these conditions will WUAs contribute to reestablishing the voice of small-scale farmers and rural communities in the governance of essential resources.

The WUAs in the Moyen Sebou irrigation scheme provide a case in point. In 1995, the Moroccan government began implementing this irrigation scheme, which is located 60 kilometers northwest of Fez (Kadiri et al. 2009, S347).[15] The development officials who designed this irrigation scheme did not seek the input of farmers who the scheme was intended to help or consider the social organization of the affected farming communities during the project's technical planning stage (Kadiri et al. 2009, S348). Indeed, development practitioners originally proposed this project as a centralized irrigation scheme with heavy infrastructure and state-controlled management. The donor agency, however, made participatory management a condition of funding. Over several years, local users transformed this scheme from a top-down imposition to an institution more closely aligned with local needs and participatory resource management (Kadiri et al. 2009).

Within this irrigation scheme, local users adapted WUAs to meet local demand through an incremental process. Initially, WUA users focused on simply making WUAs easier to use. For example, some WUAs decided to abandon inflexible fixed-payment schemes for volumetric water fees and local farmers' associations simplified WUA administrative procedures (Kadiri et al. 2009, S351–S352). Later, WUA users expanded how these WUAs operated and made them more reflective of local priorities. Thus, one irrigation board changed its regulations to finance profitable milk cooperatives (Kadiri et al. 2009, S353–S354), while other WUAs proposed replacing large water pumps, which impose heavy costs through maintenance and management, with smaller pumps that require less upkeep and oversight (Kadiri et al. 2009, S354). Perhaps most notably, the local adaptation of WUAs resulted in better local governance of essential resources. Foremost—and unlike most other WUAs—these WUAs began organizing general assemblies as soon as the irrigation scheme became operational (Kadiri et al. 2009, S352). These general assemblies are now a key community forum for debating issues of common concern. In addition, governance procedures have improved as the WUA has progressed. For example, voting now occurs through secret ballots instead of a simple show of hands (Kadiri et al. 2009).

The WUAs in the Moyen Sebou irrigation scheme provide several key findings. First, the Moyen Sebou WUAs follow a broader trend that shows WUAs in small and medium irrigation schemes are active and important to local communities, whereas WUAs in larger irrigation schemes remain largely dormant (Faysse et al. 2010, 57). This finding suggests that local participation truly determines the success of WUAs. Certainly, the relative failure of WUAs in larger irrigation schemes is attributable to a variety of factors, but a truly local institution will necessarily encounter difficulties when attempting to expand its participatory governance model into larger areas with more fractured interests and greater degrees of information and power asymmetry. In this sense, the established presence of rural notables in larger irrigation schemes and their capture of other local institutions perhaps best explain the relative failure of WUAs in larger irrigation schemes.

Second, the Moyen Sebou WUAs show the ability of younger Moroccans to revive inactive WUAs (Faysse et al. 2010, 56). One study even proposes that WUAs serve as a "school" that allows young people to learn about associative life and collective action (Kadiri et al. 2009, S353). To support this claim, researchers described a situation wherein young Moroccans organized two local development associations that began working in the region after the WUAs, and how these associations have improved community life through a variety of activities (Kadiri et al. 2009). At the very least, the desire and the ability of younger Moroccans to revive flagging WUAs shows that motivated individuals can reform these institutions to meet local demands and improve essential resource governance provided they have or can claim the autonomy to do so. Finally, these outcomes illustrate that locally adapted WUAs can help to reshape local power structures in a more equitable manner by improving local governance. This result is consistent with research that shows WUAs can improve local accountability and empower local communities (World Bank 2007, 135).

While certainly beneficial to improving essential resource governance, like all institutions, locally adapted WUAs have limitations. For one, water demand drives water scarcity within Morocco, and WUAs—which encourage more efficient water use and more equitable resource governance—may not reduce demand. Moreover, voice requires that all individuals within a community have a say in creating the rules that govern essential resources. Whether the appropriation of existing institutions can meet this lofty standard is uncertain. Finally, the combination of past agricultural policy that featured a state-centric, top-down vision of local organizations and the ongoing processes of elite capture and state co-option raise serious questions concerning the long-term viability of locally appropriated institutions.

Despite these limitations and concerns, locally adapted WUAs likely present the best available option for dealing with water scarcity in Morocco at the local level. While government efforts to reduce water demand would offer the best outcome, current socioeconomic and political circumstances make the adoption of this approach unlikely. Until circumstances change, the local appropriation of WUAs provides communities with a valuable tool for managing their water resources according to local need and through local participation. Most importantly, this approach helps communities reclaim voice and reshape narrative by demonstrating their ability to manage essential resources fairly and effectively.

CONCLUSION

How a society governs essential resources—those resources so crucial that they are indispensable for human survival—says a good deal about that society. Within postcolonial Morocco, the governance of essential resources has favored economic and political elites, initially as a compromise to secure state stability and later as the largesse of clientelist politics and elite capture. Although essential resource governance is gradually improving under King Mohammed VI, for most of its postcolonial independence, the Moroccan government has invoked specific narratives to justify inequitable resource governance, allowing a small minority to benefit at the expense of the majority. Narratives of environmental decline blamed small-scale farmers and traditional pastoralists for environmental degradation despite a lack of compelling evidence to substantiate these claims. Nonetheless, these narratives allowed elites to appropriate land and other essential resources and to suppress the voice of individuals and communities by largely denying their participation in essential resource governance.

Strong institutions based on participatory governance can provide a useful counter to such outcomes and give citizens a foothold to begin challenging these exclusionary narratives. In Morocco, locally adapted WUAs afford small-scale farmers the opportunity to regain voice. Although WUAs have generally proved disappointing for reaching their potential to increase participatory governance, the locally adapted WUAs of the Moyen Sebou irrigation scheme are an interesting exception, precisely because local communities refashioned these institutions to local needs. Of course, locally adapted WUAs are imperfect, and questions regarding their long-term sustainability remain. Nonetheless, the appropriation of these institutions to match local priorities provides a good example for how local communities can reclaim their voice for governing the resources essential to their well-being and even survival.

NOTES

1. Across North Africa, precipitation will likely decrease between 10 and 20 percent between 2011 and 2050, while temperatures will likely rise between 2 and 3°C (Paeth et al. 2009, 121).

2. The FAO also predicts that Morocco's overexploitation of groundwater will worsen, estimating a groundwater exploitation rate of 120.1 percent by 2020 (FAO 2005).

3. Diao and colleagues provide a slightly higher estimate of 85 percent (Diao et al. 2008, 119), while Richards cites the World Bank's even higher estimate of 87 percent (Richards 2008, 22).

4. Between 1953 and 1998, the amount of irrigated farmland more than doubled from 73,000 hectares to 1,471,797 hectares (He et al. 2006, 328).

5. Richards notes that dam reservoirs are silting at a rate of 1.5 percent each year (Richards 2008, 15), which suggests a continued decrease in efficiency and carrying capacity.

6. In the southern Draa Valley, a region known for date and vegetable production, salinization affects 80 percent of all agricultural soils (Davis 2006, 97–98).

7. He and colleagues provide a slightly lower estimate, finding that rain-fed agriculture characterizes 84 percent of Morocco's arable land (He et al. 2006, 328).

8. Schilling and colleagues project a 30 percent decrease in agricultural productivity by 2080 under current conditions when accounting for greater access to carbon fertilizer and a 40 percent decrease otherwise (Schilling et al. 2012, 16).

9. Here, Richards's use of the term "drought migrants" to describe rural Moroccans who abandon agriculture and move to urban centers due to deteriorating environmental conditions is particularly apt (Richards 2008, 15).

10. Throughout the 1960s and 1970s, Hassan's government used political patronage to acquire extensive amounts of the most valuable agricultural land in Morocco (Swearingen 1987b, 180). Thus, during Hassan's rule, Swearingen characterizes the "real land reform in Morocco" as "the clandestine land transfers from European settlers to Moroccan elites and the privatization of the state-controlled colonial holdings" (Swearingen 1987b, 180–181).

11. The Qur'an provides a clear statement of gender equality in sura 9, verse 71. Moreover, a number of Islamic feminist scholars and activists have engaged in a variety of projects that seek to reclaim the Islamic legal principles of egalitarianism and gender equality from patriarchal practices (Barlas 2002, 133–149).

12. Pogge makes a similar argument regarding international human rights law and global poverty: "Given that the present global institutional order is foreseeably associated with such massive incidence of avoidable severe poverty, its (uncompensated) imposition manifests an ongoing human rights violation—arguably the largest such violation ever committed in human history" (Pogge 2005, 741).

13. The widening gulf between legislators and citizens and the undue influence of special interest groups and wealthy individuals is hardly exclusive to postcolonial states or the global South. Indeed, the farcical *Citizens United* decision and the ever-increasing amount of political donations and influence of lobbyist groups raise serious questions regarding the legitimacy of democratic governance in the United States.

14. In addition to Morocco, the governments of Tunisia, Libya, Egypt, Jordan, Yemen, Oman, and Iran promote WUAs (World Bank 2007, 47).

15. The authors based their study on a survey of sixty farms in four WUAs within the Moyen Sebou irrigation scheme and several semidirected interviews of WUA board members, irrigation project staff, and government agency technicians (Kadiri et al. 2009, S348).

REFERENCES

Alkadry, Mohamad G. 2002. "Reciting Colonial Scripts: Colonialism, Globalization and Democracy in the Decolonized Middle East." *Administrative Theory & Praxis* 24 (4): 739–762.

Barlas, Asma. 2002. *"Believing Women" in Islam: Unreading Patriarchal Interpretations of the Qur'an.* Austin: University of Texas Press.

Bauwens, Daan. 2009. "Morocco: Farmers Overcome Water Scarcity." Inter Press Service News Agency, 31 July. www.ipsnews.net/2009/07/morocco-farmers-overcome -water-scarcity.

Carr, G., G. Blöschl, and D.P. Loucks. 2012. "Evaluating Participation in Water Resource Management: A Review." *Water Resources Research* 48 (WR11401): 1–17.

Charrad, Mounira. 2001. *States and Women's Rights: The Making of Postcolonial Tunisia, Algeria, and Morocco.* Berkeley: University of California Press.

Daadaoui, Mohamed. 2011. *Moroccan Monarchy and the Islamist Challenge: Maintaining Makhzen Power.* New York: Palgrave McMillan.

Davis, Diana K. 2006. "Neoliberalism, Environmentalism, and Agricultural Restructuring in Morocco." *Geographic Journal* 172 (2): 88–105.

——. 2007. *Resurrecting the Granary of Rome: Environmental History and French Colonial Expansion in North Africa.* Athens: Ohio University Press.

Diao, Xinshen, Ariel Dinar, Terry Roe, and Yacov Tsur. 2008. "A General Equilibrium Analysis of Conjunctive Ground and Surface Water Use with an Application to Morocco." *Agricultural Economics* 38: 117–135.

Faysse, Nicolas, Mostafa Errahj, Marcel Kuper, and Mohamed Mahdi. 2010. "Learning to Voice? The Evolving Roles of Family Farmers in the Coordination of Large-Scale Irrigation Schemes in Morocco." *Water Alternatives* 3 (1): 48–67.

Faysse, Nicolas, Mohamed el Amrani, Soufiane el Aydi, and Ahmed Lahlou. 2012. "Formulation and Implementation of Policies to Deal with Groundwater Overuse in Morocco: Which Supporting Coalitions?" *Irrigation and Drainage* 61 (1; supplement): 126–134.

Food and Agricultural Organization (FAO). 2005. "AQUASTAT Country Profile: Morocco." www.fao.org/nr/water/aquastat/countries_regions/mar/index.stm.

He, Lixia, Wallace E. Tyner, Rachid Doukkali, and Gamal Siam. 2006. "Policy Options to Improve Water Allocation Efficiency: Analysis on Egypt and Morocco." *Water International* 31 (3): 320–337.

Joseph, Saud. 1996. "Patriarchy and Development in the Arab World." *Gender and Development* 4 (2): 14–19.

Kadiri, Zakaria, Marcel Kuper, Nicolas Faysse, and Mostafa Errahj. 2009. "Local Transformation of a State-initiated Institutional Innovation: The Example of Water Users' Associations in an Irrigation Scheme in Morocco." *Irrigation and Drainage* 58 (3; supplement): S346–S357.

Lahlou, Mohamed, and Dale Colyer. 2000. "Water Conservation in Casablanca, Morocco." *Journal of the American Water Resources Association* 36 (5): 1003–1012.

Lekouch, I., M. Muselli, B. Kabbachi, J. Ouazzani, I. Melnytchouk-Milimouk, and D. Beysens. 2011. "Dew, Fog, and Rain as Supplementary Sources of Water in South-Western Morocco." *Energy* 36: 2257–65.

Mattei, Ugo, and Laura Nader. 2008. *Plunder: When the Rule of Law Is Illegal.* Oxford: Blackwell.

Mitchell, Robert. 2006. "Property Rights and Environmentally Sound Management of Farmland and Forests." In *Land Law Reform: Achieving Development Policy Objectives*, by John W. Bruce, Renée Giovarelli, Leonard Rolfes Jr, David Bledsoe, and Robert Mitchell, 175–226. Washington, D.C.: International Bank for Reconstruction and Development/World Bank.

Obeid, Michelle. 2006. "Women's Access and Rights to Land: Gender Relations in Tenure—Jordan, Yemen and Morocco." Scoping study, International Development Research Centre, Ottawa, July.

Oshima, Keiko. 2008. "Khattara and Water User Organizations in Morocco." In *What Makes Traditional Technologies Tick? A Review of Traditional Approaches for Water Management in Drylands*, ed. Zafar Adeel, Brigitte Schuster, and Harriet Bigas, 36–43. Hamilton, ON: United Nations University–International Network on Water, Environment, and Health.

Paeth, Heiko, Kai Born, Robin Girmes, Ralf Podzun, and Daniela Jacob. 2009. "Regional Climate Change in Tropical and Northern Africa due to Greenhouse Forcing and Land Use Changes." *Journal of Climate* 22: 114–132.

Pogge, Thomas. 2005. "Recognized and Violated: The Human Rights of the Global Poor." *Leiden Journal of International Law* 18 (4): 717–745.

Richards, Alan. 2008. "Human Capabilities in the Maghreb: Challenges and Opportunities." Keynote Address to the Maghreb Center Annual Conference: Maghreb Development, Strategic Resources and the Environment in a Globalized World, Georgetown University, Washington, D.C., 21 April 2008.

Salime, Zakia. 2011. *Between Feminism and Islam: Human Rights and Sharia Law in Morocco*. Minneapolis: University of Minnesota Press.

Salman, Salman M. A., and Daniel D. Bradlow. 2006. *Regulatory Frameworks for Water Resources Management: A Comparative Study*. Washington, D.C.: International Bank for Reconstruction and Development/World Bank.

Schilling, Janpeter, Korbinian P. Freier, Elke Hertig, and Jürgen Scheffran. 2012. "Climate Change, Vulnerability and Adaptation in North Africa with Focus on Morocco." *Agriculture, Ecosystems and Environment* 156: 12–26.

Snoussi, Maria, Johnson Kitheka, Yohanna Shaghude, Alioune Kane, Russell Arthurton, Martin Le Tissier, and Hassan Virji. 2007. "Downstream and Coastal Impacts of Damming and Water Abstraction in Africa." *Environmental Management* 39: 587–600.

Swearingen, Will D. 1987a. "Morocco's Agricultural Crisis." In *The Political Economy of Morocco*, ed. I. William Zartman, 159–72. New York: Praeger.

——. 1987b. *Moroccan Mirages: Agrarian Dreams and Deceptions, 1912–1986*. Princeton, N.J.: Princeton University Press.

Tekken, Vera, and Jürgen P. Kropp. 2012. "Climate-driven or Human-induced: Indicating Severe Water Scarcity in the Moulouya River Basin (Morocco)." *Water* 4: 959–982.

Tessler, Mark A. 1987. "Image and Reality in Moroccan Political Economy." In *The Political Economy of Morocco*, ed. I. William Zartman, 212–242. New York: Praeger.

Theesfeld, Insa. 2011. "Perceived Power Resources in Situations of Collective Action." *Water Alternatives* 4 (1): 86–103.

Thomas, Chantal. 1999. "Causes of Inequality in the International Economic Order: Critical Race Theory and Postcolonial Development." *Transnational Law & Contemporary Problems* 9 (1): 1–15.

USAID. 2010. "Country Profile: Property Rights and Resource Governance: Morocco." http://usaidlandtenure.net/sites/default/files/country-profiles/full-reports/USAID_Land_Tenure_Morocco_Profile.pdf.

——. 2014. "Morocco: Water and Sanitation." 14 March. www.usaid.gov/morocco/water-and-sanitation.

World Bank. 2007. *Making the Most of Scarcity: Accountability for Better Water Management in the Middle East and North Africa.* Washington, D.C.: International Bank for Reconstruction and Development/World Bank.

CHAPTER 14

Solving Transborder Water Issues in Changing Climate Scenarios of South Asia

A THEORETICAL ILLUSTRATION USING A PRINCIPAL-AGENT BARGAINING APPROACH

Nilhari Neupane

Water is an essential resource with multiple uses—domestic, industrial, energy-related, recreational, and agricultural—that often compete. Among the various sectors of water consumption, the agriculture sector consumes large quantities of water (70 percent of total freshwater) in comparison with other sectors such as industry (19 percent), municipal (11 percent) (Food and Agriculture Organization 2013). An increase in global population will require more food products, ultimately increasing water consumption (Johansson 2000). The world population rose from 2.5 billion in 1950 to 6.5 billion in 2010 (Alexandratos and Bruinsma, 2012). As a result, the irrigated area has increased by more than doubled and water withdrawals tripled in the past sixty years (Alexandratos and Bruinsma, 2012). The world population is expected to increase to 9.3 billion in 2050, and water demand is expected to increase accordingly from 7,200 cubic kilometers in 2006 to 13,500 cubic kilometers in 2050, which is almost twice the present water demand (IWMI 2007; Alexandratos and Bruinsma, 2012; Food and Agriculture Organization 2013). It is predicted that future water demand in developing countries will be double that of developed countries to fulfill the food demand of a growing population in the developing world (Johansson 2000).

Irrigation is an important input for crop production; it increases crop yields by 100 to 400 percent. Total irrigated land in the world is only 277 million hectares (20 percent of the total cropped area) but contributes 40 percent of the world's food. The remaining 80 percent of cropped area depends upon rainfall (Food and Agriculture Organization 2013). It may be possible to increase the crop yield by increasing the irrigated area; increasing the cultivated area is not really possible, because the cultivable area of the globe is already almost at maximum.

Nature has not divided water resources equally throughout the world (Bulkley and Antill 1971; Fisunoglu 2005). Some countries are rich in water resources and others not. Due to the high population growth rate and uneven water distribution around the globe, competition for water is high where it is scarce. Worldwide, there are already twenty-six countries that are water scarce (Johansson 2000), and many countries are going to experience more water scarcity soon.

Unlike the cases of physical water scarcity of Middle Eastern countries (Fisunoglu 2005), the water scarcity of South Asia is basically due to the lack of investment in the water sector and unequal distribution of water (Fisunoglu 2005). Furthermore, climate change has aggravated water scarcity. Due to climate change's impact on snowfall and ice, snowmelt in the Himalayas, which provides huge amounts of water for agriculture in Asia, is expected to decline significantly by 2035 (Intergovernmental Panel on Climate Change 2007; UN Water 2014). As a result, water is becoming a critical resource and is highly politicized.

There have already been 200 water-related conflicts recorded in 60 years (UN Water 2014). Around the globe, 263 rivers shared by two or more countries have been the source of conflict; violence over the use of water is rampant in every corner of the world (Mollinga 2001). The cause of most water conflicts is a sharing problem (Mollinga 2001). The amount of water sharing depends on the relative power of interest groups (Dwyer and Walker 1981). If an interest group becomes dissatisfied with the amount being shared, this can be the seed of water conflict (Gleick 1993). Studies show that the problem of water scarcity is not only caused by actual water scarcity but is also due to poor governance of water (Mehta 2000; Molle et al. 2008). Whether water is shared between or within the countries, the strongest group will normally influence the sharing process by using its relative power (Mollinga 2001). Powerful countries, regions, or individuals will have an interest in getting more water and will ultimately influence the amount of water shared, which sometimes may lead to violent conflict (Swyngedouw 2009). There is opportunity to change conflict among the riparian countries into mutually beneficial situations by designing suitable sharing schemes that will lead to win–win situations. If water sharing can be done in a more equitable way, those who are getting less water due to a power deficit will start to get more water, and ultimately, water productivity will be increased (Mollinga 2000). This study tries to incorporate the political factors into economic modeling to reflect the real situation and to identify a feasible solution.

OVERVIEW OF THE PROBLEM

This text considers transboundary water issues of the Ganga basin as a case study. The Ganga river basin originates in Tibet, crossing Nepal, India, and Bangladesh. The total basin area is 225.2 million hectares; whereas the total cropped area is 114 million hectares. The basin provides a livelihood for 747 million people (Sharma, Amarasinghe, and Sikka 2008). The Ganga basin is the twentieth longest river in Asia and the forty-first longest river in the world; there are enormous freshwater resources in this basin. Low agricultural productivity, poverty, food insecurity, water hazards (mostly flood and landslides), and migration are the common issues of the basin. The hypothesis of this study is that inequity and inefficiency in water distribution and benefit sharing is a result of the differential power position of the riparian countries.

Nepal is in the upper riparian country of the Ganga basin and holds immense potentiality in terms of hydropower and irrigation dams from the major tributaries of the Ganga such as the Koshi, Gandaki, Karnali, and Mahakali. The estimated economically feasible hydropower potentiality of Nepal from all those rivers and tributaries is 40,000 megawatts, whereas Nepal's hydropower demand is less than 1,500 megawatts. Similarly, water demand for agricultural and domestic uses is less than 5 percent of that available. Water storage reservoirs in Nepal augment river flow in the dry season and protect the downstream from flooding in the rainy season (Rogers 1993). Therefore, a large amount of water and water-related outputs can be traded with neighboring countries such as India and Bangladesh. Such countries have an extremely high electricity demand due to their increasing populations. Moreover, they use conventional sources of energy and withdraw huge amounts of underground water for agricultural purposes. The comparative advantages of Nepal being an upper riparian of the Ganga basin is that it is a mountainous country and water flows with high speed, carrying high-potential hydropower that is drastically reduced when it enters into the plains of India and Bangladesh. To take advantage of its geography, Nepal constructed two big irrigation projects at the Koshi and Gandak Rivers (tributaries of the Ganga), with the investment capital coming mainly from India. But the sharing of water looks quite inequitable.

For example, the Koshi barrage irrigates 0.96 million hectares of land in India but only 0.09 million hectares in Nepal (ten times less than India; Sharma, Upreti, and Pyakuryal 2012). Similarly, Gandak irrigates 42,000 hectares in India and only 16,000 hectares in Nepal (Beach et al. 2000).

In the absence of a purely scientific basis for water distribution, Nepal and other neighboring territories are realizing that inequity and mistrust are rampant. This fact further hinders the future development of hydro-related projects and hampers the efficiency and sustainable development of both sides. It is argued that when the upstream country in a trans-boundary river basin is a hegemon, cooperation is least likely to happen. Conversely, when the downstream country in the basin is a hegemon, the cooperation is likely to happen, but it would be in the interest of the stronger country (Dinar 2009). The latter case is applicable in this presentation. This chapter highlights transboundary water issues of the Ganga basin and presents a theoretical framework of a principal-agent bargaining model as a solution. This framework, with some modification, can be applicable to other transboundary basins of South Asia such as the Brahmaputra and Indus basins.

MODELING THE PROBLEM OF WATER SCARCITY INTO A PRINCIPAL-AGENT BARGAINING FRAMEWORK

The major attraction of the modeling approach is to manage the limited supply of water among competitive users. In the model, a powerful interest group (which may be a group of countries or states within a country or individual members of a group) is responsible for the water-related decisions and investments in irrigation infrastructures. The weaker class acts as a decision taker and cannot bargain with the powerful group (Neupane 2012). The powerful interest group enjoys property rights over water and determines the principle uses of water, though it shares some amount of water with the weaker class. Due to limited supply of water, the weaker class cannot optimize water usage and shows symptoms of water deficiency (Neupane, 2012). The aim of this model is to optimize economic benefits for both groups, taking into account the distribution of political power, water rights, and hydrological constraints in a given macroenvironment. To accomplish this, the problem is stylized as a reciprocal principal-agent model.

Nepal is an upstream country of the Ganga river basin, whereas India and Bangladesh are downstream riparian neighbors. There are four major tributaries in Nepal: Koshi, Gandak, Karnali, and the Mahakali, all of which drain to the Ganga. Being a mountainous and upstream country, Nepal has big potential for hydropower development, and other hydro-related infrastructure development, such as irrigation projects. India and Bangladesh lack this opportunity due to the flatness of their land. Both India and Bangladesh are densely populated and agro-based countries. Their electricity demand is significantly higher than the supply. In contrast, only 20 percent of total households in Nepal are receiving electricity (Hussain and Giordano 2003) and the quality of the electricity supplied is poor. Investment in large hydro-related infrastructure is currently quite difficult for an underdeveloped country like Nepal. However, the development of hydropower and irrigation projects is very important for the economies and sustainable development of all three countries, given their dependence on agriculture. Moreover, food, water, and energy are inter-dependent (Rasul 2014).[1]

In this model, Nepal can be considered the water principal, as it has the geographic advantage of developing hydro-related projects within its mountainous territory. Both India and Bangladesh can be considered agents who do not have the comparative advantage of water resources due to their lower riparian position. But they are relatively wealthier countries and more technologically advanced than Nepal. This is modeled as *information asymmetry*. One assumes that Nepal cannot invest in hydro-related projects without cooperating with other agents. This makes for the main difference from conventional principal-agent models, because here the agent has sufficient power to bargain with the principal. Hence, in this situation, bargaining power must be explicitly considered. To attract the agent, Nepal offers some incentive in the form of water or water-related products. Once the agent is ensured that it will get a reasonable quantity of water—equivalent to its resource contribution—it will participate by entering into a contract. In our case, Nepal takes the role of water principal and India and Bangladesh are the agents who provide services (i.e., technology and capital). Principal and agent have conflicting interests. The principal wants to give less water to the agent while trying to capture additional services from it. Conversely, the agent wants to contribute less service but get more water.

The principal faces difficulties in monitoring the agent. This asymmetric information can be solved within the principal-agent modeling framework (Sappington 1991). To keep matters simple, this paper will keep exogenous noise (such as variations in water quantity due to climatic conditions) as a constant.

In this model, the water principal provides water to the agent depending upon the services the agent provides, while the agent allocates services to the principal depending on the amount of water the principal provides. Principal and agent share a common resource, riparian water, but one makes decisions about the allocation, the other about services needed to generate enough water to be allocated. This is akin to the polycentric decision-making systems analyzed by Ostrom (2010) and others and acts as a solution to market failure due to the existence of asymmetrical power (Rausser and Zusman 1991). A cooperative solution, that is, a contract about sharing, is the best outcome. In our model, individual bargaining is replaced by collective bargaining. The hydro-hegemonic relationship is not universal and static. It occurs when the counterpart has a weak economy and lacks infrastructure (Zeitoun and Allan 2008). An increase in net income through a bargaining model shapes the institution and empowers the principal, through redistribution of bargaining power (Nuppenau 2000; Martimort and Semenov 2007).

The agent obtains greater benefits from access to more water supply, which in turn will allow it to obtain benefits by diversifying water use and decreasing transaction cost. Similarly, the water principal benefits from additional services provided by the agent, which helps reduce the costs of increasing the supply of water. The joint benefit for both parties is higher when they cooperate than the reference benefit when they do not cooperate (Nuppenau and Amjath Babu 2009). The two levels of benefit (with and without bargaining) will allow for measuring the power coefficient (Harsanyi 1963). Importantly, the size of the benefit depends on the size of the power coefficient (Zusman 1976). The benefit function for each class (principal and agent), the participation constraints, and the response functions will be derived algebraically. The proxies for the power coefficients for each class will be incorporated into the combined benefit function, because in this scenario, the problem is the scope of bargaining rather than a pure principal-agent relation (Zusman 1989). The objective of the principal-agent model is to cope with uncertainties and asymmetrical information that largely ignore the bargaining power of the agent and consider the contract design as only being vested in the principal (Singh 1989). This model differs from the conventional principal-agent model because of its transboundary issues, unclear property rights, sovereignty issues, and a higher transaction cost required to reach the solution. For such a specific problem, a bargaining approach is considered superior for efficient allocation of a resource (Just et al. 1998). Therefore, this paper has attempted to model this specific problem in the principal-agent bargaining framework. This power and political economy process helps in shaping international transboundary water relations (Zeitoun and Allan 2008). The objective function is maximized subject to participation and resource constraints, giving the optimized solution for this specific problem.

MODEL SETUP

Suppose Nepal has X amount of water potential for irrigation and hydropower project development. Nepal lacks services (technology and investment) to convert water into a benefit (hydropower or irrigated agriculture). Conversely, India lacks water potentiality but is strong in services (Y). The combination of water from Nepal with services from India can be converted into a shared benefit. From the total amount of water that Nepal controls (X), the country offers a fraction to India (αX) to attract the services needed to convert water into a benefit. India analyzes the offer Nepal makes and responds by offering a certain amount (quality) of services based on Nepal's offer, denoted as βY. This is essentially a principal-agent problem, because of the conflict inherent in the relation. Nepal would like to give small share of water to India and get more services, whereas India would like to take more water and give fewer services. Yet India is rich in services, capital, and experience with hydro-related projects, a factor that can be modeled as asymmetric information. In our model we allow for both parties to bargain directly for resources (water) and services. Each party's bargaining power has an impact on the final outcome, in particular on how joint benefits are shared.

Critically, property rights in water are ill defined in our scenario, because of the transborder nature of the problem. The doctrine of absolute territorial sovereignty asserts that a state enjoys exclusive authority over the waters of an international watercourse within its territory to the natural flow of the water *into* its territory (McCaffrey 2003). It follows that the principal does not have full property rights over water flowing down the Ganga and neither does the agent. Therefore, the agent is unlikely to respond to the principal's offer with a simple *yes* or *no*. In cases of overlapping, conflicting property rights—as in this case—bargaining is critical. This distinguishes our model from pure principal-agent bargaining with binary choices (Yao 2012). Specifically, the solution to conflicting or overlapping property rights can only be cooperative bargaining, as nonco-operation will give less benefit to each party.

The benefits to Nepal and India can algebraically be derived using the following notation:

Total amount of potential water (hydropower and irrigation) with Nepal $= X$

Water given to India $= \alpha(X)$

Remaining water with Nepal $= (1 - \alpha)X$

Environmental cost generated by construction of hydro-related project in Nepal $= C_1$

Total amount of services with India $= Y$

Services given to Nepal $= \beta(Y)$

Remaining services with India $= (1 - \beta)Y$

Environmental benefit for India (due to flood mitigation, replacement of conventional energy by green energy, reduction in groundwater withdrawal) $= E_1$

Environmental cost generated by construction of a hydro-related project in India $= C_2$

Therefore, the expected benefit for Nepal for participating into the contract is as follows:

$$(1 - \alpha)X \times \beta Y - C_1 = 1.0$$

The expected benefit for India for participating into the contract will be:

$$\alpha X \times 1 - \beta Y + E_1 - C_2 = 2.0$$

The combined benefit of both classes $=$ (benefit of Nepal)$^{\lambda}$(benefit of India)$^{1-\lambda}$, where λ is the power of the principal and $1-\lambda$ is the power of the agent.

The above function is maximized subject to participation and other resource constraints. Participation constraint is defined as the propensity of a party to participate in the contract, given that the benefits exceed its reservation utility. For Nepal the reservation utility is the current benefit it can derive from the water absent capital, technology, or expertise provided by India. Similarly, India's reservation utility is the benefit from employing the relevant technology, capital, or services in other sectors.

EQUITY, EFFICIENCY, AND SUSTAINABILITY

The distribution of benefits from the few existing hydro-related projects is inequitable. This might be due to India exploiting its hegemonic power position, creating rampant mistrust on the part of Nepal. As a result, further development of the projects has not occurred. Therefore, equity in benefit distribution is the main fundamental of the joint cooperative project. This equity will bring further mutual benefit for the participating groups from the joint contract.

Transborder water rights are deeply contested globally; the same applies to the Ganga basin. India, a powerful country, will translate the international water law to play to its favor. There is no external authority that defines property rights to international waters (Dombrowsky 2009). Therefore, transboundary problems can only be solved efficiently through benefit sharing rather than water sharing. The Coase theorem postulates that negotiation leads to efficient outcomes if property rights are fully defined (Coase 1960). Nepal cannot exercise full property rights of water due to its transboundary nature and the fact that the transaction cost for the allocation of property rights would increase. For this reason a principal-agent model and a principal-agent bargaining framework has been used instead of the Coase theorem (Nuppenau 2000).

This model considers principal-agent bargaining as a solution to break the ice in hegemonic power. The existence of hegemonic power is allowing only insignificant hydro-related projects in the transboundary river basin. Hegemonic power hinders cooperation, overexploits the resource, brings inequity, and does not contribute to project sustainability. Here, the power is derived exogenously. Expected benefits derived from the combined project are considered a proxy of power and are plugged into the model. There are also other sources of power that impact the bargaining; those are kept constant in this model. The assumption is that hegemonic power is a static concept and may not be universal. Having a geographic advantage, Nepal has potential with respect to bargaining and can claim its share. This model does not cover the dynamic aspect. When Nepal starts benefiting from the project, its economic condition will improve, and this economic improvement will strengthen Nepal's capital, technological strength, and, finally, bargaining power. Therefore, bargaining power is also endogenous.

The outcome suggested by the principal-agent bargaining model is theoretically more equitable than the existing situation. Similarly, getting the additional units of hydro-related output and using them as an inputs in agriculture and the industrial sectors of both countries will increase the efficiency and boost the economic development of both riparian countries.

Bihar and Uttar Pradesh are Indian states with high electricity demand currently sourced through fossil fuels (i.e., coal). Hydro-related projects could supply them with renewable energy, reduce flood risk, increase agricultural productivity, and enhance food security. In short, expanding irrigated agriculture using renewable energy could foster sustainability. Building hydro-infrastructures reduces the flow in wetlands and impacts aquatic ecosystems (Kingsford 2000). Extended cost-benefit analysis should be employed to evaluate the sustainability aspect of the wetlands before the implementation of the hydro-related projects (Turner 1991). But here, availability of additional electricity helps shift from conventional energy (wood fuel and coal) to green energy. The people in the Ganga region depend heavily on forest resources for wood fuel; forest degradation is occurring at an alarming rate in this region (Hamilton 1987; Sharma, Moore, and Vorosmarty 2000). Therefore, the net environmental benefit from the project is expected to be higher than the cost and would ultimately increase social welfare, although the community affected by reservoir inundation would also need to be provided with reasonable compensation. From the environmental perspective, the greater inequality of power causes more environmental degradation and, tending from an asymmetrical power situation to a more symmetrical situation, reduces the environmental degradation (Boyce 1994).

CONCLUSIONS

The tributaries of the Ganga River in the Nepalese area carry enormous potential for the development of hydropower and mega-irrigation projects. Nepal, an upper riparian country, could be a principal for the hydro-related goods, and other riparian countries of the Ganga basin like India and Bangladesh could be the agents. Currently, water in the Ganga basin is under exploitation due to rampant mistrust within the basin countries India, being a powerful country among the other riparian countries (popularly called the "big brother of South Asia"), has further accelerated the problem of mistrust and inefficiencies rampant in the basin. There are some combined hydro-related projects in the basin, but they are severely criticized with respect to equity. There is a widespread realization in Nepal that there is unequal benefit sharing from the existing project, but the country is unable to raise the issue due to its weak bargaining power. Based on the above constraints, therefore, this paper proposes that the principal-agent bargaining model could be the solution for sharing the cost and distributing the outcome of the project. The outcomes suggested by the model are more equitable than the existing situation. Similarly, getting the additional units of hydro-related output and using them as an input for the agriculture and industrial sectors of both India and Nepal will increase the efficiency and boost the economic development of the all riparian countries through the multiplier effect. Additionally, energy from hydropower is considered renewable and environmentally friendly. As such, it will replace conventional forms of energy such as coal. Changing rain-fed agriculture to irrigated agriculture and increasing per capita food availability and per capita electricity consumption in the project area will bring long-term sustainability to the rural and poor households of the Ganga basin. The crucial element for the both parties to go for the principal-agent model is the development of trust among the parties and improved bargaining cost. If the bargaining and negotiation are under-taken voluntarily—such a scenario is imaginable, because the number of the players in the bargaining game is only two—both parties will want to cooperate, because the outcome for both is a win-win situation.

Although this is a theoretical attempt to find a solution for the Ganga basin, this author would like to see the model implemented in the real world through a multidisciplinary team approach.

NOTES

I would like to acknowledge Prof. Dr. E. A. Nuppenau (my PhD supervisor) and Dr. Golam Rasul (International Centre for Integrated Mountain Development) for their valuable input and suggestions during this manuscript preparation. Special thank goes to Prof. Katharina Pistor and Prof. Olivier De Schutter for giving me the opportunity to present this paper at the workshop organized at Columbia Law School. I am grateful to all the participants who gave a valuable feedback on this paper during this workshop. This chapter is a part of the author's PhD work. The views mentioned here are the author's own.

1. Golam Rasul has mentioned the existence of a strong linkage between food, water, and energy in the Hindu Kush region of South Asia. Increasing per capita electricity increases water availability and, ultimately, agricultural output. The current mode of subsistence agriculture could be translated to commercial agriculture were more energy and more water available in South Asia.

REFERENCES

Alexandratos, N. and J. Bruinsma. 2012. *World Agriculture Towards 2030/2050: The 2012 Revision*. ESA Working paper No. 12-03. Rome, FAO.

Beach, H. L., J. Hammer, J. J. Hewitt, E. Kaufman, A. Kurki, J. A. Oppenheimer, and A. T. Wolf. 2000. *Transboundary Freshwater Dispute Resolution: Theory, Practice, and Annotated References*. Tokyo: United Nations University Press.

Boyce, J. K. 1994. "Inequality as a Cause of Environmental Degradation." *Ecological Economics* 11 (3): 169–178.

Bulkley, J. W., and Antill, J. 1971. "Validation of Political Simulation Models-Water Resource Projects 1." *JAWRA Journal of the American Water Resources Association* 7(5): 1071–1080.

Coase, R. H. 1960. "The Problem of Social Cost." *Journal of Law and Economics* 3: 1–44.

Dinar, S. 2009. "Power Asymmetry and Negotiations in International River Basins." *International Negotiation* 14 (2): 329–360.

Dombrowsky, I. 2009. "Revisiting the Potential for Benefit Sharing in the Management of Trans-boundary Rivers." *Water Policy* 11: 125–140.

Dwyer, F. R., and O. C. Walker Jr. 1981. "Bargaining in an Asymmetrical Power Structure." *Journal of Marketing* 45: 104–115.

Fisunoglu, H. M. 2005. "Economic and Political Perspectives for Water Resource in the Middle East : A Particular Emphasis on Turkey's South-East Anatolian Project and Syria-Iraq." NATO-CCMS Workshop Group on Integrated Water Management, Turkey.

Food and Agriculture Organization. 2013. AQUASTAT. http://www.fao.org/nr/water /aquastat/data/query/index.html?lang=en

Gleick, P. H. 1993. *Water in Crisis: A Guide to the World's Fresh Water Resources*. Oxford: Oxford University Press.

Hamilton, L. S. 1987. "What Are the Impacts of Himalayan Deforestation on the Ganges-Brahmaputra Lowlands and Delta? Assumptions and Facts." *Mountain Research and Development* 7(3) 256–263.

Harsanyi, J. C. 1963. "A Simplified Bargaining Model for the *n*-Person Cooperative Game." *International Economic Review* 4: 194–220.

Hussain, I., and M. Giordano, eds. 2003. *Water and Poverty Linkages: Case Studies from Nepal, Pakistan and Sri-Lanka*. Colombo, Sri Lanka: International Water Management Institute.

Intergovernmental Panel on Climate Change. 2007. "Climate Change 2007: Impacts, Adaptation and Vulnerability." Asia. Contribution of Working Group II to the Fourth Assessment Report of the Intergovernmental Panel on Climate Change. In ed. M. L. Parry, M. L. Palutikof, O. F. Linden, and C. E. Hanson, 469–506. Cambridge: Cambridge University Press. Downloaded from http://www.ipcc.ch /publications_and_data/ar4/wg2/en/ch10.html; accessed on 17th April, 2015.

IWMI. 2007. Looking ahead to 2050: scenarios of alternative investment approaches. Downloaded from http://www.iwmi.cgiar.org/assessment/Water%20for%20Food %20Water%20for%20Life/Chapters/Chapter%203%20Scenarios.pdf; accessed on 19th April, 2015.

Johansson, R. C. 2000. *Pricing Irrigation Water: A Literature Survey.* Washington, D.C.: World Bank. www.cepis.opsoms.org/bvsarg/i/fulltext/irrigation/irrigation .pdf.

Kingsford, R. T. 2000. "Ecological Impacts of Dams, Water Diversions and River Management on Floodplain Wetlands in Australia." *Austral Ecology* 25 (2): 109–127.

Just, R. E., G. Frisvold, V. Harrison, J. Oppenheimer, and D. Zilberman. 1998. "Using Bargaining Theory and Economic Analysis as an Aid to Trans-boundary Water Cooperation." In: R. E. Just et al. (eds.) *Conflict and Cooperation on Trans-boundary Water Resources,*411–426. New York: Springer.

Martimort, D., and A. Semenov. 2007. "Political Biases in Lobbying Under Asymmetric Information." *Journal of the European Economic Association* 5 (2–3): 614–623.

McCaffrey, S. 2003. *The Law of International Watercourses.* Oxford: Oxford University Press.

Mehta, L. 2000. "Water for the Twenty-first Century: Challenges and Misconception." IDS Working Paper 111, Institute of Development Studies, Brighton, U.K.

Molle, F., P. P. Mollinga, and R. Meinzen-Dick. 2008. "Water, Politics and Development: Introducing Water Alternatives." *Water Alternatives* 1 (1): 1–6.

Mollinga, P. P. 2001. "Water and Politics: Levels, Rational Choice and South Indian Canal Irrigation." *Future* 33: 733–752.

Mollinga, P. P., ed. 2000. "Water for Food and Rural Development: Approaches and Initiatives in South Asia." New Delhi: Sage, 349–362.

Neupane, N. 2012. "Political-Economy of Water Distribution in the trans-Himalayan Region of Nepal." Germany: Margraf, Volume 128, 221.

Nuppenau, E. A. 2000. "Public Preferences, Statutory Regulations and Bargaining in Field Margin Provision for Ecological Main Structures." *Agricultural Economics Review* 1 (1): 19–32.

Nuppenau, E. A., and T. S. Amjath Babu. 2009. "Bargaining for Risk Reduction: A Political Economy Model on the Specification of Regulations in the Use of GM Crop." In *Yearbook of Socioeconomics in Agriculture.* Swiss Society for Agricultural Economics and Rural Sociology, 113–142.

Ostrom, E. 2010. " Beyond Markets and States: Polycentric Governance of Complex Economic Systems." *American Economic Review* 100: 641–672.

Rasul, G. 2014. "Food, Water, and Energy Security in South Asia: A Nexus Perspective from the Hindu Kush Himalayan region." *Environmental Science & Policy* 39: 35–48.

Rausser, G. C., and P. Zusman. 1991. "Organizational Failure and the Political Economy of Water Resources Management." *The Economics and Management of Water Resource and Drainage in Agriculture.* New York: Springer, 735–758.

Rogers, P. 1993. "The Value of Cooperation in Resolving International River Basin Disputes." *Natural Resources Forum* 17 (2): 117–131.

Sappington, D.E.M. 1991. "Incentive in Principal Agent Relationships." *Journal of Economic Perspectives* 5 (2): 45–66.

Sharma, B. R., U. A. Amarasinghe, and A. Sikka. 2008. *Indo-Gangetic River Basins: Summary Situation Analysis.* New Delhi: International Water Management Institute.

Sharma, K. P., B. Moore III, and C. J. Vorosmarty. 2000. "Anthropogenic, climatic, and hydrologic trends in the Kosi Basin, Himalaya." *Climatic Change* 47 (1–2): 141–165.

Sharma, S. R., B. R. Upreti, and K. Pyakuryal, eds. 2012. *Nepal 2030: A Vision for Peaceful and Prosperous Nation*. Kathmandu: South Asia Regional Coordination Office of the Swiss National Centre of Competence in Research (NCCR North-South) and Department of Development Studies, Kathmandu University.

Singh, N. 1989. "Theories of Sharecropping." In: *The Economic Theory of Agrarian Institutions*, ed. P. Bardhan, 19–71. Oxford: Clarendon.

Swyngedouw, E. 2009. "The Political Economy and Political Ecology of the Hydro-Social Cycle." *Journal of Contemporary Water Research and Education* 142: 59–60.

Turner, K. 1991. "Economics and Wetland Management." *Ambio,* 20 (2) 59–63.

UN Water. 2014. UN Water home page, www.unwater.org.

Yao, Z. 2012. "Bargaining Over Incentive Contracts." *Journal of Mathematical Economics* 48: 98–106.

Zeitoun, M., and J. A. Allan. 2008. "Applying Hegemony and Power Theory to Transboundary Water Analysis." *Water Policy* 10 (2): 3–12.

Zusman, P. 1976. "The Incorporation and Measurement of Social Power in Economic Models." *International Economic Review* 17 (2): 447–462.

——. 1989. "Peasants' Risk Aversion and the Choice of Marketing Intermediaries and Contracts: A Bargaining Theory of Equilibrium Marketing Contracts." In *The Economic Theory of Agrarian Institutions*, ed. P. Bardhan, 297–316. Oxford: Clarendon.

CHAPTER 15

Voice and Reflexivity in Essential Resources

REFORMING THE COMMUNITY LAND REGIME IN KENYA

Laila Macharia

In Kenya, land can be considered an essential resource, since much of the population relies directly on it for livelihood, either as subsistence farmers or pastoralists. Most land used by these groups, particularly large swaths employed for pastoralist activity, is held communally and informally for day-to-day needs. However, some locations are also gaining importance as development sites for strategic infrastructure (such as the new Lamu port) and as reservoirs of valuable natural resources (such as oil and water in Turkana).

Despite its importance, since colonial times, community land has been administered in a haphazard manner, largely in an institutional vacuum outside the formal legal regime. In many cases, communities disregard competing rights under formal law, suggesting that the legitimacy of the latter is still contested. Some scholars consider this evidence that the assumptions driving the policy of modernization of customary land rights are not scientifically sound (Odote 2013).

Despite this, the customary land governance regime remains entrenched. Governance norms differ across communities, disposal and management decisions are often arbitrary, and administrators are seldom accountable. Local expectations for the use of community land often contradict the rights held under individual title for the same parcel of land. The result has been decades of conflict, periodically exploding into unjustified evictions and violent confrontations.

The most prominent example was the 2007–2008 post-election conflict, partially driven by a clash between the Kalenjin in the Rift Valley and immigrants from other regions of the country who had bought parcels in what the Kalenjin considered their community lands. This, among other factors, triggered a political crisis that accelerated not just the adoption of a new National Land Policy (NLP) in 2009 but also the new Constitution in 2010. From there, three critical pieces of legislation were passed: the Land Act, the Land Registration Act, and the National Land Commission Act. The outstanding piece is the Community Lands Act.

Advocates of community land reform want to see the legal infrastructure create a working framework that offers clearly defined and enforceable rights and responsibilities. This chapter examines the institutional arrangements proposed in the current slate of laws, particularly the Constitution and the Community Land Bill, and assesses the extent to which they adequately provide Voice and reflexivity as an avenue to deliver outcomes more just than those achieved in the past.

CONCEPTUAL FRAMEWORK: VOICE AND REFLEXIVITY

In Kenya, we see a typical case of the argument advanced in this volume by Olivier De Schutter and Katharina Pistor regarding the inadequacy of traditional property governance regimes when applied to essential resources. Kenya has traditionally classified land into three categories: private, public, and communal. Yet, none of the regimes has been successful in managing this essential resource efficiently, equitably, or in an environmentally sustainable way.

As a result, the land sector, starting from colonial times, has faced substantial challenges (Republic of Kenya 2004). First, land has been allocated unfairly, based first on racial and gender exclusion under the original colonial administration and then for ethnic and political patronage under post-independence regimes. Second, antiquated and opaque land laws have failed to keep up with current global practice. Related to this, systems of land registration and transfer under the Ministry of Lands and in rural registries have deteriorated over the decades.

Where land is an essential resource, independent communal land rights seem to be the solution. After all, communities may have local expertise to manage their resources, especially where livestock routes and wildlife are involved. Also, communities are likely to have an inherent interest in ensuring that resources are allocated fairly and preserved for the long term.

However, actual experience in Kenya illustrates otherwise. Community land is often managed by political authorities that lack capacity for transparent, accountable self-governance, paving the way for arbitrary holdings, extortion, and corruption. Finally, and most importantly, traditional norms often perpetuate discrimination based on affiliation, gender, and age.

For the most part, these coexisting regimes, efficient and equitable in theory, have failed to produce just outcomes. This has left many aggrieved or dispossessed. The end result has been human-wildlife conflict and, in time, actual physical conflict between communities.

To address this, article 60 (1) of the new Constitution provides that land shall be held, used, and managed in a manner that is "equitable, efficient, productive and sustainable" (Constitution). The following principles are identified as priorities: equitable access to land; security of land rights; sustainable and productive management of land resources; transparent and cost-effective administration of land; sound conservation and protection of ecologically sensitive areas; elimination of gender discrimination in law, customs, and practices related to land and property in land; and encouragement that land disputes be settled through recognized local community initiatives.

The new land governance regime offers a fresh opportunity to learn from the past. In particular, to address historical shortfalls, an ideal system should embrace two principles: Voice and Reflexivity. *Voice*, defined here as the ability to collectively choose the rules by which one wishes to be governed, is especially important in the case of community land. *Reflexivity*, by contrast, is the ability to recognize competing claims as legitimate and the willingness to accommodate them.

Two caveats are in order here. The first is the challenge of defining who represents the community's interests. As illustrated in a study on subdivision of group ranches, incentives differ for diverse players in the community (Mwangi 2005). In many cases, the tribal elite, including elected representatives, are involved in self-dealing of various kinds. While media attention is often focused on the more sensationalist cases, in which large, multinational companies in the mining, oil, or agribusiness industries move into rural areas, a more widespread phenomenon is the misappropriation of community land, often with the tacit approval or active participation of local elites. The Lamu allocations revealed in July 2014 are a case in point (Ombati 2014).

The second caveat concerns the inherent limitation of legal change. In attempting to overhaul the land governance regime, Kenya's reformers have introduced sweeping formal changes. This includes the passing of new legislation, the establishment of new organizations, and the creation of new protections and entitlements. However, as we have seen, actual practice can differ substantially, as informal norms undermine the ideal.

For these reasons, if justice is to be done, we consider Voice and Reflexivity crucial at two levels: externally, between the community and external communities, and internally, between the collective and individual community members. Accordingly, in assessing the new land regime, we ask two questions:

1. Does the regime provide a way for the community to influence the overall community land regime?
2. Does the regime provide a way for individual community members to influence the norms that govern their own land rights?

The following case study advances in twoparts. The first part provides a brief overview of the history of community land rights as a proxy for access to land as an essential resource. The second part assesses how the current push for community land reform accommodates the principles of Voice and Reflexivity.

BACKGROUND: THE HISTORY OF COMMUNITY LAND IN KENYA

To appreciate the current land reform efforts, we start with the precolonial era, when customary law prevailed in Kenya. Most of the population fell into the category of smallholder farmers, hunter-gatherers, or pastoralists, and operated under communal land regimes.

According to leading scholars, community land tenure has a number of defining features (Kameri-Mbote et al. 2012). First, land rights are embedded in a network of social relationships and units, including households and kinship networks, representing layered social identities. Second, land rights tend to be inclusive, not exclusive, in nature. Third, membership in the community determines access to land, which is administered in turn by the governance structures of that community. Fourth, access is separate from control. Fifth, management emphasizes guaranteeing access and resolving competing claims. Finally, social, political, and resource boundaries are flexible and negotiable, since the identities linked to them also evolve over time.

These principles sharply contradict those underlying the feudal English land-tenure system, which emphasizes exclusion (Kameri-Mbote et al.

2012). With the colonial advance in the late 1800s, the British government declared East Africa a protectorate, then a colony. With this, most commercially viable land, denied to Africans, was declared Crown Land, leaving native reserves and unregulated land as customary, communal land. This was the foundational principle through which informal, customary, and ancestral rights held by Africans were subordinated to formal, registered title (Odote 2013).

As the colonial era drew to a close, however, the government initiated a process of converting the customary land to individual, private ownership, either as individual property or group property. The objectives of this, implemented through the Registered Land Act, the Trust Lands Act, and the Land (Group Representatives) Act, were to develop an arms-length, commercial land market characterized by distributional efficiency (Odote 2013). These efforts were designed to address perceived weaknesses in customary land regimes but remained limited in scope and impact.

The most significant attempt was the establishment of group ranches. Unlike the arable areas of Kenya, where the colonial government aggressively pursued individuation of title, subdivision did not appear feasible in pastoralist regions, with their low population densities (Kibugi 2009). Instead, with pastoralists, the government promoted settlement schemes where the best practice was a more easily disseminated and jointly held title potentially used as collateral for commercial borrowing.

Accordingly, in 1945, the colonial government established the African Land Development Organization to help pastoralist communities develop sound ranching techniques to replace nomadic pastoralism (through modern pasture and stock management) and encourage settled agriculture. A number of grazing schemes were established on ranches of up to 20,000 acres each, equipped with paddocks and water infrastructure (Kibugi 2009).

The first, started in 1946, was Konza, intended to demonstrate improved grazing standards and stockbreeding and to introduce the Masai to stable agriculture. Ten indigent families were selected who committed verbally to adhere to the scheme's regulations. Although the target increase in herd size was achieved, selling surplus stock was culturally abhorrent to the families. Residents gradually vacated the site starting in 1954, and by 1961, Konza was totally abandoned.

This experience did not alter the overall policy of the government, which passed legislation to administer communally held land: the Land Adjudication Act (Laws of Kenya Cap. 284) for the recording of rights and interests in customary lands and their assignment to their customary users; and the Group (Land Representatives) Act (Laws of Kenya Cap. 287), providing for the governance and administration of group ranches. Under the latter, all members hold *equal, undivided* shares. They are entitled to reside on group land and to elect representatives to safeguard the rights of any person under recognized customary law. Representatives are also authorized to hold property on behalf of and to act on behalf of and for the collective benefit of all members of the group.

After independence, the vast majority of natives remained with smaller holdings in settlement schemes or in communal areas governed by customary law. Kenya's native rulers inherited this unequal state of affairs, many purchasing the properties left behind by settlers.

The early postindependence governments, in other words, continued to manage land just as the colonial governments had. The result was confusion between formal and informal customary land. In addition, corruption and mismanagement saw much community land misappropriated. This fueled discontent in the local populations and in the citizenry at large, and when agitation for democratic reform deepened, land was an important issue.

In December 2002, the multiethnic, opposition National Rainbow Coalition–Kenya won the presidential election, succeeding Daniel arap Moi, who by then had been in power for twenty-four years. Mwai Kibaki became Kenya's third president with a strong mandate and amid extremely high expectations. At the top of the agenda was economic recovery and political reform.

Land reform was an early priority. In early 2004, Kibaki appointed a commission of inquiry, led by land lawyer Paul Ndungu, to look into land management in previous administrations. It found that substantive procedures on public land allocation had been systematically flouted (Republic of Kenya 2004). In addition to the retroactive restitution, which would see the recovery of unjust proceeds from the illegal allocation and sale of public land extended to original allottees, professionals, and brokers, the Ndungu Commission acknowledged that some institutional failures needed to be addressed. The report offered very specific solutions, several of which could be immediately implemented.

In response, several civil society groups began coordinated advocacy as the government in 2004 initiated formulation of a new NLP. The process progressed in a halting manner, with factions developing outside and within government and with government not prioritizing its conclusion.

Periodically, both insiders and external observers lamented that commitment was lacking for land reform (African Center for Open Governance 2009).

The state of Kenyan land reform limped along from 2004 until 2008, when a political conflict brought land issues to the forefront. Proclamation of Kibaki's election victory against close rival Raila Odinga, amid widespread evidence of vote-rigging on both sides, triggered riots in major cities. In a few localities, neighbors from opposing ethnic groups turned on each other. For example, a clash occurred between the Kalenjin in the Rift Valley and immigrants from other regions of the country who had settled in what the Kalenjin considered their community lands. Conservative estimates found that at least 1,162 people were killed and more than 350,000 displaced during three months of sporadic ethnic violence, some of which appeared to have been orchestrated by senior political figures and was marked by widespread sexual assault and looting (Kenya National Commission on Human Rights 2008).

A panel of African elders, led by former UN secretary-general Kofi Annan, was nominated to investigate and mediate the conflict. It was agreed that the political crisis be solved by appointing Mwai Kibaki president and Raila Odinga prime minister. After broad-based reflection and consultation, the roots of Kenya's divisions were found to be complex and their resolution multifaceted. As a result, the National Accord Reconciliation Agreement, signed on 28 February 2008, identified short-term and longer-term agenda items, including land reform (Lindenmayer 2009).

The crisis also precipitated a widespread recognition that Kenya was overdue for a new social contract, symbolized by a new constitution that better reflected the maturation of the Kenyan polity and the more enlightened expectations of citizens. With both Raila and Kibaki supporting the new dispensation, the new Constitution passed in August 2010 with a 70 percent turnout and a 68.55 percent mandate (Lindenmayer 2009). The referendum was declared free and fair, and independent opinion polls showed that the majority of Kenyans (67 percent) were satisfied with the process.

Because the postelection conflict had been heavily concentrated in regions affected by multigenerational land conflicts, land-related clauses of the Constitution gained prominence. As required, a slate of new land legislation soon followed. First was the Land Registration Act of April 2012, intended to "revise, consolidate and rationalize the registration of titles to land, to give effect to the principles and objects of devolved government in land registration, and for connected purposes." This significant act repealed several constitutional relics, including the Indian Transfer of Property Act 1882, the Government Lands Act (Cap. 280), the Registration of Titles Act (Cap. 281), the Land Titles Act (Cap. 282), and the Registered Land Act (Cap. 300). Then came the Land Act of 2012, giving effect to article 68 of the Constitution, which repeals the Wayleaves Act (Cap. 292) and the Land Acquisition Act (Cap. 295). Finally, the National Land Commission was created in 2012 (Kenya National Assembly: act number 5 of 2012) to, inter alia, as provided under article 67 (2) (a) of the Constitution, to manage public land on behalf of the national and county governments.

It is difficult to overstate the significance of these changes on land administration, the complexity of which previously baffled even the most erudite legal practitioners. But it has not escaped the notice of proponents of community land reform that the Community Land Bill was not given equal priority in the Constitution. As such, this bill is still pending adoption and remains the subject of some controversy as stakeholders grapple with how best to integrate community land into a modern cash economy while also catering to those who still use land as an essential resource.

In the meantime, the urgency for reform remains high. Grievances continue to fester, fueling conflicts between holders of community land and perceived outsiders, even when the latter catalyze economic investment ostensibly of benefit to locals. In October 2013, for example, British Tullow Oil temporarily suspended exploration in Block 10BB (Ngamia 1) and Block 13T (Twiga South-1) in Turkana, when locals, reportedly led by two members of Parliament, stormed Tullow facilities (Ng'asike 2013).

And in August 2014, President Uhuru Kenyatta announced he was canceling title deeds issued to twenty-two private entities allocated more than 500,000 acres of land in Lamu County, close to the site of a proposed seaport (Ombati 2014). He elaborated that a comprehensive audit found that in just two years, between 2011 and 2012, the public land was alienated under "dubious and corrupt circumstances." The conspiracy, he added, not only dispossessed individuals and families living in the region of their land and opportunities, but also created ethnic division and helped fuel insecurity in the region.

ANALYSIS

Considering land as an essential resource in Kenya, it becomes clear that Voice and Reflexivity, two sides of the same coin, have relevance at two levels. On one hand is the ability of the community, and its unique set of land governance institutions, to hold its own vis-à-vis the formal system. On the other is the ability of individuals *within* the community to advocate for their own interests, especially when challenging the status quo. This is of particular relevance when land rights under the Constitution, such as the right of women to inherit land, violate customary norms. Accordingly, in assessing the new land regime, we ask two questions:

1. Does the regime provide a way for the community to influence the overall community land regime?
2. Does the regime provide a way for individual community members to influence the norms that govern their own land rights?

EXTERNAL VOICE AND REFLEXIVITY: DOES THE REGIME PROVIDE A WAY FOR THE COMMUNITY TO INFLUENCE THE OVERALL COMMUNITY LAND REGIME?

As we have seen, community land rights have typically been subjugated vis-à-vis formal, individuated land titles. While the new Constitution was seen as an opportunity to correct this, an early concern was that marginalized communities, and especially the illiterate, destitute, or less powerful individuals among them, would lack meaningful opportunity and clout to articulate their interests.

These fears generally proved unfounded, as the process of constitution-making provided several opportunities for meaningful input from relevant communities. First, a historical opening was created for community land rights to come to the fore. Startled by the deepening conflict, two main political factions at the national level came together in an extraordinary political coalition, highly motivated to deliver an inclusive Constitution. While this was not a panacea, it certainly provided the goodwill necessary for the process to begin on the right note.

Second, flowing from this, a committee of experts on the Constitution prepared the first draft of the Constitution after consultation and negotiation with the political leadership and community-based organizations. Any Kenyan could then have input in a highly consultative and public process in which diverse interest groups could organize themselves to influence the process, enjoying several avenues of direct access to framers of the Constitution. The result was that formerly passive groups ranging from pastoralists and squatters to manufacturers and private landowners had their input incorporated into the final legal regime.

Finally, within the land sector itself, a similar process unfolded. To coordinate input of other stakeholders in the sector, a Land Reform Transformation Unit was created within the Ministry of Lands. In theory at least, this unit was to provide a neutral, technocratic approach to conclude the NLP as well as shepherd the draft bills fronted for adoption by Parliament. Reflecting the new priority placed on land by the highest levels of political leadership, other constitutional bodies like the Commission of the Implementation of the Constitution had both the resources and the authority to advance both negotiation and implementation of land legislation.

The specific engagement of marginalized communities in the land rights debate started with the advocacy around the NLP, in which pastoralist communities, for instance, had special opportunities to offer input. One stream of activities that stand out is that of the Kenya Land Alliance (KLA; Norwegian Research Council 2010). Founded in 1999, KLA's lobbying and advocacy activities revolved around the concerns of marginalized constituents including women, internally displaced persons, squatters, and pastoral and indigenous communities. Starting in 2003, with the change in regime, KLA turned its attention to land reform. Around the NLP and later the Constitution, the KLA mobilized the Land Sector–Non-state Actors (LS-NSA) network comprising, among others, the Kenya Human Rights Commission, Federation of Women Lawyers-Kenya (FIDA Kenya), the Institution of Surveyors of Kenya, the Haki-Jamii Trust, the Resource Conflict Institute, and the Shelter Forum.

Workshops were organized countrywide, bringing together legal experts, women's rights experts, policy makers, and community organizations to deliberate on key land-tenure issues, including women's rights, historical injustices, and public land management. Recommendations were then forwarded to the government and other stakeholders. The LS-NSA thus played a key role in mobilizing community-based organizations to participate in the formulation process, ensuring key stakeholders were included.

Later, the same advocates for the NLP were closely involved in the debate on the land chapter in the Constitution. As a result, the provisions on land within the Constitution borrow heavily from both the philosophy and recommendations of the NLP. The land-related sections of the

Constitution target many of the specific ills that have disadvantaged communities that use land as an essential resource.

For example, the Constitution in article 63 mentions community land alongside public and private land. Before making reference to the required legislation, it states that any unregistered land shall be held in trust by the counties for the communities. This is intended to preempt the alienation of those properties for which communities may not have organized themselves in time to lay claim. Article 66(2) provides that investments in property must benefit local communities and their economies. Thereafter is the establishment of the National Land Commission with the mandate, inter alia, to advise the government on a program of land registration throughout the country, initiate investigations into historical injustices, and encourage the application of dispute resolution.

These clauses are all the result of sustained lobbying, and most addressed a specific historical challenge. As such, the new regime is a significant step forward from advocates of community land rights. However, in addition to specific substantive revisions, there remains an overriding concern that community land rights will continue to be sidelined vis-à-vis other forms of land rights. Commentators have already pointed out that the very act of carving out community land from the Land Act already implies that community land rights are an afterthought, marginalized and inferior as in the past. In this line of argument, an ideal resolution would be to amend the Land Act and Land Registration Act so that these incorporate provisions on community land equivalent with those for private and public land and under the same registrar (Kameri-Mbote et al. 2012).

However, with new constitutional protections and the forum of the National Land Commission expressly created to address past and future issues, much progress has been made in making community land rights more secure.

INTERNAL VOICE AND REFLEXIVITY: DOES THE REGIME ACCOMMODATE CONFLICTING CLAIMS BETWEEN INDIVIDUAL COMMUNITY MEMBERS, ESPECIALLY WHERE THE CLAIMANT COMES FROM A TRADITIONALLY MARGINALIZED GROUP OR CHALLENGES THE STATUS QUO?

Justice for a community means justice for its individual members. If both the costs and the benefits of essential resources are to be fairly shared, internal governance must function effectively. Detractors of community land rights, however, often highlight the seeming inability of communities to manage their own affairs. For instance, observers have pointed out that due to continual mismanagement, group ranch leadership faces a legitimacy crisis, eroding member goodwill and prompting subdivision (Kibugi 2009).

These opinions are hardly unfounded. The Group Ranches Act, for instance, sets out very specific rules on democratic protocol and procedure. But the reality is that these ideals are often disregarded. A survey at the Shompole group ranch, for example, showed that officeholders sometimes stay in office beyond their constitutionally pronounced electoral term (Kibugi 2009). In other locations, like the Laikipia District, no elections were reportedly held between 1972 and 2004.

Another principle is nondiscrimination. Although the Group Ranches Act provides that women must be represented in leadership bodies, few are. Indeed, reflecting the patriarchal mores of many pastoralist communities, women make a poor showing in the voting membership as well. A survey of the Shompole group ranch showed that male elders dominate discussions, while women and youth only contribute when asked. In another survey of the Olderkesi group ranch, women, it turned out, were so reluctant to participate that some refused to even answer the survey questions (Kibugi 2009). Transparency and professionalism also seem to be lacking. At Kuri Kuri and Imbirikani, among others, members expressed no confidence in their administration citing fraudulent activities, incomplete projects, and inefficiency, as well as lack of transparency and consultation.

But the Community Land Bill replicates these governance standards and strengthens them. For example, article 46 contains tough antidiscrimination provisions. Under clause 17, the committee's members must encompass community elders, women, and youth, as well as minorities. And, reflecting a general principle enshrined in article 27 (8) of the Kenyan Constitution, no more than two-thirds of members can be of any one gender.

The spirit of the Community Land Bill is also decidedly democratic. The Community Land Management Committees mandated under sections 15(1) and 16(1) must be registered, reflect the diversity of the community, and run matters transparently. Section 19 spells out procedures for "regular and democratic" elections, with all members, including minorities, having the right to stand for election and to vote. Further, accessible alternative dispute-resolution mechanisms are emphasized, and the framework provides formal channels of appeal such as the Land Dispute Tribunals and the Land and Environment Court.

In short, the Community Land Bill, particularly if the revisions proposed by experts are adopted, will reflect best practices in professional management and democratic governance. Linked to this is the Community Land Rights Recognition Model used by the Ministry of Lands to formally recognize and register community lands in a participatory and transparent process (Kameri-Mbote et al. 2012). This will provide mechanisms for individual community members to advance their own interests, a critical need for less traditionally powerful members of the community. However, as mentioned earlier, the availability of these fora does not necessarily mean they will be used. Some community members, due to factors such as illiteracy, may not have the capacity to hold their leaders accountable.

CONCLUSION

The new Constitution in Kenya has catalyzed land-related legislation and institutions, including the draft Community Land Bill, to address past shortcomings in the land governance regime. Although imperfect, this has gone a long way in providing formerly marginalized communities channels for input (Voice) and platforms through which their interests can be accommodated (Reflexivity).

To create long-term stability, the reformed regime must now enhance the ability of the communities not just to bargain with outside authorities but also to strengthen the governance within the collective. In addition, community land rights only have teeth if they are protected outside the community with formal channels of appeal to other constitutional bodies. This allows a sound framework for protection of land as an essential resource. The future challenge, however, remains in enhancing capacity where it is low, due to lack of education or exposure, so the populace can exploit the opportunity that has been provided.

REFERENCES

African Center for Open Governance. 2009. *Mission Impossible: Implementing the Ndungu Report*. Nairobi, Kenya.
Kameri-Mbote, et al. 2012. "Legal Review of the Draft Legislation Enabling Recognition of Community Land Rights in Kenya." USAID Kenya, Nairobi, Kenya.

Kenya National Commission on Human Rights. 2008. *On the Brink of the Precipice: A Human Rights Account of Kenya's Post-election Violence.* Nairobi.

Kibugi, Robert M. 2009. "Failed Land Use Legal and Policy Framework for the African Commons? Reviewing Rangeland Governance in Kenya." *Journal of Land Use & Environmental Law* 24 (2): 309.

Lindenmayer, E and Kaye, J. L. 2009. *A Choice for Peace? The Story of Forty-One Days of Mediation in Kenya.* New York: International Peace Institute.

Mwangi, E. 2005. "The Transformation of Property Rights in Kenya's Maasailand: Triggers and Motivations." CAPRi Working Paper No. 35. International Food Policy Research Institute, Washington, D.C.

Ng'asike, L. 2013. "Tullow Oil Suspends Operations Over Conflict with Locals." *East African Standard,* 28 October.

Norwegian Research Council. 2010. "The Kenya Land Alliance Case Study, Human Rights, Power and Civic Action in Developing Societies: Comparative Analyses (RIPOCA)." Norwegian Research Council, Poverty and Peace Research Programme as found in http://www.jus.uio.no/smr/english/research/projects/ripoca/workshop-april-2010/Kenya_Org_study_Kenya_Land_Alliance_Feb%202010.pdf.

Odote, C. 2013. *The Legal and Policy Framework Regulating Community Land in Kenya: An Appraisal.* Nairobi, Kenya: Friedrich Ebert Stiftung.

Ombati, C. 2014. "President Uhuru Kenyatta Revokes 500,000 Acre Title in Lamu." *East African Standard,* 1 August 1.

Republic of Kenya. 2004. *Report of the Commission of Inquiry into the Illegal/Irregular Allocation of Public Land.* Nairobi: Government Printer.

CHAPTER 16

Do Traditional Institutions Matter in Participatory
Essential Resource Governance Systems in Zimbabwe?

Manase Kudzai Chiweshe

This chapter provides a context to debate the ability of traditional institutions and indigenous knowledge to ensure sustainable and equitable
utilization of natural resources. Over the years, traditional institutions
in Africa have generally been ignored in debates on participatory and
equitable essential resource governance.[1] A review of literatures and experiences in Zimbabwe shows that despite the weaknesses of traditional
institutions (particularly the patriarchal basis of these structures, which
relegate women to inferior positions), they offer the best way of ensuring protection of natural resources. Using indigenous knowledge systems
and values, traditional leaders are best placed to implement participatory
essential resource–management systems. Traditional leadership has often
been juxtaposed with Western-style democracy, which itself is based on
the notion of political and social rights for individuals. The characteristic
of ethnic-based collectivism in African societies ensures equal participation and promotion of equity among communities (Owusu 1991). The
sidelining of traditional institutions from resource governance has led to
a lack of participation by communities using the resources. In light of
the comparative failure of the African state, undermined as it has been by
greedy and violent political elites from within and without, chieftaincy
has reemerged as an important vehicle for democracy, development, and
the potential for authentic indigenous political expression. This discussion is not an attempt to romanticize traditional or cultural forms of
organization but rather to reassert the practical and analytical value of the
efficacy of these formations in essential resource management.

The "closing out" of traditional institutions from debates on essential
resource governance goes against the continued relevance these structures

have on the everyday social organization of rural people in Zimbabwe. This paper argues for the need of a nuanced explanation of how traditional governance structures offer a way to ensure equity and local participation in essential resource access and use. In countries such as Zimbabwe, traditional leaders are influential and have the ability to manage scarce essential goods and minimize waste. As far back as 1992, the World Bank realized that Africa's institutional malaise cannot be resolved by relying exclusively on either external enclave transplant institutions or purely traditional institutions Thus, traditional governance, if fully recognized and empowered, can ensure that scarce resources are used efficiently and in a sustainable manner. Sustainability of resources is promoted by institutional arrangements that do not unduly interfere with future productivity or availability of essentials.

BACKGROUND

The management of essential resources is increasingly becoming a complex issue across the world. Various property regimes have been prescribed with varying success in Africa, yet policy makers and scholars across the continent forget that people have been part of the natural habitat for centuries. Over the years Africans have developed governance systems and knowledge geared toward protecting and revitalizing the natural environment. Ayittey (1991) argues that "westerners" and African political elites are caught up in the myth that Africa had no democratic governance institutions of its own before the arrival of the European colonialists. With colonization, industrial development, urbanization, and globalization, these systems and knowledge have been eroded. However, some institutions remain. This paper argues that for Africa, governance of natural resources should be founded on traditional institutions rooted in people's cultures and way of life. Various scholars (see e.g., Ake 1990; Wunsch and Olowu 1990; Ayittey 1991; Davidson 1992) have alluded to the failure of state structures inherited from colonial times. Such failure is fueling an increased interest in traditional leadership systems and associated indigenous knowledge.

A study by Safaids (2010) indicates that traditional leaders and structures remain influential among a large majority of the population in urban and rural southern Africa. Traditional leaders wield influence and command much respect in their communities and therefore are in many ways the gateways to any intervention seeking the participation of local people.

Kyed and Buur (2006, ii) argue that "traditional leaders now officially form part ofestablishing some kind of bottom-up benign governance based on a variety of different local, national and transnational modalities of power." The postcolonial African state has, however, remained largely centralized, with minimal devolution of power to institutions at the bottom, yet such institutions remained central to the everyday experiences of rural people. The knowledge of communities and resources built up over centuries is instilled within these structures, yet their involvement remains peripheral and token.

Mamdani (1996) theorizes that indirect rule under colonization created traditional leaders in Africa as decentralized despots. Keulder notes that traditional leaders were given extensive coercive powers and subsequently became local-level lawmakers, tax collectors, police commissioners, and judges.[2] Colonial authorities thus found a way to ensure order by using customary law and appointing the chiefs they wanted. The postcolonial state in Africa inherited this system and has continued to use chiefs to ensure political survival. In Zimbabwe, Mandondo (2000) highlights that the Traditional Leaders Act (1998) replicated the colonial roles played by chiefs and allied traditional leaders. Chiefs are appointed by the president with roles that include the supervision of headmen, promotion of cultural values, and oversight of the tax and levy collection for rural district councils. Moreover, chiefs were meant to ensure that land and natural resources were used in accordance with national legislation—especially legislation prohibiting overcultivation, overgrazing, and deforestation (Mandondo 2000). Without proper authority this institution has lost the ability to enforce environmental regulation and equal access to the commons for local communities.

When defining traditional leadership in Africa, it is important to contextualize local definitions and societal constructions. Traditional leaders and institutions are varied in their appearance and importance. They also differ in how they relate to natural resource governance and in their efficacy in resource mobilization. Traditional leadership is defined as an authentic authority that encourages decentralization with clear lines of communication and values (Wunsch and Olowu 1990). Its authenticity is derived from the fact that traditional leaders know they cannot operate in a vacuum—*nyika vanhu* or *ilizwe ngabantu* (the people make the nation)—so people are empowered and given a voice. In practice, however, traditional leadership tends to be a complex interplay of negotiation, compromise, and dictation between past customs and the modern bureaucratic state. Through colonization and postcolonial constructions these institutions have mutated in response to external pressures, but retain their core legitimacy from custom and tradition. Modern natural resource–management systems should build upon and enforce these traditional systems.

Traditional leadership systems in Africa are often described as undemocratic, antimodern, and ineffective for dealing with current challenges facing the continent. These assumptions are built on the belief that the "modernization" of Africa requires that it leave behind traditional institutions, values, and beliefs. In their introduction Olivier De Schutter and Katharina Pistor summarize the class "tragedy of the commons argument" put forward by Hardin (1968), namely that subtractive common-pool resources face collective-action problems insofar as they tend to be overexploited. In precolonial Zimbabwe, this problem did not exist, as natural resources were steeped in the spiritual linkages between the people and their ancestors and descendants (Dore 2001; Murombedzi 2003). Customs and norms were developed that ensured the protection of natural resources. For example, certain forests, rivers, water sources, and mountains were revered and protected from overuse, through norms of sharing what is now theorized as *unhu* or *ubuntu*. Eze (2010, 190–191) describes these as:

"A person is a person through other people" strikes an affirmation of one's humanity through recognition of an "other" in his or her uniqueness and difference. It is a demand for a creative intersubjective formation in which the "other" becomes a mirror (but only a mirror) for my subjectivity. This idealism suggests to us that humanity is not embedded in my person solely as an individual; my humanity is co-substantively bestowed upon the other and me. Humanity is a quality we owe to each other. We create each other and need to sustain this otherness creation. And if we belong to each other, we participate in our creations: we are because you are, and since you are, definitely I am. The "I am" is not a rigid subject, but a dynamic self-constitution dependent on this otherness creation of relation and distance.

With the increased call for endogenous development models, traditional governance structures can finally claim recognition as a truly endogenous system. Endogenous development is based on local people's criteria for development and takes into account their material, social, and spiritual well-being (Hiemstra 2010). Such an approach respects the institutions and knowledge held within communities. Such knowledge recognizes nature as an important spiritual component of the living. This type of development places local cultures at the center of interventions by allowing people to create and decide on their own paths. Hiemstra (2010) argues that the aim of endogenous development is to empower local communities to take control of their own development processes in such a way that it revitalizes ancestral and local knowledge. It is local people who then decide on external resources that best fit their local conditions. Through the utilization of this indigenous knowledge, endogenous development can lead to increased biodiversity and reduced environmental degradation.

THEORIZING TRADITIONAL LEADERSHIP IN AFRICA

The definition of traditional leadership in Africa is contested and escapes easy conceptualization. One of the major issues stems from the elusive definition of tradition. Writers such as Hobsbawm and Ranger[3] (1994) allude to how in Africa tradition is often invented to support specific ideological stances. This paper adopts Adewumi and Egwurube's (1985, 20) definition of traditional leadership.

> [The] group referred to as traditional leaders/rulers or tribal leaders/rulers are individuals occupying communal political leadership positions sanctified by cultural mores and values, and enjoying the legitimacy of particular communities to direct their affairs. . . . Their basis of legitimacy is therefore tradition, which includes the whole range of inherited culture and way of life; a people's history; moral and social values and the traditional institutions which survive to serve those values.

In a paper highlighting the role of chiefs in peace building and democracy in post colonial Zimbabwe, Makahamandze, Grand and Tavuyanago (2009, 45) argued:

> There are proverbs that remind traditional leaders to respect the people under their jurisdiction, such as *ushe varanda* (chieftaincy depends on the subjects) and *ushe vanhu* (a king depends on the people). These wise sayings stress the view that chiefs owe their status to the will of the people.

His mandate to rule rests in and is dependent on his subjects. The people therefore are the ultimate source of the king's authority.

Thus, chiefs are community leaders who derive their mandate from the people and work toward the good of their followers. In Zimbabwe they derive their authority on the basis of spiritual linkages with ancestors and should come from a designated family with a line of rulers. It is a hereditary position, but in many instances there are conflicts over the rightful heir. The Ministry of Local Government has been known to meddle with and influence the selection of heirs for chieftaincy positions.

Within this framework Weber's conceptualization of "ideal types" is instructive in noting the difference between the realities of traditional institutions and what they "ought" to be. Claude Ake (2001, 34), for example, argues that traditional African political systems in their pristine form were infused with democratic values regardless of the differences in their manifestation. Skalnik (1996, 111) further argues that:

On closer examination we will discover that those public figures designated by modern scholars as chiefs and kings were not politicians strictu senso and the institutions they embodied were not political institutions, and even less political systems. Certainly, we can speak of centralized decision making, but decisions of leaders were subject to various rules and limitations imposed by the populations which they were supposed to lead.

In practice, however, the nature and meaning of traditional leadership has evolved over the years; in certain instances it is now viewed as archaic. For example, Kuper (1986, 33) observes that nepotism is a rampant phenomenon in the leadership of the Swazi people and that "power radiates from the king to other members of the royal lineage."

Traditional institutions have often been referred to under the rubric of communal property rights. Scholars such as Ostrom (1990) note that communal property rights have a weakness in that they presuppose communities with the capacity of collective governance—conditions that may not be present where constituencies with heterogeneous interests and varying power seek access to the same resource, whether locally or globally. It is simplistic, however, to place traditional institutions within this framework. Traditional leaders occupy a unique position in postcolonial Africa that places them in arrangements such that they work on behalf of the state without really being part of the state. In essence, traditional leaders should provide a localized form of central control vested in an institution that derives authority from widely regarded customs. In countries such as Zimbabwe, these leaders continue to control most of the important rural survival strategies: allocation of land, natural resources, communal labor practices, and in some instances, law and order. They protect essential resources "through upholding the ancestral rest-day, which protects soil fertility; preparing rain rituals; get[ting] divine environmental protection through the animals, which protects species diversity; and finally, preserving holy groves, which contain the majority of intact closed canopy forests in the country" (Daneel 1996, 347).

CAN TRADITIONAL LEADERSHIP BE PARTICIPATORY?

In their introduction to this volume, Pistor and De Schutter provide a foundation for understanding how "voice" is an important aspect in the governance of essential resources. They cite Sen (1999), who argued that famines are rare in democratic countries. This assertion supposes that citizen participation engenders greater concern for the common good. It assumes that a lack of effective voice leads to inaccessibility to essential goods for vulnerable groups. This poses questions on the effectiveness of traditional institutions that do not meet strict democratic standards. Traditional institutions are based on a hereditary ruling system that does not provide for elections, though Pistor and De Schutter do not assume that voice can be only expressed in elections. Nevertheless, the ethos of traditional leadership is built on an ideology of sharing, fairness, and equity. Leaders are defined by how they treat their communities. Based on the ideology of *ubuntu*, which champions the collective over individual interests, traditional institutions are placed to ensure equitable access at the local level. They are inclined to look inward at local communities, unlike the state, which has shown a tendency of championing projects that promote external interests at the expense of local communities.[4] The concept of *ubuntu* is at the core of African social organization. Vijay Mahajan (2009) posits, as Bishop Desmond Tutu confirmed, that the Zulu word *Ubuntu* contains the meaning "I am because you are." The term connotes humanness, sharing, and community. According to the Zulu maxim, a person is a person through other persons (*Ubuntu ngubuntu ngavantu).* Success in Africa comes from recognizing and meeting the needs of African communities.

In traditional societies, social productivity that enhanced food security for all in the community was promoted. This kind of productivity is not based on individual economic advancement that places essential resources at ecological risk, but rather highlights how welfare for all was seen as a central issue. Traditional societies had an institution of *Zunde raMambo/Isiphalase Nkosi,* a social safety-net system. *Zunde raMambo* is a traditional "social welfare" system practiced by indigenous people before colonization. The word *Zunde* means a large gathering of people taking part in a common activity or may refer to plenty of grain stored for future use by people in a particular community. The traditional practice was coordinated by the chief, who provided land to his subjects to collectively produce for the granaries at his compound. Members of the community provided labor on a voluntary basis, even though they would not necessarily benefit directly from the harvest. Villagers would take turns participating in the entire production process from land preparation through to sowing, weeding, and harvesting. Although all villagers would benefit in times of need, priority was given to the vulnerable members of the community, who included the elderly, orphans and other vulnerable children, and widows. The practice was in place before colonization, was eroded by the colonial powers, and has been evolving ever since. The trend unfortunately has been an erosion of this social safety-net over the years. In recognition of the value of the *Zunde raMambo* as a social safety-net, the government made efforts to revive the practice after the devastating drought of the early 1990s and the impact of HIV and AIDS.

Linked to voice and participation is the need for sustainability of essential resources that safeguards the resources for future generations. Within traditional systems, sustainability of essential resources is guaranteed through various norms and values. Local rules and norms govern the preservation of essential resources such as natural water sources, land, and trees. These rules are based on the spiritual link between essential resources and ancestral spirits. Areas such as forests, mountains, springs, rivers, and water holes are made sacred. These are sites usually set aside for traditional ceremonies. In this way resources are preserved through the management and policing of traditional chiefs. Wanton tree cutting and starting fires are offenses punishable by fines from traditional leaders. The belief in ancestral spirits has also been an important preservative measure, as people are afraid of punishment by spirits for violating norms.

PARTRIACHIAL BASIS OF TRADITIONAL LEADERSHIP
AND WOMEN'S ACCESS TO SCARCE RESOURCES

Logan (2008) argues that patriarchal traditional systems often silenced the voices of women and youth, as in the case of the "Kgotla democracy" in Botswana, which was made up of male tribal elders from senior tribesmen. Mattes (1997, 5) contends that traditional systems can also be described as unaccountable and based on a coercive "demand for consensus," rather than freely given consent. Women's access to essential resources in Zimbabwe is mediated by a partriachial system that privileges males in the control and ownership of natural resources. Women have faced cultural and historical impediments in participating in or benefiting from resource extraction and consumption. Previous and current natural resource–management regimes have disregarded women. Zimbabwean women constitute 52 percent of the population yet remain outside the control of key resources. In 2012 Zimbabwe had five substantive female chiefs out of more than two hundred chiefs.[5] It is a male-dominated institution, as sons remain preferred heirs to chieftainship. Women thus lack representation in this key rural institution based on historical and cultural reasons. The increase of female chiefs will enhance the interests of women, which have largely been neglected. The institution of traditional leaders has been portrayed as the bastion of partriachial norms and values. It is often accused of sustaining and spearheading cultural practices that not only entrench gender inequalities but are harmful to women. In terms of resource allocation and natural resource governance, scholars have questioned how such an institution can be used to ensure gender equity in accessing and managing essential resources.

Increasing the participation of women will require a nuanced understanding of local practices and customs. Cultural contexts are important in inclusion and exclusion of women from resource management. The assumption by many is that increasing the number of women in committees and institutions will automatically lead to equal representation. A feminine presence in natural resource governance is not the same as a feminist one (Goetz 1997). While it is important to increase the number of women involved, the real challenge is institutionalizing gender equity as a shared social norm. A framework for gender equity requires strategic rather than numerical representation of women. This will include removal of partriachial norms and practices that entrench women's subordinate position. Proper advocacy and gender sensitization of traditional leaders will be crucial. The framework will be built on the understanding that women are not a monolithic group but are located in multiple and diverse relationships of subordination. As such, the needs of younger and older women or of poor and rich women are not similar. Ensuring proper representation of interests can be achieved by a democratic system that looks beyond numbers to issues.

While most traditional institutions are largely based on partriachial norms they are increasingly embracing gender equality through concerted efforts in advocacy and wider changes in society. The Zimbabwean government has promoted gender equality through the enactment of the Legal Age of Majority Act (1982), which means that women—like men—now enjoy majority status at eighteen years of age.[6] Women can now legally enter into contracts. Other policies, including affirmative action programs, have led to an increased number of women in decision-making positions, progressive laws on inheritance (Administration of Estates Act 1997), and protection with respect to domestic violence (Zimbabwe Domestic Violence Act 2008). More work is required to further entrench women-centered policies and gender equity measures. Adequate advocacy, training, and capacity building of traditional leaders on gender equity are required. This is to ensure that women and their interests are not sidelined from debates on essential resources.

TRADITIONAL INSTITUTIONS AND STATE CAPTURE IN AFRICA

One weakness often repeated about traditional governance institutions in Africa is that they have been captured by the state. Scholars have often argued that traditional leaders are mere "puppets" of the ruling elite (Mattes 1997). Von Trotha (1995) argues that chiefs continue to be subject to the pressures of the state, especially pressures to encourage local people to conform to the state's administrative policies, accept the regime's politics, and recognize the state. Other scholars have argued, however, that chieftaincy is not totally controlled by those elites that seem to have a stranglehold on states' structures. Van Rouveroy, van Nieuwaal, and Ray (1996) think of African chiefs as, if not totally uncaptured, at least in possession of great room for maneuvering, or as *chefs de manoeuvre*. Chiefs continue to draw their strengths from their local roots: they defend local culture and social order and are at the center of local political life. They are thus able to create space and ensure a certain degree of independence.

Logan (2008, 4) is of the view that "modern African leaders either undermine traditional leaders and allegiances, or politicize and thereby co-opt these potential 'vote brokers.'" She cites Van Kessel and Oomen (1997), who observe that "chiefs often align themselves, whether whole-heartedly or for tactical reasons, with the powers that seem to offer the best chances of safeguarding their positions." Williams (2004, 121) suggests that this "ability of chiefs to straddle the state-society dichotomy" and serve as necessary intermediaries for their people is a strength of the institution that helps explain its survival. There are many ways of framing the narrative on traditional leaders and state co-optation. What is necessary is to integrate all of these narratives and create an understanding of how they impact the experiences and existence of traditional systems across Africa. Such an analysis is meant to provide differing pathways to the question of essential resource management. The relationship between traditional leaders and the state must not simply be a one-way co-optation but rather a complex web of relationships and negotiation that emphasizes the agency of traditional institutions.

Since colonial times, the Zimbabwean state has co-opted the institution of chiefs as a means of control and governance. Postindependence, section 49 of the Traditional Leaders Act vests in the Minister of Local Government the responsibility to define the mandate for the chiefs. This provision makes chiefs in many ways subservient to the ruling party. The Zimbabwe African National Union–Patriotic Front (ZANU PF) has over the years manipulated chiefs to do political work and campaign on their behalf. In an editorial, Kulare (2013) argues that "ZANU (PF) has, over the years, succeeded in dishonoring and diminishing the integrity of our Chiefs by annexing them to their campaign machinery. In fact, most of the chiefs have been reduced to puppets of the former ruling ZANU (PF) party and there is urgent need to redress their image."[7] The new constitution, however, seeks to ensure that chiefs are nonpartisan. For example chapter 15.2 states: "Traditional leaders must not be members of any political party or in any way participate in partisan politics, act in a partisan manner, further the interests of any political party or cause or violate the fundamental rights and freedoms of any person." While this is progressive, the rest of the provisions in the constitution further strip traditional leaders of their powers and the ability to control and monitor natural resource exploitation in their areas.

Clause 15.3 (2) of the new constitution states: "Except as provided for in Act of Parliament, traditional leaders shall have no authority, control or jurisdiction over land except communal land or over persons outside communal land unless the cause of the action arose within the area of the traditional leader's jurisdiction." This provides inadequate powers to traditional leaders in protecting resources from outsiders. The sidelining of chiefs has followed on from colonial times. For example, laws created after independence have entrenched the role of the state in resource governance and further weakened the role of traditional institutions. The Communal Lands Act of 1982 divested the chiefs of their control over land and vested that power in the president. The act devolved its administration to rural district councils and district administrators under the then Ministry of Local Government Rural and Urban Development. In such a scenario the state has undermined the ability of grass roots institutions to respond to the lived realities of communities. This account confirms the position of De Schutter and Pistor (citing Binswanger, Deininger, and Feder 1995), who argue that centralized (state-controlled) property rights can be problematic because the power of central control guarantees neither universal nor effective access to essential resources. Moreover, any government that has the power to decide on the allocation of resources also has the power to determine who may benefit from them and to exclude others at its whim.

TRADITIONAL INSTITUTIONS AND ESSENTIAL RESOURCE MANAGEMENT IN ZIMBABWE

In precolonial Zimbabwean communities, traditional institutions were responsible for the effective management of social, political, and economic issues. The governance structures were geared toward serving the people. Leadership in traditional African societies was based on inclusiveness and sacredness. A leader was a representative of the people's power rather than having derived that power from the self. While positions of leadership were inherited, chiefs (*vana mambo*) did not rule alone but with the counsel of other elders. This ensured democratic and representative structures in which communality emerged. In the present day, rural people in Zimbabwe still depend on these traditional structures. In the absence of effective service provision from the central government, traditional institutions still provide for the needs of rural communities. Murphree (2004, 209) observes that: "Given this vacuum in effective bureaucratic institutionalism, rural populations have had to rely on management forms which derive in large part from their pre-colonial heritage of communalism, in which order is induced by 'affective' modes of personal relationships which emphasize ascriptive roles, peer pressure and collective control." The incursions of bureaucratic structures tend to be prescriptive, unenforceable, and appropriative (Murphree 2004). This is especially true in natural resource management, where systems of central control have sidelined communities from decision making. Without access or a say in the utilization of their own resources, rural people come to despise the external control imposed by outsiders. Within the Zimbabwean rural landscape, people still place faith in the traditional leadership, value local mother languages, respect norms and conventions, oversee the traditional leadership change (kugadzwakwashe), and perform community rituals.[8]

In Rhodesia, the colonial government had incorporated traditional chiefs as a means to extract human and natural resources. In essence, it was a strategy for curbing organized resistance against the colonial masters. After independence traditional chiefs faced serious challenges of mistrust and neglect from government. Makumbe (1998) shows how the formation of village- and ward-development committees after independence partially led to the disempowerment of traditional institutions, a measure purportedly adopted to punish chiefs for their pre-independence role as functionaries of colonial oppression. Meanwhile, the Communal Lands Act of 1982 had divested the chiefs of the land-allocation powers vested in them in the 1960s. These moves removed traditional institutions from direct management and control of natural resources. This institution has remained resilient, however, finding ways to somehow adapt to different contexts. It is this resilience and adaptability that can form the basis of reengineering traditional leadership structures to respond to the institutional crisis in natural resource management in Africa. Traditional leaders are already living and working with communities; they are respected and wield authority. They reach all of the grass roots levels—even places where government cannot afford to reach—and crucially have embedded knowledge on the protection and sacredness of natural resources.

Daneel (cited in van Rouveroy, van Nieuwaal, and Ray 1996) in a study on the 1980s examines the processes and factors that led Zimbabwe's traditional custodians of the land to carry out major environmental reforms in Masvingo Province through the Association of Zimbabwean Traditional Ecologists. The study shows how the historical and cultural context in which Shona chiefs' and spirit mediums' powers derived from a particular religious-political relationship that they have with their ancestor, the environment and the creator-god, *Mwari*. Hence the legitimacy of chiefs and spirit mediums depends on their guiding the community in the treatment of the land, the forest, and the water in such a way as to ensure that a correct relationship with the divine is maintained. The authority of the chiefs is thus intertwined with the environment. It is this relationship that ensures continued legitimacy of the leader. It is then surprising that such institutions, steeped in environmental protection, are sidelined from natural resource management.

Historically, postindependence Zimbabwe has largely favored a centralist approach to resource management with some attempts at grass roots involvement through the Communal Areas Management Programme for Indigenous Resources (CAMPFIRE) project. CAMPFIRE was a community-based natural resource–management system based on participatory methods, yet the power remained with state institutions at the rural district level. The Zimbabwean government, through agencies such as the Department of Parks and Environmental Management Agency, has continued to oversee the management of natural resources. Within this whole system traditional institutions are given token roles with little authority. Nemarundwe (2001) notes that with Community-Based Natural Resource Management (CBNRM), programs such as CAMPFIRE co-opted local villagers into state structures through both law and use of force in extension. CAMPFIRE was an external imposition that replaced and competed with already-existing institutions at the grass roots level. In the literature there is a glowing appraisal of how the project ensured participation of locals; yet in patriarchal communities it is curious how women were integrated into the various committees and processes. CBNRM initiatives have often been based on idyllic images of "community," assuming homogeneity and fixity in an otherwise complex and dynamic world (Nemarundwe 2001). Communities are gendered, aged, classed, and politicized to the extent that they are highly differentiated entities.

Under CAMPFIRE, the Department of National Parks and Wildlife Management awarded hunting licenses and permits, determined hunting quotas, and controlled wildlife revenues. Fifty percent of wildlife revenues was entrusted to local communities, but Murombedzi (1994) shows how the revenue was often inadequate and took a long time to be disbursed. With many institutions competing for resources, local communities and traditional leaders were often overridden by government officials. In the end, the program was more about sharing resources than management of natural resources. True ownership of resources based on local structures and knowledge ideally allows community ownership and peer checking. The biggest problem, however, is that traditional institutions and local communities were co-opted into a process over which they had little control.

The role of traditional leaders in Zimbabwe is encapsulated by the Traditional Leaders Act of 1998. The excerpt from Maturure (2008, 9) below outlines the important sections within the act that define the roles of traditional leaders in managing natural resources. It highlights how leaders are essentially powerless and have little or no control over natural resources. This act clearly shows how the postcolonial state has viewed the role of traditional leaders to be token and peripheral.

THE TRADITIONAL LEADERS ACT (CHAPTER 29: 17):

This act was enacted in 1998. The act does not mention direct administrative function of traditional leaders over mineral resources. It gives provision for the setting up of a local-level traditional institutional framework. The act confers to traditional leaders functions that promote the participation of locals in community development through the proper management of natural resources. Section 5 of the act state that a chief shall be responsible within his area for among other things "ensuring that the land and its natural resources are used and exploited in terms of the law and generally preventing the degradation, abuse or misuse of land and natural resources in his area." This function is bestowed to them with the understanding that local communities respect their leaders, and thus it is possible to influence behavior patterns of the local people through the use of traditional leaders. In the case of mining projects, the traditional leaders are key representatives of the people's views and needs during the consultation processes of environmental impact assessments. Mining projects can start in certain cases only after the necessary traditional approval and the holding of acceptance ceremonies in which the local community participates. Funding of such ceremonies is met by the project proponent (Maturure 2008, 9)

Chiefs have always been the custodians of land and natural resources in their areas of jurisdiction. They were able to enforce laws largely because of the respect they commanded within African culture and not necessarily because of the provision in the local government statutes. Yet according to Marongwe (1999), this traditional role of chiefs and headmen in the allocation of communal land was withdrawn and reallocated to the rural district councils by the central government after independence. Due to the respect they wielded in communal areas, traditional leaders continued to dispatch their traditional roles of land allocation among others in communal areas.

Traditional leaders have no control over the mineral resources or the proliferation of licenses to companies who come and extract from their land. In 2010 the government of Zimbabwe instituted the greatly contested community-share trusts to ensure that local populations benefit from their own resources. Section 14(b) of Statutory Instrument 21 of 2010 provides for the establishment of community-share ownership trusts (CSOTs) to hold shares in qualifying businesses on behalf of their respective communities. These trusts are headed by chiefs and have various members, including lawyers, accountants, and community representatives. The establishment of the CSOTs in Zimbabwe is provided for by the Indigenization and Empowerment (chap. 14.33) and Indigenization and Economic Empowerment (General) Regulations, 2010, Statutory Instrument 21 of 2010. The Mines and Minerals Act (chap. 21.05) gives no details as to how communities could benefit from mining done on their lands but leaves the question of benefits to the discretion of investors.

However, some traditional leaders who have obtained CSOTs complain of being abandoned by government. Chiefs in Mhondoro-Ngezi complained bitterly about the nature of negotiations in which the government left them on their own to negotiate with educated lawyers. Below is an excerpt of a newspaper report outlining the thoughts of the chiefs on their experiences with CSOTs. This example shows how traditional chiefs have been sidelined from decision making on extracting precious metals. It highlights how the state continues to offer token influence to traditional leaders, who are not involved in the negotiations that strip local communities of their resources.

CHIEFS IN MHONDORO COMPLAIN:

The chiefs . . . [are] left . . . at the mercy of sophisticated and business-savvy Zimplats officials as they negotiate terms of the trust. The institution of chiefs in Zimbabwe has largely remained feudal and backward characterised by leadership of elderly, generally uneducated and unsophisticated villagers. Except in a few instances where the chiefs are young and educated tertiary education graduates, the majority of us are not educated. "We are therefore, to a large extent, totally unprepared for the new phenomenon of community trusts which entails participating in management of large organisations and issues that are associated with the same. We expected the Ministry of Youth Development, Indigenisation and Empowerment to provide us or allow us to have legal representation during these meetings where we discuss formation of the trust . . . Chief Mashayamombe questioned why Government allowed Zimplats and their lawyers to drive the process while they (chiefs) have become passive actors who are just invited to sign papers whose contents they do not understand. "Zimplats has legal representation that has drawn up the deed of trust. The Ministry of Youth Development, Indigenisation and Empowerment has its legal officials and its only the community represented by the chiefs that does not have legal advice on such highly legal matters," said Chief Mashayamombe. (*Sunday Mail* 7 April 2012)

CONCLUSION

This paper provides a starting point for discussing the role traditional institutions can play in ensuring sustainable, productive, and equitable management of essential resources. It argues for the need to have a wide discussion with all possible governance regimes based on a contextual analysis. Indigenous institutions offer a great source of alternative governance regimes. Despite the weaknesses of traditional institutions (particularly their patriarchal basis), they offer important insights on ensuring protection of essential resources. The sidelining of traditional institutions from resource governance and control has led to a lack of participation in governing resources by communities living with the resources. In light of the comparative failure of the African state, undermined as it has been by greedy and violent political elites within and without Africa, to bring about democracy and development, chieftaincy has reemerged as an important vehicle for authentic indigenous political expression. This chapter has shown that empowering traditional institutions holds promise for embedding management of essential resources within local communities. Institutional synergies that include participation of local communities in which traditional leaders take the lead will allow for a resource–management system more in line with equity and sustainability than the imposition of formal property regimes.

NOTES

1. See Olivier De Schutter and Katharina Pistor's introduction for a more nuanced definition of essential resources.

2. See Keulder (2000) www.kas.de/wf/doc/kas_18730-544-2-30.pdf?100301113829.

3. An *invented tradition* constitutes a set of practices, normally governed by overtly or tacitly accepted rules of a ritual or symbolic nature, which seek to inculcate certain values and norms of behavior by repetition, which automatically implies continuity with the past. In fact, where possible, they normally attempt to establish continuity with a suitable historical past (Hobsbawm and Ranger 1994).

4. One recent example is the large-scale land acquisitions in Mwenezi and Chisumbanje that promote biofuel production by largely foreign-controlled companies at the expense of locals. See Chiweshe and Mutopo (2014).

5. See Sibongile Mpofu, "Zimbabwe Breaks New Ground in Traditional Institutions," www.africangn.net/fs-38.htm. Retrieved 12 April 2014.

6. *Age of majority* is a legal definition that means that a person is legally an adult and responsible for the majority of his or her actions. No one can be held legally responsible for all their actions.

7. See "The Role of Chiefs in the New Constitution," *The Zimbabwean*, 10 April 2013, www.thezimbabwean.co.uk/comment/30034/the-role-of-chiefs-in-the-new-constitution-.html. Retrieved 20 February 2013.

8. In 2011, 61.4 percent of Zimbabweans were resident in the rural areas (https://www.cia.gov/library/publications/the-world-factbook/geos/zi.html). Retrieved 24 March 2015.

REFERENCES

Adewumi, J. B., and J. Egwurube. 1985. "Role of Traditional Rulers in Historical Perspective." In *Local Government and the Traditional Rulers in Nigeria*, ed. Oladimeji Aborisade, 19–36. Ile-Ife, Nigeria: University of Ife Press.

Ake, C. 1990. "The Case for Democracy." *The Carter Center: African Governance in the 1990s: Objectives, Reserves and Constraints*. Atlanta, Ga.: Carter Center of Emory University.

Ayittey, G. 1991. *Indigenous African Institutions*, New York: Transnational.

Binswanger, H. P., K. Deininger, and G. Feder. 1995. "Power, Distortions, Revolt, and Reform in Agricultural Land Relations." In *Handbook of Development Economics. Vol. 3*, ed. J. Behrman and T. N. Srinivasan, 2661–2772. Amsterdam: North-Holland (Elsevier).

Chiweshe, M. K. and P. Mutopo. 2014. "National and International Actors in the Orchestration of Land Deals in Zimbabwe: What is in it for Smallholder Farmers?" In *International Land Deals in East and Southern Africa*, ed. Pascal Mihyo. Addis Ababa: OSSREA.

Davidson, B. 1992. *The Black Man's Burden*. Ibadan, Nigeria: Spectrum.

Daneel, M. L. 1996. "Environmental Reform: A New Venture of Zimbabwe's Traditional Custodians of the Land." Special Issue on the New Relevance of Traditional Authorities to Africa's future, *Journal of Legal Pluralism and Unofficial Law* 37–38: 347–376.

Dore, D. 2001. "Transforming Traditional Institutions for Sustainable Natural Resource Management, History, Narratives and Evidence from Zimbabwe." *African Quarterly* 5 (3): 1–18.

Eze, M. O. 2010. *Intellectual History in Contemporary South Africa.* New York: Palgrave MacMillan.

Goetz, A. M. 1997. *Getting Institutions Right for Women in Development.* London: Zed.

Hardin, G. 1968. "The Tragedy of the Commons," *Science, New Series,* 162, (3859): 1243–1248.

Hiemstra, W. 2010. Editorial, *Endogenous Development Magazine* 6: 1.

Hobsbawm, E., and T. Ranger. 1994. *The Invention of Tradition.* Cambridge: Cambridge University Press.

Kyed, H. M., and L. Buur. 2006. "Recognition and Democratisation: 'New Roles' for Traditional Leaders in Sub-Saharan Africa." DIIS Working Paper No. 2006/11, Danish Institute for International Studies, Copenhagen, Denmark.

Logan, C. 2008. "Traditional Leaders in Modern Africa: Can Democracy and the Chief Co-exist?" Working Paper No. 93. Cape Town: Afrobarometer Working Papers.

Keulder, C. 2000. "Traditional Leaders." *In State, Society and Democracy: A Reader in Namibian Politics.* ed. Christiaan Keulder, 150–168. Windhoek, Namibia: Macmillan Education.

Kulare, M. 2013. "The Role of Chiefs in the New Constitution." *The Zimbabwean,* 10 April 2013, http://www.thezimbabwean.co/opinions/30034/the-role-of-chiefs -in-the-new-constitution-.html, Accessed 23 February 2014.

Kuper, H. 1986. *The Swazi: A South African Kingdom.* New York: Holt, Rinehart and Winston.

Mahajan, V. 2009. *Africa Rising: How 900 Million African Consumers Offer More Than You Think.* Englewood Cliffs, N.J.: Prentice Hall.

Makahamandze, T. Grand, N. and Tavuyanago, B. 2009. "The Role of Traditional Leaders in Fostering Democracy, Justice and Human Rights in Zimbabwe." *The African Anthropologist,* 16 (1&2): 33–47.

Makumbe, J. Mw. 1998. *Democracy and Development in Zimbabwe: Constraints of Decentralization.* Harare: SAPES Trust.

Mamdani, M. 1996. *Citizen and Subject: Contemporary Africa and the Legacy of Late Colonialism.* Princeton: Princeton University Press.

Mandondo, A. 2000. "Situating Zimbabwe's Natural Resource Governance Systems in History." Occasional Paper No.32, Bogor: Centre for International Forestry Research.

Mattes, R. 1997. "Building a Democratic Culture in Traditional Society." Paper presented to the International Conference on Traditional Leadership in Southern Africa, hosted by Konrad AdenauerStiftung and University of Transkei, Umtata, South Africa, 16–18 April 1997.

Maturure, M. 2008. *A Review of the Legislative and Policy Framework for Community Based Natural Resources Management in the Mining*, Harare: Zimbabwe National CBNRM Forum.

Murombedzi, J. 2003. *Pre-colonial Conservation Practices in Southern Africa and Their Legacy Today*. Harare, Zimbabwe: IUCN.

Murombedzi, J. C. 1994. "The Dynamics of Conflict in Environmental Management Policy in the Context of the Communal Areas Management Program for Indigenous Resources." Unpublished D. Phil. diss., Center for Applied Social Sciences, University of Zimbabwe, Harare.

Murphree, M.W. 2004. "Communal Approaches to Natural Resource Management in Africa: From Whence and to Where?" *Journal of International Wildlife Law and Policy*, 7: 203–216.

Nemarundwe, N. 2001. "Institutional Collaboration and Shared Learning for Forest Management in Chivi District, Zimbabwe." In *Social Learning in Community Forest Management: Linking Concepts and Practice,* ed. E. Wollenberg, D. Edmunds, L. Buck, J. Fox and S. Brodt, 89–108. Bogor, Zimbabwe: Center for International Forestry Research.

Ostrom, E. 1990. *Governing the Commons: The Evolution of Institutions for Collective Action*. Cambridge: Cambridge University Press.

Owusu, M. 1991. "Democracy and Africa—A View from the Village." *Journal of Modern African Studies* 30 (3): 369–396.

Safaids. 2010. *The Role of Traditional Leadership Preventing Violence Against Women Towards Effective HIV Prevention in Southern Africa*. Pretoria, South Africa.

Sen, A. 1999. "Democracy as a Universal Value," *Journal of Democracy*, 10 (3): 3–17.

Skalnik, P. 1996. "Authority versus Power," *Journal of Legal Pluralism*, 37 & 38: 109–121.

van Rouveroy van Nieuwaal, E. A., and D. I. Ray. 1996. *The New Relevance of Traditional Authorities in Africa Conference; Major Themes; Reflections on Chieftaincy in Africa; Future Directions*. Leiden: African Studies Centre.

von Trotha, T. 1995. "Administrative Chieftainship: Historical and Sociological Perspectives of the Development of Modern Chieftainship." In *Proceedings of the Conference on the Contribution of Traditional Authority to Development, Human Rights and Environmental Protection: Strategies for Africa*, eds. Kwame Arhin, Donald I. Ray and E. Adriaan B. van Rouveroy, van Nieuwaal, 454–473. Leiden: African Studies Centre.

West, H. G., and S. Kloeck-Jenson. 1999. "Betwixt and Between: 'Traditional Authority' and Democratic Decentralization in Post-war Mozambique." *African Affairs* 98: 455–484.

Williams, J.M. 2004. "Leading from Behind: Democratic Consolidation and the Chieftaincy in South Africa." *Journal of Modern African Studies*, 42 (1): 113–136.

Wunsch, J., and D. Olowu, eds. 1990. *The Failure of the Centralized State: Institutions and Self-Governance in Africa*. Boulder, Colo.: Westview.

CHAPTER 17

Local Corporations

A CORPORATE FORM TO REDUCE INFORMATION COSTS AND MAINTAIN SUPPORTIVE RESOURCES

James Krueger

In this article, I make the following arguments: (1) that absolute scarcity, arising from the degradation of ecosystem services, is one of the foremost threats to essential resources; (2) that high information costs in increasingly mobile and globalized markets tend to obscure this looming scarcity and obstruct its translation into social meaning; and (3) that mobility can be reasonably limited by "local corporations" that act as combined economic and government entities with a limited power to exclude people and goods from their territory.

I agree on the importance of voice and reflexivity for the governance of essential resources (see Olivier De Schutter and Katharina Pistor's introduction to this volume) but deploy these concepts differently. Reflexivity is a call for those in power, who control access to resources, to realize the compelling needs of others and make a sacrifice to benefit them. For reflexivity to work, sacrifices must be made meaningful in the context of some particular normative community. Voice, then, is not just about a person having a say in resource decisions that affect him or her, but about a person participating in a community through which resource decisions are made meaningful. High information costs can render resource decisions less meaningful and can pose a problem for voice and reflexivity. The strategy I propose is a kind of layered governance, such that individual sacrifice for the environment has meaning in a community and community sacrifice has meaning at a national level.

The idea of local community is much maligned by the liberal focus on individuals' material needs and because of discomfort with individual sacrifice for nonmaterial ideals like community well-being. Actual community control over natural resources is threatened by the increased physical mobility of individuals in expanding labor markets, by increased influence of global markets on local resource use, and by the dominance of economic narratives of value that leave no role for community norm-leaders. Some scholars think that the talk about community is spurious and obscures more important identities and relationships (Agrawal and Gibson 1999). Yet local community is really an aspirational concept that can take many shapes.

Rather than advocating one management ideal or community type, I propose setting up a system of diverse local corporations with the flexibility to create their own internal rules. This system operates at both a local level (corporate governance) and a national level (intercorporate governance). The idea at both levels is to use communitarian techniques for saving on information costs, so that good and bad managers become more visible and sacrifices in favor of others become meaningful. Information cost savings come from community restrictions on mobility of people and goods. Local control over the movement of people and goods (i.e., defining the boundaries of the resource user group) is the first step toward effective internal community management of shared resources (Ostrom 1990). Externally, the national government can focus on intercorporate relations rather than individual members. The idea is not to impose one blueprint for corporate management but to set up and police a system that selects for better management outcomes.

Overall, information gains must be balanced against corresponding efficiency losses (of reduced mobility of individuals and goods). Yet, as in a business corporation, strong limitations on mobility (like low employee turnover, legal restrictions on firing, and promotions based on seniority) can enhance, rather than undermine, market functioning.

THE NEW RESOURCE SCARCITY

Essential resources can be subdivided into two categories: the goods necessary for human life and the natural infrastructure for all economic production.[1] The latter category of essential resources I call *supportive resources*, which include water, soils, land, forest, air, and biodiversity. Supportive resources require management for multiple goals. A forest, for example, provides timber, water filtration, carbon sequestration, soil support (nutrient cycling and erosion prevention), aesthetic beauty, cultural values, biodiversity, and so on. A tree farm may provide some water filtration but will not provide biodiversity. A "natural" forest may not provide as many livelihood opportunities today but may be essential to livelihoods of future generations. As a support for multiple activities, there is no way to "maximize" forests for all uses. Rather, there are competing interests, and trade-offs must follow some ethical standard that includes future generations. This is not a new argument. Aldo Leopold (1949) famously wrote that a new "land ethic" would be the key to a sustainable economy. I take the land ethic not as an inevitable progression in the values of landowners but as something that must be developed in a community space, through a community's attachment to land and resources.

The traditional analysis of scarcity does not apply well to supportive resources. Old scarcities, which are central to economic analysis, happen one resource at a time and assume substitutability of one resource for another and technological adaptation to meet rising demand. The new scarcity, in contrast, arises from deterioration in nonsubstitutable (and usually unpriced) inputs to production. Rising scarcity may inspire innovation, but this innovation does not address supportive resources as an interconnected system. Innovations that seem to reduce stress on one supportive resource tend rather to shift the stress to other supportive resources. For example, consumers substitute e-readers for books and thus shift demand from forest products to other things like batteries and data storage that continue the underlying stresses on land (e.g., waste dumps), water (to cool data centers), and air (carbon pollution). In addition, increases in efficiency of production that otherwise would reduce pressure on supportive resources tend to result in increased consumption of consumer goods (Lambin and Meyfroidt 2011). Efficiency gains in production often come at the expense of ecosystem services, with the "savings" focused only on priced resources, and the real environmental costs externalized onto unpriced supportive resources (Vandermeer 1996).

The new resource scarcity needs to be distinguished from the idea of relative scarcity associated with natural disasters and global warming. An example of relative scarcity is a drought. Even as crops fail in one region, they will be flourishing in another region. With a global trading system, it is possible to move food from the healthy region to the drought-stricken region (Molden 2007). Or, with greater mobility, people may move out of a drought-prone area and onto lands that can support them (Reuveny 2007). These issues have been raised in the context of climate change, as a way to address basic food needs for the world's growing population

(Beddington et al. 2011). Relative scarcity raises questions about equity and about redistribution of resources. Typically, there are sufficient resources in places outside the crisis area such that problems like poverty and malnutrition—that is, shortages in essential resources—can be solved over the short term through political will and infrastructure for redistribution. The sustainability question, as related to supportive resources, is different. Even if there are enough resources on the planet to provide every person with an essential amount, there remains the problem of resource maintenance—good management to ensure bountiful resources into the future. Redistribution (for poverty alleviation) and maintenance (for future needs) are separate and sometimes competing goals (Adams et al. 2004).

This distinction is important when discussing the necessary institutional infrastructure for supplying essential resources. Redistribution and maintenance can be separate government functions. The idea of dividing up government functions—for example, centralizing redistribution decisions and decentralizing maintenance decisions—is hardly revolutionary (see, e.g., Oates 1972). The problem of relative scarcity is a problem of insurance—the larger the pool of people paying in, the better. A global world, interconnected through market infrastructure, is better able to insure against localized crises than a compartmentalized world, in which each locality must insure itself. The problem of maintaining supportive resources, on the other hand, has worsened in this era of globalization. Greater mobility in global markets tends to sever the long-term alignment between individuals and the resources where they live. For this problem, compartmentalization makes a lot of sense. Is it possible to have compartmentalization and globalization at the same time? The premise of this paper is that, through layered governance, it is possible.

INFORMATION COSTS

THE BASIC HYPOTHESIS

Why is globalization a problem for maintaining supportive resources? Environmental deterioration (measured at the global level) proceeds apace with global market expansion (see, e.g., Foster 1992; York et al. 2003). Here I explore one possible reason for this. Global markets facilitate mobility of people and goods and lead to high information costs. These costs tend to undermine the process by which resource maintenance is made a meaningful activity.

DEFINING INFORMATION COSTS AS A SOCIAL PHENOMENON

Information cost, as applied in this article, is a social problem of collective organization, collective meaning, and collective action. From the perspective of a resource decision maker, information costs appear in the form of (1) too many people under one decision maker (making it costly to monitor, sort, and process information about them); (2) too many choices among courses of action and rules of use (making it costly and confusing to connect changes in behavior to resource outcomes); and (3) too many competing interpretive frameworks and meanings, leading to high costs of communicating.

Two overarching criticisms might be raised against an information cost analysis. First, it might be argued that resource maintenance is inherently complex (because of natural complexity of ecosystems and interdependent uses) and, therefore, that there is no way to reduce information costs to the point that resource outcomes can be predicted. This criticism is ill founded, because it is not necessary to predict outcomes with precision to act on risks. Moreover, lowering information costs will make society more responsive to its mistakes (e.g., wrong predictions) on an ongoing basis. Second, it might be argued that information technology can overcome information costs without social reorganization. This criticism is also misguided. At the same time that technology facilitates information sorting along specific variables, it greatly increases the total amount of information available. It is not clear that information savings (of computer sorting) will be greater than information costs (of more information). Supportive resources have multiple goals, multiple meanings, and multiple variables. This tends to confound the aggregation and sorting process of automated information technology. This is in contrast to online markets that can manage large numbers of buyers and sellers and sort simple information—price and quality—effectively. Governments using online forums struggle to make sense of comments collected at a broad scale. In fact, it is nonprofits—not computers—that tend to research government actions, interpret them, work out shared meanings from their membership, and communicate grievances.

GLOBALIZATION AND INFORMATION COSTS

Globalization leads to increased information costs because of increased mobility of people and goods (see, e.g., Hodgson 2003). With increased mobility, the actions of a far greater number of people become relevant to any given decision maker. Collective action becomes more difficult, because there are more people and activities to coordinate. The global economic system actually overcomes many information cost problems through the creation of a system of business firms (typified by the large publicly held corporation) that limit mobility and compartmentalize information. In matters of public management like the maintenance of supportive resources, however, there has been some breakdown in the influence of intermediate institutions (like family, community, and civic forums) that otherwise would stand between individuals and national bureaucracy and would moderate the information costs of free mobility.

Coase (1937) famously argued that high transaction costs (including information costs) explain why business firms exist at all, instead of an idealized (and more efficient) economic system of independent and highly mobile buyers and sellers (see also Williamson 1975; Demsetz 1988). To the extent that a business firm is cohesive (as measured, e.g., by low employee turnover), it holds a smaller number of people together in regular interactions, thus reducing internal information cost problems for managers. Firm managers save on information costs through a number of communitarian techniques, like face-to-face visibility (seeing what employees are doing), repeat interactions (long-term relations with employees and greater trust), use of a person's reputation as a proxy for detailed information about that person (gossip instead of research), informal oversight and peer pressure in day-to-day interactions, and imposition of standardized forms of organizing and communicating information. A system of corporations also means a reduced number of entities (corporations as compared to atomized buyers and sellers) engaged in regular interactions. An outsider dealing with a firm does not have to evaluate all firm employees. Rather, an outsider meets with the firm's agents and evaluates the firm as a whole based on its reputation. The firm's brand is a proxy for detailed information about how the firm is managed and about the quality of its products. Notably, the brand is often a firm's most valuable asset.

Another factor helping the economic system overcome information costs is standardization (of property rights, measurements, currency, contracts, and language). Standardization helps reduce information costs in government regulation as well, an example being permits that follow a standard format. I too argue for standardization as a method of reducing information costs but only at broader scales, as for example in intercorporate relations.

CORPORATIZATION AND FORMALIZING PROPERTY RIGHTS

The argument about the information cost savings of corporations is in fact drawn from very similar arguments about the information cost savings of property formalization (Hardin 1968; de Soto 2000; Merrill and Smith 2000). Formalizing property rights (private or communal) reduces information costs in that (1) it reduces multiple interests in land and resources to one owner, (2) it reduces types of ownership to one of a few standard forms (e.g., freehold, lease, etc.), and (3) it translates property uses into the uniform metric of price (such that owners make use of the property according to market demand).

With regard to maintaining supportive resources, however, the argument for formalizing property tends to break down. First, price is not an effective means of conveying information about unpriced and multifunctional supporting resources. In addition, formalizing property can fragment authority over supportive resources into many small units, making coordination of resource maintenance very expensive (Freyfogle 2002). The mobility of private owners—the ease with which they can sell their property—severs the long-term alignment of the owner's interests with the land's interests. Finally, formalized property relations cannot account well for spatial variety. Variety is a basic feature of natural ecosystems; it is also a social by-product of people having meaningful relationships with nature (Graham 2011). Land and resources cannot be crammed into standardized property forms, because they have a personal (and local) component (Radin 1981; Jacobs 1989).

The underlying argument about information costs may still hold, however, for local corporations. Local corporations represent larger blocks of land and resources. They restrict rather than facilitate mobility by having inalienable territory and by limiting who can enter and exit. Moreover, corporate formalization is less intrusive into the complex web of resource interdependencies among its members. Property formalization attempts to simplify this web (Meinzen-Dick and Mwangi 2008). Corporate formalization, on the other hand, need not dissolve complex internal rules of management. The key is to carve out some independent rule-making authority for local managers, such that they have a role in creating and guaranteeing rights to resources. The corporate form can mediate the downsides of standardization, as it allows for both internal variety in corporate management and external standardization vis-à-vis outsiders and national government.

WHY NO "PUBLIC" FIRMS TO DEAL WITH INFORMATION COSTS IN BIG MARKETS?

If the business corporation has been successful at reducing information costs and making economic transactions work in a globalized system, why are there no local corporations—a form of local self-government—to address information costs for residents concerned with the public problem of resource maintenance? The simple answer is that there is no enabling legislation that allows people to form local corporations. In a broader sense, though, there are two big obstacles to this corporate form: the tendency of law to micromanage sub-state governance, and our inability to conceive of (relative) sub-state autonomy in a market system.

The tendency among lawyers is to specify a response in law to every potential management problem within a corporation. Such micromanagement re-creates many of the information problems that the corporate form is there to solve. The problem of micromanagement is apparent in proposals to formalize customary authority. South Africa, for example, allows indigenous groups to incorporate and hold communal land as a corporation (Fitzpatrick 2005). The legal procedures for forming this corporation are arduous, requiring a specific type of management structure that is democratic, transparent, and nondiscriminatory (Fitzpatrick 2005; Klug 2006). Facing complex legal requirements, indigenous groups in South Africa enlist NGOs to help write their corporate constitutions (Klug 2006). The community then lacks buy-in into their own rules, and government in any case cannot enforce the rules from the outside (Fitzpatrick 2005).

Micromanagement can be compared to formalization programs that look for measurable results (like sustainability) rather than standard rules. Haldar and Stiglitz (2013) compare two formalization programs: de Soto's program for state recognition of informal property claims and Yunus's program organizing loan applicants into groups and extending credit to one person based on the reputation of the group. De Soto's program requires land demarcation and legal titling according to state procedures, in the end replacing informal relations with a title deed, guaranteed by the state. Yunus's microcredit program, on the other hand, is results oriented. It holds individuals responsible for one another vis-à-vis outsiders, without specifying the form of internal governance. Yunus's method is more effective, in part because it incentivizes rather than replaces informal monitoring and enforcement among peers in a group.

As for the second obstacle, the idea of relative local autonomy is difficult to grasp, as it involves layered governments with some overlapping jurisdiction. Local governments are commonly thought of as having only as much authority as national or regional governments give them. Conflicts in rules are resolved in favor of national government. The idea that local governments might have an independent power, based in part on economic activities, is somewhat foreign to modern thinking (Frug 1980).

Frug (1980) illustrates the tension between national rights and autonomous collectives with the interesting example of the medieval town. He asks how one might revive town autonomy in the modern liberal state to mediate between individual rights and state government. The medieval town was neither a public entity nor a private business but a different kind of corporation combining economic, political, and communal functions. The town had a degree of sovereign power over its members and maintained areas of independence against state action. What is interesting in the medieval town is the fiercely independent and coercive nature of the collectivity, based in large part on its economic independence. Inevitably, "the exercise of corporate power infringes individual rights protected by the state" (Frug 1980, 1124). Similarly, though, "the exercise of state power infringes individual rights protected by independent corporations" (Frug 1980, 1124).

Greif (2004), also exploring the history of the medieval town, argues that autonomous towns, far from hindering markets, were important to the rise of commercial economies in Europe. Greif highlights the strangeness to modern thinking of one important aspect of the territorial corporation: collective responsibility. Greif explains how all the members of a medieval town could be held liable for trade losses of one of their members. As Greif points out, collective responsibility gives rise to strong internal policing. It can also provide a basis for trust in the marketplace, inbetween autonomous communities, since an individual carries his or her collective identity with him or her as a guarantor against his or her unfair or opportunistic behavior. Outsiders put their trust in the community name, rather than the individual.

ESSENTIAL FEATURES OF LOCAL CORPORATIONS

OVERVIEW

Local corporations are distinguished from business corporations mainly by rootedness in territory and by having members as shareholders (and outsiders only as lenders and investors). The main features of the local corporation are: (1) territory; (2) ability to engage as a collectivity in various economic activities; (3) formal relationship with the state, including personhood status and registration and reporting requirements; (4) informal internal order that is mostly free from state control, to maximize participation and ecological adaptability; (5) collective responsibility to outsiders, to incentivize internal policing and facilitate trust in intercorporate transactions; and (6) some control over entry and exit.

INITIAL SETUP AND BOUNDARIES

The corporate territory I have in mind is a town or small city along with surrounding rural land. Nonetheless, people living in a neighborhood of a global megacity might also create a local corporation. Perhaps the most perplexing initial problem of creating a local corporation is defining its boundaries. It would be impossible to get every person in a given locality to agree to join. Rather, there would have to be a referendum through majority vote. This would be very much like converting an existing local government jurisdiction to a corporate form. Those not joining would then have the option of joining or exiting. For those exiting, the corporation would exercise eminent domain (forced purchase of their property, subject to state-level review) or line up purchasers who are either already members or who are interested in joining (voluntary sale). In addition, enabling legislation would have to specify a minimum and maximum population for a local corporation. The initial management structure and allocation of "shares" would be for members to decide.

INFORMAL INTERNAL GOVERNANCE

The local corporation has a dual nature, being more informal and communal on the inside and more formal and standardized on the outside. The idea is to insert an intermediate body between the state and the individual, so that the state can focus on the broader natural resource problems among intermediate bodies (e.g., spillover effects) and the intermediate body can leverage informal rules to govern individual members inside the corporate territory. I use "informal" here as shorthand for norms that govern day-to-day relations among members of a geographically defined community. Informal rules are embedded in social relations and are enforced mostly in a decentralized manner (see Cleaver 2002).

These rules may reduce some administrative costs—for example, making communication between managers and members easier—but need not replace the planning processes that are necessary for the long-term management of any business or local government. In addition, informal rules can function alongside corporate constitutions and bylaws that may be applied in (formal) local courts.

Moore (1973) provided a compelling model for how a sub-state group (here, the corporation) can generate its own informal rules while operating under national law. Moore puts forward the idea of "semi-autonomous social fields." The social field is only semi-autonomous because of the persistent influence of some outside rules (like law) but is nonetheless autonomous to the extent that the group generates its own rules and achieves compliance. Referring to the work of Max Weber, Moore suggests that "private" groups achieve compliance largely by threatening to exclude people who break rules (or, in the positive, offering greater inclusion in the group as an incentive for following rules).

For resources like land falling exclusively within its jurisdiction, the local corporation would have the primary power to set rights and responsibilities. The local corporation thus would have freedom to tinker with different arrangements for public, private, and communal property. The corporation might allow private ownership of the land surface but retain subsurface rights as public (corporate owned). Other assets, like a mine or a factory, might be owned by an individual, a group, or the local corporation. The forms of property are unique to each corporation, much like customary land tenure, but they do not present a problem of information cost to outsiders, because outsiders go through the standardized corporation in order to get access to local resources.

The forms of property internal to the corporation might also include new environmental rights, like conservation easements or carbon credits for carbon-saving land uses (like maintaining forest). The local corporation would be the holder of the rights and would bear responsibility for monitoring individual members. Along these lines, Rieser (1999) proposes that the national government allocate fishing quotas to entire communities instead of to individuals. The community then would be responsible to the state for not exceeding the allowable catch and would face collective punishment for failing to restrain individual members. This arrangement eases some of the inherent monitoring problems of environmental rights: individuals are responsible to the corporation (and are easier to monitor at this level because of reduced information costs), and the corporation is collectively responsible to the state and to outsiders in rights markets. The national government, for example, might compensate the corporation for its aggregate conservation or carbon savings, much as it does now through tax breaks to individuals.

FORMAL CONTROL FROM THE OUTSIDE

The rules governing corporations in their interactions with outsiders are different from the internal rules. At this level, corporations can afford legal experts and can finance more complex adjudication. National law will govern corporate interactions with outsiders. A local corporation can sue and be sued, can be subject to criminal investigation and sanctions, and in extreme cases can even be forced to dissolve. The corporate brand too, unlike the personal reputation of individual members within a corporation, is protected by formal law, as is common in trademark law.

Unfortunately, it is not so clear what corporate governance issues are "internal" and subject to (mostly) informal corporate management and what matters are "external" and subject to national law. Of course, if a local corporation polluted a national river, this would be an externality, subject to national regulation. On the other hand, each local corporation might release a de minimis amount of fertilizer into local waters that, when accumulated at a river delta, has disastrous effects on (national) aquatic ecosystems. Since today's de minimis harm can be tomorrow's externality, the state must retain the power to identify externalities on an ongoing basis and, among externalities, determine which are matters for national regulation and which for intercorporate bargaining. One limitation on the state is that it must not dictate methods of internal governance but rather should only require results from local corporations, like a minimum amount of pollution.

The national government has some incentive to protect local autonomy, because the local corporation system provides information cost savings to the national government too. If ten individuals from a local area pollute a river, the state must gather information about each of them and prosecute each of them individually. In the local corporation model, if the state detects pollution leaving the corporate territory, the state can penalize the corporation without bothering to investigate which individual is responsible. The corporation in turn would investigate individuals and punish them. Similarly, if upper riparian users and lower riparian users each were organized into local corporations, the state would be able to negotiate with representatives over water sharing, rather than trying to work out a solution among multiple resource users.

CONTROL OVER ENTRY AND EXIT

Local corporations must have some control over who is a member, that is, over entry and exit. This is true of business corporations also; they have the power to hire and fire employees (within limits). Control over entry and exit is important for several reasons. It limits mobility and serves as the basis for repeat interactions, for habit and tradition, and for reputation mechanisms of informal governance. Also, as in Moore's model of the semi-autonomous social field, control over entry and exit is a primary means of enforcing nonstate rules. Obedient members move closer to the center of power, and disobedient members are pushed out. Finally, easy entry and exit will tend to diminish people's incentive to participate in local government (Komesar 2001). A person who can easily exit has less at stake in local decision making.

In the context of a territorial corporation, however, total control over entry and exit is also dangerous. Unhappy members, trapped in a local community, will not make the best cooperating partners and can easily become victims of local prejudice. Dagan and Heller (2001) argue that liberal exit (i.e., mobility) can be cooperation enhancing, if one guards against incentives for waste. This point is well-taken, although the question should not be presented as a choice of alternatives, liberal exit versus rootedness, but rather as a problem of community design, of limited exit. Total freedom to move is an illusion in any society. People may be indirectly tied to territory for any number of reasons—job, family, poverty, and so on.

In a territorial corporation, as in a commons, the main entry-exit problem is that members wanting to exit might be forced to sell land, resources, and even their shares in corporate economic enterprises at a loss. A member selling his or her property may not be able to find a willing buyer. When no existing members want to purchase the property, sales involve a two-step process, with the seller finding a buyer and then the corporation deciding whether to accept the buyer as a member. Such community screening processes are already in existence, as in, for example, community land trusts (Bassett 2005). In cases of extreme and patent prejudice against the person leaving or the person seeking to join, the person must have an option to resort to national courts. This is particularly important in the case of local corporations exercising eminent domain, as the local corporation may refuse to provide adequate compensation to an expelled (and possibly disliked) member. Of course, the individual will have assets at stake in the local corporation, some of which are not fungible. For example, an individual may invest labor into common or corporate property. Such things are very difficult to provide compensation for. Arguably it is good for both the corporation and the person leaving to suffer slight losses, as a small (but not total) barrier to exit.

There are entry-exit problems for goods as well as people. With control over territory, the corporation can prevent some consumer import products from being bought and sold within corporate territory. In some cases, the corporation might make bulk purchases of goods, like infrastructure building materials, to reduce costs. It could secure a corporate loan from a national bank and then turn around and function as a bank itself, loaning money to individual members. However, when bank loans to individuals come only through the local corporation where those individuals live—the only real consumer choice—minor difficulties may be encountered. If, for instance, individuals want to use a different bank, they must either convince their local corporation to transact with a different bank or exit the local territory. Such an arrangement is not as extreme as it may seem. The trade-off for limiting consumer choice is reduced information costs. Indeed, an individual in a local corporation has a real voice in making local rules. Moreover, joining a local corporation does not cut off participation in the broader national and international economy. Rather, it interposes the corporation to represent some (but not all) of the individual's interests in the broader economy.

COLLECTIVE RESPONSIBILITY

Part of membership in a local corporation is collective responsibility. In dealing with outsiders, a local corporation puts all of its members' assets at risk. A corporation could suffer a loss or be fined, and then could turn around and fine its individual members (or tax them) and reach into members' private assets. At first glance, it might seem unfair to punish individuals for the faults of their leaders. Indeed, it is not enough for an individual to protest the group's decision; the only way to avoid collective responsibility is to exit the group before the decision takes effect. Of course, individual responsibility is somewhat illusory anyway, as we all can suffer financially from bad leadership in our communities, in our companies, and in our nations. Embracing the reality of collective responsibility does not absolve individual leaders of responsibility either, but rather allows us to have layered discipline. The corporation pays as a collectivity to outsiders but then can turn around and punish individual wrongdoers internally.

A SYSTEM THAT SELECTS FOR GOOD MANAGEMENT

The success of any particular locality at maintaining local resources depends on a number of factors, including such elusive things as good leadership, ecological sensibility, and personal restraint. The internal design features of local corporations—their relatively small size and control on mobility—do not guarantee good internal governance (as should be obvious from small-scale environmental disasters of the past, like Easter Island). What matters then is not that every local corporation is successful but rather that the system is set up to select for those corporations that are successful. The key ingredients of such a system are: diversity (different types of local corporations), visibility (so that people know which corporations are successful), multiple memberships (overlapping commitments by individuals to their local corporations, their jobs, their nations, and so on), and incentives to improve governance.

Corporate management strategies must be diverse if corporations are to serve as laboratories for different environmental policies. Diversity comes out of local autonomy. Members can adapt corporate management to the natural environment in their locality, to environmental and social change, to group character, and to particular preferences and economic needs (on the adaptability of local institutions, see, e.g., Lane and McDonald 2005; Ostrom 2010). Adaptability may be temporary and may run up against a contrary tendency in institutions toward path dependency—or traditionalism—over time. But with diversity of local corporations, those management structures that do not adapt or otherwise do not serve members' interests may be eliminated, for example, by competition.

Visibility is also key to improved resource governance. One of the main purposes of reducing information costs, from the perspective of national regulators, is to give regulators the ability to expose corporate actions. This does not happen automatically. Rather, with lower information costs, the national government will have an opportunity to increase the visibility of corporate actions, via control over brands, public stigmas, fines, and reporting requirements. Big actors in the marketplace also have a greater ability to expose one another: managers from different firms engage in regular transactions with one another and gossip about other corporations' quality of performance.

It is very important that individual members of local corporations have other loyalties and other memberships. This is to deal with the old problem of factions, of governing relations among various small, cohesive communities. Geertz (1963) describes the problem as one of "primordial attachments" in modern pluralist states. If members are too insular, they will have great difficulty negotiating agreements to share national resources (e.g., a national river). Instead of thinking of mutual or shared benefits, each group becomes very sensitive of the advantages that another group might have over it. In short, members of insular groups, without other memberships, might make decisions based on feelings of affiliation rather than on (nationally agreed) reasonable goals.

The territorial aspect of public firms makes overlapping memberships harder to conceptualize. In the case of business corporations, multiple memberships are common. A person may work for a corporation as his or her main job while still holding financial interests in other enterprises (e.g., as a stockholder), joining a food or agriculture cooperative, or participating in condominium housing or neighborhood activities. So also, members in a local corporation might work outside the local corporation, might participate in various civic groups or national-level political parties, might transact on an individual basis (or invest) in other local or business corporations, and so on. The only thing that members cannot share with outsiders is their fundamental responsibility for land and resources in their territory.

Incentives for members to improve resource governance, or to follow the most successful local corporations, are various. They include: marketplace competition (the discipline that comes to people engaged in a joint economic enterprise to make profit), yardstick competition (when members of one corporation see members of another corporation enjoying greater environmental health and push for their own corporation to change its ways), concerns about group reputation (national-level social pressure to be a successful group), and the pressure for long-term planning (coming from people who are more rooted in place). The national government must play a role in managing these incentives, for example, through its tax structure, through fines, and through national recognition and awards.

CONCLUSION

I have emphasized the role of local corporations in reducing information costs in big markets and in maintaining supportive resources. Because of this emphasis, it may seem that local corporations are about local power over national government power. This is inaccurate. It bears repeating that government functions can be divided among different units and that the national government plays many roles not discussed in detail here, like insurance, redistribution of revenue, market regulation, management of national public lands, and so on.

There is a gap in discussions about environmental governance between those who understand something about environmental science and therefore recognize the gravity of current risks to the environment and those who think of scientists as one of many interested parties in a policy debate that involves also businessmen, economists, lawyers, and others. If scientists' assessments of risk are taken seriously, as I think they should be, then the situation demands a coming to terms with the failure of current governing institutions to respond to the obvious risks. A system of local corporations—if not a panacea—at the very least is an attempt to match institutional reform to the scale of the problem. Moreover, it is a proposal to enable a new institutional form, so that people at least have the option to try it. Finally, it is an institutional form that is not totally unfamiliar and that can operate within the market framework.

NOTES

1. I borrow here from Schlager's distinction between environmental infrastructure and the common and private goods derived from this infrastructure. See Edella Schlager, chapter 3 in this volume.

REFERENCES

Adams, William M., Ros Aveling, Dan Brockington, Barney Dickson, Jo Elliott, Jon Hutton, Dilys Roe, Bhaskar Vira, and William Wolmer. 2004. "Biodiversity Conservation and the Eradication of Poverty." *Science* 306: 1146–1149.

Agrawal, Arun, and Clark C. Gibson. 1999. "Enchantment and Disenchantment: The Role of Community in Natural Resource Conservation." *World Development* 27: 629–649.

Bassett, Ellen M. 2005. "Tinkering with Tenure: The Community Land Trust Experiment in Voi, Kenya." *Habitat International* 29: 375–398.

Beddington, J., M. Asaduzzaman, A. Fernandez, M. Clark, M. Guillou, M. Jahn, L. Erda, T. Mamo, N. van Bo, C.A. Nobre, R. Scholes, R. Sharma, and J. Wakhungu. 2011. *Achieving Food Security in the Face of Climate Change: Summary for Policy Makers from the Commission on Sustainable Agriculture and Climate Change.* Copenhagen: CGIAR Research Program on Climate Change, Agriculture and Food Security.

Cleaver, Francis. 2002. "Reinventing Institutions: Bricolage and the Social Embeddedness of Natural Resource Management." *European Journal of Development Research* 14: 11–30.

Coase, Ronald. 1937. "The Nature of the Firm." *Economica* 4: 386–485.

Dagan, Hanoch, and Michael A. Heller. 2001. "The Liberal Commons." *Yale Law Journal* 110: 549–623.

Demsetz, Harold. 1988. "The Theory of the Firm Revisited." *Journal of Law, Economics, and Organization* 4: 141–161.

de Soto, Hernando 2000. *The Mystery of Capital: Why Capitalism Triumphs in the West and Fails Everywhere Else.* New York: Basic.

Fitzpatrick, Daniel. 2005. "'Best Practice' Options for the Legal Recognition of Customary Tenure." *Development and Change* 36: 449–475.

Foster, John Bellamy. 1992. "The Absolute General Law of Environmental Degradation Under Capitalism." *Capitalism, Nature, Socialism* 3: 77–82.

Freyfogle, Eric T. 2002. "The Tragedy of Fragmentation." *Valparaiso University Law Review* 36: 307–337.

Frug, Gerald E. 1980. "The City as a Legal Concept." *Harvard Law Review* 93: 1057–1154.

Geertz, Clifford. 1963. "The Integrative Revolution: Primordial Sentiments and Civil Politics in the New States." In *Old Societies and New States: The Quest for Modernity in Asia and Africa*, ed. Clifford Geertz, 105–157. New York: Free Press.

Graham, Nicole. 2011. *Lawscape: Property, Environment, Law.* New York: Routledge.

Greif, Avner. 2004. "Impersonal Exchange Without Impartial Law: The Community Responsibility System." *Chicago Journal of International Law* 5: 109–138.

Haldar, Antara, and Joseph E. Stiglitz. 2013. "Analyzing Legal Formality and Informality: Lessons from Land Titling and Microfinance Programs." In *Law and Economics with Chinese Characteristics: Institutions Promoting Development in the Twenty-First Century*, eds. David Kennedy and Joseph E. Stiglitz, 112–148. Oxford: Oxford University Press.

Hardin, Garrett. 1968. "The Tragedy of the Commons." *Science* 162: 1243–1248.

Hodgson, Geoffrey M. 2003. "Capitalism, Complexity, and Inequality." *Journal of Economic Issues* 37: 471–478.

Jacobs, Harvey M. 1989. "Localism and Land Use Planning." *Journal of Architectural and Planning Research* 6: 1–18.

Klug, Heinz. 2006. "Community, Property and Security in Rural South Africa: Emancipatory Opportunities or Marginalized Survival Strategies? In *Another Production Is Possible: Beyond the Capitalist Canon (Reinventing Social Emancipation: Toward New Manifestos)*, ed. Boaventura de Sousa Santos, 123–145. London: Verso.

Komesar, Neil K. 2001. *Law's Limits: The Rule of Law and the Supply and Demand of Rights.* Cambridge: Cambridge University Press.

Lambin, Eric F., and Patrick Meyfroidt. 2011. "Global Land Use Change, Economic Globalization, and the Looming Land Scarcity." *Proceeding of the National Academy of Sciences USA* 108: 3465–3472.

Lane, Marcus B., and Geoff McDonald. 2005. "Community-based Environmental Planning: Operational Dilemmas, Planning Principles and Possible Remedies." *Journal of Environmental Planning and Management* 48: 709–731.

Leopold, Aldo. 1949. *A Sand County Almanac: And Sketches Here and There.* New York: Oxford University Press.

Meinzen-Dick, Ruth, and Esther Mwangi. 2008. "Cutting the Web of Interests: Pitfalls of Formalizing Property Rights." *Land Use Policy* 26: 36–43.

Merrill, Thomas W., and Henry E. Smith. 2000. "Optimal Standardization in the Law of Property: The Numerus Clausus Principle." *Yale Law Journal* 110: 1–70.

Molden, David, ed. 2007 *Water for Food, Water for Life: A Comprehensive Assessment of Water Management in Agriculture.* Washington, D.C.: Earthscan.

Moore, Sally Falk. 1973. "Law and Social Change: The Semi-autonomous Social Field as an Appropriate Subject of Study." *Law and Society Review* 7: 719–746.

Oates, Wallace E. 1972. *Fiscal Federalism.* New York: Harcourt Brace Jovanovich.

Ostrom, Elinor. 1990. *Governing the Commons: The Evolution of Institutions for Collective Action.* Cambridge: Cambridge University Press.

——. 2010. "Polycentric Systems for Coping with Collective Action and Global Environmental Change." *Global Environmental Change* 20: 550–557.

Radin, Margaret Jane. 1981. "Property and Personhood." *Stanford Law Review* 34: 957–1015.

Rieser, Alison. 1999. "Prescriptions for the Commons: Environmental Stewardship and the Fishing Quotas Debate." *Harvard Environmental Law Review* 23: 393–421.

Reuveny, Rafael. 2007. "Climate Change-induced Migration and Violent Conflict." *Political Geography* 26: 656–673.

Vandermeer, John. 1996. "Tragedy of the Commons: The Meaning of the Metaphor." *Science & Society* 60: 290–306.

Williamson, Oliver E. 1975. *Markets and Hierarchies: Analysis and Antitrust Implications.* New York: Free Press.

York, Richard, Eugene A. Rosa, and Thomas Dietz. 2003. "Footprints on the Earth: The Environmental Consequences of Modernity." *American Sociological Review* 68: 279–300.

Olivier De Schutter and Katharina Pistor

How would a shift in the debate about resource management from efficiency to essentiality affect institutional choice and the governance of scarce resources? This question motivated this book project and was posed to the contributors to this volume, who brought perspectives from different disciplines and different social and geographic settings to the analysis. The question may at first appear as a mere play on words. Yet as this volume demonstrates, moving from efficiency to essentiality forces a change in perspective from the resource or asset to the people whose survival and well-being depends on access to it. It introduces a different normative dimension into the allocation of resources: Even if paying the highest prices in general can be taken as an indicator for efficient use of an asset, it does not reflect the human price paid by those excluded from its use—and the more *essential* the resource, the more attention ought to be paid to the consequences of exclusion.

For the purpose of this book project we have focused only on resources that most would deem essential, that is, as indispensable for survival: drinking water, food, and shelter. We left open the possibility of extending the concept to include other resources that may be critical to ensure that all members of a society have the opportunity to live the lives they have reason to value (Sen 1999; Nussbaum 2011). Essentiality thus cannot be fully determined objectively. It is a normative concept, the contours of which can and should be subject to debate and contestation. The major work it does is to emphasize the normative commitments societies and communities ought to make to their most vulnerable constituencies. As such, the concept of "essentiality" is markedly different from the "basic needs" approach framed by the International Labor Organization as discussed in our introduction. The latter assumes that basic needs are objective categories and is largely agnostic as to who provides the means for covering the basic needs for the world's poor.

The emphasis on essentiality requires a shift in the choice and design of governance regimes away from both a purely market-based system for allocating resources and ex post redistribution to cover basic needs. The normative aspiration embedded in the concept of essentiality places a different demand on the design of governance: Voice and Reflexivity, that is, a process of institutionalization, learning and recognition of competing claims and a commitment to sharing.

The contributions found in this volume have wrestled with the concept and have brought to the fore important insights that we hope will stimulate future debates. Here, we summarize the core insights we have taken away from extensive collaboration with the contributors at the workshop and in conversations, comments, and countercomments on drafts and revised drafts since.

First, the concept of essentiality brings factors other than price and quantity to the debate about how best to allocate scarce resources. The concept's major contribution is to serve as a conceptual bridge between economics with its focus on scarce resource allocation on one hand, and moral philosophy and its emphasis on norms that shall govern individual and collective lives on the other. It infuses resource allocation with normative questions and highlights the need to accommodate resource scarcity as binding constraints in moral discourse.

Second, the contours of the concept remain vague, but unavoidably so. We may all agree that drinking water is a hard-core essential resource; yet even here we find that what constitutes drinkable water is contested. Also contested are the conditions under which land, electricity, or other resources may qualify as essential. To some this may appear a weakness of the concept. We suggest that it reflects its strength: Governing access to essential resources necessarily entails debate about what resources are essential for mere survival, whether this is all a given society wishes to afford for its most vulnerable constituencies, or what else to include. The concept alone does not deliver answers, much less easy institutional solutions; it poses a question that requires that societies aspiring toward social justice cannot afford to leave unanswered.

Third, we argue that the shift from allocative efficiency to essentiality points toward Voice and Reflexivity as guiding principles for developing appropriate governance regimes. Allocating resources deemed essential requires more than partial redistribution to avoid human catastrophe. It necessitates recognition of the human need to access essential resources even by those who lack the material means for attaining them. Moreover, it demands willingness by those who possess such means to engage in the search for solutions to meet these needs in a collective, other-regarding process. A space for essential resources must be carved out that responds to rules of allocation different from the pricing mechanism. The decommodification of essential resources makes room for Voice and Reflexivity as the guiding principles for devising new modes of governance: Voice points to the need for deliberative processes that allow all, including the underprivileged, to have their views taken into account. Reflexivity means that participants in the design of new governance regimes have the opportunity to reflect critically upon the origins of their preferences and to reassess and change them in light of the needs and demands of other constituencies. As such, Reflexivity can be seen as a condition for Voice to be effective and a means to overcome blockages in deliberation.

Fourth, our insistence on Voice and Reflexivity may sound naïve. Indeed, many case studies included in this volume demonstrate that Voice is often muffled and power relations trump Reflexivity. And yet, we find sufficient counterexamples to suggest that alternatives are possible. Comparative analyses of different water- or land-management regimes indicate that some governance regimes are more in line with Voice and Reflexivity than others. Those that lead to a competitive race to the bottom and deplete resources for current and future generations are highly problematic. Not infrequently, this scenario is associated with private access rights to common-pool resources. However, private property rights and market mechanisms can be meaningfully employed in the allocation of even essential resources, provided they are embedded in a normative framework that establishes collective priorities for their use.

Fifth, we are acutely aware that increasing pressure on resources such as water and arable land are more likely to lead to cutthroat competition and/or violent uprisings than peaceful governance based on Voice and Reflexivity. The historian Richard Parker reminds us that the civil unrests, wars, uprisings, and turmoils that characterized the seventeenth century coincided with severe weather conditions around the globe that brought famine and deprivation (Parker 2008). Experimenting with more inclusive forms of governance becomes more, not less, difficult as these resources become ever more scarce. Yet even if we may not be able to avoid this dire endgame scenario, we should strive to postpone it.

We hope this volume has made a modest contribution to rethinking governance of essential resources—a debate we can hardly avoid given their increasing scarcity.

REFERENCES

Nussbaum, Martha. 2011. *Creating Capabilities: The Human Development Approach.* Cambridge, Mass.: Belknap.

Parker, Geoffrey. 2008. Crisis and Catastrophe: The Global Crisis in the Seventeenth Century Reconsidered. *American Historical Review* 113 (4):1053–1079.

Sen, Amartya K. 1999. *Development as Freedom.* New York: Random House.

Nikhil Anand is an assistant professor of Geography, Environment, and Society at the University of Minnesota. His research examines how cities are materialized and governed through hydraulic infrastructure networks. His first book, *The Hydraulic City: Public Systems and the Social Life of Water in Mumbai*, is currently under review at Duke University Press. Framed by anxious debates about urbanization in the south, on one hand, and disappearing water resources, on the other, the book is a careful ethnographic account of how water is moved to and through Mumbai and accessed by those living in its settlements.

Vanessa Casado-Pérez is a lecturer in law and the Teaching Fellow of the Environmental Law and Policy Program at Stanford Law School. Her research focuses on management of natural resources, particularly water. She is analyzing different legal mechanisms to mitigate water scarcity in prior appropriation.

Manase Kudzai Chiweshe is currently a senior lecturer at the Institute of Lifelong Learning and Development Studies at Chinhoyi University of Technology, Zimbabwe. He is an expert in African gender theory and has focused his research on natural resource management, food security, sexuality, urban poverty, human rights, rural and urban spaces, social networks, social movements, survival strategies, and grassroots organizations.

Michael Cox studies community-based natural resource management, environmental governance, and the determinants of resilience and vulnerability in social-ecological systems. He has conducted empirical fieldwork-based analyses of irrigation systems in the southwestern

United States, Peru, and Kenya. More recently he has participated in an analysis of small-scale fisheries management in the Dominican Republic. He is currently conducting a synthetic analysis of large-scale environmental governance, the details of which can be found at http:// sesmad.dartmouth.edu.

Hanoch Dagan is the Stewart and Judy Colton Professor of Legal Theory and Innovation at Tel Aviv University Faculty of Law, a senior fellow at the Israel Democracy Institute, and a member of the American Law Institute and of the International Academy of Comparative Law. Prior to becoming dean of the Faculty of Law (2006–2011), he was the founding director of the Zvi Meitar Center for Advanced Legal Studies, the director of the Cegla Center for Interdisciplinary Research of the Law, and the editor in chief of *Theoretical Inquiries in Law*. Among his numerous publications are the books *Property: Values and Institutions* (2011) and *Properties of Property* (with Gregory S. Alexander; 2012). In recent years, Dagan has served as a visiting professor at Columbia University, Yale University, University of Michigan, Cornell University, and University of Toronto.

Olivier De Schutter teaches human rights law and jurisprudence at the University of Louvain and at Sciences Po in Paris. Between 2008 and 2014 he was the UN Special Rapporteur on the right to food, and he is now a Member of the UN Committee on Economic, Social and Cultural Rights. He has published widely at the intersection of economic globalization, the theory of governance, and economic and social rights.

Alain Durand-Lasserve is an emeritus research director with the CNRS. He works on attachment to the Les Afriques dans le Monde laboratory, a combined research unit of the CNRS and the Bordeaux Institute of Political Studies. He is a member of the Technical Committee on Land Tenure and Development (French Development Agency and Ministry of Foreign Affairs). He specializes in research on land tenure and housing policies in the developing-country context, with a particular focus on the regularization and integration of informal settlements, land title registers and the dynamics of real estate markets. He has worked mainly in Southeast and southern Asia and in sub-Saharan Africa (French-speaking and English-speaking countries and South Africa).

Michael B. Dwyer is a postdoctoral fellow in the Center for International Forestry Research's Governance Program. He has studied resource development and regulation in Southeast Asia since 2004, focusing on property as a meeting point for multiscalar and multitemporal questions related to agrarian change, state formation, and international relations.

Derek Hall is an associate professor in the Department of Political Science and the Balsillie School of International Affairs at Wilfrid Laurier University in Waterloo, Ontario. His research focuses on the political economy of land, food, agriculture, and the environment, especially in Japan and Southeast Asia. He is the author of *Land* (Polity, 2013) and, with Philip Hirsch and Tania Murray Li, of *Powers of Exclusion: Land Dilemmas in Southeast Asia* (NUS Press and University of Hawai'i Press, 2011). In 2009–2010 he was an S.V. Ciriacy-Wantrup Visiting Research Fellow in the Department of Environmental Science, Policy, and Management at the University of California, Berkeley.

John Hursh is an independent legal researcher. He holds an LL.M. from McGill University Faculty of Law, a J.D. from Indiana University Maurer School of Law, and an M.P.A. from Indiana University School of Public and Environmental Affairs. He has also completed research fellowships at the University of Cambridge Lauterpacht Centre for International Law and the McGill University Centre for Human Rights and Legal Pluralism. His research interests include land and natural resource rights in the Maghreb and land reform in southern Africa.

James Krueger is a doctoral candidate in environmental studies at the University of Wisconsin–Madison. Currently he is in Kenya on a Fulbright-Hays dissertation research fellowship. His research focuses on interactions among formal law and informal institutions, and national and local levels of natural resource governance in East Africa. He previously taught environmental law and natural resources law at Haramaya University in Ethiopia.

Laila Macharia is the founder of Scion Real, an investment firm focused on urban Africa. Previously, she worked in the United States, managing portfolios, most recently at the New York office of Clifford Chance. Since returning to East Africa, Laila has led several projects to reform the transport and building sectors, including a project for which she acted as a senior regional advisor to USAID. She is currently a director at Centum, the largest listed private equity firm in East Africa, and also teaches at the Woodrow Wilson School of Princeton University. She is also a fellow of the Aspen Institute's Africa Leadership Initiative.

Scott McKenzie is a doctoral student in resource management and environmental studies at the University of British Columbia. He has a bachelor of arts degree in environmental studies, philosophy, and American studies from the University of Kansas and a juris doctorate from the University of Iowa. His work considers the relationships between the natural environment, human development, and law.

Nilhari Neupane is an economic analyst for the Koshi Basin Programme of the International Centre for Integrated Mountain Development (ICIMOD) and the Australian Aid Agency for International Development (AusAID). The Koshi River is a transboundary river crossing China, Nepal, and India, and the program aims to enhance regionally coordinated management of the river basin. His dissertation provided a political and economic analysis of water resource distribution in Nepal. He recently served as an intern for the sustainability component of the World Food Program in Nairobi, Kenya.

Eva Pils is Reader in Transnational Law at King's College London. She studied law, philosophy, and sinology in Heidelberg, London, and Beijing; qualified as a lawyer in Germany; and holds a doctorate in law from University College London. Her scholarship focuses on human rights and the law in China, with publications addressing the role and situation of Chinese human rights lawyers, land and eviction rights, criminal justice, access to justice, and conceptions of justice in China. Eva's publications on these topics have appeared in academic publications as well as in the popular press; her book *China's Human Rights Lawyers: Advocacy and Resistance* was published in November 2014. Before joining King's in September 2014, she was an associate professor at the Chinese University of Hong Kong Faculty of Law. She is also a nonresident senior research fellow at the U.S.-Asia Law Institute of New York University Law School.

Katharina Pistor is the Michael I. Sovern Professor of Law at Columbia Law School. She is also the director of the Law School's Center on Global Legal Transformation and has served as a member of Columbia University's Committee on Global Thought since its inception. She is principal investigator of the Global Finance and Law Initiative, a collaborative research project aimed at reconceptualizing the relation between finance and law, funded by INET. In 2012 she received the Max Planck Research Award for her contributions to international financial regulation. In 2014 she was awarded the Allen & Overy Best Paper Prize by the European Corporate Governance Institute for her paper "A Legal Theory of Finance."

Edella Schlager is a professor at the University of Arizona School of Government and Public Policy and the Institute of the Environment, an interdisciplinary program that focuses on solutions to environmental challenges. Her research focuses on comparative institutional analyses of water laws and policies, property rights, and water governance compacts in the western United States. She has written extensively on the design and performance of polycentric systems of water governance and how such systems adapt to changing environmental, legal, and social circumstances, and she coauthored two books on Western water governance: *Common Waters, Diverging Streams: Linking Institutions and Water Management in Arizona, California, and Colorado* (with William Blomquist and Tanya Heikkila) and *Embracing Watershed Politics* (with William Blomquist).

Vamsi Vakulabharanam is currently an associate professor of economics at the University of Hyderabad, India. He was assistant professor of economics at Queens College, City University of New York, between 2004 and 2007. He was also a fellow at the India China Institute at the New School in New York between 2008 and 2010. His research interests center around the nature and changing dynamics of inequality in the contemporary economies of India and China. Specifically, he has worked on globalization and agrarian change in India and consumption and wealth inequality during the period of economic reforms in India and China. One of the major arguments in his work is that during the current promarket economic regime, both countries have tended to neglect their agricultural sectors, thereby causing agrarian distress to millions of farmers as these two economies witnessed a sharp increase in rural–urban divide over the recent decades.

climate change, 289
close corporation, 84
Club of Rome, 3
Coase, Ronald H., 34, 37–38
coercion, 141–42
collective mobilization, 112
collective responsibility, 349–50
colonialism: Africa relating to, 275–76,
    317–18; land tenure regimes relating
    to, 305–7; Mumbai water governance
    relating to, 109; in New Zealand, 96
Colorado, 220; prior appropriation and
    quantity-based property rights in,
    224–26, 227
Colorado River basin, 12
Committee on Economic, Social and
    Cultural Rights (CESCR), 15
Committee on World Food Security
    (CFS), 22
commodities, 65n4
common-interest communities, 86
common-law property, 10–11
common-pool resource management,
    21; water management and, 243; in
    Zimbabwe, 319
common-pool resources, 67–68;
    demand for, 70–71, 74–77;
    infrastructure relating to, 68–69;
    policies, environmental services, and,
    70–77
common property: definition of, 83; in
    India, 206–7
Communal Areas Management
    Programme for Indigenous Resources
    (CAMPFIRE), 329–30
Communal Lands Act, 327, 328
communal property rights, 25–26,
    28; issues with, 27; traditional
    institutions relating to, 321–22
commune, 182n15
communism, 130
community: common-interest, 86;
    globalization and, 22; imagined,
    22; irrigation, 220–23, 243–44, 246;
    land rights and, 36; local, 336–37;

makhzen, 273–74; reflexivity and, 22;
    rural, 90–91, 94–95, 244–45; water
    management relating to, 243–47
Community-Based Natural Resource
    Management (CBNRM), 329
community land: background on,
    305–9; Group Ranches Act relating
    to, 313; in Kenya, 302–3, 305–14; land
    governance of, 303–14; land rights
    for, 305–6
Community Land Bill, 309, 313–14
community-share ownership trusts
    (CSOTs), 331
compact laws, 75–76, 79n7
compartmentalization, 339
compensation, for expropriation, 18,
    140–41, 142
competition: antitrust laws on, 97;
    globalization and, 9; markets and,
    94–95; for water, 289
condemned property, 98
conflict, 357; expropriation protests
    and, 143–46, 152n35; in Kenya,
    302–3, 307–9; in Mumbai water
    governance, 118–19; over property,
    91–94, 170; over territory, 54; over
    water, 289–90
conservation, 73–74
Constitutional Court, German, 21
constitutional governance, 253; for
    water, 256–58
consumption, 338
control rights, 26
cooperative alternatives, on property,
    98–99
Cooperative Framework Agreement
    (CFA), 261
corporate management strategies, 350–51
corporations: close, 84; public, 343–44.
    See also local corporations
Cox, Michael, 12, 34
CSOTs. See community-share
    ownership trusts
customary land, 163–64, 169, 176–77,
    182n11